Marketing Planning

PEARSON
Education

We work with leading authors to develop the strongest educational materials in marketing, bringing cutting-edge thinking and best learning practice to a global market.

Under a range of well-known imprints, including Financial Times Prentice Hall, we craft high quality print and electronic publications which help readers to understand and apply their content, whether studying or at work.

To find out more about the complete range of our publishing please visit us on the World Wide Web at: **www.pearsoned.co.uk**

A Companion Website accompanies *Marketing Planning: principles into practice* by Marian Burk Wood

Visit the *Marketing Planning: principles into practice* Companion Website at www.booksites.net/wood_mp to find valuable learning material including:

For Students:

- Online resource links to research sites mentioned in the text, arranged by topic
- Complete glossary of marketing planning terms
- Link to Palo Alto Software for more information about *Marketing Planning Pro* software

Marian Burk Wood

Marketing Planning
principles into practice

FT Prentice Hall
FINANCIAL TIMES

An imprint of **Pearson Education**
Harlow, England • London • New York • Boston • San Francisco • Toronto
Sydney • Tokyo • Singapore • Hong Kong • Seoul • Taipei • New Delhi
Cape Town • Madrid • Mexico City • Amsterdam • Munich • Paris • Milan

Pearson Education Limited
Edinburgh Gate
Harlow
Essex CM20 2JE
England

and Associated Companies throughout the world

Visit us on the World Wide Web at:
www.pearsoned.co.uk

First published 2004

ISBN 0 273 68679 8

British Library Cataloguing-in-Publication Data
A catalogue record for this book is available from the British Library

Library of Congress Cataloging-in-Publication Data
A catalog record for this book is available from the Library of Congress

10 9 8 7 6 5 4 3 2 1
06 05 04 03 02

Typeset by Pantek Arts Ltd, Maidstone, Kent
Printed by Ashford Colour Press Ltd., Gosport

Brief contents

Full contents

Website Resources

For students:

- Online resource links to research sites mentioned in the text, arranged by topic

- Complete glossary of marketing planning terms

- Link to Palo Alto Software for more information about *Marketing Plan Pro*
  software

For Lecturers:

- A password-protected site with complete, downloadable Instructor's Manual

- Correlation guides showing how this text integrates with chapters in leading
  Pearson marketing texts

Preface

The first step on the road to marketing success in today's highly dynamic environment is a creative, realistic marketing plan. Although most marketing textbooks explain the principles of marketing planning and discuss what marketing plans should cover, few include sufficient detail to guide student marketers through the actual planning process. Yet effective marketing planning is all about putting principles into practice. This text shows how, by taking students step-by-step through the structured process of researching, developing and controlling a marketing plan.

Step-by-step with *Marketing Planning: principles into practice*

Special features in each chapter help students move through all the steps involved in formulating a sound marketing plan:

- *Directions*. The 'how to' format explains the decisions and issues to be addressed in researching and writing a marketing plan.

- *Definitions*. Students learn the language of marketing through key term definitions in every chapter. For quick reference, all definitions are presented in the Glossary at the end of the book.

- *Comprehension outcomes, application outcomes*. Comprehension outcomes indicate what students will know after studying each chapter. Application outcomes indicate what students will be able to do after studying each chapter. Both types of outcomes are necessary for students to put principles into practice.

- *Practical marketer checklists*. Chapter checklists summarise key questions for students to consider as they proceed through the planning process.

- *Online resources*. A listing of Internet sites in each chapter gives students a valuable starting point for researching markets, competitors and other aspects of marketing planning.

- *Cases and examples*. Numerous recent examples show how companies and non-profit organisations around the world actually put important marketing principles into practice.

- *Pedagogy.* Questions for discussion and analysis check students' understanding of chapter material. 'Apply your knowledge' exercises challenge students to put principles into practice by analysing a specific organisation's marketing decisions and activities. 'Build your own marketing plan' exercises direct students to use each chapter's principles in formulating all the parts of a workable marketing plan. These exercises can be completed using the accompanying software.

- *Sample marketing plan.* The Appendix presents a detailed, realistic sample marketing plan for a fictional company, Lost Legends Luxury Chocolatier.

Convenient planning with *Marketing Plan Pro* software

Students can conveniently organise and document their own marketing plans using the accompanying *Marketing Plan Pro* software. This academic version of the award-winning program from Palo Alto Software is easy to use and contains numerous sample marketing plans for manufacturing businesses, service firms, retailing and non-profit organisations. Its spreadsheet and charting capabilities simplify the systematic preparation of budgets, breakeven calculations and other complex financial tasks required for effective planning. The software is not only interactive and customisable, it is useful for tracking progress from strategy to implementation to results. Students can also refer to the sample marketing plan in the text (Appendix) as a model for recording marketing decisions and strategies.

Real-world view of marketing planning

Seeing how different organisations have actually applied marketing principles in different situations can provoke new thinking and lead to more realistic marketing plans. How does Ryanair use marketing to implement a smart corporate strategy (Chapter 1)? What are Danone's plans for marketing yoghurt to targeted market segments (Chapter 4)? How is HSBC banking on a global growth strategy (Chapter 5)? Why is Virgin putting special emphasis on planning brand management (Chapter 6)? How does Zara use forecasting to get the right fashions to the right stores at the right time (Chapter 11)? These and many more up-to-date cases and examples demonstrate that good marketing can be found anywhere in the world; in consumer markets and business markets; in large companies, small companies, e-commerce companies and non-profit organisations.

In line with this real-world view, the examples have been chosen to reinforce that marketing plans are subject to change at any time: Budgets may be cut or shifted; marketing staff may be transferred or made redundant; new competitors may emerge or strong competitors grow weaker. Thus, students who learn to apply the principles of marketing planning will have more than a good plan on paper: they will have a good plan for the market.

Bringing organisation to marketing planning

Marketing Planning: principles into practice is divided into 12 chapters, each covering a specific aspect of the planning process. Chapters 1–3 introduce marketing planning, explain how to analyse the current marketing situation and discuss how to research markets and customers. Chapter 4 examines the use of segmentation, targeting and positioning in consumer and business markets. Chapter 5 looks at setting strategic direction, objectives and marketing strategy. Chapters 6–9 focus on the marketing mix: product, place (channels and logistics), price and promotion (integrated marketing communication). Chapter 10 shows how to use customer service and internal marketing to support the marketing mix. Chapters 11 and 12 present techniques for forecasting, budgeting, measuring marketing performance and controlling plan implementation.

More features on companion website

Visit www.booksites.net/wood_mp to access the following valuable supplements:

- *For students*. Students can link to any of the online resources listed in the text, which are arranged by topic on the companion website. Students can also link to the Palo Alto Software site for technical information about the accompanying *Marketing Plan Pro* software.

- *For lecturers*. Lecturers can access the Instructor's Manual on the password-protected instructor section of the website. Lecturers can also examine correlation guides showing how *Marketing Planning: principles into practice* integrates with chapters in leading Pearson marketing texts.

Acknowledgements

Many people were involved in bringing this book from concept to the classroom. I greatly appreciate the assistance of the following academic reviewers who were kind enough to read and comment on parts of the manuscript during the formative stages:

Declan Bannon – University of Paisley Business School
Jill Brown – University of Portsmouth Business School
Paul Oakley – University of Brighton Business School

John Rudd – Aston Business School
Heather Skinner – Glamorgan Business School

I am especially grateful to Tim Berry of Palo Alto Software, whose *Marketing Plan Pro* software accompanies this text, for his marketing savvy and his gracious permission to use illustrations and other copyright material. My gratitude, also, to Sabrina Parsons of Palo Alto Software for her insights and guidance regarding the software's inner workings and application.

Many thanks to the talented professionals at Pearson Education whose hard work and dedication made this book possible. On the Marketing Publishing Team, I particularly appreciate the expert guidance and enthusiastic stewardship of Senior Acquisitions Editor Thomas Sigel; the knowledgeable leadership of Sadie McClelland, Editor in Chief for Business and Economics; the marketing insights of Marketing Executive John Henderson and Marketing Manager Leigh-Anne Graham; and the skilful support of Editorial Assistant Peter Hooper. I also want to thank Senior Editor Verina Pettigrew; Adam Renvoize who was responsible for the text design and the cover; Kay Holman the Production Controller; Susan Faircloth, freelance copy editor; Helen Baxter, freelance proof-reader and Melanie Beard, Electronic Projects Editor, who produced the website accompanying the book.

This book is dedicated with love to the youngest consumers in my extended family: Amelia Biancolo, Ella Biancolo, Gabriel Wood, Michael Werner, Nathan Hall and Charlie Hall.

—Marian Burk Wood MarianBWW@netscape.net

About the author

Marian Burk Wood has held vice-presidential level positions in corporate and non-profit marketing with Citibank, Chase Manhattan Bank and the National Retail Federation. She has extensive practical experience in marketing planning, having developed and implemented dozens of marketing plans over the years for a wide range of goods and services. Her US book, *The Marketing Plan Handbook*, has been used by thousands of students across North America and has been translated for use by colleges in the Netherlands and Eastern Europe.

Wood holds an MBA in marketing from Long Island University in New York and a BA from the City University of New York. She has worked with prominent academic experts to co-author undergraduate textbooks on principles of marketing, principles of advertising and principles of management. Her special interests in marketing include ethics, segmentation, channels and business buying.

Publisher's acknowledgements

We are grateful to the following for permission to reproduce copyright material:

Fig. 1.5 after *Strategic Marketing for Non-profit Organisations*, 6th edn, Prentice Hall (Andreason A.R. & Kotler P. 2003). Copyright © 2003. Adapted by permission of Pearson Education, Inc., Upper Saddle River, NJ; Fig. 2.5 from *Market-Based Management: Strategies for Growing Customer Value*, 2nd edn, Prentice Hall (Best R.J. 2000). Copyright © 2000. Reprinted/Adapted by permission of Pearson Education, Inc., Upper Saddle River, NJ; Fig. 3.2, Fig. 11.5, Checklist 5 and Checklist 11 adapted from *The Marketing Plan: A Handbook*, Prentice Hall (Wood M.B. 2003). Copyright © 2003. Reprinted/Adapted by permission of Pearson Education, Inc., Upper Saddle River, NJ; Fig. 3.5 from *Principles of Marketing*, Pearson Education (Brassington F. 2003); Fig. 4.2 and Fig. 4.3 from *Strategic and Competitive Analysis*, Prentice Hall (Fleisher C.G. and Bensoussan B.E. 2003). Copyright © 2003. Reprinted/Adapted by permission of Pearson Education, Inc., Upper Saddle River, NJ; Fig. 4.6 adapted from, Fig. 6.6 after, and Checklist 6 adapted from *Strategic Brand Management* 2nd edn, Prentice Hall (Keller K.L. 2003). Copyright © 2003. Reprinted/Adapted by permission of Pearson Education, Inc., Upper Saddle River, NJ; Fig. 5.1 adapted from *On Target: The Book on Marketing Plans*, 2nd edn, Palo Alto Software (Berry T. and Wilson D. 2001) ©1993 Timothy J. Berry; Fig. 6.3 from *Marketing Management*, Pearson Education (Hollandson S. 2003); Fig. 7.2 and Fig. 11.4 from *Market-Based Management*, 2nd edn, Prentice Hall (Best R.J. 2000). Copyright © 2000. Reprinted/Adapted by permission of Pearson Education, Inc., Upper Saddle River, NJ; Fig. 8.1 from, and Fig. 8.6 adapted from *The Strategy and Tactics of Pricing*, 3rd edn, Prentice Hall (Nagle T.T. and Holden, R.K. 2002). Copyright © 2002. Reprinted/Adapted by permission of Pearson Education, Inc., Upper Saddle River, NJ; Fig. 8.4 from *Marketing Management*, 11th edn, Prentice Hall (Kotler P. 2003) Copyright © 2003. Reprinted/Adapted by permission of Pearson Education, Inc., Upper Saddle River, NJ; Fig. 9.3 after *Consumer Behaviour*, 5th edn, Prentice Hall (Solomon M.R. 2002). Copyright © 2002. Reprinted/Adapted by permission of Pearson Education, Inc., Upper Saddle

River, NJ; Checklist 8 text adapted from *The Strategy and Tactics of Pricing*, 3rd edn. Upper Saddle River: NJ: Prentice Hall, (Nagle T.T. and Holden, R.K. 2002) and *Marketing Management*, 11th edn, Prentice Hall (Kotler P. 2002). Copyright © 2002. Reprinted/Adapted by permission of Pearson Education, Inc., Upper Saddle River, NJ.

1 Introduction to marketing planning

Comprehension outcomes

After studying this chapter, you will be able to:

- Explain the relationship among the three strategy levels
- Discuss how a mission statement is used and what it should contain
- Define marketing planning and outline the seven stages in the process

Application outcomes

After studying this chapter, you will be able to:

- Analyse and prepare a mission statement
- Start documenting a marketing plan using *Marketing Plan Pro* software or an appropriate written format

OPENING CASE: THE RYANAIR REVOLUTION

Who says low price and no frills mean no service? Welcome to the Ryanair revolution, where fares are surprisingly low, service quality is surprising high and the profits are flowing. This Dublin-based airline's strategy, modelled after the strategy of Southwest Airlines in the United States, is to give travellers the most value for their money. 'Fare-cutting is the principal factor', states CEO Michael O'Leary. 'But we're also the number one customer service airline in Europe. We're number one for on-time flights, number one for fewest cancellations, number one for fewest lost bags and number one for fewest customer complaints.'[1]

Profitably transforming such a strategy into action is far from easy in the turbulent airline industry. Ryanair must battle well-established competitors such as British Airways as well as ambitious discounters such as easyJet and simultaneously overcome highly variable demand for air travel. Sometimes passenger loads are up, sometimes down, but the airline has been generally successful in its first decade.

How does Ryanair do it? Its flight plan for building market share among price-sensitive leisure travellers relies heavily on low pricing based on low costs. The airline serves smaller, secondary airports (even former military bases, where landing costs are lower); uses its fleet more productively (it flies only one type of jet, allows only 20 minutes between flights); flies limited schedules to selected European destinations (to attract high passenger loads); and sells nearly all tickets online (at an operational cost of less than one penny per ticket sold). Low prices are so important that when O'Leary acquired the discount airline Buzz from KLM, he was able to slash prices by 50 per cent and still enjoy an operating margin of 31 per cent (more than triple the margin of easyJet or Southwest Airlines).

Ryanair now carries more than 16 million passengers annually, double the number of passengers who flew with the airline just two years ago. O'Leary is aiming to double the number of passengers again, to 30 million within a few years, through further fare cuts, dozens of new routes and quality service. His strategy is not only resetting travellers' expectations of air fares, but dramatically transforming industry competition throughout Europe and beyond. No-frills airlines have begun challenging major carriers in Australia, India and the Pacific with low costs and low ticket prices – both hallmarks of the Ryanair revolution.[2]

CHAPTER PREVIEW

Ryanair is a very visible example of carefully crafted strategy at the corporate level translated into effective strategy at the business and marketing levels. Before the first jets took off – even before any were ordered – Ryanair's executives were assessing travellers' needs and expectations, analysing the competition, weighing the effect of industry deregulation and determining how the new airline could profitably serve its chosen market. Decisions at the corporate level laid the foundation for business decisions (such as which cities to serve) and marketing decisions (such as how to price each flight and what the website would look like). Yet the coordinated set of decisions that add up to a successful strategy for Ryanair will not necessarily work for easyJet or for any other rival, nor will it remain unchanged in the highly dynamic global environment.

This chapter introduces you to the marketing planning process, starting with a description of how strategy and plans are developed at three levels within an organisation. The next section covers the contents, application and importance of an organisational mission statement, which guides the development of strategy and ultimately the marketing plan. After a discussion about how marketing plans are documented, the chapter offers an overview of the seven stages in the marketing planning process. *As you read this chapter, think about how to apply the principles in developing a practical marketing plan that will satisfy customers and meet organisational needs.*

MARKETERS AS STRATEGISTS AND PLANNERS

For Ryanair to build profitable customer relationships, it must show, through marketing, that it is doing something differently than its competitors – doing something *better* – to satisfy the needs of air travellers. This type of customer orientation starts at the top, with an awareness that taking steps to understand and satisfy customers will ultimately lead to satisfying shareholders and other stakeholders.[3] In a very real sense, marketing is a priority and concern of everyone in a customer-oriented organisation. Yet the hard details of *who*, *what*, *when*, *where*, *how* and *how much* are the responsibility of marketers whose skill as master strategists and planners will have a great deal to do with the organisation's success.

Although consumer packaged goods corporations such as Beiersdorf (maker of Nivea skin products) employ marketers as master strategists and planners, business-to-business (B2B) companies also rely on marketing expertise to build and maintain strong relationships with corporate customers. Airbus is a good example: it markets aircraft to airlines around the world, including Emirates in the Middle East and Grupo Taca in Central America. Airbus exemplifies business-to-government (B2G) marketing as well, because it markets military aircraft to Belgium, Britain, France, Turkey and Spain, among other governments. Fierce competition from Boeing means that Airbus must take special care with its marketing strategies in order to win multi-million euro orders from business and government customers.[4]

Online businesses need to plan marketing strategies for profits, not just create flashy websites and clever advertising campaigns. Highly publicised failures such as that of the clothing retailer boo.com have reinforced this essential point. Smaller e-commerce enterprises have even less margin for error. The online retailer eShopAfrica, based in Ghana, sells high-quality textiles and other fair-trade African goods to a global customer base. Despite significant expenses for Web hosting, product sourcing and shipment, founder Cordelia Salter-Nour invests in marketing to reach interested buyers and stimulate more sales transactions for improved turnover and – ultimately – better profitability. Yet at any time, adverse economic conditions, higher costs or other potential problems can drain profits and threaten eShopAfrica's future.[5]

As a marketer, even if you craft and implement a successful strategy, you should expect to make changes from time to time. Consider the situation at J. Sainsbury.

MARKETING IN PRACTICE: J. SAINSBURY

One of the largest and best-known UK grocery chains, J. Sainsbury, has long focused on quality foods to differentiate itself from traditional rivals like Tesco. These days, however, the environment is changing, with aggressive price competition from the Asda discount chain; uncertain economic conditions; and consolidation among the top supermarket chains. Analysts note that Sainsbury's emphasis on quality actually makes the retailer seem higher priced, even though its prices are barely above those of competing chains. Moreover, time-pressured customers can buy many non-food products at competing stores, whereas Sainsbury has kept non-foods to just 13 per cent of turnover. Finally, more competition is coming from rival Tesco's increasingly popular online grocery service, which makes 24,000 deliveries daily. To increase turnover and profits in this evolving environment, Sainsbury may have to review and revamp its long-standing 'quality foods' marketing strategy.[6]

Ongoing changes in the environment can affect more than customer needs and competitive battles. Among the most important developments is the drive to balance social and environmental responsibilities through commitments to a broader stakeholder base. Public pressure and corporate leadership are encouraging a growing number of companies to adopt **sustainable marketing**, 'the establishment, maintenance and enhancement of customer relationships so that the objectives of the parties involved are met without compromising the ability of future generations to achieve their own objectives'.[7] This poses difficult choices for organisations seeking to balance decisions affecting the long-term good with the short-term realities of today's budgets and performance requirements. Royal Dutch/Shell, for instance, has made a corporate commitment to sustainability in the many countries where it operates. 'Whatever you do, economic, social or environmental, you have to be thinking sustainably', stresses Clive Mather, the petrol company's global head of learning.[8]

Sustainability can, of course, be expensive at the outset. The express delivery company FedEx, for instance, will replace every one of its 30,000 delivery vans with more costly low-emission hybrid diesel/electric vans over the coming decade. Still, the payback to society is that the new fleet will pollute far less. The payback to FedEx is that it will save enough on diesel fuel and maintenance to offset the cost of the entire fleet by the time all the vans are on the road. Publicity related to the changeover is giving FedEx a greener image, too.[9]

Decisions such as those by Shell and FedEx, made at the top levels of the organisation, are intended to pave the way for stronger bonds with many stakeholder groups. These decisions are an integral part of successful marketing built on a foundation of top-down and floor-up strategies.

One organisation, three levels of strategy

At the top level, **organisational** (or **corporate**) **strategy** governs your organisation's overall purpose and its long-range direction and goals; establishes the range of businesses in which it will compete; and shapes how it will create value for customers and other stakeholders (including shareholders). In turn, organisational strategy and goals provide a framework for the set of decisions made by business managers who must move their units forward toward the goals, given the organisation's resources and capabilities. The **business strategy** indicates the scope of each unit and how it will compete; what market(s) it will serve; and how unit resources will be allocated and coordinated to create customer value. In establishing business strategy, senior managers must determine what portfolio of units is needed to support the organisation's overall goals and what functions should be emphasised or possibly outsourced.

Once the portfolio of business units is in place, **marketing strategy** is used to determine how each unit will use the *marketing-mix* tools of product, place, price and promotion – supported by customer service and internal marketing strategies – to compete effectively and meet unit objectives. Because marketing is the organisational function closest to customers and markets, it is in the pivotal role of implementing higher-level strategies while simultaneously informing the market and customer definitions of these strategies. Thus, marketing integrates floor-up, customer-facing knowledge of the market and the current environment with top-down development, direction and fine-tuning of organisational and business strategies. Figure 1.1 illustrates key strategic decisions and how they apply at each of the three levels.[10]

Strategy level	Decisions covered	Examples of application at Unilever
Corporate	• Purpose	• To achieve sustainable, profitable growth and create long-term value for consumers, shareholders, employees
	• Direction	• Growth
	• Long-range goals	• 5–6% annual growth
	• Business definition	• Consumer goods
	• Value creation for customers	• Brand-name, quality products that meet and anticipate everyday customer needs
Business (implementing corporate strategy)	• Unit scope	• Foods, home and personal care divisions
	• Competitive approach	• Leverage brands for market leadership in high-demand product categories
	• Markets served	• Build relationships with consumers in Europe, Asia, the Americas, other markets
	• Allocation of resources for value	• Emphasise research and development to meet emerging consumer needs
Marketing (implementing business strategy, supporting corporate strategy)	• Product strategy	• Reinforce brand names in chosen categories (such as Magnum ice cream, Knorr soup)
	• Pricing strategy	• Offer quality and value
	• Channel/logistics (distribution) strategy	• Reach consumers through food wholesalers, retailers, restaurants, hotels
	• Integrated marketing communication (promotion) strategy	• Build brands through media advetising, online presence and various other techniques
	• Service	• Fill channel orders completely, on time
	• Internal marketing	• Build commitment and cooperation for marketing through ongoing communication and meetings

FIGURE 1.1   Levels of strategy

Anglo-Dutch Unilever, famous for brands like Dove soap and Omo detergent, is a good example of strategy in action.

MARKETING IN PRACTICE: UNILEVER

Even a global company has limited resources to invest for the purpose of achieving sustainable, profitable growth and creating long-term customer value. Under its corporate strategy, a multi-year 'Path to Growth', Unilever has designated the businesses in which it competes. At the business level, this strategy is being implemented by eliminating slower-performing product categories and refocusing resources on a core of 400 master brands in two main divisions. At the marketing level, this strategy is being implemented by increasing advertising spending for the most promising power brands, introducing additional products under successful brand names such as Bertolli and using additional tactics to satisfy customer needs, build sales and boost profits.

Without the market-sensing activities for which its marketing personnel are responsible, Unilever would have insufficient data about customer needs, trends and markets on which to base strategic decisions about value creation and business definition. Similarly, Unilever's business strategists draw on competitive and customer data gathered by marketing personnel and systems when making decisions that affect each division. In the foods division, for example, these decisions include directing research and development activities to create new products under SlimFast and other brands. Results of the actions at each level are used for feedback to adjust strategies and implementation (and sometimes objectives).[11]

Although Unilever uses a formal process for developing, documenting and implementing strategy at all three levels, smaller organisations sometimes take a less formal approach. Luis Carlos Faria is an entrepreneur in Divinopolis, Brazil, who single-handedly sets, adjusts and implements his strategies as the environment evolves. Faria's company, Peeky, exports military uniforms to government customers in Chile, the Dominican Republic, the United States and other countries. His corporate strategy is to build profits by meeting customers' exacting specifications while outsourcing the actual production. On the business and marketing levels, Faria concentrates on determining customers' needs, finding distributors in new markets and investigating opportunities for new products. Being ready to adjust strategies at any time gives Faria an edge over larger, more bureaucratic companies that require time-consuming hierarchical reviews and approvals for significant strategic changes.[12]

Marketing and the organisational mission statement

The starting point for any marketing strategy you might develop – indeed, all management decisions – is the **mission statement** stating the organisation's purpose and pointing the way toward a future vision of what it aspires to become. In practice, a mission statement should be more than mere words on a page. A good mission statement clarifies priorities and sets the tone for all organisation members – including marketing staff – by touching on five vital areas: [13]

- *Customer focus.* Who will the organisation exist to serve? Businesses generally serve consumers, other businesses or government customers; non-profit organisations serve clients (such as patients, in the case of hospitals); government agencies serve constituents. The customer focus should be specific enough to guide organisational decisions and actions. For instance, Belgium's Médecins Sans Frontières (MSF) is an international non-profit organisation with the mission of 'providing medical aid wherever needed, regardless of race, religion, politics or sex and raising awareness of the plight of the people we help'.[14] This mission guides decisions about sending medical assistance to anyone in need and about publicising the human impact of these emergencies.

- *Value creation.* How will the organisation create value for its customers and other stakeholders in a competitively superior way? Companies make sales (and profits) only when their offerings add value that customers need or want. Etsuo Miyoshi, president of Swany Corporation in Japan, used his own difficulties in dragging luggage through airports to develop a bag that any traveller, even someone older or physically challenged, could handle. The Stickchaircart bag has four wheels, rolls in any direction, contains a small fold-out seat and has a sturdy handle that is also a backrest. This bag creates value for customers who want the benefits of its unique features – and its ever-higher sales create value for employees (in the form of jobs) and shareholders (in the form of profits).[15]

- *Market scope.* Where and what will the organisation market? Defining the market scope helps management properly align structure, strategy and resources. SABMiller, for example, markets beer in selected European, Asian and North American markets. The company recently bought a majority stake in the Italian brewery Peroni to add strength in that country, one of only two Western European nations in which beer consumption is rising. Now SABMiller will profit from domestic sales of Peroni as well as from importing its other beers for sale in Italy.[16]

- *Guiding values.* What values will guide managers and employees in making decisions and dealing with stakeholders? What does the organisation want to stand for? Consider the values inherent in the mission of Tetra Pak, a company based in Lausanne, Switzerland, that markets equipment and packaging for milk, juices and other foods. The company follows this mission statement: 'We work for and with our customers to provide preferred processing and packaging solutions for food. We apply our commitment to innovation, our understanding of consumer needs and our relationships with suppliers to deliver these solutions, wherever and whenever food is consumed. We believe in responsible industry leadership, creating profitable growth in harmony with environmental sustainability and good corporate citizenship.'[17] Tetra Pak's mission statement identifies principles its marketers should apply (as well as defining the customer focus, value creation and market scope).

- *Core competencies*. What employee, process and technological capabilities give your organisation its competitive edge? These are its **core competencies** (sometimes known as *distinctive competencies*) – capabilities that are not easily duplicated and that differentiate the organisation from its competitors.[18] The clothing retailer Zara, which has its headquarters in Spain, has grown to more than 600 stores because of two core competencies: an unusually short design-to-production-to-store cycle, based on customer buying patterns and current styles; and a constant stream of new products that keep store inventories fresh. With more than 11,000 new items of clothing flowing into Zara stores around the world, customers have good reason to return again and again for the latest fashions.[19] Note that competencies are 'core' when they are based on specific organisation capabilities *and* contribute to competitive differentiation, as in Zara's case.

Use the practical marketer checklist No. 1, at the end of this chapter, to develop or review your organisation's mission statement.

The role of marketing planning

The mission drives strategy at all levels and ultimately leads to plans outlining decisions about marketing activities and resource allocation. As shown in Figure 1.2, organisational strategy results in a long-term strategic plan; the strategy for each business unit results in a business plan for as long as three to five years; and marketing strategy results in a marketing plan, which typically covers the coming year (but may cover multiple years).

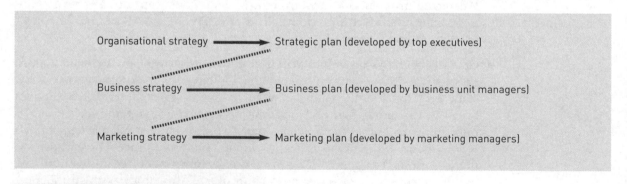

FIGURE 1.2   Plans as outputs of strategies

Marketing planning is the structured process that links the mission, organisational strategy and business strategy to marketing decisions and actions as you:

- research and analyse the marketing situation, markets and customers
- develop marketing direction, objectives, strategies and programmes for the targeted customer segments
- determine how to support marketing strategies through customer service and internal marketing
- implement, evaluate and control marketing programmes to achieve the desired objectives.

Using this process, you can examine any number of suitable opportunities for satisfying customers and moving your organisation closer to its goals, as well as various potential threats to successful performance. After systematically considering the different possibilities and outcomes, you and your managers will agree on one course of action and record it in the **marketing plan**. This internal document outlines the marketplace situation and describes the marketing strategies and programmes that will support the achievement of business and organisational goals. Necessarily the business plan and the marketing plan overlap to some extent. Sir George Bull, chairman of J. Sainsbury, stresses that the marketing plan, which is based on marketing strategy and planning, is distinguished from the business plan by its focus. 'The business plan takes as both its starting point and its objective the business itself', he explains. In contrast, 'the marketing plan starts with the customer and works its way round to the business'.[20]

Kotler stresses that rather than try to stimulate purchases one at a time, marketers should use **relationship marketing** to build ongoing connections with customers (and other key stakeholders).[21] When you use relationship marketing, you start from the premise that if you look beyond the immediate transaction to build trust with customers and meet their long-term needs, they are more likely to remain loyal. Cultivating long-term relationships with profitable customers in particular will help a company reach its financial objectives and defend against competition.

The marketing plan is not simply an account of what you as a marketer hope to accomplish in the coming year. Given the changes that inevitably occur in the marketing environment, your plan must allow for measuring progress toward the objectives and for making adjustments if actual results vary from projections. For example, new competitors may enter the marketplace, regulations may evolve, economic situations can improve or worsen and customer needs may change, among other shifts. Any or all of these changes can affect marketing performance. A good marketing plan will anticipate likely changes and provide guidelines for how to react with customer relationships in mind. You should, in fact, have several alternative plans in mind that might be implemented if significant changes occur.

Consider the marketing challenges posed by the fast-changing mobile phone market in Japan.

MARKETING IN PRACTICE: NTT DOCOMO

NTT DoCoMo, the largest mobile phone company in Japan, has revised its marketing plans over and over to combat increasingly intense competition and lower prices for voice calls. In recent years, DoCoMo's marketers have responded to such pressures with changed marketing plans emphasising non-voice features such as online photo and video transfers, downloadable colour maps, customised ring tones and remote control phone capabilities. These marketing plans also call for promoting 3G mobile phone technology through wider availability and incremental price cuts to encourage usage. DoCoMo's constant customer-oriented innovation has kept its mobile phone subscriber base well above 43 million customers – higher than projected in the company's marketing plans – despite a maturing market.[22]

Documenting a marketing plan

Although some marketing plans may be recorded in only a few pages, larger companies generally require detailed marketing plans for each unit, brand and product. This allows executives to review and approve the strategies and programmes within the context of the strategies and goals of each business as well as the entire organisation. Most marketing plans consist of the main sections shown in Figure 1.3. In practice, marketers cannot write the executive summary until all other sections have been completed, because its purpose is to offer a quick overview of the plan's highlights. With that exception, each section of the marketing plan is developed in order, building to the details documented in the financial plans and the implementation controls at the end of the plan. And when marketers change one section of the marketing plan in response to competitive shifts or other environmental trends, they need to re-examine and change other sections as well.

Rapid environmental changes can prompt a company to revamp an existing marketing plan or create a new plan when a new opportunity suddenly emerges. For example, Standard Chartered Bank spotted an opportunity to do business in post-war Afghanistan. Management spent just two months examining the possibilities and threats before implementing a marketing plan for opening a Kabul branch. The first step was to apply for government permission to operate a branch in Kabul. While the application was being processed, Standard Chartered was finalising the services to be offered. This branch, the first by a foreign bank entering the Afghan market in the post-war period, helped the UK company move closer to its goal of becoming a major financial services provider in Middle Eastern and Southern Asian countries.[23]

Section	Purpose
Executive summary	To describe the plan's objectives and main points briefly
Current marketing situation	To provide background about markets and customers, products, previous plans and results, competition, external opportunities and threats, environmental trends and internal strengths and weaknesses in the context of the organisational mission statement
Objectives and issues	To show what the marketing plan is designed to achieve in terms of marketing, financial and societal objectives; to identify and explain key issues that could affect the plan's implementation and success
Target market	To indicate who will be targeted and how the organisation, product or brand will be positioned for the selected segment(s)
Marketing strategy	To describe the broad strategic approach that the plan will apply in moving toward the objectives that have been set
Marketing programmes	To describe the set of coordinated actions that will be implemented for product, place, pricing, promotion, customer service and internal marketing
Financial plans	To back up the programmes with specifies about projected costs, revenue and sales forecasts, expected profit
Implementation controls	To show the marketing organisation needed for implementation; marketing responsibilities; next steps to initiate implementation; monitoring progress toward objectives; and contingency plans to consider if results vary from projections

FIGURE 1.3   Contents of a typical marketing plan

For convenience, you can document your marketing plans and complete the 'Build your own marketing plan' exercises at the end of each chapter using the *Marketing Plan Pro* software on the CD that accompanies this book. *Marketing Plan Pro* also includes brief sample plans showing the results of the marketing planning process undertaken by different types of businesses and non-profit organisations. If you use a written format rather than the software on the CD, look at the sample marketing plan in the Appendix as a guide to content and sequence of topics.

THE MARKETING PLANNING PROCESS

Standard Chartered needed only two months to assess the situation in Afghanistan and draw up a marketing plan for entering the market. Except for such unusual circumstances, most organisations begin the marketing planning process many months before a marketing plan is scheduled to take effect. This process covers seven distinct stages, as shown in Figure 1.4. The following sections will give you an overview of these seven stages.

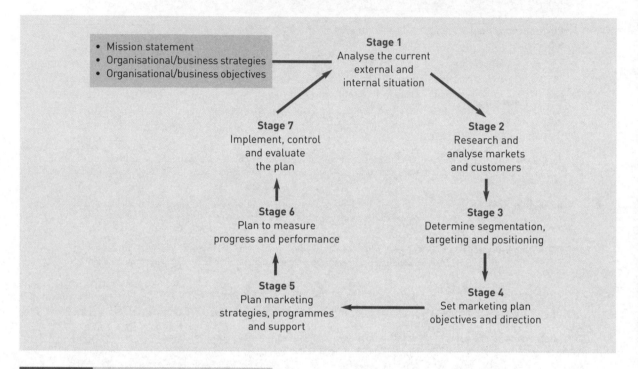

The marketing planning process

Stage 1: Analyse the current external and internal situation

In the first stage of the marketing planning process, you will study the overall situation outside and inside the organisation. Using an *external audit*, you study trends and changes in the broad political–legal, economic, social–cultural and technological environment (abbreviated as *PEST* or, if ordered differently, as *STEP*). You also research any ecological, competitive and demographic changes that might affect marketing and performance. This includes researching how issues, threats and opportunities might influence your ability to put the marketing plan into action and achieve good results. In addition, you need an *internal audit* to examine the current situation within the organisation, including resources, offerings, capabilities, important business relationships and – an important way of learning from the past – the results of earlier plans.

In crafting a solid marketing plan, you should be realistic about your competitive situation, as the experience of YesAsia.com illustrates.

MARKETING IN PRACTICE: YESASIA.COM

Joshua Lau, founder of YesAsia, knew his business needed a very focused marketing plan to thrive in an e-commerce world dominated by Amazon.com, Yahoo! and other giants. In considering how to differentiate YesAsia, Lau came to the realisation that expatriates, immigrants and students living abroad had different needs from those of consumers at home. Therefore, he developed a plan to market Asian entertainment products – such as Korean videos, Japanese graphic novels and Asian music – online to Asian consumers in Europe and the United States. Later he adapted his plan to market English-language entertainment items to English-speaking consumers in Asia. By maintaining warehouses in California and Hong Kong, the company can buy from suppliers and ship to customers in the most economical way. Keeping its marketing plan updated for the latest product trends and delivering the value that customers want has helped YesAsia prosper as it serves 200,000 buyers worldwide.[24]

Chapter 2 discusses how to assess the current situation by collecting and analysing internal and external data.

Stage 2: Research and analyse markets and customers

After analysing the current situation, you can begin researching your markets and customers (consumers, businesses, clients or constituents). This entails investigating trends in market share, product demand, customer needs and perceptions, demographics, product demand, buying patterns and customer satisfaction. Through research, you will seek to answer questions such as: Who is buying or would buy the product being marketed, and why? How are buying patterns changing, and why? What is in demand, when is it in demand, where is it in demand and how is demand expected to change over time?

Gathering data about customer needs, interests and buying behaviour is faster and easier with technology. For example, Google and Yahoo! (among other online search sites) list trends based on rankings of Web searches conducted on their sites.[25] As another example, Otis Elevator, the US-based maker of lifts, uses software to analyse how business customers and prospects use its website. The software is sophisticated enough to show that architects, for instance, tend to click on certain sections of the site. It can also help Otis track which businesses make purchases after using the site. 'Our efforts are to get as close to our customers and what they are doing as possible', states the company's senior manager of e-business.[26]

Yet using technology to track customer activities and behaviours raises ethical questions about invasion of privacy. When the Benetton Group disclosed plans to test clothing labels fitted with tiny radio transmitters, for instance, public reaction was swift and negative. Critics feared that such tracking would enable companies to monitor product usage in homes and at the individual level. A similar backlash prompted Wal-Mart, the world's largest retailer, to halt an in-store test of radio-enhanced tags designed for merchandise tracking and theft control.[27]

Regardless of the technology used, marketers must be careful not to overdo customer research. Not long ago, different groups within IBM were conducting dozens of surveys to assess customer satisfaction; one survey involved 40,000 interviews conducted in 58 countries. Some IBM customers complained about being surveyed up to five times a year. As a result, IBM combined some surveys and made the response data available across the corporation. 'When you're the CEO of one of our major customers, and you hear from IBM three times in a month on a survey that sounds identical to the last one you answered, you get a little annoyed', says IBM's director of worldwide customer satisfaction management.[28]

See Chapter 3 for more about the process of researching and analysing markets and customers.

Stage 3: Determine segmentation, targeting and positioning

No organisation has the resources (people, money or time) satisfactorily to serve every customer in every market. You will therefore use your research and customer knowledge to identify which specific subgroups that can be effectively targeted through marketing. To do this, you group customers into **segments** based on distinct characteristics, behaviours, needs or wants that affect their demand for or usage of the product being marketed.

A segment may be as small as one consumer or business customer or as large as millions of customers in multiple nations. More companies, for example, are viewing the pre-teen market for toys as a global segment. Research by the toymaker Mattel found that girls in the United Kingdom, Italy, Spain, South Korea, China, Japan and other countries were all interested in playing with blonde-haired, blue-eyed dolls like Barbie. 'The general, overriding belief was that kids are different' from country to country, observed the president of Mattel Brands. 'But we discovered that wasn't the case. Kids are more alike than they are different.'[29] Accordingly, Mattel's marketers formulated a comprehensive marketing plan for simultaneously introducing a new Rapunzel Barbie doll around the world, supported by advertising and in-store promotions. The doll quickly became one of the most popular toys in many European countries. Demand was so strong, in fact, that Carrefour and other retailers ran out during the holiday selling season.[30]

Next you will decide on your **targeting** approach. Will you focus on a single segment, on two or more segments or on one entire market? How will these segments be covered through marketing? You also need to formulate a suitable **positioning**, which means using marketing to create a competitively distinctive place (position) for the product or brand in the mind of targeted customers. The purpose is to set your product apart from competing products in a way that is meaningful to customers.

For example, in consumer markets, Prêt À Manger differentiates its sandwiches and other ready-to-eat foods using the positioning of 'made fresh daily'. Burberry positions its clothing and accessories on the basis of recognisably elegant style. In business markets, Rolls-Royce positions its jet engines on the basis of quality. Your chosen positioning must be conveyed consistently through all marketing programmes as a way of reinforcing the competitive differentiation.

Chapter 4 discusses segmentation, targeting and positioning in further detail.

Stage 4: Set marketing plan objectives and direction

Now you are ready to set the direction of your marketing plan, based on the organisation's mission statement and higher-level goals. Most companies use marketing plans to support a direction of growth. As shown in Figure 1.5, there are six approaches to growth: penetrating existing markets, expanding within existing markets, adding new markets, offering existing products, modifying existing products and offering entirely new products.[31] Some companies strive for growth through more than one of these expansion strategies. Diageo, based in London, has both created new alcoholic beverages for existing markets (such as Ciroc vodka) and entered new geographical markets with existing brands (such as Baileys).[32] When an organisation chooses growth, its marketing plan defines objectives in financial terms (such as achieving higher turnover or profits) and marketing terms (such as achieving higher market share). In addition, many companies define societal objectives (for example performance in areas of social responsibility, ecological protection and stakeholder relations).

| FIGURE 1.5 | Growth grid |

Source: After Alan R. Andreasen and Philip Kotler, *Strategic Marketing for Non-profit Organisations*, 6th edn (Upper Saddle River, NJ: Prentice Hall, 2003), p. 81.

Instead of choosing a growth strategy, companies trying to protect their current profit situation or their market share may use their marketing plans to sustain the current turnover level. Those under severe financial strain may develop plans to retrench by selling off units. For example, Edesur, the electrical utility serving southern Buenos Aires, chose not to pursue growth until a government-imposed price freeze was lifted, inflation slowed, the currency stabilised and thefts of equipment and materials were controlled.[33] Some companies prepare a marketing plan for downsizing the marketing activities of a business unit (or the entire organisation) in an orderly manner.

Goals and objectives are not the same, although the words are often used interchangeably. **Goals** are longer-term targets that help a business unit (or the entire organisation) achieve overall performance and fulfil its mission; **objectives** are shorter-term performance targets that lead to the achievement of goals. Thus, your marketing plan should aim to achieve objectives that, in turn, bring your organisational closer to its goals. As Ambler notes, key corporate goals must be connected throughout the organisation, all the way down to the marketing plan and individual marketing programmes, if the company is to succeed.[34]

See Chapter 5 for more information about establishing the marketing plan's direction and objectives.

Stage 5: Plan marketing strategies, programmes and support

In this stage, you will plan marketing strategies and tactics to achieve the objectives you set earlier. You will look not only at how to deliver value that meets customers' needs but also at the coordination of the basic marketing mix tools of product, place, price and promotion within individual marketing programmes. In addition, you should determine how to support the marketing effort with customer service and internal marketing. For practical reasons, you probably will not finalise all the details of these marketing-mix strategies until your marketing plan has been approved and funded and is ready for implementation.

Product

The product offering may be a tangible good such as a television or an intangible service such as expert tax-preparation assistance. Often, however, an offering combines the tangible and the intangible, as when a mobile phone company markets phones (tangible) along with phone service (intangible) or a manufacturer markets robotic assembly equipment (tangible) and provides repair services (intangible). The brand is another intangible but extremely important aspect of the product offering. In planning product strategy, you need to consider all the components of the offering, how customers will perceive the product offering, how its benefits will satisfy customers' needs and how it should be marketed from introduction on through the product's life.

Figure 1.6 lists some of the elements and processes to consider when planning for product offerings (specifics vary from organisation to organisation and product to product). See Chapter 6 for more about developing product and brand strategy for a marketing plan.

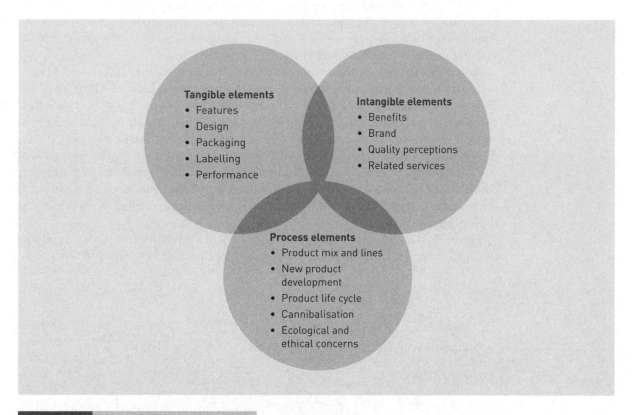

Tangible elements
- Features
- Design
- Packaging
- Labelling
- Performance

Intangible elements
- Benefits
- Brand
- Quality perceptions
- Related services

Process elements
- Product mix and lines
- New product development
- Product life cycle
- Cannibalisation
- Ecological and ethical concerns

FIGURE 1.6   Planning the product offering

Channel and logistics

Channel and logistics strategy – place strategy – is concerned with how customers gain access to the product offering, regardless of whether it's a tangible good or an intangible service. Will you market directly to your chosen customer segments, the way Dell uses its website and direct mail campaigns to sell personal computers to consumers and businesses? Or will you use indirect channels by working with intermediaries to make your products available, the way Vespa works with dealers to market its motor scooters? B2B companies also face similar choices: Will they market through wholesalers, distributors or agents that sell to business buyers? Should they deal directly with some or all of their business customers?

Your decisions will relate not only to elements of the channels themselves, as shown in Figure 1.6, but also to the logistics involved in making products available, including shipping, inventory management, order fulfilment and related functions. Current channel and logistical arrangements should be evaluated as part of the internal audit before you plan channel strategy for any new marketing plan. And, as with all other marketing mix tools, the needs, expectations and preferences of customers should be deciding factors in decisions about adding value through channels and logistics.

In the early 1990s, for example, after decades of distributing milk and dairy products through supermarkets and convenience stores, Japan's Morinaga Milk Industry Co. sensed growing public interest in home delivery. Its marketers developed marketing plans to take advantage of this change by promoting the reliability and convenience of home delivery, along with nutrient-rich milk drinks developed especially for this direct channel. Within ten years, Morinaga was delivering milk to nearly two million households. This channel strategy not only differentiated the company from competitors, but it also enhanced company revenue and allowed management consistently to predict and meet demand for the delivery-only products.[35]

Figure 1.7 shows some of the elements to consider when planning channel and logistics strategy. These topics are covered more thoroughly in Chapter 7.

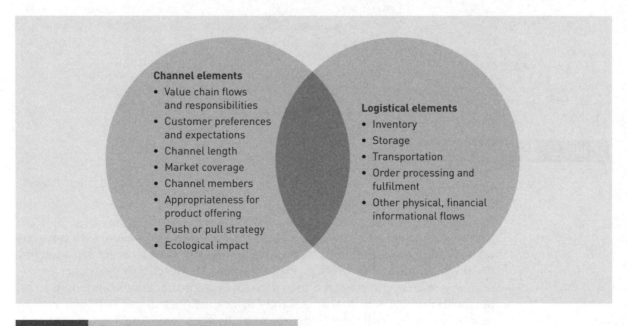

Channel elements
- Value chain flows and responsibilities
- Customer preferences and expectations
- Channel length
- Market coverage
- Channel members
- Appropriateness for product offering
- Push or pull strategy
- Ecological impact

Logistical elements
- Inventory
- Storage
- Transportation
- Order processing and fulfilment
- Other physical, financial informational flows

FIGURE 1.7　Planning channel and logistics strategy

Price

What should you charge for your product offering? In planning price strategy, marketers must answer a number of key questions, including: How do customers perceive the value of the good or service? How can price be used to reflect the positioning of the product, brand or organisation? What costs must be considered when calculating revenues and profitability? How does the price fit with other marketing mix decisions? How will competitive pressures affect pricing? And how can pricing bring the organisation closer to its objectives and goals?

Pricing is a vital ingredient in the marketing plan that 7-Eleven recently devised for attracting price-conscious shoppers who buy imported beer.

MARKETING IN PRACTICE: 7-ELEVEN

This huge convenience store chain, which is under Japanese ownership, operates thousands of outlets in Japan and the United States. Not long ago, its US marketers recognised that many shoppers were buying lower-priced store brands. In the category of imported beer, however, few retailers were offering low-priced alternatives and Mexico's Corona beer remained the top imported beer in the United States. The 7-Eleven marketers therefore developed a plan to import beer from El Salvador's Cerveceria La Constancia brewery, market it in a distinctive bottle under the Santiago brand and price it noticeably lower than Corona. Now 7-Eleven is closely tracking revenue figures for its Santiago beer and watching for any changes in sales of its other beer products, as well. 'We wanted to create a brand that would be as popular as any other beer inside the import category', explained the vice president of merchandising.[36]

Because customers with Internet access can easily compare prices, you should allow for price adjustments and more flexibility, such as participating in online auctions as appropriate. When companies cut prices too low, however, they can hurt profits, which is why pricing is such an integral and important part of the marketing planning process. Figure 1.8 summarises some of the elements involved in price strategy. See Chapter 8 for more about price and value.

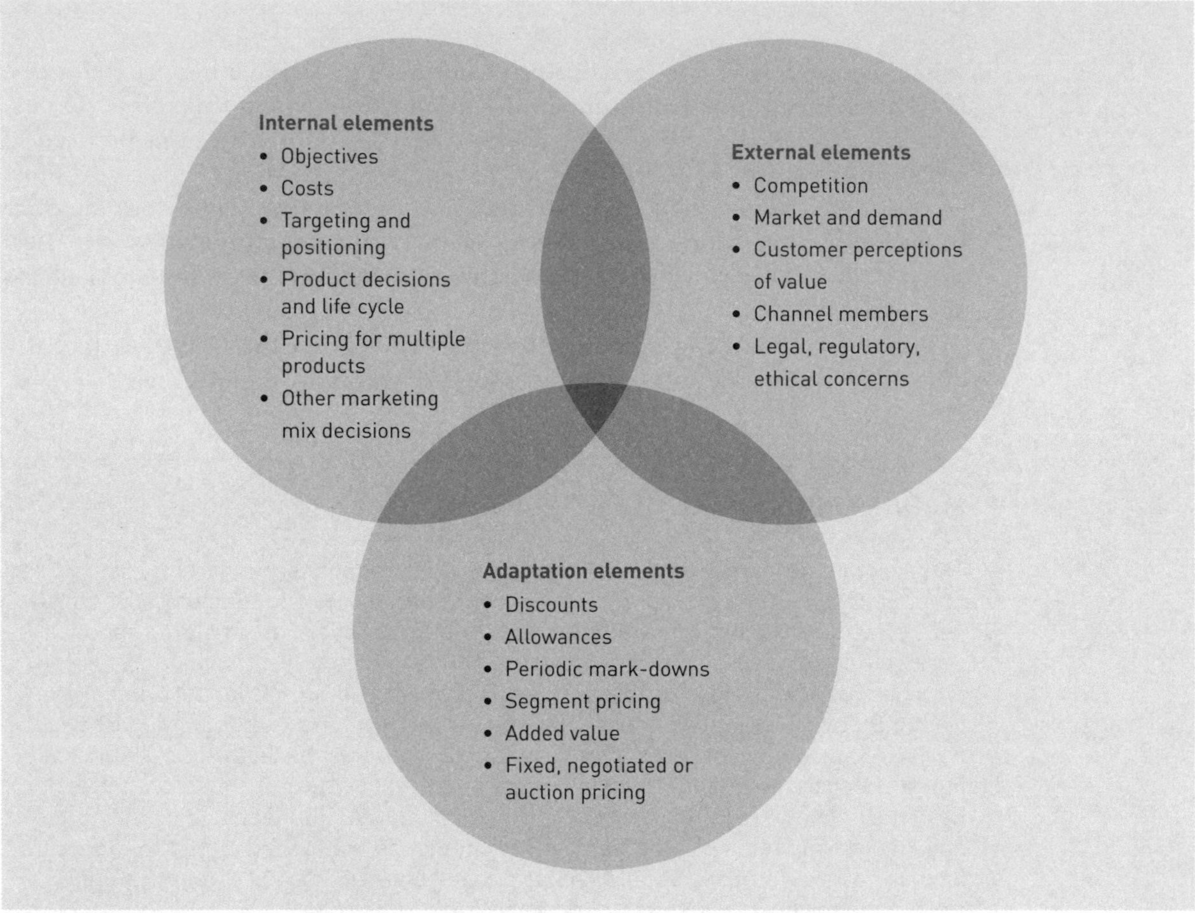

Internal elements
- Objectives
- Costs
- Targeting and positioning
- Product decisions and life cycle
- Pricing for multiple products
- Other marketing mix decisions

External elements
- Competition
- Market and demand
- Customer perceptions of value
- Channel members
- Legal, regulatory, ethical concerns

Adaptation elements
- Discounts
- Allowances
- Periodic mark-downs
- Segment pricing
- Added value
- Fixed, negotiated or auction pricing

FIGURE 1.8   Planning price strategy

Integrated marketing communication

Integrated marketing communication strategy – also called promotion strategy – covers all the tools you use in reaching out to your targeted segments. Media and online advertising are among the most visible and sometimes the most flamboyant; other tools include: public relations, sales promotion, personal selling and direct marketing techniques such as messages delivered via e-mail, mobile phone and post. Given the needs, interests, expectations and buying patterns of customers in targeted segments, most organisations allow for a variety of messages and media in their marketing plans. However, you should be sure that the content and impact of the entire promotion strategy is consistent, unified and supportive of your positioning and objectives.

Because consumers and business customers are constantly bombarded with promotions, many companies look for out-of-the-ordinary ways of reaching targeted segments. Peugeot, for instance, is promoting its family cars through special arrangement with Tussauds' UK theme parks. Visitors to Alton Towers Theme Park and other Tussauds' parks can try out a World Rally Championship car simulator, look over new car models and redeem discount tickets received from test-driving Peugeot cars at local dealerships. Peugeot is also telling customers about the deal through its *Rapport* magazine. A company manager calls the arrangement 'an ideal medium in which to communicate our range of family vehicles to the right target market'.[37]

Figure 1.9 presents some of the many elements to consider when developing an integrated marketing communication strategy. See Chapter 9 for more on this topic.

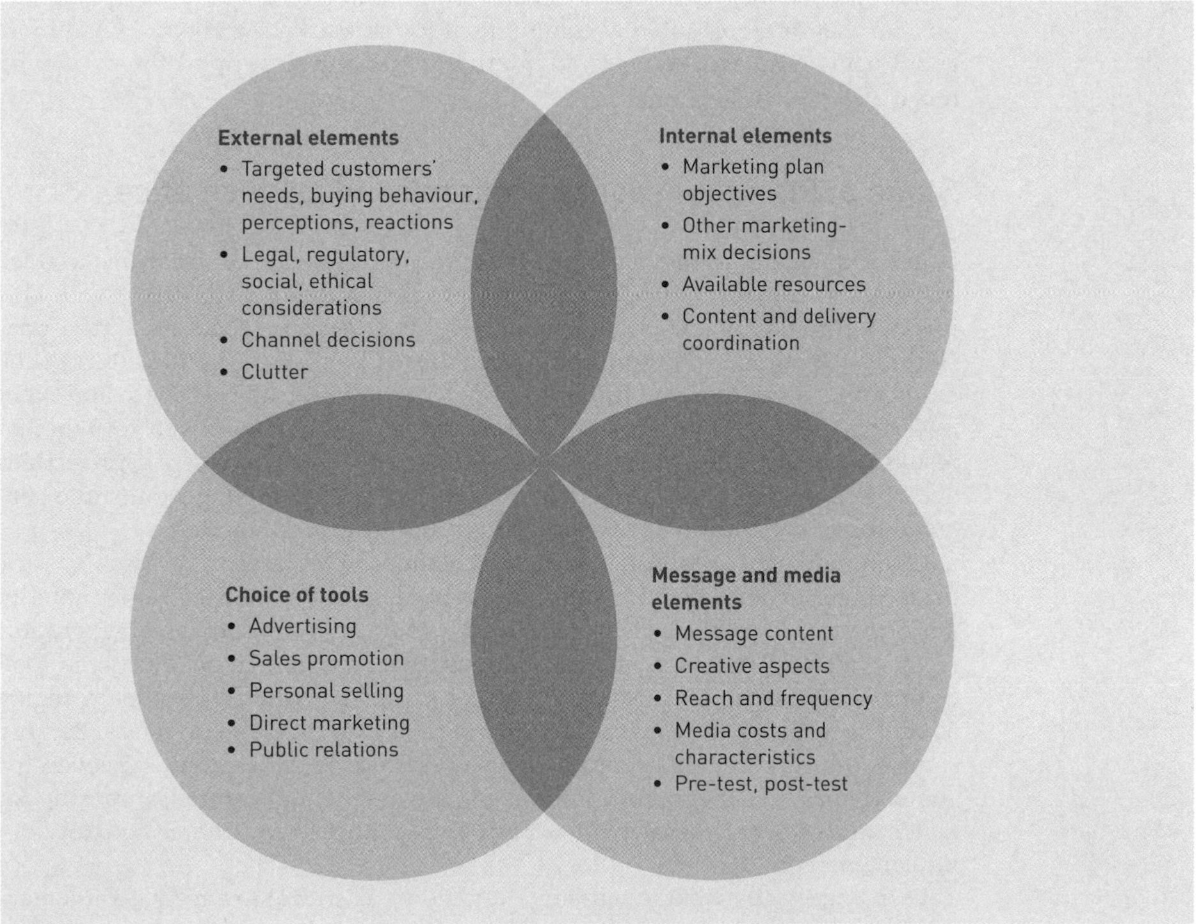

External elements
- Targeted customers' needs, buying behaviour, perceptions, reactions
- Legal, regulatory, social, ethical considerations
- Channel decisions
- Clutter

Internal elements
- Marketing plan objectives
- Other marketing-mix decisions
- Available resources
- Content and delivery coordination

Choice of tools
- Advertising
- Sales promotion
- Personal selling
- Direct marketing
- Public relations

Message and media elements
- Message content
- Creative aspects
- Reach and frequency
- Media costs and characteristics
- Pre-test, post-test

FIGURE 1.9   Planning integrated marketing communication (promotion) strategy

Marketing-mix support

You can plan to support your product, place, price and promotion strategies in two main ways. First, you should decide on an appropriate customer service level, in line with the chosen positioning, resource availability and customers' needs or expectations. B2B customers often require service before, during and after a purchase, from tailoring product specifications to arranging installation to maintaining and repairing the product years later. As an example, Legend Holdings, China's largest computer manufacturer, provides pre-purchase service to help companies and schools configure systems tailored to their unique needs and post-purchase repair service during the warranty period. Legend also provides customer service support for consumers, including warranty coverage.[38]

Second, you will need the commitment and cooperation of others to implement and control your plan. This requires *internal marketing*, activities designed to build relationships with colleagues and staff members backed up by personnel policies that reinforce internal commitment to the marketing effort.[39] Read more about using customer service and internal marketing to support the marketing mix in Chapter 10.

Stage 6: Plan to measure progress and performance

Before implementing the marketing plan, you must decide on measures to track marketing progress and performance toward achieving your objectives. This involves developing and documenting budgets, forecasts, schedules and responsibilities for all marketing programmes. You will also forecast the effect of the marketing programmes on future turnover, profitability, market share and other measures that signal progress toward objectives. The purpose is to see whether results are better than expected, lagging expectations or just meeting projections and objectives. For perspective, it is important to put marketing results into context through comparisons with competitors and the overall market.

Often marketers establish quantifiable standards (*metrics*) to measure specific marketing outcomes and activities. In many cases, these metrics look at interim performance of specific brands, individual products or product lines, geographic results, financial results, customer relationship results and so on. The Swiss food company Nestlé, for instance, has metrics for analysing interim results by region as well as by product, category, brand, profitability and major currencies. Because some products carry different tracking codes in different regions, however, the company has launched a new initiative to streamline and centralise tracking for faster and easier measurement of results and, therefore, tighter control over implementation.[40]

Deciding exactly what to measure – and how – is critical to effective implementation and control of a marketing plan. Here is what managers at the online auction firm eBay do.

MARKETING IN PRACTICE: EBAY

'If you can't measure it, you can't control it', emphasises Meg Whitman, eBay's CEO. Whitman recently set a five-year goal of achieving $3 billion in revenues; in monitoring performance, she and her marketers use measures such as the number of registered users, the gross monetary value of auction sales hosted and the revenue eBay earns on each transaction. The CEO personally monitors how many people visit and use the site daily, how long each person remains on each visit, even what users are saying about the site (and its management) on eBay discussion pages.

When an interim measurement indicates improvement is needed, Whitman and her team take action. For instance, eBay compared the speed at which it introduces new website features to that of similar sites. Finding that others added new features at a speedier pace, the company pinpointed this area for improvement. On the other hand, Whitman warns, 'You have to be careful because you could measure too much'.[41]

Check Chapter 11 for more about planning to measure marketing progress and performance.

Stage 7: Implement, control and evaluate the plan

The real test of any marketing plan's effectiveness comes at implementation. For effective control, you will start with the objectives you have set, establish specific standards for measuring progress toward those targets, measure actual marketing performance, analyse the results and take corrective action if results are not as expected. Businesses generally apply several types of marketing control at different levels and intervals. The outcome of this stage feeds back to the beginning of the marketing planning process, paving the way for changes as needed.

The marketing control process is iterative: you will check your results against standards at designated points during implementation to identify variances so you can realign performance with expectations before programmes are complete. When the Uganda Red Cross participated in International Red Cross Week, for example, it launched a programme to receive donations of 5,000 units of blood nationwide. To reach this week-long objective, each regional centre was assigned to collect a specific number of units. Midway through the week, however, after comparing donations with objectives, officials found that some regions were running behind projections. They then sought additional publicity to reinforce the urgent need for blood and encourage more donors to volunteer in those areas so the overall objective could be achieved.[42]

Depending on your organisation's instructions, you may compare results with standards daily, weekly, monthly and quarterly; you may even compare results with standards on an hourly basis if you need to maintain extremely tight control over marketing. In addition, you and your managers will evaluate the marketing plan's overall performance after all programmes are complete. See Chapter 12 for more about how to prepare for effective implementation and control of your marketing plan.

CHAPTER SUMMARY

1. *Explain the relationship among the three strategy levels.*
   Organisational (corporate) strategy sets the organisation's overall purpose, long-term direction, goals, range of businesses and approach to value creation. Within this framework, business strategy sets the scope of individual units and proposes how each will compete, what markets each will serve and how unit resources will be used. Marketing strategy is concerned with how each unit uses the marketing-mix tools plus service and internal marketing to achieve objectives. Marketing strategy implements and supports higher-level strategies and simultaneously provides market and customer information for the development and fine-tuning of the organisational and business strategies. Each level of strategy results in a plan covering a specific period; typically, a marketing plan covers one year, whereas business plans may cover three to five years and strategic plans cover longer periods.

2. *Discuss how a mission statement is used and what it should contain.*
   The mission statement outlines the organisation's fundamental purpose, describes a future vision of what it strives to become, clarifies priorities and sets the tone for all organisation members. It is used to drive strategy and planning decisions at the organisational, business and marketing levels. A good mission statement should summarise the organisation's customer focus, competitively superior approach to value creation for customers and other stakeholders, market scope, guiding values and core competencies.

3. *Define marketing planning and outline the seven stages in the process.*
   Marketing planning is the structured process that links the mission, organisational strategy and business strategy to the decisions and actions made by marketing managers. The resulting course of action is documented in the organisation's marketing plan. The marketing planning process consists of seven stages: (1) analyse the current external and internal situation; (2) research and analyse markets and customers; (3) determine segmentation, targeting and positioning; (4) set marketing objectives and direction; (5) plan marketing strategies, programmes and support; (6) plan to measure progress toward objectives and performance; (7) implement, control and evaluate the plan.

KEY TERM DEFINITIONS

business strategy Strategy determining the scope of each unit and how it will compete, what market(s) it will serve and how unit resources will be allocated and coordinated to create customer value

core competencies Organisational capabilities that are not easily duplicated and that serve to differentiate the organisation from competitors

goals Longer-term targets that help a business unit (or the organisation as a whole) achieve performance

marketing plan Internal document outlining the marketplace situation and the marketing strategies and programmes that will help the organisation achieve its business and organisational goals

marketing planning Structured process that links the mission statement, organisational strategy and business strategy to marketing decisions and actions

marketing strategy Strategy used to determine how the marketing-mix tools of product, place, price and promotion – supported by service and internal marketing strategies – will be used to meet objectives

mission statement Statement of the organisation's fundamental purpose, pointing the way toward a future vision of what it aspires to become

objectives Shorter-term performance targets that lead to the achievement of organisational goals

organisational (or corporate) strategy Strategy governing the organisation's overall purpose, long-range direction and goals, the range of businesses in which it will compete and how it will create value for customers and other stakeholders

positioning Use of marketing to create a competitively distinctive place (position) for the product or brand in the mind of the target market

relationship marketing Marketing geared toward building ongoing relationships with customers rather than stimulating isolated purchase transactions

segments Customer groupings within a market, based on distinct needs, wants, behaviours or other characteristics that affect product demand or usage and can be effectively addressed through marketing

sustainable marketing The establishment, maintenance and enhancement of customer relationships so that the objectives of the parties involved are met without compromising the ability of future generations to achieve their own objectives

targeting Determination of the specific market segments to be served, order of entry into the segment and coverage within segments

THE PRACTICAL MARKETER CHECKLIST NO. 1:
ORGANISATIONAL MISSION STATEMENT

Content

Who will the organisation focus on as customers, clients or constituents?

How will the organisation create value for customers and other stakeholders?

What main markets (geographic, product) will the organisation serve?

What guiding values will the organisation adopt?

What core competencies will the organisation apply for competitive advantage?

Application

Does the mission statement provide direction for decisions, actions and resource allocation?

Is the mission statement capable of rallying employees and inspiring stakeholders?

Is the mission statement too broad or detailed as a foundation for strategy and marketing planning?

Is the mission statement forward-looking and enduring to guide the organisation into the future?

ONLINE RESOURCES

Marketing planning and mission statements

- www.booksites.net/wood_mp – Provides instructions about using *Marketing Plan Pro* and other planning aids.

- Palo Alto's *Marketing Plan Pro* site (www.paloalto.com) – Offers dozens of sample plans, FAQs, technical support and other information; especially valuable for users of the software on the CD that accompanies this book.

- Startups UK (www.startups.co.uk) – Covers the fundamentals of marketing and offers general information for small businesses.

- University of Bradford (www.brad.ac.uk/acad/mancen/micromods/market/plantext.htm) – Discusses the nature, contents and usage of marketing plans.

- Know this.com (www.knowthis.com) – Provides links to a variety of marketing plan guides plus general information about marketing techniques.

- Internet Non-profit Centre (www.nonprofits.org/npofaq/03/21.html) – Discusses mission statements for non-profit organisations and presents several examples.

QUESTIONS FOR DISCUSSION AND ANALYSIS

1. Why would all kinds of organisations (businesses, non-profit organisations and some governmental agencies) benefit from defining their mission?

2. What are the arguments for and against an e-commerce business preparing and following a yearly marketing plan? What would you recommend?

3. Why is a marketing plan considered an internal document only, not for public disclosure?

APPLY YOUR KNOWLEDGE

Choose a particular industry (such as banking or soft drinks) and research the mission statement and recent marketing activities of two competing businesses.

- What do the mission statements say about the customer focus, value creation, market scope, guiding values and core competencies of these companies?

- For each company, how do specific marketing actions appear to relate to the stated mission? As an example, does the advertising reflect the customer focus in the mission statement?

- What changes would you suggest to make the mission statement of one of the companies more effective as a guide for the marketing planning process or as an inspiration for managers and employees?

- Prepare a brief oral or written report summarising your comments.

 ## BUILD YOUR OWN MARKETING PLAN

This is the first of 12 exercises designed to give you hands-on experience in building a marketing plan. By the end of this course, you will know how to work through all the stages in the marketing planning process and how to document a marketing plan. Depending on your lecturer's instructions, you will base your marketing planning on an actual organisation (as if you were one of its marketing executives) or prepare a marketing plan for a hypothetical company or non-profit organisation.

As you complete each of these cumulative exercises, record your findings and decisions in a marketing plan prepared using Marketing Plan Pro *software. As an alternative, you can write your plan following the order of topics shown in Figure 1.3. In subsequent chapters, consider how your decisions will work with earlier marketing decisions and how you can shape the overall marketing plan to achieve its objectives.*

Start by defining the mission of your hypothetical organisation or analysing the mission statement of the organisation you have chosen. If necessary, amend an existing organisation's mission statement so it covers all five content areas in checklist No. 1 and can be used to guide marketing decisions. What does this mission statement suggest about the organisation's purpose? Include information about the mission statement when writing about the current marketing situation in your marketing plan. In preparation for later stages of the marketing planning process, make notes about how the mission affects the markets and customers to be served, the product offering, the competition and higher-level strategy. Also look at the general direction you expect the marketing plan to take: will it drive a growth strategy, sustain current turnover or support retrenching? Finally, write a few lines about what the marketing plan needs to accomplish in order to lead the organisation closer to its strategic goals. Save your notes for use in completing later assignments.

CLOSING CASE: VOLKSWAGEN REVS UP ITS MARKETING PLAN

Can a carmaker known for low-priced, utilitarian cars successfully market to more affluent customers? Volkswagen, based in Wolfsburg, Germany, is all geared up to find out. True to its name, which means 'the people's car', the company built its reputation making affordable, driver-friendly cars. Gradually the world's fourth-largest carmaker expanded its corporate and business strategies until it now offers something for nearly everyone under brands such as VW, Škoda, Seat, Audi, Bentley, Bugatti and Lamborghini.

Lately, VW has had a bumpy ride. CEO Bernd Pischetsrieder faces both flattening demand in some markets and shrinking share in Europe, although VW is the largest foreign carmaker operating in the burgeoning China market. Under the previous corporate strategy, the company produced multiple models based on one vehicle platform. As a result, individual models were not always clearly differentiated from one another and VW's brands often competed for the attention of the same customer segment. VW's strategy needed a tune-up.

Pischetsrieder started by having his staff chart the major customer segments against all VW models. They found that VW was strong in some areas, such as hatchbacks and compact cars, but weak in other areas. For example, the company offered neither convertibles nor compact minivans – both increasingly popular among European customers. And despite definite customer interest, VW's first sport-utility vehicle (SUV) – a four-wheel drive vehicle with off-road capability and a sporty appearance, which was developed in partnership with Porsche – came to the market well after rivals BMW and Mercedes introduced their own SUVs.

To compete more effectively and pursue growth, Pischetsrieder decided on a strategic move upmarket to meet the needs of more customers and to improve profitability. At the business level, the original VW Beetle was one of the first casualties of this corporate strategy. Although the Beetle had long been popular in Mexico, few were rolling off local assembly lines by the time the model was discontinued in 2003. Meanwhile, the marketing strategy put more emphasis on high-end models such as the Phaeton, priced as high as £68,000, and the Touareg, a luxury SUV model. New roadsters, convertibles and station wagon–minivan hybrids would give VW traction in market segments with strong demand. But VW is not abandoning current customers; it recently launched an updated version of its best-selling Golf model.

A highlight of the marketing mix is VW's clever advertising, which stresses each model's particular features and benefits, including the Touareg's powerful V10 diesel engine option. Already, VW sells more diesel vehicles in the United Kingdom than any other carmaker. However, moving upmarket will not happen overnight and it will be costly. 'It's an investment in the future', observes the VW executive board member in charge of strategy. 'It takes time to change people's perceptions.'[43] And this is just the start, says CEO Pischetsrieder: 'The strategy of VW is not complete yet. We have only started at the top end.'[44]

Case questions

1. What shifts in the external environment does VW seem to be addressing with its upmarket marketing strategy?

2. How would you suggest that VW build on its reputation and history as the maker of 'the people's car' as it markets to more affluent customers?

ENDNOTES

1. Quoted in 'Michael O'Leary', *Newsweek International*, 23 June 2003, pp. 64ff.

2. Based on information from: 'Low-Fare Airline EasyJet Loses More Ground to Ryanair As Growth Dips', *Evening Standard*, 7 July 2003, www.thisislondon.co.uk; 'Michael O'Leary', *Newsweek International*; Kerry Capell, 'Ryanair Rising', *Business Week*, 2 June 2003, pp. 40–1; 'Michael O'Leary', *Business Week*, 13 January 2003, p. 61; Phil Davies, 'Ryanair to Follow Southwest Example', *Travel Trade Gazette UK & Ireland*, 2 March 1994, p. 15; Branwell Johnson, 'Ryanair Axes Entire Buzz Marketing Team', *Marketing Week*, 20 March 2003, p. 5; Trish Saywell and Scott Neuman, 'Budget Air Carriers Are Flying High in Asia', *Wall Street Journal*, 3 July 2003, www.wsj.com.

3. Tim Ambler, *Marketing and the Bottom Line* (London: Financial Times Prentice Hall, 2000), pp. 19–20.

4. Charles Duhigg, 'Airbus Gets Qatar Order, Building Lead Over Boeing', *Washington Post*, 20 June 2003, pp. E3ff.; Tony Smith, 'It's Boeing vs. Airbus in Big Battle Over Brazil', *New York Times*, 3 June 2003, p. W1; John Tagliabue, 'Airbus in $24 Billion Deal for Military Jets', *New York Times*, 28 May 2003, p. W1.

5. Cordelia Salter-Nour, 'E-Commerce from Ghana', in Judy Strauss, Adel El-Ansary and Raymond Frost, *E-Marketing*, 3rd edn (Upper Saddle River, NJ: Prentice Hall, 2003), pp. 510–11.

6. 'The Mediocre Middle', *The Economist*, 28 June 2003, p. 67; 'Secret Shopper Supermarkets', *Internet Magazine*, April 2003, pp. S38ff.

7. Frances Brassington and Stephen Pettitt, *Principles of Marketing*, 3rd edn (Harlow, Essex: Financial Times Prentice Hall, 2003), p. 19.

8. Alison Maitland, 'Shell Takes Its Vexed Dilemmas to Business School', *Financial Times*, 7 May 2003, www.ft.com.

9. Charles Haddad, 'FedEx and Brown Are Going Green', *Business Week*, 11 August 2003, pp. 60–2.

10. Based on information in Deborah Ball, 'It Makes Dove, But Attracts Bears', *Wall Street Journal*, 31 July 2003, pp. C1, C3; Stephanie Thompson, '"Master" Plan: Bestfoods Strategy Results in Shakeup', *Advertising Age*, 7 July 2003, p. 3.

11. Ball, 'It Makes Dove, But Attracts Bears'; Thompson, '"Master" Plan: Bestfoods Strategy Results in Shakeup'.

12. Jonathan Karp, 'Tiny Firm Exporting Fatigues Holds Key to Brazilian Future', *Wall Street Journal*, 1 May 2003, www.wsj.com.

13. Adapted from Stephen J. Porth, *Strategic Management* (Upper Saddle River, NJ: Prentice Hall, 2003), pp. 53–4; Forest R. David and Fred B. David, 'It's Time to Redraft Your Mission Statement', *Journal of Business Strategy*, January–February 2003, pp. 11ff.

14. Médecins Sans Frontières website, www.msf.org.

15. Campbell Robertson, 'Making a Bag Travellers Can Lean On', *New York Times*, 15 June 2003, sec. 3, p. 2.

16. Heather Timmons, 'Owner of Miller Beer to Buy Most of Big Italian Brewer', *New York Times*, 15 May 2003, p. W1.

17. Quoted on Tetra Pak website, www.tetrapak.com.

18. Stephen J. Porth, *Strategic Management* (Upper Saddle River, NJ: Prentice Hall, 2003), pp. 85–6.

19. John Tagliabue, 'A Rival to Gap That Operates Like Dell', *New York Times*, 30 May 2003, pp. W1–W7.

20. Quoted in Sir George Bull, 'What Does the Term Marketing Really Stand for?', *Marketing*, 30 November 2000, p. 30.

21. See Philip Kotler, *A Framework for Marketing Management*, 2nd edn (Upper Saddle River, NJ: Prentice Hall, 2003), p. 9.

22. Phred Dvorak, 'Beyond 1.0 Megapixel', *Wall Street Journal*, 17 June 2003, pp. B1, B11; Yoshio Takahashi and Ron Harui, 'NTT DoCoMo Swings to Profit of $1.83 Billion', *Dow Jones Newswires*, 8 May 2003, www.dowjones.com.

23. Erik Portanger, 'U.K.'s Standard Chartered Plans Afghan Branch', *Wall Street Journal*, 27 June 2003, p. A10.

24. Geoffrey A. Fowler, 'Target: Expats', *Wall Street Journal*, 16 June 2003, p. R6.

25. Lee Gomes, 'Web Allows People Just Like You and Me to Spot Trends. Uh-Oh', *Wall Street Journal*, 28 July 2003, p. B1.

26. Quoted in 'Otis Elevator Company Creates the Ultimate Web Data Mining Solution Using Sane Solutions' Net Tracker', *Internet World*, January 2003, p. 14.

27. Heather Green, 'Bugging the World', *Business Week*, 25 August 2003, pp. 100–1; James Covert and Christina C. Berk, 'Consumer Groups Rip Tracking Chips', *Wall Street Journal*, 30 July 2003, p. B3D.

28. Quoted in Kevin J. Clancy and Peter C. Krieg, *Counterintuitive Marketing* (New York: Free Press, 2000), pp. 199–201.

29. Quoted in Lisa Bannon and Carlta Vitzthum, 'One Toy Fits All', *Wall Street Journal*, 29 April 2003, www.wsj.com.

30. Bannon and Vitzthum, 'One Toy Fits All'.

31. H. Igor Ansoff, 'Strategies for Diversification', *Harvard Business Review*, September–October 1957, pp. 113–24; Ade S. Olusoga, 'Market Concentration versus Market Diversification and Internationalisation: Implications for MNE Performance', *International Marketing Review*, vol. 10, no. 2 (1993), pp. 40–59; Alan R. Andreasen and Philip Kotler, *Strategic Marketing for Non-profit Organisations*, 6th edn (Upper Saddle River, NJ: Prentice Hall, 2003), pp. 80–1.

32. Christopher Lawton and Deborah Ball, 'Liquor Giant Targets System Dating to End of Prohibition', *Wall Street Journal*, 8 May 2003, www.wsj.com; Gerry Khermouch and Kerry Capell, 'Spiking the Booze Business', *Business Week*, 19 May 2003, pp. 77–8.

33. Michael Casey, 'Rain Brings Hope', *Wall Street Journal*, 13 August 2003, p. B5B.

34. Tim Ambler, 'Set Clear Goals and See Marketing Hit Its Target', *Financial Times*, 29 August 2002, p. 8.

35. Taiga Uranaka, 'Got Milk Delivery? Doorstep Service Doubles in Last 10 Years', *Japan Times*, 24 July 2003, p. 8.

36. Quoted in Christopher Lawton and Ann Zimmerman, '7-Eleven Cracks Open a Private-Label Brew', *Wall Street Journal*, 2 May 2003, www.wsj.com.

37. Quoted in 'Peugeot Sponsors Tussauds Parks', *Marketing*, 17 April 2003, p. 5.

38. Justine Lau, 'Legend Launches Defence of PC Business', *Financial Times*, 2 June 2003, www.ft.com.

39. See Ambler, *Marketing and the Bottom Line*, Chapter 6.

40. Deborah Ball, 'Nestlé Hits Its Target for Sales, Affirms Growth Forecast for '04', *Wall Street Journal*, 25 October 2003, p. B6; Deborah Ball, 'Nestlé Craves Fatter Profits', *Wall Street Journal*, 19 August 2003, p. B5.

41. Information and quotations in Adam Lashinksy, 'Meg and the Machine', *Fortune*, 1 September 2003, pp. 68–78.

42. Esther Namugoji, 'Hundreds Donate Blood in Red Cross Week', *Africa News Service*, 12 May 2003, www.allafrica.com.

43. Quoted in Gail Edmondson, 'Will Yankee Drivers Buy VW Luxury?', *Business Week*, 3 November 2003, p. 51.

44. Quoted in Neal E. Boudette, 'After Luxury Drive, Volkswagen Breaks Down on Several Fronts', *Wall Street Journal*, 8 May 2003, pp. 1ff.; other information from: Clay Chandler, 'China Goes Car Crazy', *Fortune*, 1 September 2003, pp. 120–2; Mark Lander, 'A German Town Tells Volkswagen: We Are Family', *New York Times*, 31 August 2003, sec. 3, p. 4; 'Adwatch: Volkswagen's "Skulls" Imply Animal Power of V10 Engine', *Marketing*, 5 June 2003, p. 21; 'VW's Brand Statement on Wheels', *Marketing*, 15 May 2003, p. 19; Gail Edmondson, 'VW Needs a Jump', *Business Week*, 12 May 2003, pp. 24ff.; 'The Last Love Bug: The Volkswagen Beetle', *The Economist*, 12 July 2003, p. 59.

2 Analysing the current situation

Comprehension outcomes

After studying this chapter, you will be able to:

- Discuss the use of internal and external audits
- Explain the main factors in the internal environment that can affect marketing and performance
- Explain the main factors in the external environment that can affect marketing and performance
- Understand the use of SWOT analysis in marketing planning

Application outcomes

After studying this chapter, you will be able to:

- Identify sources for environmental scanning and analysis
- Conduct internal and external audits
- Prepare a SWOT analysis

OPENING CASE: CHANGE BRINGS CHANGE AT CIBA SPECIALITY CHEMICALS

Marketing chemicals is at least as much of a challenge as marketing colas. Consider the challenges faced by Ciba Speciality Chemicals. This B2B company, with its headquarters in Basel, Switzerland, makes a wide variety of chemicals and coatings used by manufacturers of plastics, rubber, textiles, home and personal care products. To achieve corporate goals for growth and profitability, Ciba's managers have to track developments inside and outside the company carefully, identify and analyse shifts in demand and other environmental changes, then adjust internal capabilities and marketing accordingly.

For instance, a worldwide economic slump was dampening demand for some Ciba products not long ago, which in turn restrained the company's revenue growth. Unfortunately, predicting the short-term course of economic changes that affect demand is tricky if not impossible. So as some business customers slowed the pace of ordering to reduce their inventories, Ciba's marketers could not forecast with any certainty when demand for their products would rebound.

Because the company does business in more than 120 nations, fluctuation in currency exchange rates is another economic concern. Ciba's managers recently found that one quarter's sales of plastic additives, coating products and products for home and personal care was higher when measured in local currencies than when translated into Swiss francs, due to the effect of prevailing exchange rates. Yet by putting more internal emphasis on tight cost controls and operational productivity, Ciba's managers have been able to keep the company on track for net income performance as measured in Swiss francs.

Ciba is also responding to questions raised about the ecological impact of Irgarol, a paint additive designed to keep boat hulls free of algae and barnacles. Ciba conducted studies and found that the product does not damage sea life. However, a few countries have put restrictions on Irgarol use because of concerns about potential harm, and product sales would suffer if Irgarol is further restricted or – in the most extreme case – banned in some or all markets.

Finally, managers have been assessing how Ciba's internal resources and capabilities can support a corporate push to double the turnover growth rate. On the basis of this evaluation, they have initiated a multi-year innovation scheme. By increasing the budget for research and development and putting more resources toward marketing new products in new markets, Ciba is strengthening its ability to grow despite challenging external conditions.[1]

CHAPTER PREVIEW

Like their counterparts at Ciba Speciality Chemicals, all marketing managers need a thorough understanding of the organisation's current situation before they can create appropriate strategies and programmes. Ciba's managers have to determine where the company and each product stands before they can work out where they want to go and how to get there. Using internal sources, they can analyse results by product and product category, by country and by currency. These results are heavily influenced by economic and ecological factors, among other environmental factors. It is up to Ciba's marketing managers to identify the intricate connections among environmental factors that could affect performance. For instance, questions about the potential ecological repercussions of a Ciba product may also influence public opinion (a social–cultural factor) and legal or regulatory actions (a political–legal factor).

Many decisions – sometimes many jobs – depend on the conclusions marketers reach in this stage in the marketing planning process. Ciba's managers, for instance, decided to cut costs by closing some plants after concluding that, based on environmental analysis, the economic situation would not dramatically improve in the near future. The point is not to collect data and fashion it into a fact-filled report, but to work out which environmental factors are important to the organisation's marketing and performance. The factors that are most important to one organisation may be far less important to another, just as the effect on marketing and performance can vary a great deal from one organisation to another.

This chapter looks at how and why you will collect and interpret data about the environment inside and outside the organisation as a prerequisite for developing marketing strategy. First there is an overview of environmental scanning and analysis, including an overview of how marketers use internal and external audits to identify important aspects of the environment. The section also suggests sources that marketers can consult when gathering environmental data. After a discussion of particular factors in the internal and external environment that can make a difference to marketing and performance, the chapter closes with a look at how marketers use the data they collect to evaluate their organisation's strengths, weaknesses, opportunities and threats. *As you read this chapter, think about how you can apply the principles to develop a practical, effective marketing plan.*

ENVIRONMENTAL SCANNING AND ANALYSIS

In this first stage of the marketing planning process, you will look at the organisation's current situation within the context of the mission, higher-level strategies and higher-level goals. This is accomplished through **environmental scanning and analysis**, the systematic (and ongoing) collection and interpretation of data about both internal and external factors that may affect marketing and performance. When learning about the situation inside the organisation, marketers use an **internal audit**; when learning about the situation outside the organisation, they use an **external audit**.

All the relevant information is accumulated, evaluated and distilled into a critique reflecting the organisation's primary strengths, weaknesses, opportunities and threats, known as the **SWOT analysis**. In addition, many marketers conduct a SWOT analysis of their main rivals (and some companies that may become more important over time) to clarify the competitive situation. With this background and understanding, you are in a much better position to develop marketing strategies that leverage internal strengths, bolster internal weaknesses, take advantage of competitors' main weaknesses and defend against competitors' strengths, as shown in Figure 2.1.

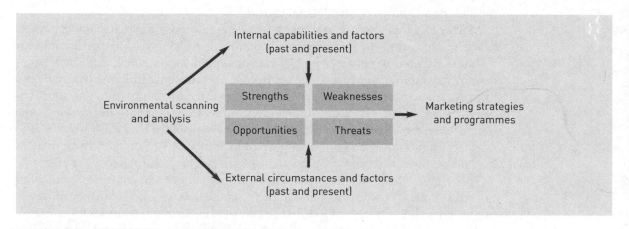

| FIGURE 2.1 | Environmental scanning and marketing strategy |

Details count in any environmental scan, but professional judgement plays a vital role as well. It is possible for marketers to be so thorough in their data collection and examination that 'analysis paralysis' sets in, preventing the organisation from using the information in a timely manner. Yet change – sometimes rapid, often unpredictable – is the one constant that every organisation must confront. In practical terms, then, you must use your best judgement (supported by expert models and other decision-making tools when available) to develop the most reasonable marketing plan under the circumstances. Looking ahead, you also should continue to monitor the current situation and make contingency plans if changes warrant.

Interpreting the data revealed by environmental scanning can be extremely challenging. For one thing, understanding the significance of and reason for a trend is not easy, even when a mound of details has been collected, simply because you may lack sufficient evidence to detect and correctly decipher one or more environmental patterns. Moreover, you rarely are able to foresee accurately the intensity or duration of a particular trend, let alone how it might evolve. You also need the ability to discern the combined influence of various internal and external factors. Finally, you must learn to conceptualise the likely effect of these factors and trends on the organisation and its marketing strategies, whether positive, negative or neutral – and recognise how the effect might change over time.[2]

Internal audit: strengths and weaknesses

The internal audit covers organisational resources and capabilities, current offerings, previous performance, business relationships and key issues. These internal factors, individually and in combination, are instrumental in the way a company fulfils its mission, serves its customers and competes in the marketplace. And – just as important – they contribute to the organisation's strengths and weaknesses in dealing with opportunities and threats.

A **strength** is an internal capability or factor that can help support the organisation in achieving its objectives, making the most of opportunities or deflecting threats. For example, one of Nintendo's great strengths has been its technical innovation, exhibited in the popular Game Boy and other electronic products. Another is its sizeable cash position, which supports innovative new product development and other internal activities. A **weakness** is an internal capability or factor that may prevent the organisation from achieving its objectives or effectively handling opportunities and threats. For Nintendo, one weakness could be changes in its business relationships: when its GameCube sales fell short of Nintendo's projections, some game development companies chose to reduce the number of new games they created for the console.[3]

An internal factor or capability might be considered a weakness within a certain competitive context. For instance, Nintendo sold millions of GameCubes during one recent year. Worldwide, however, its sales were far outdistanced by the market-leading Sony PlayStation 2 consoles.[4] And in Europe and the United States, Microsoft Xbox consoles outsold Nintendo GameCubes. Looking at this competitive situation, the developers might have cut back on making games for the GameCube because they were disappointed in the sales potential.

Where can you search for data when conducting an internal audit? Among the most productive sources are:

- *internal information systems* storing data about current offerings, finances, personnel and skills, technological capabilities, supplier relations, distributor connections, partnerships and other relevant details

- *internal documents and files* containing information about previous marketing plans and their results

- *managers, employees and staff specialists* who are knowledgeable about the organisation and can identify issues that may turn the situation favourable or unfavourable over time

- *outside or expert outside views* of the organisation, its strengths and its weaknesses, to supplement internal data and provide perspective.

External audit: opportunities and threats

The external audit covers political–legal factors, economic factors, social–cultural factors and technological factors (known as *PEST* or *STEP* if the order is rearranged) plus ecological and competitive factors that may present opportunities or pose threats. An **opportunity** is an external circumstance or factor that the organisation can attempt to exploit for higher performance. Nintendo is already taking advantage of an opportunity created by strong demand for games like *Pocket Monsters Ruby and Sapphire* that internal game developers have created for its GameCube and Game Boy products. Not only is game software less expensive than the game machines for Nintendo to create, it is more profitable.[5]

A **threat** is an external circumstance or factor that could inhibit organisational performance, if not addressed. Nintendo faces the threat of changing market demand for electronic game equipment and games. The market for children's electronic games – Nintendo's targeted segment for consoles – is growing more slowly than the market for teenage and adult electronic games. If growth in the targeted segment slows further or stops, Nintendo may change its focus. Competition is another threat, especially from Sony's PlayStation Portable, which directly challenges Nintendo's popular line of Game Boy Advance handheld game machines, and from the indirect competition offered by Nokia's game-equipped mobile phones.[6]

Sources that can be consulted for an external audit include:

- *internal information systems* storing data about customers, suppliers, industry trends, market share, technical standards and other relevant details

- *customer feedback* received through satisfaction surveys, advisory panels, customer service records, customer suggestions and other methods

- *government, academic or syndicated studies* about the market, demographic trends, competition and so on

- *industry groups* that publish studies or convene meetings about technological developments, political–legal issues and other external factors

- *internal personnel, suppliers, distributors and partners* who have knowledge of customer trends, competitive pressures and other opportunities and threats

- *media and online coverage* of external factors affecting the industry and the organisation

- *special interest groups* that monitor or get involved with ecological developments and other external factors
- *publicly available* materials about the competitive situation.

THE INTERNAL ENVIRONMENT

During an internal audit, you will scan and analyse five main factors looking for clues to strengths and weaknesses, as shown in Figure 2.2. The following sections discuss these factors in more depth. See this chapter's practical marketer checklist for a summary of questions to ask when conducting internal and external audits as background for further marketing planning.

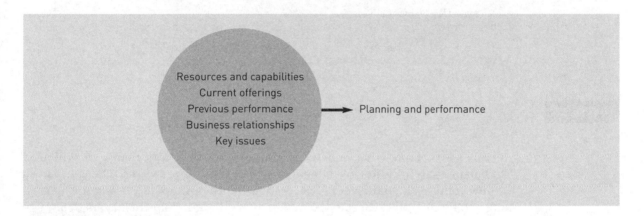

Resources and capabilities
Current offerings
Previous performance
Business relationships
Key issues

Planning and performance

FIGURE 2.2   Factors in the internal environment

Organisational resources and capabilities

As noted in Chapter 1, core competencies are internal capabilities that contribute to competitive superiority yet are not easily duplicated. Such capabilities are traced to the organisation's human, financial, informational and supply resources, as shown in Figure 2.3. One reason Wal-Mart de México, for example, has boosted its turnover and its profit margin is its core competency in logistics management. The retailer's enviable efficiency in planning inventory, warehousing goods and getting merchandise to the right store at the right time has helped it increase market share and continue growing even in challenging economic times.[7]

Human resources

- Workforce knowledge, skills, morale, turnover
- Top management support
- Individual commitment, initiative, entrepreneurial spirit
- Recruitment, training, development, rewards

Informational resources

- Data capture and storage systems
- Analysis tools
- Organisation-wide access to information

Financial resources

- Funding for marketing-mix activities
- Funding for marketing research
- Funding for internal support
- Anticipated funding for multi-year programmes

Supply resources

- Ample supply of materials, parts, components and service
- Supply chain relationships
- Inventory management

FIGURE 2.3   Areas of focus in organisational resources

Because no company has unlimited resources, you and your managers will need to balance carefully the investment and allocation of resources. The company's values, ethical standards and social responsibility position also affect this balancing act. From a practical standpoint, the internal audit helps managers determine the resources they have, the resources they can obtain and where their resources are currently committed. This is the starting point for identifying any resource gaps and determining how best to allocate resources in support of the marketing plan.

Outsourcing, strategic alliances and supply chain realignment are three ways that organisations can gain or supplement resource arrangements to bridge any gaps for added strength. Rather than devote internal resources to certain research-and-development (R&D) questions, some companies are outsourcing these. To illustrate, BASF, based in Germany, has posted scientific problems on the InnoCentive website and rewarded independent researchers or companies that respond with creative solutions. Other companies using R&D outsourcing for particular projects include Eli Lilly and Procter & Gamble.[8] Even product design and assembly can be outsourced. European carmakers such as Saab have contracted with Canadian-based Magna Steyr, for example, to design and put together some new models.[9]

Current offerings

Here, you review and analyse the goods and services that your organisation currently offers, another way of finding out where you stand before making plans to move ahead. Although the exact analysis depends on the organisation, companies generally examine the following, looking at historic trends and current position:

- composition of product mix and product lines

- product and line sales, market share

- customer needs satisfied by features and benefits

- product pricing and profitability

- product age and position in product life cycle

- links to other products

- proportional contribution to organisational performance.

In the course of this analysis, you need to determine how your organisation's offerings relate to its mission and organisational resources. Are the current offerings in line with the customer focus and vision in the mission statement? Are the firm's resources being allocated effectively and efficiently to current offerings? Answering these questions helps you apply the lessons learned in planning to exploit promising opportunities and defend against threats. Porsche, for example, found after examining its current offerings that it was not addressing an important marketplace opportunity: buyers of sport-utility vehicles (SUVs) (sporty four-wheel drive vehicles with off-road capability). As a result, the company planned the Cayenne, a speedy, powerful and luxurious SUV model. Customer response has been so positive that Porsche's profits have risen by 18 per cent since the introduction of the Cayenne.[10]

Previous performance

Although past performance is never a guarantee of future performance, looking at previous results can reveal insights about internal strengths and weaknesses. The purpose is to build on past marketing experience in planning new marketing activities. At a minimum, you will analyse these performance indicators:

- prior year sales (in units and monetary terms)

- prior year profits and other financial results

- historic trends in sales and profits by product, geographic region, customer segment, etc.

- results of previous marketing plans

- customer acquisition, retention and loyalty trends and costs.

Some companies also analyse the deals that got away. For instance, marketers at Samsung Electronics America carefully scrutinise data from 10,000 distributors to see how many and what kind of orders have been lost to rivals. By studying orders from customers in the health-care industry, the company learned that one competitor had won 40 per cent of the orders that Samsung did not get. This analysis of previous performance convinced Samsung to strengthen relations with hardware firms targeting computer buyers in the health-care field.[11] Many companies are taking a closer look at costs related to customer relationships, to avoid spending too much or attracting the wrong kinds of customers.

Business relationships

As the Samsung example suggests, good business relationships can act as strengths, helping organisations make the most of opportunities or defend against threats and profitably satisfy customers. Among the areas of business relationships to be examined during an internal audit are:

- value added by suppliers, distributors and strategic alliance partners

- internal relationships with other units or divisions

- capacity, quality, service, commitment and costs of suppliers and channel members

- changes in business relationships over time

- level of dependence on suppliers and channel members

The existence of a business relationship is not in and of itself a strength. Moreover, not having strong connections with vital suppliers or channel members can be a definite weakness when an organisation is seeking aggressive growth or simply struggling to survive. On the other hand, close connections – with internal divisions or with channel members and suppliers – can help with customer satisfaction and serve as a competitive advantage, as in the case of two Web-based companies, eBags.com and QVC.com.

MARKETING IN PRACTICE: EBAGS.COM AND QVC.COM

Supplier relations are a particular strength for e-commerce retailers such as eBags.com (which sells luggage) and QVC.com (which sells jewellery and other items). Both companies use the drop-shipping method of delivery: when an online purchase is made, they electronically transmit the order to the appropriate supplier for direct despatch to the customer. This allows the retailers to offer thousands of products without carrying extensive inventory or handling shipping.

Drop-shipping is popular among US-based Web retailers and is slowly gaining ground in Asia and other regions. However, if a supplier fails to despatch or despatches late, the retailer looks bad and risks losing the customer. This is why QVC staff members personally visit suppliers' facilities and occasionally place orders anonymously to see how suppliers perform. At eBags.com, managers closely monitor more than 150 suppliers to be sure orders are despatched no later than two days after purchase. If problems recur, the company ends the supplier relationship in order to preserve its customer relationships.[12]

Key issues

What specific issues could interfere with the organisation's ability to move toward its mission and goals, and what are the warning signs of potential problems? What specific issues are pivotal for organisational success? Some organisations look at key issues more closely, according to customer segment, market or product. For example, Alberto-Culver, which makes personal care products, has identified weather as a key issue that influences sales of certain products. Recently Alberto-Culver hired a company that specialises in long-term weather projections so it can have the information it needs to better match production and promotion of its Static Guard (which controls clothing static cling) to higher demand in hot, humid periods.[13]

At times, you may need marketing research to get a more complete picture of the issues, potential threats, emerging opportunities and alternative paths to success. For e-commerce businesses, encouraging visitors to keep clicking and ultimately buy online is a key issue. But a particularly important question is why some customers fail to complete the check-out process. To find out, the travel and holiday website 11thHourVacations.com hired a marketing research firm. Not only did the researchers look at which Web pages were visited and in what order, they examined whether visitors were scrolling to read entire pages and which links were most popular. Based on this research, the company tested different page designs, forms and instructions and implemented more than three dozen site changes to increase the odds that visitors would actually buy.[14]

THE EXTERNAL ENVIRONMENT

In contrast to the five factors in the internal environment, which offer clues to strengths and weaknesses, the six factors in the external environment offer clues to opportunities and threats (*see* Figure 2.4). These factors also suggest additional lines of inquiry for researching and analysing markets and customers, as discussed in Chapter 3. The following sections look at external environmental factors in more detail.

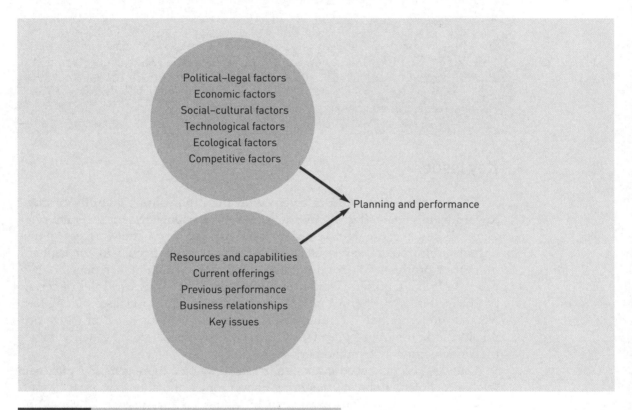

Political–legal factors
Economic factors
Social–cultural factors
Technological factors
Ecological factors
Competitive factors

Planning and performance

Resources and capabilities
Current offerings
Previous performance
Business relationships
Key issues

FIGURE 2.4   Factors in the external and internal environment

Political–legal factors

In this part of the external audit, you research and analyse the political, legal and regulatory guidelines that affect your marketing and operations. Depending on where your organisation is based and where it does business, political–legal factors can lead to profitable opportunities or potential threats (or both). Political instability can pose a threat to ongoing operations; laws, regulations and governmental actions can affect product purity and labelling, promotion, pricing, distribution, competitive behaviour and consumer choices.

For example, Société Générale, based in France, and Raiffeisen Bank, based in Austria, both identified opportunities in Russia because of a new law governing private bank accounts. In the past, only accounts at the state-run Sberbank were covered by deposit insurance. As Russia implemented legal changes so deposits in other banks would have insurance cover, the foreign banks projected increased customer demand for other bank services and accelerated plans for local branches and online banking.[15]

On the other hand, political action posed a threat to the future of mining by foreign companies in Chubut Province, Argentina, after a non-binding vote in the town of Esquel showed resident opposition. Some critics worried that mining might hurt water quality; others wanted Argentine companies, not foreign companies, involved. In response, the US-based company Meridian Gold began investigating how its proposed mine could affect water supplies and set up a fund to address any accidental impact on local ecology. But Patagonia Gold, owned in part by a UK exploration firm, stopped prospecting nearby. 'It's no use exploring if you can't turn the land into a mine', explained a vice president.[16]

Economic factors

In the interconnected global economy, recession or recovery in one region can have a cascading effect on the purchasing patterns of consumers and businesses near and far. Consider the lengthy recession in Japan, which prompted many Japanese tourists to postpone or scale back holiday trips to other nations. Airlines and tour companies catering to these travellers were greatly affected by the resulting change in demand. Thus, regional, national and international economic trends can be just as important as local economic conditions for some organisations.

Economic factors influence customer buying power because of the effect on consumer and business income, debt and credit usage. Economic slowdowns often discourage businesses from spending heavily on upgrading their plants, for instance; depending on economic conditions, some government agencies may postpone purchases or spread them over a longer period. Even if the home country economy is growing slowly, however, a company may look for opportunities in countries where the economic outlook seems more favourable, as Metro is doing.

MARKETING IN PRACTICE: METRO

Metro, a retail company based in Germany, has opened several superstores in Vietnam because of that nation's economic growth and higher consumer buying power. In the past decade, Vietnam's economy has grown at an annual rate of nearly 7 per cent. Projections suggest that the average annual per capita income in Vietnam will outpace that of nearby nations, especially Thailand, by 2020. Small wonder that Metro's marketing strategy calls for opening more stores in Hanoi and Ho Chi Minh City in the coming years. Given the expenses associated with new-store openings, Metro's management is realistic about waiting for profits as it makes marketing plans to gain a higher share of this fast-growing market.[17]

Social–cultural factors

Social–cultural factors are among the most dynamic in the external environment, affecting the size and composition of markets and segments as well as customers' requirements, characteristics, attitudes and perceptions. Population shifts due to higher or lower birth rates, longer life spans and immigration can create, expand or shrink markets. Along with these shifts come changes in demand and usage of different goods and services. Consider how Seiko is dealing with demographic changes in the global market for wristwatches.

MARKETING IN PRACTICE: SEIKO

Seiko, with its headquarters in Japan and an international customer base, has long been known for its quality wristwatches. When its marketers recognised that younger consumers were interested in wristwatches as fashion accessories, they decided to make a number of changes to marketing strategy. They began heavily promoting more stylish wristwatches to young adults in multiple markets. At the same time, they aggressively courted younger, tech-savvy Japanese consumers by partnering with NTT DoCoMo to test-market a wristwatch mobile phone styled like a bracelet that unfolds to reveal a display and an extendable antenna. How will these changes affect Seiko's relations with its current customer base? 'We are very viable to the 45–50 year old customer and we aren't going to walk away from that', says the vice president of marketing, 'but we can't ignore the relevance of targeting the younger customer – it's a new market, and everyone who is a little older aspires to be younger'.[18]

You should also examine demographic details such as gender, education, occupation, ethnic and religious composition, household size, household composition and household income – any and all of which can affect product purchase and usage. Specific products may demand a closer look at particular characteristics, such as how a consumer segment uses technology (important for marketing on the Internet, for example) or whether a household includes children (important for marketing toys, for example).

Consumers are real people, not numbers; they have distinct feelings and attitudes toward companies, brands and products, which in turn influence how they act. Paid promotions play a role in establishing a positive reputation, but consumers may give more credence to word-of-mouth communication about quality, service and other aspects of the offering. 'Word of mouth is still important because it reaches people who many not be e-commerce shoppers yet', explains a spokesperson for the online retailer Amazon.com. 'Word of mouse is important because on the Web you can reach so many more people beyond your circle of friends.'[19]

Marketers for B2B companies look closely at social–cultural trends that affect purchasing patterns, such as the size and growth of the industries to which they sell, as measured by number of companies, number of locations or outlets, workforce size, turnover and profitability. Trends in new business formation can suggest opportunities to market goods and services such as networking systems, legal and accounting services and telecommunications equipment. Palo Alto Software, which makes the *Marketing Plan Pro* software that accompanies this text, tracks new business formation as an indicator of demand for its marketing planning software as well as its *Business Plan Pro* business planning software and other products.

Technological factors

Fast-changing technology has an effect on customers, suppliers, competitors, channel members, marketing techniques and organisational processes. Moreover, competing technology standards (at times coupled with government-imposed standards) have become major factors in particular product categories. To illustrate, mobile phones in some parts of the world operate on a standard known as GSM, whereas CDMA is the standard in other areas. Standards for wireless Internet communication are evolving, as well, which affects what manufacturers make and where they can market their mobiles, handheld personal digital assistants and personal computers.[20]

The Internet has led to increased opportunities for retailing to consumers and stimulated business purchases of infrastructure equipment; it has also raised questions about privacy and security, among other issues. Still, technology touches virtually every element of marketing, from digitally enhanced advertisements to new packaging materials and methods and beyond, making this an increasingly vital part of the external environment.

During the marketing planning process, you should look at these aspects of technology as a starting point:

- how rapidly innovations are spreading or evolving

- how technology is affecting customers, suppliers, distributors, marketing and processes

- how technology is affected by – or generating – industry-wide standards and government regulations

- what and when technology is prompting substitute products or improved products that compete with established products

- how much the industry and important competitors are investing in research and development.

The purpose of analysing technological factors is to discern potential threats (such as discovering that a competitor's R&D budget has been dramatically increased) and possible opportunities (such as planning to be among the first firms to incorporate a new technological standard).

Ecological factors

Ecological factors can influence organisations in numerous ways. Manufacturers will be unable to perform as expected if vital raw materials needed for production, such as water, timber, oil or minerals, are unavailable. A steady source of non-polluting energy is problematic for businesses and non-profit organisations in certain regions. Further, government regulations and public attitudes are doing more to shape the way organisations interact with the natural environment. European Union rules, for instance, require carmakers to pay for recycling of their vehicles and electronics manufacturers to eliminate heavy metals such as lead from their products.[21]

Due to higher social consciousness of ecological issues, more companies are disclosing how their marketing and operations affect ecological conditions; they are also striving to meet stricter environmental standards. Although disclosures are mainly voluntary, public sentiment is putting pressure on companies to issue more detailed reports about progress toward sustainability. In line with this movement, Crédit Lyonnais and nine other banks now require that the major infrastructure projects they finance satisfy criteria for minimising ecological impact.[22] Business customers are also pressuring suppliers over ecological conditions. Ricoh and other Japanese companies, for instance, said they would stop buying paper from Asia Paper & Pulp if it failed to protect forests near its mill in Indonesia.[23]

Competitive factors

Every organisation, not just businesses, faces competition. Charities must compete with other charities for a share of donors' contributions, and governments compete with each other when trying to attract businesses to create jobs in an area, for example. In the business world, a SWOT analysis is only one facet of competitive analysis. As a marketer, you should examine three sets of industry forces to gauge the competitive attractiveness of the industry: (1) how easily competitors can enter or leave the market; (2) how much power buyers and suppliers have; and (3) whether substitutes are available for the company's products and the resulting effect on industry rivalry (*see* Figure 2.5).

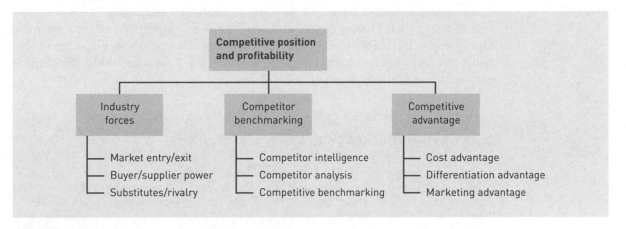

| **FIGURE 2.5** | Competitive position and profitability |

Source: Adapted, with permission, from Roger J. Best, *Market-Based Management: Strategies for Growing Customer Value and Profitability*, 2nd edn (Upper Saddle River, NJ: Prentice Hall, 2000), p. 127.

According to Michael Porter's model,[24] when rivals can easily enter the market, the industry may become suddenly and unpredictably more competitive, which complicates the marketing planning process and can affect the company's ability to achieve planned objectives. When buyers and suppliers have relatively little power, the competitive environment is likely to be less pressured and the market may have more profit potential. And when there are few substitutes for the company's product and few rivals in the market, the company will feel less pressure and be better positioned for profit potential. Microsoft, for example, dominates the market for personal computer operating software because the barrier to entry is quite high, buyers and suppliers do not have inordinate power and few widely available substitutes exist.

Next, you will gather information on rivals using competitive intelligence, analyse the data and use benchmarking to set targets for equalling or exceeding what competitors do in key areas. Consider what your customers value as well as what your organisation needs to achieve its objectives and goals. For example, one of the benchmarks used by South Korea's SK Telecom is average revenue per user. Even if SK Telecom's average revenue per user drops in a given quarter, it can research the average revenue per user reported by competitors to compare company results with industry results.[25] Such an analysis can help you focus on strengths and identify weaknesses that must be addressed. You may decide to go further, searching for world-class performers outside the industry against which to benchmark for more efficiency and higher customer satisfaction.

The third set of competitive factors relates to how the organisation achieves competitive advantage. Companies like Asda (retailing) and Dell (computers) strive for cost advantage, seeking to lower their costs and price products lower than competitors. Companies like Luxottica (spectacles) and Nokia (mobile phones) derive competitive advantage from quality, style or another point of differentiation by positioning their products as superior in delivering innovative features and desirable benefits valued by customers. Companies like Sony (electronics) and Walt Disney (entertainment) derive competitive advantage from highly cost-effective marketing due to broad brand recognition, widespread distribution and other marketing-related efficiencies. Consider how H&M builds competitive advantage in world markets.

MARKETING IN PRACTICE: H&M

Hennes & Mauritz – better known as H&M – has built a global empire based on affordable fashion. The Swedish retailer minimises overhead and operating costs to keep prices low. Staff designers choose from 900 outside suppliers and are willing to rotate suppliers for a better deal. The company keeps little inventory in warehouses, shaving costs by speeding up cycle time from design to production to delivery of products. As a result, new styles are constantly arriving in H&M's 800+ stores, which brings shoppers back again and again. H&M's competitive advantage has become so powerful that its turnover and profits are soaring even as some retailer chains are struggling. 'When I joined in 1972', remembers Chairman Stefan Persson, 'H&M was all about price. Then we added quality fashion to the equation, but everyone said you could never combine [them] successfully. But we were passionate that we could.'[26]

Many marketers tend to focus on current competitors that follow similar strategies, typically within the same industry. However, you also need to scan the environment for trends that might change the future competitive situation and for companies that might soon be able to satisfy customer needs in an entirely new or different way.[27] For example, Internet-based travel sites have increased competitive pressure to the point that many smaller store-based travel agencies have gone out of business. One of the Internet competitors is the travel website Lastminute.com, which uses cost advantage to compete with traditional holiday packagers. In this competitive environment, some travel specialists are innovating for differentiation advantage and profit. Space Adventures, for example, markets tours to the International Space Station – a unique out-of-this-world experience that sells for millions and attracts an exclusive clientele.[28]

THE SWOT ANALYSIS

Once you have data from internal and external audits, you will prepare a SWOT analysis to make sense of what you have learned and interpret it in the context of the organisation's situation, mission and goals. As discussed earlier, strengths and weaknesses are internal capabilities and factors that may support or hinder performance. The purpose of a SWOT analysis is to match key strengths with promising opportunities and see how strengths can guard against weaknesses and threats in supporting marketing strategies and programmes.

How can you determine whether a particular internal capability, resource or factor is a strength or a weakness? Four criteria can be used:[29]

1. *Previous performance.* How has the factor affected earlier performance, as measured by trends in profitability, market share, employee productivity or other appropriate standards? Are prior trends and performance likely to continue?

2. *Outcomes.* How has the factor contributed to specific outcomes defined by objectives and goals? Will the factor be likely to influence short- and long-term outcomes in the future?

3. *Competitors.* How does the factor compare with that of competitors, and is significant change likely to occur in the future?

4. *Management judgement.* How do organisational managers currently view the factor? Do they believe their view will change in the coming months or years, and why?

The point is not to analyse every capability, resource or factor but to single out the most important as strengths (to be employed) and weaknesses (to be counteracted). For example, operational efficiency is one of Honda's greatest strengths. The car-maker has tackled threats such as economic downturns and intense competition by streamlining its supply chain, carefully managing parts inventories and making its factories more flexible. High productivity keeps costs under control and allows Honda quickly to adjust its output and its prices as needed.[30]

Opportunities cannot be profitably exploited unless the organisation possesses strengths to take full advantage of the situation, as managers at Siemens' transport division found out. Customers that bought its electrical systems for trains began expressing interest in buying fully assembled locomotives. Lacking the capabilities to manufacture locomotives, Siemens responded by acquiring companies in that industry. Now this strength is helping the transport division profitably satisfy customers' needs.[31]

As shown in Figure 2.6, you will systematically examine each important strength and weakness to determine its source and its effect on an opportunity or a threat and the implications for marketing strategy. Remember, however, that opportunities that lead your organisation away from its mission and strategic goals are not viable, regardless of applicable strengths or competitive pressures. You can confirm the suitability of identified opportunities when you further analyse markets, customer needs and customer behaviour in Stage 3 of the marketing planning process (*see* Chapter 3).

Strength or weakness (brief description)	Internal source (resource, capability or factor)	Effect (on an opportunity or a threat and implications for marketing strategy)
Strength:		
Strength:		
Weakness:		
Weakness:		

FIGURE 2.6   The effect of strengths and weaknesses

CHAPTER SUMMARY

1. *Discuss the use of internal and external audits.*

   Marketers use an internal audit to examine the situation within the organisation. This audit should cover resources and capabilities, current offerings, past results, business relationships and key issues that could affect marketing and performance. The external audit examines what is occurring outside the organisation, covering political–legal factors, economic factors, social–cultural factors, technological factors, ecological factors and competitive factors. On the basis of the internal and external audits, marketers proceed to prepare a SWOT analysis of the organisation's primary strengths, weaknesses, opportunities and threats.

2. *Explain the main factors in the internal environment that can affect marketing and performance.*

   Organisational capabilities are based on human, financial, informational and supply resources. Marketers look at current resources, available resources and resource commitment to identify gaps and decide on marketing allocations. An examination of current offerings covers product mix and lines, sales, share, need satisfaction, pricing and profitability, age and position in life cycle, links to other products and contribution to organisational performance. Previous performance covers unit and monetary sales and profits, financial trends, results of earlier marketing plans and customer relationship trends and costs. This yields insights about strengths and weaknesses and highlights experience that can be applied to new marketing programmes. When analysing business relationships, marketers look at suppliers, channel members and strategic alliance partners. In particular, they consider value added, quality and service, capacity and commitment, costs, relationship changes over time and level of dependence. Key issues can either hamper performance or act as keys to success.

3. *Explain the main factors in the external environment that can affect marketing and performance.*
Political–legal factors can open the door to opportunities or pose threats by affecting marketing activities, customer behaviour and competitive behaviour. Local, regional, national and international economic factors can influence the purchasing patterns of both consumers and businesses. Social–cultural factors can affect the size and composition of markets and segments as well as customers' requirements, characteristics, attitudes, perceptions, product purchases and usage. Technological factors can create opportunities and threats by influencing product standards, marketing, purchasing and customer behaviour. Ecological factors can affect resources such as raw materials and energy, operations, costs and relations with the public and other stakeholders. Three sets of competitive factors can determine whether a market is competitively attractive: (1) ease of market entry and exit; (2) power of buyers and suppliers; and (3) availability of substitutes and the effect on industry rivalry.

4. *Understand the use of SWOT analysis in marketing planning.*
After completing the internal and external audits, marketers analyse and distil the relevant data into a critique summarising the organisation's primary strengths, weaknesses, opportunities and threats, examined in the context of its mission and goals. Some marketers also prepare a SWOT analysis of key competitors. An internal capability, resource or factor is a strength if it: previously helped performance and is likely to continue doing so; has contributed to specific outcomes and is likely to continue doing so; is superior to that of competitors and is likely to remain so. Managers must believe it is and will continue to be a strength. Using a SWOT analysis helps marketers better match strengths with promising opportunities and understand how strengths can guard against weaknesses and the threats when exploited in marketing programmes.

KEY TERM DEFINITIONS

environmental scanning and analysis The systematic and ongoing collection and interpretation of data about internal and external factors that may affect marketing and performance

external audit Examination of the situation outside the organisation, including political–legal factors, economic factors, social–cultural factors, technological factors, ecological factors and competitive factors

internal audit Examination of the situation inside the organisation, including resources, offerings, previous performance, important business relationships and key issues

opportunity External circumstance or factor that the organisation aims to exploit for higher performance

strength Internal capability or factor that can help the organisation achieve its objectives, capitalise on opportunities or defend against threats

SWOT analysis Evaluation of an organisation's primary strengths, weaknesses, opportunities and threats

threat External circumstance or factor that may hinder organisational performance if not addressed

weakness Internal capability or factor that may prevent the organisation from achieving its objectives or effectively addressing opportunities and threats

THE PRACTICAL MARKETER CHECKLIST NO. 2:
INTERNAL AND EXTERNAL AUDITS

Internal audit

Does the organisation have appropriate human, informational, financial and supply resources to support and advance its marketing efforts?

What do recent and historic trends in marketing results and overall performance suggest about the effectiveness of previous marketing strategies? How can previous results be applied to planning for future programmes?

What mix, price and volume of goods and services are currently being offered and how are they affecting turnover and profits?

How do the organisation's offerings deliver value to customers – and is this value competitively superior?

Are the offerings suitable for the organisation's mission, goals and resources?

What are the trends in customer needs, acquisition, retention and loyalty?

How do relationships with suppliers, channel partners and other businesses affect capacity, quality, costs and availability?

What key issues might be warning signs of future problems or especially pivotal for success?

What marketing research does the organisation need to better define the issues in preparation for completing the marketing plan?

What assumptions and conclusions from the internal audit can be applied to formulating marketing strategy?

External audit

What developments and changes in the political–legal environment can or will affect the organisation and, specifically, its marketing decisions and actions?

How are local, regional, national and international economic conditions affecting demand and customer buying power?

In what ways are trends in demographics, social values, popular culture, customer attitudes and customer perceptions influencing demand, markets and segments?

How are technological innovations affecting customers, competitors, suppliers, channel partners, marketing and internal processes such as research and development?

What emerging and ongoing ecological concerns may affect the organisation's materials, suppliers, energy access, processes, marketing programmes and public reputation?

What is the current competitive situation and how is it changing (or likely to change)?

What are each main competitor's market share, strengths, weaknesses, opportunities, threats, resources and competitive advantages?

Is the industry competitively attractive, what benchmarks can be used for competitive performance and on what basis can the organisation achieve competitive advantage?

What assumptions and conclusions from the external audit can be applied to formulating marketing strategy?

 **ONLINE RESOURCES**

THE EXTERNAL ENVIRONMENT

- Social Science Information Gateway (http://sosig.ac.uk) – Links to numerous websites with information about social–cultural developments.

- Eurostat (http://europa.eu.int/comm/eurostat) – Provides statistics about demographics, social trends and other social–cultural factors affecting the European Union.

- United Nations statistics links (www.un.org/ecosocdev/topicse/statiste.htm) – Links to reports and statistics about economic and social development around the world.

- UK Trade Partners (www.tradepartners.gov.uk) – Offers country-specific and industry-specific information on exporting opportunities, currency issues and more.

- Society of Competitive Intelligence Professionals (www.scip.org) – Explains legal and ethical issues in competitive intelligence.

- Business for Social Responsibility (www.bsr.org) – Posts discussions and links related to social responsibility and sustainability issues.

- Institute of Business Ethics (www.ibe.org.uk) – Monitors business ethics issues and offers examples of ethical codes of conduct.

- *The Economist* (www.economist.com) – Covers the latest worldwide business and financial news and trends.

- *Financial Times* (www.ft.com) – Updated every business day, presents economic and business news.

- BBC News (http://news.bbc.co.uk) – National and international news about business, economic issues, politics plus country profiles and more.

- CyberAtlas (http://cyberatlas.internet.com) – Offers statistics and demographics related to Internet usage, especially important for e-commerce companies.

QUESTIONS FOR DISCUSSION AND ANALYSIS

1. Why is it important for marketers to analyse their organisation's relationships with suppliers and partners as well as with channel members?

2. Why would a capability or resource that is a strength for one organisation not necessarily be a strength for another?

3. What factors in the internal and external environment should a charitable organisation examine before preparing a marketing plan to attract new contributors?

APPLY YOUR KNOWLEDGE

Research and analyse the forces shaping the industry of a company that is facing intense competitive pressure.

- How powerful are suppliers to this industry? What are the implications for the company's business relationships?

- How powerful are buyers in this industry? What are the implications for the company's pricing strategy?

- Can customers substitute other goods or services for the company's offerings? What are the implications for customer loyalty to this company?

- Can the company or competitors easily exit the industry? Can more rivals easily enter the industry? What are the implications for the company if environmental conditions threaten profitability?

- Prepare a brief oral or written report summarising your comments.

BUILD YOUR OWN MARKETING PLAN

Continue the marketing planning process for a hypothetical organisation or an actual organisation you have chosen, using the concepts and tools from this chapter. Start with an internal audit of resources, offerings, previous performance, business relationships and key issues. If the organisation is a start-up, examine the recent performance of direct competitors and discuss what the trends might mean for your organisation. Next, look at relevant political–legal factors, economic factors, social–cultural factors, technological factors, ecological factors and competitive factors in the external environment. On the basis of these audits, put together a SWOT analysis explaining how the main strengths and weaknesses relate to specific opportunities or threats and their implications for marketing strategy. Before you record your conclusions, take a moment to consider how these latest ideas will help you develop a practical, successful marketing plan. Then enter your work in *Marketing Plan Pro* software or in a written marketing plan.

CLOSING CASE: FASHIONING THE FUTURE AT AUSTIN REED

For more than a century, Austin Reed has made and sold upmarket clothing for men and women. Its original London store was established in 1900 and the company now operates more than 50 stores in airports, city centres and other locations. Recently, however, the company has faced formidable challenges caused by changes in the internal and external environment.

Austin Reed's traditional strengths include its quality and its well-known brand. Although many business executives continue to favour Austin Reed suits, the company has also introduced new product lines and new brands to take advantage of trends toward more casual and edgier clothing. Profit performance has moved up and down in recent years, reflecting the difficult external environment. Yet after a costly 13-month renovation of the main London store in Regent Street, which contributes 18 per cent of the company's turnover, senior managers are anticipating better performance ahead.

Despite these strengths, Austin Reed is confronting a number of threats. Trendier brands and boutiques are drawing customers, especially younger ones, away from Austin Reed. Also, the company's city stores and airport outlets are not as busy when international travel drops, as in the aftermath of terrorist attacks or following health scares. Moreover, an economic slowdown has hurt the buying power of some customers, affecting demand for Austin Reed's classic clothes. With profitability at stake, cost management has emerged as a key issue. Nonetheless, after suspending print campaigns for a time, senior managers decided to invest in advertising for the main store's reopening. They also upgraded logistics to speed the movement of clothing from factory to sales floor, which is important for restocking when styles prove especially popular.

Still, Austin Reed may not be able to remain independent for long if it cannot achieve consistently higher financial performance. Some entrepreneurs and retail chains have already looked into buying the company, and investors are likely to keep pushing for better returns. Based on the current situation, Austin Reed's marketers and managers will have to wring the most out of every strength and opportunity as they plan for the future.[32]

Case questions

1. From a competitive standpoint, how attractive is the retail clothing industry, based on the three sets of forces in Figure 2.5?

2. What role do you think Austin Reed's business relationships and resources might play in the initiative to improve logistics?

 ENDNOTES

1. Based on information from: David Firn, 'Ciba Warns of Tough Trading as Profits Fall', *Financial Times*, 20 August 2003, www.ft.com; 'Ciba Speciality Chemicals', *Ink World*, July 2003, p. 18; Cheryl Lyn Dybas, 'Paint for Smooth Sailing Can Stall Marine Life', *Washington Post*, 31 March 2003, p. A6; Patrick Raleigh, 'Ciba Sets Up Distributors for Rubber Additives', *European Rubber Journal*, March 2003, p. 16; Sean Milmo, 'Ciba Unveils Aggressive Growth Plans', *Chemical Market Reporter*, 10 February 2003, pp. 4ff.

2. Craig S. Fleisher and Babette E. Bensoussan, *Strategic and Competitive Analysis* (Upper Saddle River, NJ: Prentice Hall, 2003), pp. 269–83.

3. 'Nintendo', *Financial Times*, 8 April 2003, www.ft.com; Paul Abrahams, 'Microsoft to Cut Price of Xbox in Europe', *Financial Times*, 10 April 2003, www.ft.com; Barney Jopson, 'Nintendo Trims Forecast on Sluggish Sales', *Financial Times*, 7 April 2003, www.ft.com.

4. Ibid.; also Jay Greene, 'Xbox Problems? Microsoft's Not Singing the Blues', *Business Week*, 19 May 2003, p. 64.

5. 'Nintendo's Profit Slides 37% on Weak GameCube Sales', *Wall Street Journal*, 22 May 2003, www.wsj.com.

6. 'Nintendo's Profit Slides 37% on Weak GameCube Sales', *Wall Street Journal*; 'Nintendo', *Financial Times*; Jopson, 'Nintendo Trims Forecast on Sluggish Sales', *Financial Times*.

7. Kerry A. Dolan, 'It's Nice to Be Big', *Forbes*, 1 September 2003, pp. 84–5.

8. Paul Kaihla, 'Building a Better R&D Mousetrap', *Business 2.0*, September 2003, pp. 50–2.

9. John Turrettini, 'Made to Order', *Forbes*, 1 September 2003, pp. 78–80.

10. John Tayman, 'The Profit Machine', *Business 2.0*, September 2003, pp. 172–3.

11. Mitch Betts, 'Unexpected Insights', *Computerworld*, 14 April 2003, p. 34.

12. Donna Fuscaldo, 'B-to-B – Looking Big: How Can Online Retailers Carry So Many Products? The Secret Is "Drop-shipping"', *Wall Street Journal*, 28 April 2003, p. R7.

13. Andy Raskin, 'Can This Weatherman See Your Future?', *Business 2.0*, August 2003, pp. 97–100.

14. Catherine Arnold, 'Usage Analysis Converts Visitors to Sales', *Marketing News*, 26 May 2003, pp. 6–7.

15. Jason Bush, 'Retail Banking Renaissance', *Business Week*, 1 September 2003, p. 45.

16. Quoted in Leslie Moore, 'A Town's Protests Threaten Argentina's Mining Future', *New York Times*, 20 April 2003, sec. 3, p. 6.

17. Catherine McKinley, 'Vietnam Has a Market for Superstores', *Wall Street Journal*, 13 August 2003, p. B3A.

18. Quoted in 'Seiko Announces New Direction, Aggressive Marketing Plan', *American Time*, June–July 2003, p. 8; other source: Yoshiko Haro, 'Paging Dick Tracy: DoCoMo to Test-market Seiko's Wristwatch Phone', *Electronic Engineering Times*, 31 March 2003, p. 24.

19. Quoted in Nicholas Thompson, 'More Companies Pay Heed to Their "Word of Mouse" Reputation', *New York Times*, 23 June 2003, p. C4.

20. 'How Code-Division Multiple Access (CDMA) Technology Emerged as the World's Standard for Mobile Phones', *The Economist*, 21 June 2003, pp. 22–4.

21. Samuel Loewenberg, 'Europe Gets Tougher on U.S. Companies', *New York Times*, 20 April 2003, sec. 3, p. 6.

22. Jonathan Finer, 'Monitoring Corporate Standards', *Washington Post*, 5 June 2003, p. E4.

23. Tom Wright, 'Paper Company Executes Moves to Save Forests', *Wall Street Journal*, 27 August 2003, p. B3C.

24. Discussion based on theories in Michael Porter, *Competitive Advantage* (New York: Free Press, 1985), pp. 11–26; and Roger Best, *Market-Based Management: Strategies for Growing Customer Value and Profitability*, 2nd edn (Upper Saddle River, NJ: Prentice Hall, 2000), Chapter 6.

25. 'SK Telecom's Net Profit Rises 1%', *Wall Street Journal*, 6 May 2003, www.wsj.com.

26. Quoted in Kerry Cappell, 'Hip H&M', *Business Week*, 11 November 2002, pp. 106–10.

27. Fleisher and Bensoussan, *Strategic and Competitive Analysis*, Chapter 11.

28. 'New Routes to the Beach', *The Economist*, 2 August 2003, pp. 55–6.

29. Mary K. Coulter, *Strategic Management in Action* (Upper Saddle River, NJ: Prentice Hall, 1998), Chapter 4.

30. 'Rising Above the Sludge', *The Economist*, 5 April 2003, pp. 61–3.

31. 'Rising Above the Sludge', pp. 61–3.

32. Based on information from: James Hall, 'Austin Reed Refashions Its Image', *Wall Street Journal*, 8 September 2003, p. A13A; Sophy Buckley, 'Austin Reed Tries on a New Set of Clothes', *Financial Times*, 24 August 2003, www.ft.com; Peter John, 'Austin Reed Sales Hit by Store Redevelopment', *Financial Times*, 24 May 2003, www.ft.com.

3

Analysing customers and markets

Closing case: McDonald's invites families to dine

Endnotes

Comprehension outcomes

After studying this chapter, you will be able to:

- Understand why marketers examine markets according to definition, changes and share

- Explain the main influences on customers in consumer markets

- Explain the main influences on customers in business markets

- Describe the use of secondary and primary research in marketing planning

Application outcomes

After studying this chapter, you will be able to:

- Define and describe the market for a product

- Identify sources of information about consumer and business markets

- Calculate market share for a product

- Analyse customer behaviour influences in consumer and business markets

OPENING CASE: NESTLÉ PURINA COURTS PET OWNERS

The global pet food market is both large and lucrative: in the United Kingdom alone, pet owners buy nearly £2 billion worth of food yearly for their cats and dogs. Now, with its acquisition of Purina, Nestlé is marketing a number of pet food brands for different segments and regions, including Felix (for cats) and Alpo (for dogs).

To keep its pet food brands in front of pet owners and build customer loyalty, Nestlé Purina mounts a constant stream of promotions, sometimes in partnership with retailers and veterinary surgeons. For example, the company has teamed up with Tesco supermarkets to mail cat care tips and Felix discount coupons to pet owners. It has also offered free samples of its Felix and Bonio pet foods in Tesco, Sainsbury's and other grocery chains while promoting free dental check-ups for dogs and cats at local veterinary surgeries. In addition, Nestlé Purina regularly advertises its brands in print and broadcast media and has sponsored a prime-time television programme to reach out to pet-owning families. All this marketing activity has helped the Felix brand – which covers 40 product varieties – capture a sizeable share of the cat food market in the United Kingdom (where it is strongest) and in 12 other European countries.

In South Africa and other regions within Africa, however, commercial pet food brands such as Alpo represent only a small share of the overall market. One reason is that pet owners have little disposable income to spare; another is that some brands are of lower quality, which affects pet health and inhibits overall market growth. Recently, the share of speciality pet foods marketed through veterinary practices has been rising and now accounts for about one-third of all commercial pet foods sold in South Africa. To help pet owners take care of their pets, learn about pet nutrition and publicise Nestlé Purina's brands, the company has partnered with veterinary surgeons to operate six pet clinics in South African towns. The result: higher awareness of Alpo and other company brands among pet owners who can buy the brands locally. As the African market for commercial pet food grows, Nestlé Purina will be well positioned to compete and to increase its market share.[1]

CHAPTER PREVIEW

Nestlé Purina's marketers define their market as people with pets who can afford to buy commercial pet foods and have local access to the company's products. This definition narrows the market from everyone to only those who keep pets, have sufficient disposable income and live or work in areas where Nestlé Purina's brands are available through veterinary surgeries and retail locations. Yet another aspect of the company's marketing focuses on customer buying behaviour and how to encourage purchases of its brands rather than competing brands once a pet owner has decided to switch to commercial pet food.

This chapter discusses the second stage in the marketing planning process, in which marketers prepare for later decisions by analysing markets and customers. The chapter begins by explaining how and why markets are defined as a first step toward choosing specific markets and segments to be targeted. Next you'll see how market share is calculated and used, and this discussion is followed by a closer look at the analysis of needs and behaviour in consumer and business markets. The final section explores the use of secondary and primary marketing research to fill information gaps. *As you read this chapter, think about how these concepts can be combined with principles from earlier chapters for effective marketing planning.*

ANALYSING CONSUMER AND BUSINESS MARKETS

People make a **market**, the group of potential customers for a good or service. The **consumer market** consists of individuals and families who buy goods and services for their own use. Described in the broadest terms, Nestlé Purina's market consists of pet owners who buy pet food for their household dogs and cats. In contrast, the **business (organisational) market** consists of companies, institutions, non-profit organisations and government agencies that buy goods and services for organisational use. Despite this definition, B2B marketers are not dealing with faceless organisations: buying decisions are, of course, made by people. Even when a company or institution develops an automatic system for reordering without human intervention, it still relies on a manager, employee or team to establish decision rules for when to buy, what to buy and from which supplier. As Figure 3.1 indicates, market analysis provides valuable background for understanding who might buy the product, what their needs are and what influences their buying behaviour.

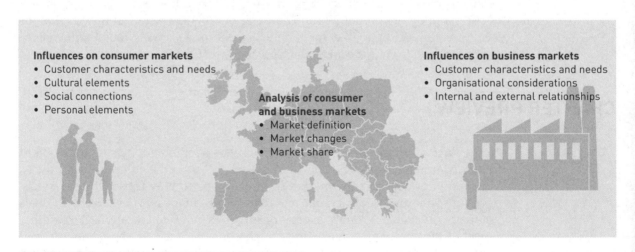

Influences on consumer markets
- Customer characteristics and needs
- Cultural elements
- Social connections
- Personal elements

Analysis of consumer and business markets
- Market definition
- Market changes
- Market share

Influences on business markets
- Customer characteristics and needs
- Organisational considerations
- Internal and external relationships

FIGURE 3.1   Consumer and business market analysis

Consider how Panasonic sees the business market for 'ruggedised' laptop computers.

MARKETING IN PRACTICE: PANASONIC TOUGHBOOK

Not everyone needs or wants to pay for a notebook computer so well built that it can operate in extreme heat or cold, resist repeated spills on the keyboard and start up properly after being dropped again and again. Panasonic's Toughbook notebook computers offer all these benefits and more. The firm, owned by Japan's Matsushita Electric Industrial Co., understands that the business market for such products is a tiny fraction of the market for all notebook computers.

Still, government agencies are willing and able to pay a bit more for reinforced notebooks that law enforcement officers, military specialists and others can use even under the harshest conditions. As one example, the New York City Police Department has been purchasing Toughbooks to equip its patrol cars. Panasonic enjoys higher profits on these notebook computers in part because their unique benefits command higher prices and in part because of lower costs by sourcing components from the parent company. This small market therefore represents a good marketing opportunity.[2]

You will look at three things during your preliminary analysis of a consumer or business market: (1) market definition, (2) market changes and (3) market share.

Market definition

Defining the market helps you narrow the marketing focus to consumers or businesses that are qualified to be or already are buyers of a particular type of product. The broadest level of market definition is the potential market; within this are four subsets: the available, qualified available, target and penetrated markets.[3] The **potential market** is all the customers who may be interested in that good or service. However, some customers in this market may be unaware of the product; some may have no access to it; some may not require its benefits; some may not be able to use it; and some may not be able to afford it. Thus, the potential market represents the *maximum* number of customers who might buy the product – but not the number who will *realistically* buy.[4]

Part of the potential market is the **available market**, all the customers who are interested and have both adequate income and adequate access to the product. A subset of that is the **qualified available market**, all the customers who are qualified to buy based on product-specific criteria such as age (for alcohol and other products that may not legally be sold to under-age consumers). The **target market** is the segment of customers within the qualified available market that an organisation decides to serve. The smallest market of all is the **penetrated market**, all the customers in the target market who currently buy or have bought a specific type of product. Figure 3.2 shows how a car-hire company might define its market according to these levels.

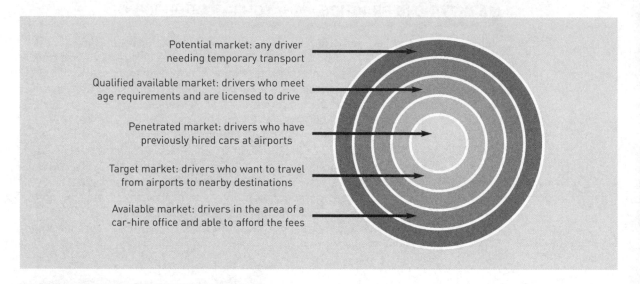

| FIGURE 3.2 | Five levels of market definition |

Source: After Marian Burk Wood, *The Marketing Plan: A Handbook* (Upper Saddle River, NJ: Prentice Hall, 2003), p. 39.

For planning purposes, you should define your potential market by more than the product. Many organisations use geography and customer description in their market definitions. 'The UK consumer market for credit cards' is a general description of one potential market for the British bank Abbey National. If offering credit cards beyond UK borders, the bank would define each new market geographically, such as 'the Western European consumer market for credit cards'. If the bank wanted to restrict its marketing to certain areas, it would describe each market more precisely: 'the London consumer market for credit cards' and 'the Manchester consumer market for credit cards'. And if the bank determined that one of its strengths was evaluating applications from consumers who have previously defaulted on loans, it might describe a market even more precisely: 'the higher-risk London consumer market for credit cards'.

Now you can narrow your focus by researching customer needs and buying behaviour within the potential market, yielding a more specific definition of the available and the qualified available markets. Research will help you understand what your customers value and what aspects of marketing strategy will best support competitive differentiation in a given market. For example, Vespa's marketers realise that consumers in its qualified available market need and want more than mere transportation. Style is therefore an important part of the company's competitive advantage, as are engineering and affordability.[5]

Market changes

Although Vespa has been marketing scooters for nearly 60 years, the company has tracked ongoing changes in its market and responded accordingly. One change is increased interest in safety features; another is the desire for fuel efficiency. In response, Vespa has introduced advanced braking systems and engines that take riders further on a tank of petrol. Vespa's marketing is a good example of the rule that no market remains static for very long. Every day, consumers and business customers leave or enter an area; every day, consumers begin or stop buying a product. For this reason, you will need to research expert projections and track overall market trends.

Two key changes that affect the size and nature of a market are:

* *Number of customers.* Is the consumer population (or number of businesses) increasing or decreasing, and by how much?

* *Purchases.* How many products are all companies in the industry estimated to buy in the next year and later years? How has the trend in purchases changed?

The purpose is to determine how changes, trends and projections are likely to affect customers in the market and the implications for your marketing decisions. For example, the number of corporate users of instant messaging software is projected to more than triple worldwide by 2007, creating a tempting target for Microsoft and other companies that market such products.[6] If the market were shrinking at that same rate, however, companies would be much less eager to target corporate buyers.

Market share

Going beyond current and projected market size and trends, you will want to estimate your product's or brand's market share and the share held by competitors. Remember that your share will change as the market grows or shrinks and rivals enter, expand, reduce their presence or leave. Still, market share serves as a baseline against which you can track market dynamics and measure the progress of your marketing plan results.

Market share is defined as the percentage of sales within a market accounted for by a company, brand or product, as calculated in terms of units or money (or both, if the data can be obtained). The basic formula is: divide the company's or brand's unit or monetary sales by the entire market's unit or monetary sales of that type of product. Thus, if you sell three million units and overall market sales by all competitors selling that type of product are 12 million units, you hold a 25 per cent share. Your share would be 15 per cent if your product sales totalled £15 million or €15 million and overall sales of that type of product in that market totalled £100 million or €100 million.

Markets can and do change all the time, which means your market share calculation will reflect the relative positions of key industry players during a particular period only. Consider the market for air travel within Colombia.

MARKETING IN PRACTICE: DOMESTIC AIR TRAVEL IN COLOMBIA

The market for domestic air travel in Colombia is constantly changing as new airlines begin operation or existing airlines go out of business. Not long ago, the Colombian Aces airline had a 15.5 per cent share of the market before it was liquidated, second only to the 37.5 per cent share of market leader Avianca. After the liquidation, the market shares of the eight remaining carriers changed immediately. However, two more airlines received government permission to enter the market shortly afterward. This change in competition meant that the share positions of all carriers were likely to change very soon. Thus, each carrier was keenly interested in tracking how much of the defunct airline's share it was able to capture while defending against the newcomers.[7]

Market share is one of the vital signs of a product or brand that you can track over time to spot potential problems and opportunities. You will want to calculate or at least estimate the share for each product in each market on a regular basis to detect any significant shifts. Examining both market changes and market share changes can give you a better picture of what customers are doing, what rivals are doing and where the market is going so your marketing plan does not involve attracting an increasingly large share of an ever-shrinking, less profitable market. You can also identify less-competitive markets and markets where purchases are projected to rise rapidly.

Bear in mind that changes in share are not the only indicators – or even the most important indicators – of competitive standing in a market nor do they necessarily warrant immediate attention. Usually you will use share standings as one of a number of standards for measuring progress in marketing programme implementation and to signal the need for adjustments, as discussed in Chapters 11 and 12.

ANALYSING CUSTOMER NEEDS AND BEHAVIOUR

Once you have a preliminary definition of the market, understand market changes and know your market share, you are ready to look more closely at customer demographics, needs, buying behaviour and attitudes. This will help you decide which markets and specific segments to target; the most appropriate positioning for each product in each segment; and the marketing strategies and programmes likely to satisfy customers profitably. For example, the owner of Tuk-Tuk Foods has based her marketing decisions on observations of consumer behaviour in Sweden.

MARKETING IN PRACTICE: TUK-TUK FOODS

Sawanee Engblom was teaching in Stockholm when she observed what happened when students came back from visits to Thailand. 'Many Swedes gained a liking for Thai foods after travelling to Thailand', she notes.[8] However, the returned travellers had difficulty finding dishes prepared in the authentic Thai manner. Understanding this behaviour convinced the teacher-turned-entrepreneur to start Tuk-Tuk Foods, a small business producing microwave-ready Thai foods based on her own recipes. Tuk-Tuk Foods employs 16 and has a daily output of 3,000 packaged dishes such as Panaeng Moo and Kaeng Kaew Wan Kai. The foods are sold through grocery chains in Stockholm with colourful labels featuring the founder in traditional Thai attire. Tuk-Tuk factory will soon be exporting meals to Denmark, Norway and Finland as consumers in those countries develop a taste for Thai foods.[9]

As the Tuk-Tuk Foods example shows, what customers buy and how many customers buy can be influenced by different factors and experiences. Although you may start out with aggregated data to form a picture of the average customer, technology is available to help you identify and understand customer behaviour at the individual level. To illustrate, Mexico's Banco Azteca was formed by the head of a retail chain with a 50-year history of selling appliances on credit to working families. Each of the bank's 3,000 loan representatives carries a handheld computer full of individual customers' credit data and other details needed for banking decisions. Customers who come to the branches inside parent Grupo Elektra's stores need no passbooks: their account pops up on branch screens at the touch of a finger, thanks to fingerprint identification technology. Thus the bank can analyse its market and customers at both the macro and micro levels. 'We know this segment of Mexican society better than anyone else', states the bank's president.[10]

Consumer markets

In the process of analysing customers in consumer markets as a prelude to developing market targeting and strategy, you should research the following influences on consumer behaviour: characteristics and needs; cultural elements; social connections; and personal elements. Figure 3.3 summarises these influences.

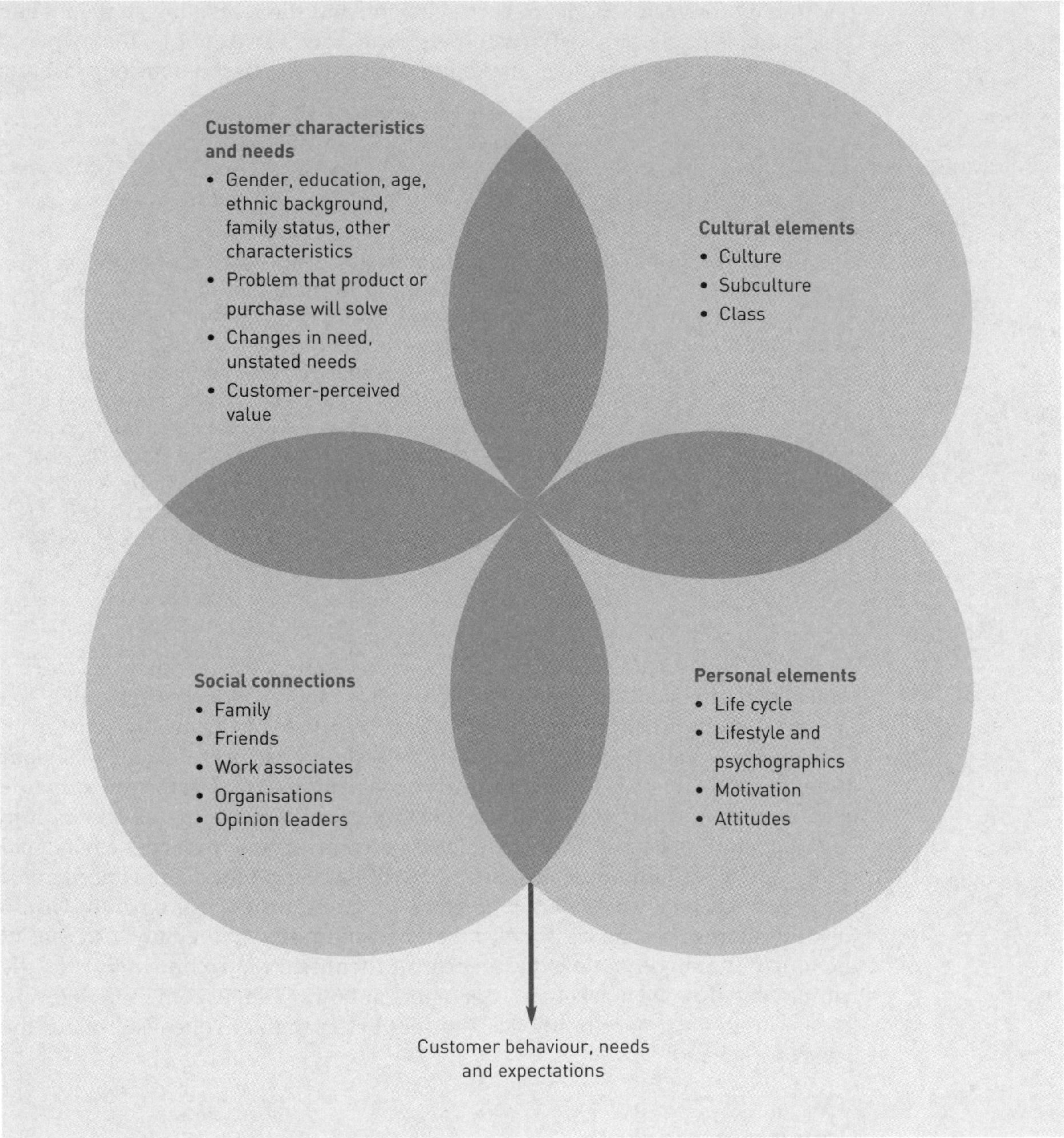

Customer characteristics and needs
- Gender, education, age, ethnic background, family status, other characteristics
- Problem that product or purchase will solve
- Changes in need, unstated needs
- Customer-perceived value

Cultural elements
- Culture
- Subculture
- Class

Social connections
- Family
- Friends
- Work associates
- Organisations
- Opinion leaders

Personal elements
- Life cycle
- Lifestyle and psychographics
- Motivation
- Attitudes

Customer behaviour, needs and expectations

FIGURE 3.3   Influences on consumer behaviour

Characteristics and needs

Often some characteristic, such as gender, family status, age, education or ethnic background, affects what consumers need and buy. Gender, for example, is a key factor in marketing clothing and personal care products geared to women. Similarly, Huggies and other disposable nappies are marketed to families with babies. Before conducting extensive marketing research, try to learn more about the characteristics of particular consumer markets from a variety of secondary sources. (See this chapter's online resources listing for some ideas.)

As you assess consumers' needs, ask: What problem do customers want to solve by buying a particular product? What are customers requesting now that they haven't requested in the past? What changes in need are suggested by developments revealed through internal and external audits? Do customers have unstated needs and wants (such as boosting status) that can be uncovered through marketing research and satisfied through marketing?

Closely related is the value that consumers receive when they buy products to satisfy their needs. **Value** is defined as the difference customers perceive between the benefits they derive from a product and the total price they pay for the product. Customers perceive more value from a good or service that seems to deliver more benefits for the money. For example, many consumers place a high value on the benefit of convenience. Thus, in the UK market for entertainment products, more consumers are buying popular books, CDs and DVDs in local supermarkets as they shop for food, rather than making separate trips to bookshops or music chains. Because of this shift in perceptions of value, the book and entertainment retailer WH Smith is now looking to attract shoppers with products that deliver value by providing other benefits.[11]

Cultural elements

The beliefs, customs and preferences of the culture in which consumers were raised – and the culture where they currently live – can have an influence on consumer buying behaviour. It is a mistake to assume that customers everywhere have the same wants, needs and buying patterns as you. Marketing research is a crucial way for marketers to avoid this misconception.[12] For example, marketers for the appliance manufacturer Daikin, based in Japan, cannot take for granted that consumers in France are just as interested in buying home air conditioners as consumers in Japan. In fact, French consumers buy fewer air conditioning units because of concerns about ecological effects, energy consumption and health. Understanding this cultural difference helps Daikin make better decisions about targeting and marketing programmes.[13]

Within a larger culture are **subcultures**, each a discrete group that shares a particular ethnicity, religion or lifestyle. The subculture can affect consumer buying behaviour, which in turn affects marketing strategy. As an example, many marketers see teens as a distinct global subculture. Consumers in this age group have much in common regardless of geography, including a shared interest in pop music and fashion. Television and the Internet have only intensified the commonalties of this subculture, which has an immense collective spending power. The casual clothing retailer Benetton, with branches from Naples to New York and beyond, is one of many companies that uses its knowledge of this subculture to market to style-conscious teens around the world.[14]

Class distinctions – more subtle in some cultures than in others – are yet another influence on consumer behaviour. Consumers in a certain class tend to buy and use products in similar ways. At the same time, consumers who want to emulate a different class – such as those who strive to move into a higher class – may adopt that class's buying or usage behaviours. Only by researching how such distinctions affect consumers' intentions, attitudes and purchases can you make informed marketing decisions.

To illustrate, as part of BMW's research prior to marketing a new Rolls-Royce model, an engineer spent months driving a Rolls-Royce around Great Britain and talking with upper-class consumers about the brand. He learned that these consumers were concerned about car quality and wanted new Rolls-Royce models to perform in much the same way as older models. They stressed that new models, like older models, should be able to accelerate quickly and easily to high speed without any apparent strain. Understanding the concerns and requirements of this class was essential to planning a suitable marketing strategy. 'Rolls customers are almost invisible to start with', the engineer noted, 'and if you approach them in the wrong way they will just disappear'.[15]

Social connections

Social connections such as family members, friends, work associates and non-work groups can influence how, what and when consumers buy. You will want to determine whether any of these connections are relevant to a particular product's purchase or usage and how they affect buying behaviour. Parents and children, for example, may have different ideas of how to spend a holiday week. To appeal to both, the Hyatt Resorts chain markets Camp Hyatt programmes for children along with more sophisticated attractions for parents.[16]

Just as some consumers follow the buying behaviour of another class to which they aspire, some consumers follow the buying behaviour of different social groups to which they aspire. Youngsters often imitate the clothing and accessory choices of their older siblings; employees seeking job advancement may imitate the attire of higher-level managers. People who are especially admired or possess special skills may be seen as **opinion leaders** in each social group and therefore exert more influence over the purchasing decisions of others. Sports figures are frequently viewed as opinion leaders for athletics wear and equipment. They are also considered opinion leaders for clothing and accessories, as are rock stars and movie stars, among others. Knowing this, Matthew Mellon launched his London business, Harry's Shoes, by arranging for Elton John, John Travolta and other well-known stars to wear his upmarket shoes. He emphasised this marketing approach rather than paying for advertising because, he says, 'there is no better endorsement than a celebrity'.[17]

Personal elements

The fourth category of influences in consumer markets relates to personal elements such as life cycle, lifestyle, motivation and attitudes. An adult's *life cycle* is his or her changing family status over time. People may be single, single parents, single but co-habitating, engaged, married, married with children, divorced, divorced with children and so on. Consumers have different needs, behaviour patterns and buying priorities in each of these life-cycle phases – which, in turn, translate into marketing opportunities. Marketers for the global furniture retailer IKEA, for example, see opportunity in reaching singles who are setting up their first households; single, co-habitating adults who buy furniture together; young married couples furnishing a home or flat; first-time parents who need children's furniture; and consumers in other life-cycle phases.

Lifestyle is the pattern of living reflecting how consumers spend their time or want to spend their time. Through research, you can learn more about how lifestyle influences what and when purchases are made in your market, how purchase transactions are planned and completed, who is involved in the purchase and other aspects of consumer buying behaviour. The UK company Joe Bloggs, for example, markets clothing and bed coverings for teenagers, based on its knowledge of their lifestyle. 'We are bringing fashion into the bedroom because teenagers spend such a lot of their time there', says the company's marketing director.[18]

Lifestyle data helps you create a detailed picture of who your consumers really are and how they actually behave. This is what Burton Snowboards does.

MARKETING IN PRACTICE: BURTON SNOWBOARDS

To Jake Burton Carpenter, snowboarding is as much a lifestyle as it is a sport, and he believes that many young adults share this view. Carpenter founded Burton Snowboards in 1977 to make snowboarding equipment for enthusiasts like himself. Over the years, he has broadened his product line to include anoraks, trainers and clothing items for consumers aged 25 and under who like the snowboarding life. Carpenter and his marketers get many new product ideas from talking with professional snowboarders. The founder even took nine-months' leave to snowboard around the world and stay in touch first-hand with the needs, interests and preferences of the snowboarder segment. Understanding the lifestyle of this segment of the consumer market has helped Burton sell its products to snowboarders in the United States, Europe and Japan.[19]

By analysing consumer behaviour using a complex set of lifestyle variables related to activities, interests and opinions – collectively known as **psychographic characteristics** – you can better understand the roots and drivers of consumer behaviour. Claritas Europe and CACI are two companies that collect and analyse data about consumers' interests, media consumption, reading habits and other lifestyle variables useful for marketing purposes.

Psychological factors such as motivation and attitudes are also important influences on consumer buying. **Motivation** is the internal force that drives a consumer to act in a certain way and make certain purchases as a way of satisfying needs and wants. **Attitudes** are the consumer's assessment of and emotions about a product, brand or something else, which can affect actions. Manchester United, the world's most popular football team, markets itself on the basis of motivation and attitudes – in this case, consumers who have such positive attitudes that they are highly motivated to attend matches and buy team merchandise. Fans are so loyal, in fact, that Man U's 67,000-seat stadium is filled to capacity whenever the team plays at home. Even after David Beckham moved to Real Madrid, Man U fans were motivated to keep buying tickets, watching televised matches and spending millions of euros on branded team merchandise.[20]

Business markets

Individuals or groups make buying decisions for businesses, government agencies and non-profit organisations. Sometimes these decisions involve huge sums of money and involve months of internal review and approval that spans multiple management layers. Business buying behaviour is generally influenced by: the organisation's characteristics and needs; relationships inside and outside the organisation; and considerations that are unique to each organisation (*see* Figure 3.4).

Characteristics and needs

Organisations with different characteristics have different needs and buying patterns, so your first step as a B2B marketer is to gather general information about the markets you are considering. You want to determine the common needs and concerns of organisations in each industry and see which characteristics affect these needs (and how). One way to do this is by categorising organisations according to characteristics such as type of industry, annual turnover, number of employees, location of facilities and geographic focus.

In Europe, the European Commission's Eurostat system provides a standardised method for researching, describing and categorising statistics by industry. Similarly, the North American Industry Classification System (NAICS) provides a method for researching the characteristics of companies in specific industries in the United States, Mexico and Canada. Data organised according to UN industry standard classifications and other international and national industry standards systems is available, as well.

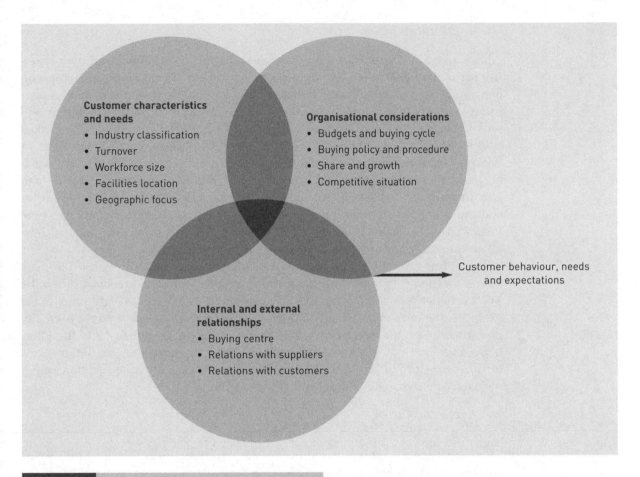

FIGURE 3.4   Influences on business customer behaviour

To gather more data about industries, characteristics of businesses, non-profit organisations or government agencies and business products, you can consult numerous sources, including:

- national and international trade organisations

- country consulates

- multinational banks

- university sources

- magazines, newspapers and other publications that follow international business developments.

Organisational considerations

Although a few organisations buy without budgets, most plan ahead by budgeting for certain purchases during a specified period. Thus, after gathering and analysing general data about a business market, your next step is to learn something about the size of each organisation's budget and the timing of its purchases, which can vary widely within an industry. In addition, research each organisation's buying policy and procedure, its share situation and growth plans or prospects and its competitive situation – all of which can influence what, when and how much the organisation buys. If a multinational corporation's policy is to encourage decentralised or local buying, for example, you will have to plan for communicating with more buyers than if the policy is to centralise buying at the headquarters level. If a business insists on online buying, that policy must also be taken into account during the marketing planning process.

Budgeting and buying cycles are particularly important factors for B2B marketers that sell to non-profit organisations and government agencies. When the Boston Ballet reduced the number of performances in a cost-cutting move, for example, the lower budget and shorter season affected purchases from a variety of suppliers, such as the printer that produces its programmes.[21] On the other hand, rapidly growing cities and countries tend to increase their annual budgets for infrastructure improvements, creating opportunities for construction companies, telecommunications firms and other suppliers.

Internal and external relationships

Many internal and external relationships can affect an organisation's buying patterns. Particularly in large organisations, a group of managers or employees may be responsible for certain purchases. Different individuals within this **buying centre** play different roles in the buying process, as shown in the example in Figure 3.5. Moreover, every member of the buying centre may not participate in every purchase, and different participants may be involved for different purchases. Thus, you should investigate relationships within the buying centre so you can market to the right participants at the right time.

Also research the organisation's relations with current suppliers to find out whether long-term contracts are the norm; whether certain future purchases are already committed to current suppliers; what standards suppliers are expected to meet; and how suppliers are evaluated. In some cases, a company cannot become a supplier until it has met certain criteria and been approved. Even if prior approval is not needed, you should determine what criteria the business customer uses to select suppliers so you can plan accordingly.[22]

Buying centre participant	Example of influence on buying
User	Machine breaks down; operator reports it, thus initiating the buying process. May also be asked for help with specifications for replacement
Influencer	Users may influence this participant, who may also involve R&D staff, accountants, suppliers, sales reps and external consultants
Decider	May be a senior manager with either an active or passive role in the whole process. May also be the buyer and/or influencer
Buyer	Handles the search for and negotiations with suppliers
Gatekeeper	Administrative staff preventing influencers or others from reaching the decision maker; or R&D staff controlling access to information

FIGURE 3.5   How buying centre participants affect a purchase

Source: Adapted from Brassington and Stephen Pettitt, *Principles of Marketing*, 3rd edn (Harlow, Essex: Pearson Education, 2003), p. 161.

For example, Thomas Cook and other companies based in Europe and North America are outsourcing selected operations to companies in India as a way of cutting costs.[23] When making outsourcing decisions, companies use standards such as whether the supplier has sufficient staff able to communicate in a particular language and whether its staff have the expertise to complete projects properly and on time. The CEO of RMSI, an Indian company that markets outsourcing services to the insurance industry, explains: 'The advantage is not just in our lower costs – it is in the easy availability of highly qualified English-speaking technicians.'[24]

Clearly, cost is not the only criterion in a B2B buying decision. Staff expertise, quality, reliable delivery and other considerations can be important criteria by which buying centre participants choose among competing suppliers. Also, by looking at how an organisation deals with its customers, you can get a sense of the value you must add to help satisfy your customers' customers. In fact, organisations often look carefully at the extra value that individual suppliers can add.

Consider the value added by Pan-European Fish Auctions, which has its headquarters in Belgium. Its online fish auction website, www.PEFA.com, benefits all participants by making purchases fast and convenient. Instead of personally attending auctions in 18 different European ports every day, buyers and sellers of Baltic herring and other fresh fish varieties transact business online at www.PEFA.com. The electronic marketplace adds value by reducing the time and effort involved in getting fresh fish through the distribution system to restaurants, food processors, fish retailers and ultimately onto consumers' plates. 'Everyone loves it – the fishermen, the ports and the buyers', says Karl Johannesson, PEFA's marketing director. The added value is so appealing that the site now auctions more than €200 million worth of fish in a year.[25]

RESEARCHING MARKETS AND CUSTOMERS

When researching markets and customers, you will usually start by consulting **secondary research** – information previously collected for another purpose. You can glean basic facts and figures from secondary research more quickly and cheaply than through **primary research**, studies undertaken to address specific marketing questions or situations. This chapter's listing of online resources shows some websites with access to secondary research about business and consumer markets and customers. (*See* Figure 3.6 for questions to ask as you consult secondary sources of research.)

Question	Purpose
What is the date of the research?	To determine whether the research is outdated
What is the source of the research?	To determine whether the source is unbiased, legitimate and qualified
Why was the information originally collected?	To determine whether the information is appropriate for use in this situation
Can the data and conclusions be verified through another source?	To determine whether the research can be relied upon
Does the research include contact information?	To determine whether it is possible to obtain more clarification or detail from the source

FIGURE 3.6 Questions to ask when using secondary research

Secondary research can give you an overview of markets and customers, but often you will need primary research to support the development of specific marketing strategies and activities. Heineken, the Netherlands-based brewing company, uses a variety of primary research methods to gain in-depth knowledge of its customers' needs, unstated wants, attitudes and characteristics. Heineken's marketers undertake this research by travelling around the world to sip beer and chat with the younger consumers they want to attract plus the core market of middle-aged beer lovers who drink Heineken, Amstel, Tiger, Birra Moretti and other company brands.[26] **Ethnographic research** – observing customers' behaviour in real situations rather than experimental surroundings – has become increasingly important for learning about needs and preferences not easily articulated.[27]

Indicate any need for primary research in your marketing plan and allow for the time and money in your schedules and budgets. In addition to researching customer needs and market conditions, plan for research to test programmes and track marketing progress, including customer satisfaction surveys, market-share studies and promotion pre- and post-tests. These kinds of studies can yield insights to help you develop segmentation, targeting, positioning and marketing-mix strategies.

CHAPTER SUMMARY

1. *Understand why marketers examine markets according to definition, changes and share.*
   Marketers examine markets to narrow their focus to a general subset of consumers or businesses that are qualified to buy or currently buyers of a particular type of good or service. They start at the broadest level of the potential market (all customers who may be interested in that product). Then they define the available market (those who have income and access to the product), the qualified available market (those who meet product-related criteria for buying the product), the target market (which the organisation wants to serve) and the penetrated market (customers who already buy or have previously bought that type of product). Next, they research and analyse market changes (because markets are not static) and market share (to determine competitive standing and measure marketing progress).

2. *Explain the main influences on customers in consumer markets.*
   There are four main influences on customers in consumer markets. First, consumer behaviour is affected by needs stemming, in part, from characteristics such as gender and age. In assessing needs, marketers should think about how their product addresses a consumer problem, request, unstated need or unstated want. Second, the consumer's national or regional culture, subculture and class can influence buying behaviour. Third, social connections with family, friends, work associates and non-work organisations can influence consumer buying behaviour. Opinion leaders within a social group may exert more influence over certain consumer purchases. Fourth, personal elements such as life cycle, lifestyle, motivation and attitudes are influential in consumer buying behaviour. Lifestyle is the pattern of living reflecting how consumers spend their time or want to spend their time. Motivation drives consumers to satisfy needs and wants by buying certain products. Attitudes are the consumer's assessment of and emotions about a brand or product, which in turn influence how customers act.

3. *Explain the main influences on customers in business markets.*
There are three main influences on customers in business markets. First, the organisation's characteristics, such as industry, turnover and number of employees, influence needs and buying patterns. Second, organisational considerations, such as budgets, the timing of purchases, buying policies and buying procedures, affect business buying behaviour. Third, internal relationships, such as those among participants in the buying centre, influence business buying behaviour, as do external relationships with current suppliers and the value that buyers are seeking in order to satisfy their customers.

4. *Describe the use of secondary and primary research in marketing planning.*
Secondary research, which is information previously collected for a different purpose, can give marketers basic facts and figures about markets and customers both quickly and cheaply. In addition, marketers often need to use primary research, which is conducted to address specific marketing questions or situations. Any primary research that is needed should be mentioned in the marketing plan and included in the plan's budgets and schedules.

 **KEY TERM DEFINITIONS**

attitudes Consumer's assessment of and emotions about a product, brand or something else

available market All the customers within the potential market who are interested, have adequate income to buy and adequate access to the product

business (organisational) market Companies, institutions, non-profits organisations and government agencies that buy goods and services for organisational use

buying centre Group of managers or employees that is responsible for purchases within an organisation

consumer market People and families who buy goods and services for personal use

ethnographic research Observing customer behaviour in real-world situations

lifestyle The pattern of living reflecting how consumers spend their time or want to spend their time

market The group of potential buyers for a specific product

market share The percentage of unit or monetary sales in a particular market accounted for by one company, brand or product

motivation Internal force driving a consumer's behaviour and purchases to satisfy needs and wants

opinion leader Person who is especially admired or possesses special skills and therefore exerts more influence over certain purchases made by others

penetrated market All the customers in the target market who currently buy or previously bought a specific type of product

potential market All the customers who may be interested in that good or service

primary research Research undertaken to address a particular situation or question

psychographics Complex set of lifestyle variables related to activities, interests and opinions that marketers study to understand the roots and drivers of consumer behaviour

qualified available market All the customers within the available market who are qualified to buy based on product-specific criteria

secondary research Information collected in the past for another purpose

subculture Discrete group within an overall culture that shares a common ethnicity, religion or lifestyle

target market All the customers within the qualified available market that an organisation intends to serve

value From the customers' perspective, the difference between the perceived benefits and the perceived price of a product

THE PRACTICAL MARKETER CHECKLIST NO. 3:
ANALYSING CONSUMERS AND BUSINESS CUSTOMERS

In the consumer market

What consumer needs must the product and product category address?

How can customers in each consumer market be described (by demographics, geography, etc.)?

How is customer behaviour affected by cultural elements such as subculture and class?

How is customer behaviour affected by social connections such as family and friends?

How is customer behaviour affected by personal elements such as lifestyle, motivation and attitudes?

What do these influences mean for segmentation, targeting and marketing strategy?

In the business market

What customer needs must the product and product category address?

How can customers in each business market be described (by demographics, buying policies, etc.)?

Who participates in the buying centre and what is each participant's role?

How does each business customer solicit, qualify and assess suppliers?

How do current supplier arrangements affect competition for orders?

What other relationships and considerations affect business buying behaviour?

What do these influences mean for segmentation, targeting and marketing strategy?

What are the implications of these influences for marketing programmes targeting business and government buyers?

 **ONLINE RESOURCES**

Sources for secondary research

- Global Statistics (www.geohive.com) – Provides access to demographic information about consumers in various regional markets.

- National Statistics Online, UK (www.statistics.gov.uk) – Web gateway to UK government-maintained statistics about consumer and business markets.

- National Institute for Statistics and Economic Studies, France (www.insee.fr) – Web gateway to statistics about consumer and business markets in France.

- Istituto Nazionale di Statistica (http://demo.istat.it/e/) – Posts past, present and projected demographic characteristics for the Italian population.

- Youth at the United Nations (www.un.org/esa/socdev/unyin/index.html) – Shows children's demographics by country plus links to social and economic data.

- OffStats (www2.auckland.ac.nz/lbr/stats/offstats/OFFSTATSmain.htm) – Offers links to statistics about regions, individual nations and industries.

- Eurostat (http://europa.eu.int/comm/eurostat) – Provides European business statistics categorised by standard industry classifications plus links to other organisational classification systems.

QUESTIONS FOR DISCUSSION AND ANALYSIS

1. Why are market definitions and general descriptions only a starting point for formulating marketing strategy?

2. Is it possible or desirable for a marketer to examine the influence of an extremely small subculture within the overall culture?

3. How is the influence of internal and external relationships on business buying behaviour similar to the influence of social connections on consumer buying behaviour?

APPLY YOUR KNOWLEDGE

Research the general definition of a particular market, such as the consumer market for mobile phones or the business market for desktop computers.

- How can this market be described broadly in terms of product, geography and demographics?

- If you are researching a consumer market, approximately how many people, families or households are in the market?

- What characteristics such as age, gender, family status and other descriptions relevant to the product apply to consumers in this market?

- What, specifically, are the main influences on buying behaviour in this consumer market?

- If researching a business market, approximately how many and what type of organisations are in the market for the product?

- What characteristics such as turnover, number of employees and other descriptions relevant to the product apply to customers in this business market?

- What changes are currently affecting (or will soon affect) this consumer or business market?

- What relationships and organisational considerations have the most influence on buying in this business market?

- Prepare a brief oral or written report summarising your comments.

BUILD YOUR OWN MARKETING PLAN

Continue the marketing planning process for a hypothetical organisation or an actual organisation you have chosen by broadly describing the market and the influences on customer buying behaviour. First, identify the five levels of market definition that apply, from the potential market to the penetrated market. Also determine the criteria by which you would consider customers to be in the available market and in the qualified available market. Next, research the most important changes that are currently affecting or are expected soon to affect this market. Look at market share trends to understand the competitive situation. Then examine the major influences on customer needs and behaviour in this consumer or business market. Finally, list any primary and secondary research needed to enable you to understand your markets or customers better. Document what you have learned and the implications for segmentation, targeting and marketing strategy in *Marketing Plan Pro* software or in a written marketing plan. Be sure to consider how these analyses will help you formulate and implement appropriate marketing strategies.

CLOSING CASE: MCDONALD'S INVITES FAMILIES TO DINE

Think Happy Meals, think family. Understanding how much influence children can have over a family's choice of fast-food restaurant, the marketers at McDonald's use a wide variety of marketing tactics to reach children. During one recent year, the fast-food chain introduced a series of new Happy Meals toys geared to hit children's movies and television shows. Working with Sega, McDonald's also launched a Happy Meals video game. The result: Happy Meals turnover rose by more than 10 per cent as children repeatedly returned to McDonald's with their families. In fact, CEO Jim Cantalupo notes that McDonald's has been successful in Europe because 'we are one of the few restaurants where kids and families are welcome. And you can get in and out at a reasonable price and have some fun, and have a family get to-together', he adds.[28]

In an ongoing quest to gain market share in the fast-food industry, McDonald's has spread its red-and-yellow logo far and wide. Toyshops are a particularly good place to reach children. Now children can dress Barbie dolls in a McDonald's uniform and play with toys shaped like Chicken McNuggets and other items on the McDonald's menu. After years of in-store and media exposure, Ronald McDonald is one of the most familiar characters in the world, reminding youngsters of the fast-food chain with every appearance. But the company also supports many socially responsible initiatives such as promoting bicycle safety and raising money for charity. In turn, these initiatives give parents a good feeling about taking their children to McDonald's.

Despite the enormous popularity of fast food, some parents are becoming concerned about their children's nutrition. Lawsuits over obesity have drawn even more media attention to this issue. Reacting to market change, McDonald's has started offering yoghurt, apple juice and other healthy foods as part of the Happy Meals package, not just burgers and chips. Still, intense competition and slower growth in mature markets are keeping the pressure on McDonald's. By appealing to the influence of children, can it encourage more family trips to McDonald's restaurants and lay the foundation for profitably serving tomorrow's adult customers – and their families?[29]

Case questions

1. What are some of the needs and unstated wants that influence the way parents and children decide on a fast-food restaurant?

2. What specific questions about the influence of family and other social connections would you suggest that McDonald's marketers seek to answer through primary research?

 ENDNOTES

1. Based on information from: 'Nestlé Purina Sponsors Pet Smile Month', *Marketing*, 1 May 2003, p. 12; 'Felix in Link with Tesco for Co-branded Mailing', *Marketing*, 24 April 2003, p. 8; 'Nestlé Overhauls Felix Identity Across Europe', *Marketing*, 6 March 2003, p. 10; Larry Claasen, 'Nestlé Zooms in on Local Pet Food Market', *Africa News Service*, 17 January 2003, www.comtexnews.com; 'Felix in TV Sponsor Debut with You've Been Framed', *Marketing*, 2 May 2002, p. 6.

2. Peter Burrows, 'The Humvee of Laptops', *Business Week*, 21 April 2003, p. 74; Marc Spiwak, 'Panasonic Notebooks "Tough" It Out', *Computer Reseller News*, 10 March 2003, p. 41.

3. Based on Gary L. Lilien and Arvind Rangaswamy, *Marketing Engineering*, 2nd edn (Upper Saddle River, NJ: Prentice Hall, 2003), p. 159.

4. Roger J. Best, *Market-Based Management: Strategies for Growing Customer Value and Profitability*, 2d edn (Upper Saddle River, NJ: Prentice Hall, 2000), pp. 59–62.

5. 'Design Choice – Vespa Granturismo', *Marketing*, 7 August 2003, p. 10.

6. Steve Hamm, 'Tech Comes Out Swinging', *Business Week*, 23 June 2003, pp. 62–6.

7. Bill Ordine, 'Airlines Vie for Aces Market Share', *The America's Intelligence Wire*, 25 August 2003.

8. Quoted in Krissana Parnsoonthorn, 'Thai-Owned Producer of Food Business Set for Rapid Expansion in Scandinavia', *Bangkok Post*, 20 February 2003, www.bangkokpost.com.

9. Parnsoonthorn, 'Thai-Owned Producer of Food Business Set for Rapid Expansion in Scandinavia'.

10. Geri Smith, 'Buy a Toaster, Open a Bank Account', *Business Week*, 13 January 2003, p. 54.

11. Alison Smith, 'The Middle Road Gives WH Smith a Rough Ride', *Financial Times*, 29 August 2003, www.ft.com; Alison Smith, 'WH Smith Warns and Signals US Withdrawal', *Financial Times*, 28 August 2003, www.ft.com.

12. Andrew Gershoff and Eric Johnson, 'Avoid the Trap of Thinking Everyone Is Just Like You', *Financial Times*, 28 August 2003, www.ft.com.

13. John Tagliabue, 'Europe Decides Air-Conditioning Is Not So Evil', *New York Times*, 13 August 2003, pp. W1ff.

14. Arundhati Parmar, 'Global Youth United', *Marketing News*, 28 October 2002, pp. 1, 49; Gail Edmondson, 'Has Benetton Stopped Unravelling?', *Business Week*, 30 June 2003, p. 76.

15. Quoted in Scott Miller, 'British Blue Bloods Instruct BMW on Retooling the Rolls', *Wall Street Journal*, 11 October 2002, www.wsj.com.

16. Martha Stevenson Olson, 'Hotels Aim for Families', *New York Times*, 20 July 2003, sec. 5, p. 4.

17. Quoted in Cecilie Rohwedder, 'In Step with Famous Feet', *Wall Street Journal*, 27 June 2003, pp. B1, B7.

18. Quoted in 'Joe Bloggs Unveils Teen Interiors Range', *Marketing*, 7 August 2003, p. 2.

19. Cathy Horyn, 'To Balance a Business, He Rides a Snowboard', *New York Times*, 24 August 2003, sec. 3, p. 5.

20. Stanley Holmes, 'Can Man U Score in America?', *Business Week*, 23 June 2003, pp. 108–9.

21. Michelle Higgins, 'When the Show Doesn't Go On', *Wall Street Journal*, 27 August 2002, pp. D1–D2.

22. William Band and John Guaspari, 'Creating the Customer-Engaged Organisation', *Marketing Management*, July–August 2003, pp. 35–9.

23. Nick Huber, 'Outsourcing: Thomas Cook Puts Ticketing Out to India', *Computer Weekly*, 22 July 2003, p. 8.

24. Quoted in Dan Roberts and Edward Luce, 'Service Industries Go Global', *Financial Times*, 19 August 2003, www.ft.com.

25. Quoted in Andy Reinhardt, 'Europe's Borderless Market: the Net', *Business Week*, 12 May 2003, p. 52.

26. Jack Ewing, 'Waking Up Heineken', *Business Week*, 8 September 2003, pp. 68–72.

27. Virginia Matthews, 'How to Dig Deeper in the Consumer Mind', *Financial Times*, 8 October 2003, www.ft.com.

28. Quoted in Neil Buckley, 'Interview with McDonald's CEO Jim Cantalupo', *Financial Times*, 28 August 2003, www.ft.com.

29. Based on information from: Buckley, 'Interview with McDonald's CEO Jim Cantalupo'; Parija Bhatnagar, 'Is McDonald's Summer of Fun Over?', *CNN Money*, 28 August 2003, http://money.cnn.com/2003/08/27/news/companies/mcdonalds_toys; David Barboza, 'If You Pitch It, They Will Eat', *New York Times*, 3 August 2003, sec. 3, pp. 1, 11.

4

Planning segmentation, targeting and positioning

Closing case: Danone means dairy and more

Endnotes

Comprehension outcomes

After studying this chapter, you will be able to:

- Explain the benefits of segmentation, targeting and positioning
- Identify segmentation variables for consumer and business markets
- Discuss the use of undifferentiated, differentiated, concentrated and customised target marketing
- Describe the criteria for effective positioning

Application outcomes

After studying this chapter, you will be able to:

- Apply segmentation variables in consumer and business markets
- Evaluate segments and select appropriate targeting approaches
- Formulate a meaningful positioning for competitive power

OPENING CASE: PEPSICO PURSUES GROWTH SEGMENT BY SEGMENT

Everyone drinks soft drinks – right? For decades, soft drink marketers like PepsiCo and Coca-Cola thought in terms of mass markets. They marketed their colas to just about every thirsty consumer, regardless of age, culture, buying patterns or other differences. Later they created and marketed diet versions of their colas for calorie-conscious consumers. Today, however, PepsiCo is pursuing a growth strategy by sharpening its marketing focus. Rather than trying to reach all potential buyers with one or two brands, PepsiCo's marketers are aiming at smaller, specific segments on a country by country, brand by brand basis.

Consumers in their teens and twenties are high on the list of customer segments that PepsiCo is working to reach in different regions. Through research, the company has learned that these customers are eager to try new flavours and are sceptical of traditional marketing tactics. This means that PepsiCo's marketers must find appropriate ways of communicating with such consumers, apart from the one-size-fits-all advertising campaign. Pepsi Max, for example, is aimed at the segment of the UK market defined by gender (male), age (young) and lifestyle (active). PepsiCo promotes Pepsi Max using communication techniques geared to this segment's interests. For instance, it has arranged sponsorship contracts with top athletes such as David Beckham who are seen as opinion leaders by these consumers.

In the United States, one of PepsiCo's biggest hits among young adults is Mountain Dew Code Red, a cherry-flavoured soft drink packed with caffeine. Instead of launching Code Red with a massive advertising campaign, PepsiCo's marketers allowed consumers to 'discover' the new product through sampling at youth-oriented sporting events. The resulting word-of-mouth buzz helped Code Red sell 100 million cases in its first full year on the market. Although Code Red represents a tiny fraction of PepsiCo's annual turnover, the brand is successfully appealing to women and city dwellers as well as African Americans – who, research shows, are particularly big buyers of carbonated soft drinks.

PepsiCo targets diverse market segments using lifestyle elements such as popular culture as a unifying theme because, says Giuseppe D'Alessandro, director of multicultural marketing, 'The multicultural mind-set is more about your interests, like music', than about race or national origin.[1] As one example, Pepsi commercials featuring the Colombian-born star Shakira are broadcast in English and Spanish in North American markets. 'The era of the mass brand has been over for a long time', observes Pepsi-Cola marketing executive David Burwick. 'It took our category longer than most to accept that.'[2] Now PepsiCo is counting on segmentation and targeting to keep global turnover growing into the future.[3]

CHAPTER PREVIEW

Not so very long ago, a multinational marketer like PepsiCo might have hesitated to invest significant resources in products like Mountain Dew Code Red, which attract a limited customer base compared to the almost ubiquitous Pepsi-Cola. Now, facing the reality that the mass market for soft drinks is fragmenting into a series of smaller market segments, PepsiCo and its chief rival Coca-Cola are battling for market share and profits one segment at a time. The reason: just as not everyone has a taste for Pepsi-Cola (or Coca-Cola), no single marketing strategy is effective for all customers.

This chapter discusses the third stage in the marketing planning process. First, the chapter discusses the benefits of market segmentation, targeting and positioning. Next is a look at the market segmentation process and how it is applied to consumer and business markets. Following a section about the targeting process, the chapter concludes by discussing the use of positioning for competitive power. *In reading this chapter, look carefully at how the principles can be applied, along with principles from earlier chapters, to support the development of a realistic marketing plan.*

BENEFITS OF SEGMENTATION, TARGETING AND POSITIONING

Market segmentation involves grouping consumers or business customers within a market into smaller segments based on similarities in needs, attitudes or behaviour that marketing can address. PepsiCo segments its markets on the basis of similarities it has found in consumers' tastes and interests. By eliminating inappropriate markets and identifying appropriate market segments for more thorough research, the company can better understand customers in these segments and more effectively respond to their needs. This process also helps PepsiCo's marketers decide which segments to target for marketing activities, and in what order. Finally, it helps them determine how to create a meaningful and competitively distinctive position in the minds of the customers in each targeted segment. Figure 4.1 shows how segmentation, targeting and positioning (STP) are applied in marketing planning, along with the major benefits.

Segmentation is hardly a marketing panacea. In fact, it makes sense only when:

- the customers within each segment have something identifiable in common

- different segments have different responses to marketing efforts

- the customers in segments can be reached through marketing

- competitive advantage can be gained by focusing on segments

- organisational goals such as profitability can be achieved by focusing on segments.

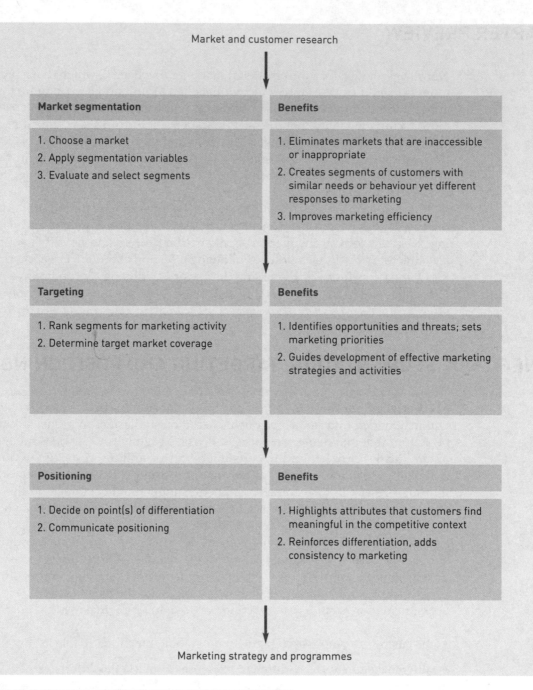

FIGURE 4.1 Applying segmentation, targeting and positioning

A segment may consist of millions of people, yet still be a select subset of a much larger market. Customers within each segment will have similar behaviour and needs or be seeking the same benefits from a product. Taking segmentation one step further, you may be able to distinguish **niches**, small sub-segments with distinct needs or requirements. Consider the success that many companies are enjoying by focusing on soy milk niches.

MARKETING IN PRACTICE: SOY MILK

From Texas to Tokyo, a small but growing number of consumers have started buying soy milk during the past 20 years. The dominant US player in this segment is White Wave, maker of Silk Soymilk, which has built a $200 million business based on three niches. One is the group of consumers who cannot digest cow's milk or are allergic to it; a second is the group of consumers seeking the health benefits of soy; and a third consists of customers interested in organic foods.

'We look at our market as mainstream but very niche specific', comments Silk's president.[4] Indeed, the soy milk segment is growing in size and opening new niche opportunities for enterprising companies. More than four dozen companies now compete in the US soy milk market, mirroring the increase in competition around the world. In Japan, Kibun Food Chemifa markets four flavoured soy milk drinks; Takara Shuzo offers thick soy milk drinks and other variations. In addition to flavour, companies are varying their marketing mixes to appeal to niches created by preferences for refrigerated or longlife, unrefrigerated packages and purchases at supermarkets or health-food stores.[5]

Taken to the extreme, you may be able to segment a market to create niches of one. In the past, marketing to such a small niche would not be profitable. Now you can use technology to discern the specific needs, behaviours and responses of individual consumers or business customers. In some industries, the potential size of and profit from a single order make it worthwhile to segment and target single-customer niches.

Airbus, for example, carefully studies the needs of each airline or government interested in buying aircraft. One recent multi-jet purchase by Qatar Airways, for example, was valued at over £3 billion; another, from Korean Air, added up to nearly £1 billion. No two airlines' needs are alike, no two respond to marketing in exactly the same way and no two have identical aircraft configuration preferences. Therefore, Airbus can better serve the market and compete more effectively by segmenting down to niches of one, targeting each individually and positioning itself on the basis of the needs of each.[6]

THE MARKET SEGMENTATION PROCESS

You will follow three steps to segmenting a market, as Figure 4.1 indicates. The first is to choose the market to be segmented; the second is to apply appropriate segmentation variables; and the third is to evaluate and select segments for targeting. Your decisions in all three steps depend on understanding your mission and long-term goals as well as on detailed, current information drawn from internal and external audits (*see* Chapter 2) plus thoughtful analyses of markets and customers (*see* Chapter 3).

Choose the market

With your market definitions as a starting point, you begin the segmentation process by determining which markets you will investigate further and which you will eliminate. Although the specific criteria differ from organisation to organisation, you may want to consider eliminating markets based on:

- formidable legal, political, social or competitive pressures

- extreme logistical difficulties

- lack of purchasing power or other serious economic challenges

- troubling ethical controversies

- persistent ecological concerns.

For years, many marketers eliminated China from their list of viable markets because of then-insurmountable legal hurdles regarding ownership and currency. Once China became a member of the World Trade Organisation and allowed more access by foreign firms, however, the country rejoined the list of markets being considered by companies around the world. Further legal changes, being phased in, are encouraging companies like Netherlands-based ING Group to establish plans for doing business in China.[7]

Apply segmentation variables

Once you have eliminated inappropriate markets, look for ways to distinguish meaningful segments within your chosen markets. The point is to form consumer or business segments that are internally homogeneous yet exhibit some differences (compared with other segments) that can be addressed through marketing. If you find no differences, segmentation is pointless, because you will not need to vary your marketing approach for each segment's unique needs, characteristics or behaviour patterns.

You can segment consumer and business markets using a number of variables, as discussed in the following sections.

Consumer market variables

Customer characteristics and product-related behavioural variables can be used to group consumers into segments within a market (*see* Figure 4.2). You will rarely apply a single segmentation variable; for more specific segment definition, you should apply a combination of appropriate variables. User-based customer characteristics are easier to identify and apply, yet behaviour-based, product-related approaches – which are not as easy to isolate and analyse – typically give you more insight into potentially effective marketing approaches for each segment.

The most appropriate variables for each consumer market may not be obvious or intuitive. For example, L'Oréal, the French beauty products company, uses price perceptions – specifically, interest in higher quality at a higher price for a luxury feeling – as one segmentation variable for hair colouring and other beauty products. A second variable is gender and a third is place of usage. By gearing its product features, packaging, promotion and distribution strategies to different segments – women willing to spend a bit more to pamper themselves at home, men using skin-care products for a sense of well-being, women having their hair dyed at salons and so on – L'Oréal has become the global market leader in its industry.[8]

Customer characteristics – consumer

One reason to apply consumer segmentation variables, which describe the buyer or user in some way, is because they are easy to identify within a market. (See this chapter's online resources section for sources of demographics on consumers and businesses.) L'Oréal's marketers apply the demographic variable of gender as a segmentation variable for cosmetics. Marketers for LVMH Moët Hennessy–Louis Vuitton and Richemont apply the socioeconomic variables of income and class to segment the market for their luxury brands. Geographic and lifestyle variables are also important to LVMH, which recently turned its focus to segments in Japan and Canada, seeking to reach wealthy consumers who travel less often.[9]

You can also apply geographic variables when you want to enter or increase sales in specific regions or climates; avoid specific countries or regions because of competitive challenges or other threats; or leverage your organisation's strengths for competitive advantage in those areas. For example, the Ask Central restaurant group has opened only a few of its 156 ASK and Zizzi restaurants in central London. Instead, most of the chain's restaurants are located in other UK cities, where operating costs are lower and their 'value for money' concept is especially appealing to consumers.[10]

However, avoid the pitfalls of viewing customers as merely a bundle of 'characteristics' and ignoring differences that transcend geography. People are more

Customer characteristics – a user-based approach that asks, 'Who purchases what?'

Demographic
- Age
- Family size
- Marital status
- Gender

Socioeconomic
- Income
- Class
- Vocation
- Education
- Religion
- Ethnicity

Geographic
- Global, hemispheric, national, state, city, postal code
- Climate
- Rural vs. urban

Lifestyle/personality
- Attitudes/opinions
- Interests
- Avocations
- Tastes and preferences

Product-related approaches – a behavioural approach that asks, 'Why do they purchase?'

User types
- Regular
- Non-user
- First-time
- Potential

Price sensitivity
- Low-cost orientation
- Higher-cost quality/ differentiation focus

Consumption patterns/ usage frequency
- Low
- Medium
- Strong

Perceived benefits
- Performance
- Quality
- Image enhancement
- Service

Brand loyalty
- Loyal/satisfied
- Experimenters
- Unsatisfied/Defectors
- Unaware

Application

Purchase occasion/ buying situation

Media exposure

FIGURE 4.2 Variables for segmenting consumer markets

Source: Adapted from Craig S. Fleisher and Babette E. Bensoussan, *Strategic and Competitive Analysis* (Upper Saddle River, NJ: Prentice Hall, 2003), p. 173.

complex and their buying motivations are driven by numerous factors; even those who share a particular characteristic will not necessarily respond in the same way to the same marketing activities. Likewise, applying non-geographic variables such as gender, age or vocation can reveal viable segments across geographic boundaries. And, because consumer reactions are often heavily influenced by product-related variables, you should apply those in addition to characteristics and other variables.

For example, Starwood Hotels uses a number of variables to segment the market for hotel accommodation. One segment it has identified is that of consumers who (1) own dogs, (2) prefer driving holidays and (3) are not price-sensitive. Despite these similarities, people in this segment may have few other characteristics in common. Starwood communicates how it meets the needs of this segment by publicising its policy of allowing guests to bring their dogs to more than 700 hotels worldwide. This policy is not just good public relations: according to the company's research, dog owners will show loyalty to a hotel chain that accepts their pets.[11]

Consider how S.C. Johnson & Son Canada combines consumer variables to market its line of insect repellents.

MARKETING IN PRACTICE: S.C. JOHNSON & SON CANADA

The leader in the lucrative Canadian market for insect repellents is S.C. Johnson & Son Canada, which makes popular products such as Deep Woods Off! Company marketers use seasonal weather as one segmentation variable, because demand is highest during the warm summer months when consumers on holiday spend more time outdoors. It applies consumer attitudes toward chemical ingredients as another variable. To reinforce the company's brands and remind consumers about the benefits of insect repellent, S.C. Johnson's marketers boost advertising expenditures during summer months.

Responding to consumers' concerns about the harmful effects of the chemical repellent DEET, Johnson's marketers developed an alternative formula marketed as Off! Botanicals. In recent years, fear of West Nile virus – spread by mosquitoes – has dramatically increased demand for insect repellents, prompting S.C. Johnson to expand production. The company has also hired specialists to pinpoint locations of infected insects, information that is posted on the S.C. Johnson website. 'Hiring experts doesn't give us any brand recognition, but it does provide credibility', explains Neil Chin, vice president of marketing.[12]

Product-related variables – consumer

On the most basic level, you can segment a market according to users and non-users, such as those who use insect repellent and those who do not. You should look deeper to determine how and why a consumer uses or does not use a product – behaviour related to the product – which helps you identify signs of underlying wants or needs that may be addressed through marketing strategies. One advantage to using variables such as consumption patterns and purchase occasion is that they are easily observed, measured and analysed. For example, marketers for Suntory's chain of Pronto cafés have effectively segmented the Japanese market using the variable of consumption patterns. During the day, the cafés operate as coffee shops, catering to the country's pattern of heavy coffee consumption. During the evening, however, the cafés are transformed into bars, catering to the popular habit of stopping for a drink and meal after work.[13]

Here is how Zespri International applied the variable of purchase occasion/buying situation when entering a new market.

MARKETING IN PRACTICE: ZESPRI INTERNATIONAL

Zespri International, owned by New Zealand farmers, has segmented by geography, ethnicity, purchase frequency and a taste for sweet fruit to establish its Zespri Gold brand of golden kiwi fruit in far-flung markets. This is not the usual green, tart, hairy kiwi fruit: it's sunny yellow, nearly hairless and has a mango-like flavour. Zespri's marketers used geographic segmentation to decide on which markets to enter in Europe, Japan, South Korea, Taiwan and the United States. For US markets, they also applied product-related variables and customer characteristics. Through research, they learned that Latino consumers in the United States shop for fresh fruits and vegetables twice as often as other US consumers and that these consumers like the sweet taste of tropical fruits. In response, Zespri's initial Spanish-language campaign ran only in US cities with high Latino populations – and it was so successful that demand temporarily outstripped supply.[14]

Increasingly, companies are seeking to build stronger, longer-term relationships with customers by identifying segments whose stated or unstated needs they can satisfy and who are likely to be brand loyal as a result. Look at Barclays Bank of Kenya, which segments its national market according to customer characteristics (personal wealth), behavioural variables (need for personalised services) and benefits (interest in banking with a recognised institution). The bank has designed products, marketing communications and services to respond to this segment's needs and reinforce customer loyalty. [15]

Note that different segmentation variables are appropriate for different markets and products. In the Korean market for mobile phone services, for instance, some companies are successfully segmenting using the variable of variety-seeking behaviour. The companies have noticed that Korean teenagers (like their counterparts in many countries) constantly use their mobile phones to download the latest ring tones, background music and pop recordings. Thus, variety-seeking behaviour is a good segmentation variable for phone companies and content providers who offer new music and ring tones. In a country with 32 million mobile phone users, downloaded music is generating impressive industry-wide annual revenues, shared among phone companies and content providers.[16]

Business market variables

As in consumer markets, business markets can be segmented using both customer characteristics and product-related approaches that probe behaviour (*see* Figure 4.3). Customer characteristics describe the organisation from the outside, whereas behavioural variables look at activities and dynamics below the surface. Generally B2B marketers apply both types of variables to form segments of organisational customers that are internally homogeneous but have different needs or different responses to marketing when compared with other segments.

Customer characteristics – a user-based approach that asks, 'Who purchases what?'

- Industry type: e.g. SIC codes
- Geographic
- Industry position

- Company size
- Technology employed
- Business age
- Ownership structure

Product-related approaches – a behavioural approach that asks, 'Why do they purchase?'

- Consumption patterns/ usage frequency
- End use application
- Perceived benefits
- Size of purchase

- Relationship between seller/purchaser
- Psychodemographics of purchaser
- Purchasing policies

FIGURE 4.3   Variables for segmenting business markets

Source: Adapted from Craig S. Fleisher and Babette E. Bensoussan, *Strategic and Competitive Analysis* (Upper Saddle River, NJ: Prentice Hall, 2003), p. 174.

Customer characteristics – business

As a B2B marketer, you can apply demographics such as industry type, geography and annual turnover to narrow the dimensions of a market before you apply behavioural variables. For example, the anti-plagiarism service Turnitin.com uses industry and geography to sharpen its focus. Not every organisation is a potential buyer for a service that screens students' assignments to identify plagiarised passages. Therefore, Turnitin.com segments according to industry (colleges and universities) and geography (serving more than 50 countries) as well as the specific need for anti-plagiarism services. Oxford, Cambridge and some 700 other public universities are now among Turnitin.com's UK customers.[17]

From the standpoint of customer characteristics, businesses typically have different needs and responses from those of non-profit organisations and government agencies; likewise, larger or older organisations tend to have different needs and responses from those of smaller or newer organisations. Some organisations rely more heavily on certain technologies (such as e-commerce or customer contact software) than others, another indicator that can help you segment your market. In general, look carefully at how certain characteristics reveal differences that you can build on when planning marketing activities.

Product-related variables – business

When you segment a business market by product-related variables, especially in combination with customer characteristics, you can uncover important customer needs and buying patterns. As an example, Mitsubishi Fuso Truck and Bus Corp., one of Japan's largest truck manufacturers, recently had success segmenting its market by one variable – perceived benefits. It found that commercial truckers were eager to buy new trucks before the government implemented new vehicle emissions standards. Applying this variable to create marketing keyed to the desired benefits boosted the company's annual turnover by 25 per cent before the new standards came into effect.[18] You can also use frequency, size, timing and method of purchasing to segment business markets, along with variables reflecting purchasing policies and authorised buyers. Consider the situation of the US industrial distributor W.W. Grainger.

MARKETING IN PRACTICE: W.W. GRAINGER

With 500,000 products, 1.5 million business customers, 600 outlets and more than €4.5 billion in annual turnover, W.W. Grainger is far larger than its closest competitor. From mops to microchips, Grainger's product assortment is as broad as its customer base, which ranges from corporate giants to government agencies to tiny sole traders. Some corporations have thousands of authorised buyers; some customers want to buy and receive goods on the same day or the next day.

To deal with this market complexity, Grainger uses both customer characteristics (industry, company size, geographic location) and product-related variables (who is doing the purchasing, end use application, purchasing patterns, benefits sought) for segmentation. More specifically, the company knows that many corporations seek the benefits of (1) purchasing efficiency and (2) one-stop solutions. American Airlines became a customer not just because of attractive prices and convenient service but because Grainger's staff were willing to tackle the logistical problems associated with consolidating the airline's maintenance purchases.[19]

Evaluate and select segments for targeting

The next step in the segmentation process is to assess the attractiveness of each segment in terms of opportunity, environment, reach and response and see how each fits with internal considerations such as mission, image, strengths, core competencies, resources and performance. The purpose is to eliminate undesirable segments and evaluate the possible opportunity inherent in the remaining segments. At this point, you can screen out segments with insufficient profit potential, intense competition or other complications. Top managers of the Fast Retailing chain, for instance, decided against continuing to focus on certain geographic segments after experiencing increased competition and lower profits in those segments. On the basis of this decision, the Japanese retailer closed a number of stores in the United Kingdom but retained hundreds of stores in Japan, five in London and three in Shanghai.[20]

It is important to investigate the possibilities thoroughly even when a segment appears unrealistic at first glance. The Tiffindell resort, located in Africa's Drakensberg mountain range, illustrates this principle in action. Five companies tried unsuccessfully to promote skiing here before Ivan van Eck established Tiffindell to appeal to the segment of young, fun-loving, affluent skiers. He found a marketing angle that goes beyond skiing (mostly on artificial snow) by adding lively night-life activities. Although Tiffindell has not been consistently profitable, it has operated every winter for a decade despite intermittent snowfall, a remote location and rough access roads.[21]

Ideally, you want to be active in segments that play to your organisation's strengths and do not stretch your resources too thin. This is what Alpha M.O.S., based in Toulouse, France, is doing. Alpha makes electronic devices for sensing smells and tastes; because of its relatively small size, the company has limited resources to invest in customising devices for individual business customers. Therefore, Alpha looks for attractive, sizeable industry segments such as food producers, breweries and wineries where customers are interested in the benefit of electronically testing for quality and can justify the cost.[22] This chapter's checklist gives specific questions to ask when evaluating segments.

THE TARGETING PROCESS

After you drop unattractive or unsuitable segments from consideration, you are ready to rank the remaining segments in priority order for marketing attention, on the basis of research and analysis. You can do this in several ways. For example, you might assign relative weights to each of the evaluation criteria and calculate the total scores segment by segment. The sample ranking shown in Figure 4.4 shows how you might score three segments based on the four criteria categories, along with a total score per segment. As in this sample, a segment may merit a high score for opportunity yet have a much lower score for environment or another of the criteria.

	Segment A	Segment B	Segment C
Opportunity	8	6	5
Environment	3	5	5
Reach and response	6	4	7
Internal considerations	9	7	4
Total score	26	22	21

FIGURE 4.4   Sample segment ranking

Note: Weighted scores range from 1 (extremely unattractive) to 10 (extremely attractive).

To decide which segment should be your top priority, look at the total score and, if necessary, set minimum scores for individual criteria. In the sample ranking, Segment A has the highest total score and, if the organisation does not require a minimum score of 5 or higher on all criteria, would be the highest priority. Note that Figure 4.4 is only an example; organisations vary widely in their evaluation criteria, weighting and ranking systems. One organisation might rank segments according to similar customer characteristics or needs, in line with its product manufacturing or distribution strengths. Another might put more weight on the opportunities for competitive advantage within segments. A third might be more concerned with **customer lifetime value**, the total revenue (or profit) a particular customer relationship represents to the organisation over time. The choice depends on your unique situation, your chosen market and your customer knowledge. If possible, use sensitivity analysis to adjust criteria weights under differing forecasts and confirm priority rankings by testing prospective strategies before moving ahead with full-scale marketing plans.

After selecting and prioritising segments, you next decide on a coverage strategy: how many segments will you target and with what marketing approach? As shown in Figure 4.5, targeting coverage strategies include undifferentiated marketing, differentiated marketing, concentrated marketing and customised marketing.

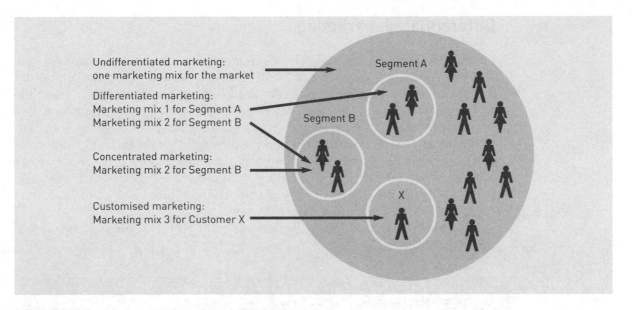

Undifferentiated marketing:
one marketing mix for the market

Differentiated marketing:
Marketing mix 1 for Segment A
Marketing mix 2 for Segment B

Concentrated marketing:
Marketing mix 2 for Segment B

Customised marketing:
Marketing mix 3 for Customer X

Segment A

Segment B

X

FIGURE 4.5 Segment targeting coverage strategies

Undifferentiated marketing

Essentially a mass-marketing approach, **undifferentiated marketing** means targeting the entire market with the same marketing mix. This assumes that all customers in a particular market, regardless of any differences in characteristics or behaviour, will respond in the same way to the same marketing attention. Undifferentiated marketing is less expensive than other coverage strategies, due to the lower costs of developing and implementing only one marketing mix. However, today's markets are rarely so homogeneous; even slight differences can serve as clues to underlying needs in segments where an organisation can gain competitive advantage, encourage customer loyalty and ultimately return profits.

Consider the increasingly fragmented market for salt. Industry giants Cargill (owner of the Diamond Crystal brand) and Morton (owned by Rohm & Haas) have segmented what was once assumed to be a homogeneous market according to type of customer (consumers, restaurants and institutional customers) and specific cooking uses and occasions. The result is an avalanche of products such as sea salt, coarse crystal salt, natural mineral rock salt and other variations, promoted differently to different segments. Meanwhile, La Baleine and Flower of the Ocean are two of many brands entering the market with gourmet salts for smaller niches within the larger salt market. In short, if you were competing in that industry, you would avoid undifferentiated marketing because the mass market for salt no longer exists.[23]

Differentiated marketing

With **differentiated marketing**, you formulate a separate marketing mix for each segment you target. You may not target all segments in a given market, but for those you rank as priorities, you will need different marketing mixes geared to each segment's unique characteristics and behaviours. The assumption is that you can provoke a different response from each segment by using different marketing mixes. Customers benefit because their specific needs are being addressed, which increases satisfaction and encourages customer loyalty. Moreover, you can compete more effectively by tailoring the marketing mix for each segment, although this is much more costly than undifferentiated marketing and may overburden resources if not carefully managed.

Look at how Emirates, one of the world's most profitable airlines, uses differentiated marketing.

MARKETING IN PRACTICE: EMIRATES AIRLINE

The dominant carrier based in Dubai, Emirates airline segments the overall market for international air travel by destination, service and price sensitivity. Within that market, the airline uses differentiated marketing to appeal to different segments with different marketing mixes. First-class and business-class passengers flying to Dubai, who pay more for their tickets, receive free car service to the airport in London and 14 other cities. On the plane, they settle into roomy, comfortable seating; can choose among 48 movies on a personal screen; and savour gourmet meals with free wine. Economy-class passengers, who pay less, are only slightly less pampered. They receive no car service but can choose among 17 movies and 18 video games. Every segment, however, receives the high-quality service that gives Emirates airline its competitive edge. In the words of one passenger, 'on this airline they really treat you like a human being, not just a number'.[24]

Concentrated marketing

As you saw in Figure 4.5, **concentrated marketing** involves targeting one segment with one marketing mix. The idea is to compete more effectively and efficiently by understanding and satisfying one set of customers, rather than spreading organisational resources across multiple marketing activities for multiple segments. As long as the targeted segment remains attractive, this can be a profitable coverage approach. However, uncontrollable and unexpected factors such as new competition or changes in customer needs can make the targeted segment less attractive or even unfeasible. Thus, focusing on only one segment can be an advantage for a time but is potentially risky over the long term.

Customised marketing

You may be able to tailor marketing mixes to individuals within certain targeted segments, an approach known as **customised marketing**. Airbus, as noted earlier in this chapter, uses this targeting approach. Its marketers can identify all the potential buyers in the jet aircraft market, get to know their needs and specifications, then develop a separate marketing mix for each. The market is not so large that this is impractical, and the potential profit from each order is so great that customised marketing makes sense for Airbus.

If you have the right technology, you can opt for **mass customisation** and create products tailored to individual customers' needs on a larger scale, as Canada Post does with personalised postage stamps. Consumers simply fill out an order form, submit a non-copyrighted photo and include payment. In three weeks, sheets of 25 personalised stamps arrive, at a price double that of an ordinary stamp. Thousands of Canadian consumers order stamps every week, submitting photos of children, pets or other images. Small businesses are even ordering stamps bearing company logos. And the response? 'The buzz has tipped us off that we are really onto something big', comments a Canada Post spokesperson.[25]

THE POSITIONING PROCESS

With positioning, you use marketing to create a competitively distinctive position for your product in the minds of targeted customers. You need marketing research to understand how your targeted customers perceive your organisation, product or brand and your competitors. Research can also help determine which attributes matter most to the targeted customers. Regardless of how you see your products, it is the customer's view that counts. Procter & Gamble, for example, once marketed its Dash brand of laundry detergent in the United States by emphasising its low-sudsing quality. This positioning was aimed at the segment of US consumers who owned front-loading washing machines, which could not use high-sudsing detergents. Over time, top-loading machines became more popular in US households, and Dash became less popular because consumers saw it as strongly associated with front-loading machines.[26] (Now that front-loading washing machines are regaining popularity in America because they use less water, should P&G reintroduce Dash with a new 'low-sudsing' campaign?)

Deciding on differentiation

P&G's experience with Dash illustrates the importance of deciding on a point of difference that is not only competitively distinctive but also relevant and believable (*see* Figure 4.6). Dash was not like other laundry detergents – it was different and better because it did not produce a lot of suds and was therefore well suited to front-loading washing machines. This point set Dash apart from rivals in a credible way and, just as important, it was important to customers. Once front-loaders began disappearing, however, Dash's low-sudsing quality became irrelevant because customers stopped worrying about a detergent's volume of suds.

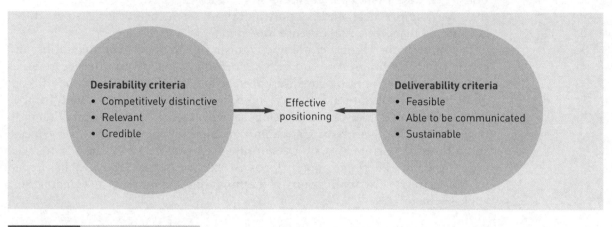

| FIGURE 4.6 | Effective positioning |

Source: Adapted from Kevin Lane Keller, *Strategic Brand Management*, 2nd edn (Upper Saddle River, NJ: Prentice Hall, 2003), p. 143–4.

You should base your product's positioning on all three criteria – criteria that are meaningful and desirable from the customer's perspective yet competitively distinctive. Here are some examples of effective positioning based on desirable criteria:

- Swatch: unique fashion watches

- Carrefour: wide merchandise selection at low prices

- Ryanair: low-cost, no-frills air travel.

Applying positioning

In addition to satisfying the three desirability criteria, you must actually carry through the positioning in your product's marketing and performance. Determine first whether your organisation can, realistically, develop and market a product that will live up to meaningful points of difference. Second, consider whether the points of difference can be communicated to the targeted segments. And third, determine whether you can sustain the product's performance and continue to communicate a meaningful point of difference over time.

To illustrate, look at how the online movie rental company Netflix applied its original positioning of convenience. Netflix required customers to visit its website, set up a list of DVD movies they wanted to rent, receive DVDs by mail and pay for rentals one at a time. If DVDs weren't returned within a week, customers had to pay a late charge. Even after Netflix lowered its rental fee and liberalised the return period, however, it attracted few loyal customers. Why? Although convenience was a relevant, credible and distinctive point of difference, customers did not think Netflix was any more convenient than renting from a neighbourhood store. To enhance feasibility, Netflix changed the offer to match the positioning by charging a monthly subscription fee, allowing customers to rent three DVDs at a time and eliminating late fees and deadlines. Delivering on the positioning worked: Netflix now serves more than one million customers.[27]

In short, positioning is the driver behind all your marketing-mix strategies and tactics. With differentiated marketing, you develop a positioning appropriate to each segment and apply that positioning through your marketing decisions for each segment. With concentrated marketing, you establish one positioning for the single segment you target. Remember that positioning is not a one-time decision: as markets and customers' needs change, you must be prepared to reposition a product, if necessary, for desirability and deliverability.

CHAPTER SUMMARY

1. *Explain the benefits of segmentation, targeting and positioning.*
   Segmentation helps marketers rule out inappropriate markets, identify appropriate market segments for more study and gain a more in-depth understanding of the customers in those segments so the organisation can more easily respond to their needs, which in turn benefits customers. Evaluating segments enables the organisation to decide which to target and in what order to market to each. The process also provides a basis for creating a meaningful and competitively distinctive position in the minds of each target segment's customers.

2. *Identify segmentation variables for consumer and business markets.*
   In consumer markets, organisations can apply two categories of segmentation variables: user-based consumer characteristics (demographic, geographic, socioeconomic and lifestyle/personality) and product-related behavioural approaches (user types, consumption patterns and usage frequency, brand loyalty, price sensitivity, perceived benefits and more). Business markets can be segmented using customer characteristics (industry type, geographic, industry position, company size and more) and product-related behavioural approaches (consumption patterns/usage frequency, end use application, perceived benefits and more).

3. *Discuss the use of undifferentiated, differentiated, concentrated and customised target marketing.*

When organisations use undifferentiated marketing, they are targeting the entire market with the same marketing mix, on the assumption that all will respond in the same way to the same marketing attention. When using differentiated marketing, the organisation creates a separate marketing mix for each targeted segment, assuming that customers in each segment will respond differently to these different marketing mixes. With concentrated marketing, the organisation targets only one segment with a single market mix. With customised marketing, the organisation customises a marketing mix for each individual customer within the targeted segment.

4. *Describe the criteria for effective positioning.*

Effective positioning must satisfy three desirability criteria (be competitively distinctive, relevant and credible) as well as three deliverability criteria (the positioning must be feasible, able to be communicated and sustainable).

 ## KEY TERM DEFINITIONS

concentrated marketing Targeting one segment with one market mix

customer lifetime value Total long-term revenue (or profit) that an organisation estimates it will reap from a particular customer relationship

customised marketing Tailoring marketing mixes to individual customers within targeted segments

differentiated marketing Targeting different segments with different marketing mixes

market segmentation Process of grouping consumers or businesses within a market into segments based on similarities in needs, attitudes or behaviour that marketing can address

mass customisation Developing products tailored to individual customers' needs on a large scale

niche market Sub-segment within a larger segment that has customers with distinct needs or requirements

undifferentiated marketing Targeting the entire market with one marketing mix

THE PRACTICAL MARKETER CHECKLIST NO. 4:
EVALUATING MARKET SEGMENTS

Segment opportunity

What is the current size of the segment and how is it changing?

What potential do you see for sales and profits in this segment and how is this changing?

Would the cost of marketing to this segment outweigh the payback?

How might this segment's opportunity contribute to the organisation's goals?

Segment environment

How many competitors serve the segment and how is competition likely to affect performance?

Can the organisation realistically capture or defend market share in this segment?

What threats exist or could emerge to prevent success in this segment?

Segment reach and response

Can customers in the segment be reached through appropriate marketing activities?

Are customers in this segment likely to respond to different marketing activities than customers in other segments?

Internal considerations

Can the organisation's strengths and core competencies make a difference in this segment?

Does the organisation have the resources to serve this segment?

Will serving this segment interfere with operations or performance in other segments?

Does the segment fit with the organisation's mission and image?

ONLINE RESOURCES

Demographic sources for consumer and business markets

- Eurostat (http://europa.eu.int/comm/eurostat) – Offers research on demographic characteristics of European businesses.

- National Statistics Online, UK (www.statistics.gov.uk) – Provides demographic statistics about UK consumer and business markets.

- CyberAtlas (http://cyberatlas.internet.com) – Presents demographics of consumers who use the Internet.

- Youth at the United Nations (www.un.org/esa/socdev/unyin/index.html) – Shows youth demographics by country.

- Global Statistics (www.geohive.com) – Posts demographics of consumer markets in various geographic markets.

- Asia-Pacific.com (www.asia-pacific.com) – Posts links to demographics and other data resources for researching Asian markets.

QUESTIONS FOR DISCUSSION AND ANALYSIS

1. What are the advantages and disadvantages of using concentrated marketing to target a niche segment?

2. Why should marketers go beyond demographic variables when segmenting consumer and business markets?

3. Under what circumstances would a marketer want to change a product's positioning?

APPLY YOUR KNOWLEDGE

Research the segmentation, targeting and positioning of a particular company active in consumer or B2B marketing, using its products, advertising, website and other activities as clues.

- Based on the organisation's marketing, what market(s) and segment(s) appear to be targeted?

- Is this company using differentiated, undifferentiated, concentrated or customised marketing? How do you know?

- What benefits are featured in the company's marketing, and what customer needs are they designed to satisfy? How might the targeted segments be described in terms of needs?

- Analysing the marketing clues you have observed, what product-related variables do you think this company is using to segment its market(s), apart from benefits sought?

- In one sentence, how would you summarise the positioning this company is trying to reinforce in one of the targeted segments?

- Prepare a brief oral or written report summarising your comments.

BUILD YOUR OWN MARKETING PLAN

Proceed with the marketing plan for a hypothetical organisation or an actual organisation that you have chosen. During the segmentation process for this organisation, what markets would you eliminate from consideration, and why? What specific segmentation variables would you apply to the remainder of the market, and how would you expect them to create segments that make sense from a marketing perspective? What further research would support this segmentation? What criteria would you use to evaluate the segments you identify? Given the organisation's overall goals, strengths and resources, what targeting approach would you choose? Finally, what positioning would you want to reinforce for the customers in each targeted segment? Be sure that these ideas are appropriate in light of your earlier decisions, then document your choices (and explain how they affect your strategy) in *Marketing Plan Pro* software or in a written marketing plan.

CLOSING CASE: DANONE MEANS DAIRY AND MORE

Although yoghurt, water and biscuits are entirely different products, Groupe Danone competes effectively in all three categories. The French company is the world's largest maker of yoghurt products; its brands include Actimel in Europe, Danone in South America and Dannon in the United States. In addition to dairy products, the company markets bottled water (under Evian and other brands) and biscuits (under Jacob's and other brands). Clearly Danone's marketers cannot target every customer in every market, so they study the needs that drive consumer behaviour and reach out to targeted segments through differentiated marketing.

In the yoghurt market, company marketers identified segments based a diversity of needs and wants: some consumers want health benefits, some want a low-calorie snack, some prefer a fruity or creamy taste and so on. In response, Danone makes dozens of varieties of yoghurts with higher or lower levels of active cultures, sweetener, flavourings, fruits and other ingredients. Its yoghurt packages come in different sizes and shapes to accommodate buyers who want portable snacks, to eat yoghurt at home and who display other consumption behaviours. Also Danone offers smoothies and enriched dairy drinks for those who prefer to sip their yoghurt rather than eat it with a spoon.

Needs and perceptions can change over time, as Danone's marketers are well aware. After the company acquired Shape, which was positioned in the United Kingdom as a diet yoghurt brand, marketers researching consumer perceptions found that diet products were seen as less relevant than healthy foods. Meanwhile, Shape was facing more competition from Onken, Benecol and other diet dairy brands. Armed with this information, Danone's marketers decided to change Shape's positioning by changing its marketing. They designed a new logo, packaging and advertising to appeal to customers seeking healthy foods (a positive association) rather than those avoiding higher-calorie foods (a negative association).

Interest in healthy eating has also become a major factor in food-buying patterns among Chinese consumers. Spotting this opportunity, Danone's managers bought a majority interest in China's Hangzhou Wahaha Group, which makes enriched milk drinks, expanded capacity and used the company's brand and distribution system to break into the bottled water market. Now China is Danone's largest market for water, with annual purchases of more than four billion bottles.

Like their counterparts in other countries, some consumers in China prefer to support to local businesses. This worked to Danone's advantage when the government asked the parent to assist Wahaha in developing a local cola soft drink, Future Cola, which the company positioned as 'the Chinese people's own cola'. The drink quickly gained enough market share to take the number-three position (behind Coca-Cola and Pepsi-Cola) – an especially striking achievement because Danone is not involved with soft drinks in any other market.[28]

Case questions

1. Of the evaluation criteria in Checklist No. 4, which seem to have strongly influenced Danone's decision to eliminate the diet foods segment?

2. How did positioning contribute to Danone's success in marketing Future Cola?

ENDNOTES

1. Quoted in Laurel Wentz, 'Pepsi Puts Interests Before Ethnicity', *Advertising Age*, 7 July 2003, p. S4.

2. Quoted in Gerry Khermouch, 'Call It the Pepsi Blue Generation', *Business Week*, 3 February 2003, p. 96.

3. Based on information from: Brian Steinberg, 'Pepsi Puts Its Hopes on Plain Vanilla', *Wall Street Journal*, 15 August 2003, p. B4; Martin Peers, 'Spend It Like Beckham', *Wall Street Journal*, 19 June 2003, p. B1; 'Soft Drinks Struggle, But Flavours Shine', *Beverage Industry*, July 2003, pp. 16ff.; Elizabeth Brewster, 'The New Multicultural Mainstream', *Beverage Industry*, February 2003, p. 32; 'Cola Giants' NPD Frenzy', *Marketing*, 28 November 2002, pp. 26ff.; www.pepsi.com; Wentz, 'Pepsi Puts Interests Before Ethnicity'; Khermouch, 'Call It the Pepsi Blue Generation'.

4. Quoted in Susan Greco, '1 + 1 + 1 = the New Mass Market', *Inc.*, January 2003, pp. 32–3.

5. Christina C. Berk, 'Health-Food Maker Hain Faces Rivals', *Wall Street Journal*, 13 August 2003, pp. 1ff.; Dina ElBoghdady, 'Soy Milk Spilling into the Mainstream', *Washington Post*, 15 March 2003, pp. E1ff.; 'New Soy Milk Products from Tully's and Others', *New Food Products in Japan*, 25 May 2003, n.p.; Greco, '1 + 1 + 1'.

6. Charles Duhigg, 'Airbus Gets Qatar Order, Building Lead Over Boeing', *Washington Post*, 20 June 2003, pp. E3ff.; Tony Smith, 'It's Boeing vs. Airbus in Big Battle Over Brazil', *New York Times*, 3 June 2003, p. W1.

7. 'Strings Attached', *The Economist*, 8 March 2003, pp. 67–8.

8. Kenneth Maxwell, 'L'Oréal CEO Sees New-Product Boost', *Wall Street Journal*, 10 September 2003, p. B4A; 'The Colour of Money: The Beauty Business', *The Economist*, 8 March 2003, p. 59.

9. Alan Cowell, 'Luxury Wobbles on Legs of Dollars and Yen', *New York Times*, 25 May 2003, sec. 3, p. 4.

10. 'Ask Delivers Record Profits', *Ananova*, 4 September 2003, www.ananova.com.

11. Jane Engle, 'Starwood Opens Its Doggie Door', *Los Angeles Times*, 31 August 2003, p. L3.

12. Quoted in John Intini, 'The Profits in Repellents', *Maclean's*, 1 July 2003, pp. 58ff.

13. Jason Singer and Martin Fackler, 'In Japan, Adding Beer, Wine to Latte List', *Wall Street Journal*, 14 July 2003, pp. B1, B3.

14. Debbi Gardiner, 'Selling Kiwis Without Tears', *Business 2.0*, October 2002, p. 62.

15. 'Barclays Unveils Marketing Plan', 28 May 2003, www.comtexnews.com.

16. Mark Russell, 'Musical Mobiles', *Newsweek*, 9 September 2003, p. 12.

17. Michael Hastings, 'Cheater Beaters', *Newsweek*, 8 September 2003, p. E16.

18. James B. Treece, 'Japan's No. 3 Truckmaker Sees a Surge in Profits', *Automotive News*, 21 July 2003, p. 20.

19. Victoria Fraza, 'Making Integrated Supply Work', *Industrial Distribution*, April 2003, pp. 69ff.; Nancy Syverson, 'Inside Grainger', *Industrial Maintenance & Plant Operation*, November 2002, pp. 20ff.

20. Bayan Rahman, 'Fast Retailing Lifted by Better News at Uniqlo', *Financial Times*, 6 May 2003, www.ft.com; Bayan Rahman, 'Fast Retailing Makes Fast Exit from UK Market', *Financial Times*, 7 March 2003, www.ft.com.

21. 'No Business Like Snow Business', *The Economist*, 2 August 2003, p. 57.

22. John Tagliabue, 'Sniffing and Tasting with Metal and Wire', *New York Times*, 17 February 2002, sec. 3, p. 6.

23. Allison Askins, 'Salt Has an Ancient History and a Bright Future', *The State* (Columbia, S.C.), 2 June 2003, www.thestate.com; Michael J. McCarthy, 'Little Umbrella Girl Watches Her Back in Kosher Salt War', *Wall Street Journal*, 10 June 2002, pp. A1ff.

24. Quoted in Joseph B. Treaster, 'Flying with Panache and at a Profit, Too', *New York Times*, 5 January 2003, sec. 3, p. 5.

25. Quoted in James Brooke, 'Topple the Queen! Enthrone Yourself on a Stamp', *New York Times*, 27 June 2000, p. A4; also: Alicia Henry, 'You Oughta Be In . . . Stamps?', *Business Week*, 25 August 2003, p. 14.

26. This positioning section and the example draw on Kevin Lane Keller, *Strategic Brand Management*, 2nd edn (Upper Saddle River, NJ: Prentice Hall, 2003), Chapter 3.

27. Christopher Null, 'How Netflix Is Fixing Hollywood', *Business 2.0*, July 2003, pp. 41–43.

28. Based on information from: David Haffenreffer, 'Danone Restructures Products Portfolio', *America's Intelligence Wire*, 30 July 2003; 'Danone Opens New Production Line in Budapest – Extended', *Europe Intelligence Wire*, 3 July 2003; 'Danone Brings in Bloom to Revamp Shape Diet Image', *Marketing*, 6 February 2003, p. 3; Hannah Booth, 'Bloom Researchers Yoghurt to Update Its Pack-Shape', *Design Week*, 6 February 2003, p. 5; Sherri Day, 'Yoghurt Makers Shrink the Cup, Trying to Turn Less into More', *New York Times*, 3 May 2003, pp. C1ff.; Leslie Chang and Peter Wonacott, 'Cracking China's Market', *Wall Street Journal*, 9 January 2003, pp. B1ff.

5 Setting a direction, objectives and marketing strategy

Comprehension outcomes

After studying this chapter, you will be able to:

- Explain how marketing plans are driven by direction and objectives
- Describe the three broad directions that can shape a marketing plan
- Discuss the characteristics of effective objectives
- Explain the distinctions and linkages between financial, marketing and societal objectives

Application outcomes

After studying this chapter, you will be able to:

- Set the marketing plan's direction
- Formulate effective marketing plan objectives

OPENING CASE: HSBC HOLDINGS BANKS ON GLOBAL GROWTH

With more than 6,000 offices worldwide, HSBC Holdings is banking on profitable growth for its global future. The London-based company serves both consumers and businesses through units under the HSBC name and various regional names. Its offerings range from credit cards and savings accounts to commercial loans and investment management, among many others. Regardless of location, every HSBC unit sets specific objectives and uses marketing to move toward the corporation's overriding goal of growth.

For example, the HSBC unit in South Korea, which has 11 branches, is aiming to grow by increasing market share. One objective is therefore 'to be the most preferred foreign bank operating in the country', says the unit's head of personal financial services.[1] Other objectives are to increase the amount of money that the bank lends by 35 per cent and to double the amount of money managed for customers. To accomplish these objectives, the South Korean unit has more than doubled the number of sales representatives it employs, introduced an array of new products and more aggressively promoted its wealth-management business.

HSBC Bank Malaysia Bhd is also on the path to growth. This unit recently set an annual objective of increasing the number of credit cards issued by 20 per cent, which it can meet only by approving 500,000 new credit accounts. The five-year objective is to attract one million new customers – not a simple task, according to the general manager of personal banking services: 'The greatest challenge for the bank will be to gain market share in a slow growth market environment and increasing competition. This will be achieved through clear segmentation of our customer base and reaching out to them in meeting their needs through relationship management.'[2]

The HSBC unit in Hong Kong, the Hong Kong and Shanghai Banking Corporation, is seeking growth by attracting new customers (especially affluent consumers), introducing new products and persuading current customers to sign up for more of the bank's products. Despite nearly doubling the number of credit cards issued over the past three years, the general manager plans to increase the number issued by 10 per cent annually for the next two years. However, he warns, 'It's not just about competing in terms of the number of cards, profitability is more important.'[3]

As important as profits may be, the bank is also concerned about ecological protection. It recently donated $50 million to conservation efforts by the Earthwatch Institute and other non-profit groups. In line with its social responsibility objectives, it is also sending 2,000 employees to participate in global ecological projects over the next five years. 'The environment is something that people feel very strongly about, and the reality is that we can make some difference there because of our scale', points out Amanda Combes, who manages HSBC's community programmes.[4]

CHAPTER PREVIEW

The global growth HSBC Holdings seeks is reflected in marketing plan objectives set unit by unit, market by market and product by product. HSBC wants to achieve growth by a number of measures, including higher turnover, higher profits, higher market share and a larger customer base. From the top down, management is expanding geographically by acquiring other banks and opening new branches in new areas. At the local level, HSBC units move in the direction of growth through strategies to offer existing products in existing markets; modify existing products for new markets; market new products in existing markets; and offer new products in new markets.

To do this, the units must plan to initiate relationships with new customers, strengthen relationships with current customers and, if possible, reinvigorate relationships with customers who were thinking about switching or have already switched to other banks. The marketing plan for each HSBC unit documents strategies and programmes with corresponding objectives to support the parent's overall growth strategy. As one example, when HSBC's Bangkok unit planned a mortgage marketing programme to enlarge the customer base and build profitability, its objective was to make 300 new loans in three months.

This chapter discusses marketing plan objectives and direction, which make up the fourth stage in the marketing planning process. The chapter opens by examining how direction and objectives drive the marketing plan to help the organisation achieve its longer-term goals. Next is a discussion of marketing plan direction, covering both growth and non-growth strategies. Finally, the chapter closes by explaining how to set effective marketing, financial and societal objectives, with examples. *As you study this chapter, think about how you can combine the principles with information from earlier chapters in developing a workable marketing plan.*

HOW DIRECTION AND OBJECTIVES DRIVE MARKETING PLANNING

No marketing plan is developed in isolation. As Chapter 1 noted, marketing plans are actually an integral part of the hierarchy of strategies at the organisational, business and marketing levels. Higher-level strategies reflect the organisation's direction, which in turn are supported by marketing objectives, strategy and tactics. As a marketer, you will make programme-level decisions based on the direction and objectives of your marketing plan. The strategy pyramid illustrated in Figure 5.1 shows this linkage.

If the objectives in your marketing plan are explicit and clearly connected to higher-level objectives and long-term goals, the plan is more likely to produce the desired performance.[5] Thus, each objective, marketing strategy and marketing programme must be consistent with the plan's direction as well as with both organisational and business objectives. Consider how Carrefour uses marketing to move its retail empire in the direction of growth.

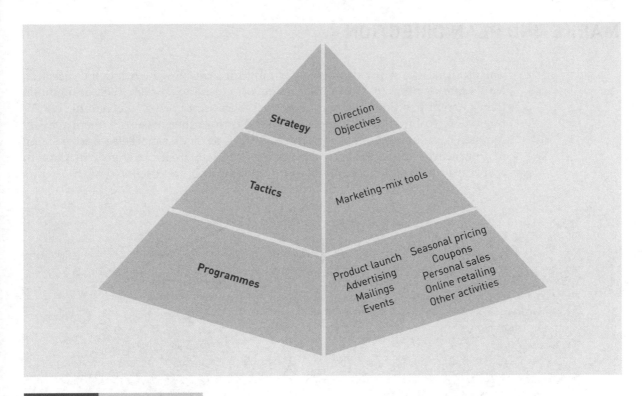

FIGURE 5.1   Strategy pyramid

Source: After Tim Berry and Doug Wilson, *On Target: The Book on Marketing Plans*, 2nd edn (Eugene, OR: Palo Alto Software, 2001), p. 107.

MARKETING IN PRACTICE: CARREFOUR

Ever-higher turnover is the goal of the Paris-based discount retailer Carrefour, which operates more than 9,000 hypermarkets, supermarkets and discount stores in Europe, Asia and South America. Carrefour constantly looks for opportunities to open new stores in Indonesia, China and other places where population and income are rising. Each opening is supported by marketing programmes designed to draw shoppers, build revenues and ultimately yield profits. The chain also supports growth by relying on discount pricing as a point of differentiation. As one example, Carrefour stores hang banners and use other promotional techniques to draw attention to their low prices during France's two annual sales periods.

Further, the company has a customer loyalty programme, Ticket One, to encourage higher shopper spending in and regular patronage of its stores as paths to growth. Finally, although the company tailors each store's merchandise selection to local needs, it is known for carrying a vast array of foods, household products and other items. This wide selection brings shoppers back again and again, supporting Carrefour's relentless push for growth.[6]

MARKETING PLAN DIRECTION

Carrefour is, like many companies, aiming for growth, which sets the direction for its marketing plans. In contrast, some organisations merely seek to maintain their current position, postponing growth because of adverse economic conditions, fierce competition, financial problems or for other reasons. Others actively retrench by selling off units or products, exiting particular markets or downsizing in other ways – often for survival purposes or to prepare for later growth. Growth and non-growth strategies, summarised in Figure 5.2, are discussed next.

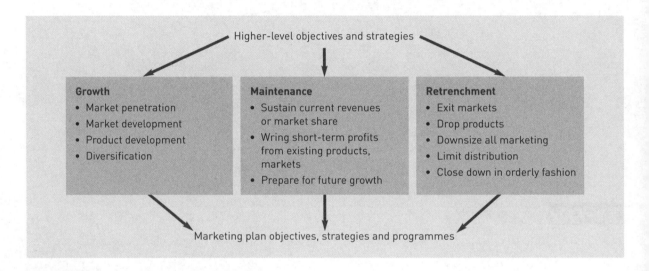

Higher-level objectives and strategies

Growth
- Market penetration
- Market development
- Product development
- Diversification

Maintenance
- Sustain current revenues or market share
- Wring short-term profits from existing products, markets
- Prepare for future growth

Retrenchment
- Exit markets
- Drop products
- Downsize all marketing
- Limit distribution
- Close down in orderly fashion

Marketing plan objectives, strategies and programmes

FIGURE 5.2 Choices of marketing plan direction

Growth strategies

If your organisation wants to grow, you will choose among the four main growth strategies proposed by Ansoff: market penetration, product development, market development and diversification.[7] With **market penetration**, you offer existing products to customers in existing markets. This increases unit and/or monetary sales and simultaneously reinforces the brand or product's strength in each market. It also connects customers to the organisation with more ties and strengthens the relationship. As the opening case in this chapter noted, Hongkong and Shanghai Bank uses market penetration by cross-selling additional financial services to customers who are already doing business with the bank. Shiseido, the Japanese cosmetics manufacturer, also does this to increase sales of skin-care products, lipsticks and other beauty items to customers in China and other Asian countries where demand is rising.[8]

With **product development**, you market new products or product variations to customers in existing markets. This only works when you can develop a steady stream of product innovations appropriate for the needs of customers in those markets. Heinz used this strategy when it developed Top Down Tomato Ketchup. Based on research indicating that 70 per cent of consumers store ketchup bottles upside down so the ketchup flows more easily, this new package is designed to stand on its lid and cut the flow of ketchup after users stop squeezing. Introducing the new product across Europe and in the United States is helping Heinz achieve its growth objectives for higher sales and profits.[9]

With **market development**, you pursue growth by marketing existing products in new markets and segments. Such a strategy builds on the popularity of established products and allows organisations to expand their customer base either geographically or by segment. The Canadian supermarket chain Loblaw's, for example, created its President's Choice store brand to give shoppers a lower-priced yet quality alternative to manufacturers' brands. The first product under this brand, a chocolate chip cookie, quickly became the best-seller in its category. More products followed, and after this success in Canada, the company pursued higher growth by marketing President's Choice products in the United States.[10]

The fourth growth strategy is **diversification**, which means marketing new products in new markets or segments. You can diversify by (1) distributing new products in new markets through existing channel arrangements, (2) initiating new marketing activities in new markets or (3) acquiring companies to gain access to new products and new markets. London-based Hanson, once part of a larger conglomerate, has recently been growing through diversification within the building materials industry. By buying brick companies in North America, cement companies in Australia and related businesses in other areas, the company can offer a wider range of construction products in Europe, the Americas, Australia and the Pacific.[11]

MARKETING IN PRACTICE: BARNES & NOBLE

One of the world's largest book retailers, Barnes & Noble has been diversifying to fuel growth in the face of mature markets and intense competition. In one diversification initiative, the company acquired a publisher that releases 600-plus new titles every year. This provided access to the publisher's distribution channels and to new customer segments. In another diversification move, the company began publishing art books priced lower than competing books. Thanks to well-placed displays in the chain's superstores, these books sold steadily; a few publishers finally stopped releasing art books because they were unable to compete.

Publishing is becoming such an important driver of growth that sales of Barnes & Noble's own books are expected to contribute up to 12 per cent of the chain's annual turnover by 2008. Some publishers have adapted to this competition by agreeing to co-publish books with Barnes & Noble. 'We're competing against ourselves', says the president of one publishing firm, 'but if I didn't do this, somebody else would'.[12]

Diversification can open doors to new opportunities but may also cause conflict with suppliers, customers or channel members. That was the consequence of diversification by the New York-based book retailer Barnes & Noble.

Non-growth strategies

Sometimes growth is not an appropriate direction. Pressured by severe economic or competitive conditions, insufficient resources, ambitious expansion, lower demand or stagnant revenues and profits, organisations may follow a maintenance strategy or even retrench. You might therefore create a maintenance marketing plan to keep revenues, market share or profits at current levels, if possible, or at least defend against deterioration. Rather than invest in improving products, targeting new markets, developing new promotions or other marketing activities, your organisation could try to harvest short-term profits from existing products and markets as a way of conserving resources and building a stronger foundation for later growth.

Organisations that cannot maintain their current levels may be forced into making marketing plans to retrench or, in the extreme, to shut down entirely. As shown in Figure 5.2, some common choices here are to withdraw from certain markets, eliminate particular products, downsize all marketing efforts, shrink distribution or go out of business. And, if the retrenchment effort goes well, the company will soon be able to start planning for a turnaround through a new growth strategy.

Brio's retrenchment strategy is a good example. The Swedish company has long been known for high-quality, expensive toys such as wooden trains. Besides designing and producing its own toys, it eventually owned a regional toy chain, distributed toys in Scandinavian countries and marketed board games, among other activities. Then IKEA, Tesco and other large retailers began selling wooden trains at lower prices, just as the number of independent toy stores – a key distribution channel – plummeted in the United States and other markets. Brio's sales and profits suffered. Finally, management decided on retrenchment. By outsourcing production, focusing product development and cutting costs, Brio planned to become, in a few years, 'a smaller company but profitable', said one of the company's owners.[13]

Clearly, the marketing plan for Brio's retrenchment strategy will be completely different from the marketing plan for Barnes & Noble's diversification strategy and the plan for Shiseido's market penetration strategy. Each has chosen a different path and therefore needs different marketing plan objectives – achieved by the implementation of appropriate marketing strategies and programmes – to guide its movement toward the desired direction.

MARKETING PLAN OBJECTIVES

Marketing plan objectives are short-term targets that, when achieved through implementation of appropriate strategies and programmes, will bring the organisation closer to its longer-term goals. Some companies use broad organisational performance measures such as the **Balanced Scorecard**, which seeks to balance financial performance and performance affecting other stakeholders (such as good community citizenship or employee safety). In such cases, the marketing plan objectives should be aligned to support these broader measures of performance.

To be effective, your marketing plan objectives must be:

- *Relevant*. Be sure your objectives relate to the chosen direction and higher-level strategies and goals. Otherwise, your marketing strategy and programmes to achieve objectives will not support organisational needs. Although most businesses set objectives for revenues and profits, non-financial objectives such as those relating to corporate image are also important because they help build long-term stakeholder relations.

- *Specific and measurable*. Vague targets will not help you determine what you need to accomplish and how. Simply calling for 'growth' is not enough. To be effective, your objectives should indicate, in quantitative terms, what the marketing plan is being developed to achieve.[14] As mentioned in the opening case, HSBC Bank Malaysia's marketing plan for growth set an objective of increasing the number of credit cards issued by 20 per cent each year, which meant opening 500,000 new accounts.[15] The bank's marketing managers can check their progress toward this objective at any time by counting the number of accounts opened and cards issued.

- *Time defined*. What is the deadline for achieving the objective? You will plan differently for objectives that must be achieved in six months compared with objectives that must be achieved in 12 months or longer. Setting an open-ended objective is like setting no objective at all, because you will lack a schedule for showing results – and will not be accountable. During one recent year, the Swiss food company Nestlé set an objective of raising annual sales volume by 4 per cent over the prior year. Knowing the deadline, the company had time to adjust its marketing plans when it found that six-month growth was 3.5 per cent.[16]

- *Realistic*. A marketing plan geared to attaining market dominance in six months is unlikely to be realistic for any business – especially for a start-up. Thus, your marketing plan objectives should be realistic to provide purpose for marketing and to keep organisational members motivated. For example, BT Retail, part of the British Telecom phone company, recently declared a two-year goal of attracting one million customers for its BT Mobile Home Plan. Because the UK mobile phone market is nearly saturated and the four largest competitors each serve up to 13 million customers, BT's objective seems realistic.[17]

- *Challenging*. Realistic objectives need not be easy to attain. In fact, many marketers set aggressive yet realistic marketing plan objectives so they can expand more quickly than if their objectives resulted in incremental growth. Objectives that are too challenging, however, may discourage the marketing staff and tie up resources without achieving the desired result.

- *Consistent*. Is the objective consistent with the organisation's mission, goals, strategy, strengths, core competencies and interpretation of external opportunities and threats? Are all objectives consistent with each other? Inconsistent objectives can confuse staff members and customers, detract from the marketing effort and result in disappointing performance.

When G.R. Gopinath prepared for the launch of Air Deccan in India, he set specific, challenging and time-defined objectives to guide the new company's marketing.

MARKETING IN PRACTICE: AIR DECCAN

'We're going to connect cities that are poorly connected by roads and trains', founder and managing director G.R. Gopinath said in announcing his no-frills airline, Air Deccan.[18] The entrepreneur, formerly an Indian Army pilot, has planned flights to and from Bangalore, Hubli, Mysore, Salem and other cities in South India. His idea is to take advantage of a potentially profitable opportunity to serve India's growing middle-class segment of price-sensitive business travellers, families and sightseers with low air fares and scheduled services to regional airports. These people usually travel by train because they regard traditional airlines as too expensive.

In targeting this segment, one of Gopinath's key objectives is to fill 80 per cent of the seats on each flight; his first-year objective is to attract 700,000 customers. To accomplish these objectives profitably, Gopinath plans to keep costs low by selling tickets directly to customers and offering no in-flight food or other amenities, in the manner of Ryanair and other discount carriers. Although positive publicity and word-of-mouth communication will help increase demand over time, Air Deccan still faces competition from established carriers such as Jet Airlines. Will the carrier be able to reach its objectives and fly high in its chosen market segment?[19]

You can set marketing plan objectives in three categories. **Financial objectives** are targets for achieving financial results through marketing strategies and programmes. **Marketing objectives** are targets for achievements in marketing relationships and activities, which in turn directly support attainment of financial objectives. **Societal objectives** are targets for accomplishing results in areas related to social responsibility; such objectives indirectly influence both marketing and financial achievements. The choice of marketing plan objectives and specific targets will, of course, be different for every organisation.

Financial objectives

Companies usually set marketing plan objectives for external results such as unit, monetary, product and channel sales plus internal requirements such as profitability, return on investment and breakeven deadlines. Figure 5.3 shows the focus and purpose of financial objectives commonly used by businesses. Non-profit organisations typically set objectives for short-term and long-term fund-raising as well as other financial targets. To achieve the organisation's financial objectives, you will need to coordinate other compatible objectives dealing with relationships between buyers and sellers, suppliers and distributors, donors and recipients.

Focus of financial objective	Purpose and examples
External results	To provide targets for outcomes of marketing activities such as: • Increasing unit or monetary sales by geographic market • Increasing unit or monetary sales by customer segment • Increasing unit or monetary sales by product • Increasing unit or monetary sales by channel • Other objectives
Internal requirements	To provide targets for managing marketing to meet organisational requirements such as: • Achieving breakeven status • Achieving profiability levels • Achieving return on investment levels • Other objectives

FIGURE 5.3   Focus and purpose of financial objectives

A company might set a financial objective for external results such as: *to achieve a minimum weekly sales volume of $1,000 for each new product*. Notice that this objective is relevant (for a profit-seeking organisation); specific; time-defined; and measurable. Whether it is realistic, challenging and consistent depends on the company's particular situation. A financial objective related to internal requirements might be: *to achieve an average annual profit margin of 13 per cent across all products*.

Because such objectives are measurable and time-defined, you can check progress, adjust your targets or change your marketing if necessary. Mercedes-Benz,

for example, originally set an objective of selling 1,000 Maybach cars in its introductory year, at a price of about €300,000 each. When unfavourable economic
conditions dampened demand for super-luxury vehicles, however, the company
lowered its first-year objective to a more realistic 800 cars and set 1,000 cars as the
second-year objective.[20]

Marketing objectives

Connections with customers and channel members are particularly critical to
organisational success, which is why every marketing plan should include objectives for managing these external relationships. Looking at the life cycle of a
customer relationship, the organisation would begin by approaching the customer
to explore a possible relationship; establishing a relationship and adding more ties
to strengthen it; reigniting customer interest if purchases plateau or loyalty wavers;
saving the relationship if the customer signals intention to switch to another product or brand; and restarting the relationship if the customer is open to switching
back. This life cycle applies to relations with channel members, as well.[21]

Focus of marketing objective	Purpose and examples
External relationships	To provide targets for managing relations with customers and other stakeholders such as: • Enhancing brand, product, company image • Building brand awareness and preference • Stimulating product trial • Acquiring new customers • Retaining existing customers • Increasing customer satisfaction • Acquiring or defending market share • Expanding or defending distribution • Other relationship objectives
Internal activities	To provide targets for managing specific marketing activities such as: • Increasing output or speed of new product development • Improving product quality • Streamlining order fulfilment • Managing resources to enter new markets or segments • Conducting marketing research • Other objectives

FIGURE 5.4   Focus and purpose of marketing objectives

Many businesses establish explicit objectives for building their customer base; enhancing customers' perceptions of the brand, product or company; holding on to existing customers; boosting or defending market share; strengthening ties with key distributors; improving customer satisfaction; and so on, as in Figure 5.4. As one example, British Airways sets marketing objectives for customer satisfaction as well as financial objectives for number of seats sold by flight and by route.[22]

Here is how Procter & Gamble pursued the marketing objective of gaining share in the US nappy market.

MARKETING IN PRACTICE: PROCTER & GAMBLE

Procter & Gamble's Pampers brand has long battled its arch-rival Kimberly-Clark's Huggies brand for a share of the US nappy market. In monetary terms, Huggies is the share leader, holding nearly 45 per cent of the US market. A few years ago, when Pampers' market share was hovering under 35 per cent and overall market growth seemed limited, its marketers decided on more aggressive share objectives. At the time, Kimberly-Clark was reducing the number of nappies in each Huggies package – and lowering prices slightly – to stimulate sales and profits.

Pampers' marketers cut prices but not the number of nappies per package and, in pursuit of higher market share, began emphasising this advantage in splashy new promotions. They intensified the pressure even further by increasing the value of discount coupons and adding the word 'Compare' to Pampers packages. The plan worked: Pampers gained market share even as Huggies lost some ground. The following year, with financial objectives in mind, Pampers' marketers followed Kimberly-Clark's lead and reduced the number of nappies per package.[23]

The Pampers marketers recognised that boosting marketing spending to increase the brand's short-term share of the nappy market was not compatible with higher long-term profitability. So once they had achieved their immediate marketing objective, they sought to meet financial objectives by packing fewer nappies in each box, which improved profits. This illustrates an important point: in practice, you need to avoid conflicts between your marketing objectives and your financial objectives. P&G could not significantly increase market share and simultaneously raise profitability. Therefore, for competitive reasons, the company first focused on share and then addressed profitability.

Non-profit organisations also set marketing objectives for attracting contributors, sponsors and other key relationships. For instance, the Canadian office of Doctors Without Borders set a one-year marketing objective of adding 1,000 new donors who would contribute at least once – and possibly more than once – to the organisation's cause. The related financial objective was to break even on fundraising costs within four months or less.[24]

Many e-commerce companies set objectives for new customer relationships measured first by number of site visitors and time spent browsing the site and then by objectives for conversion – the proportion of website visitors who actually make a purchase, enter an online contest or take other actions. Transforming casual visitors into repeat visitors and then into customers will ultimately support achievement of financial objectives such as sales and profit growth.

In conjunction with objectives aimed at external relationships, you may formulate objectives covering internal activities such as increasing the accuracy or speed of order fulfilment; adjusting the focus, output or speed of new product development; and arranging the resources for entering new segments or markets. Planning for these activities helps lay the groundwork for achieving relationship objectives and the financial objectives that depend on those relationships.

Societal objectives

Because businesses in particular are increasingly mindful of their responsibilities to society – and the way their actions are viewed by stakeholders – a growing number are setting societal objectives to be achieved through marketing. Such objectives are addressed in marketing plans because they indirectly help the company strengthen ties with customers (achieving marketing objectives) and increase or maintain sales (achieving financial objectives). As shown in Figure 5.5, societal objectives may relate to ecological protection or to social responsibility and stakeholder relations. The list of online resources at the end of this chapter is a starting point for finding information about corporate social responsibility activities.

Many businesses fulfil their societal objectives by donating money, goods or services to charities or good causes. This helps polish their image and demonstrates their commitment to the community and to society at large. The Manila Electric Co., for example, gives free computers, printers and computer literacy training to teachers in the Philippines. The company also sponsors an annual book drive in which employees donate reference books and other educational materials to local schools. Surveys confirm that customers notice and appreciate the energy company's activities. 'This definitely inspires us to work even harder and have more projects for social and national development', says CEO Manuel M. Lopez.[25]

Some companies set specific societal objectives for **cause-related marketing**, in which the brand or product is marketed through a connection to benefit a charity or other social cause. When Krispy Kreme Doughnuts opened stores in the United Kingdom and Ireland, for example, it brought its cause-related marketing tradition of helping non-profit organisations raise funds through the sale of doughnuts bought at a large discount.[26]

Focus of societal objective	Purpose and examples
Ecological protection	**To provide targets for managing marketing related to ecological protection and sustainability:** • Reducing pollution with natural or 'greener' products, ecologically friendly processes • Doing business with 'greener' suppliers and channel members • Reducing waste by redesigning products and processes for recycling, other efficiencies • Conserving use of natural resources • Other objectives
Social responsibility and stakeholder relations	**To provide targets for managing marketing related to social responsibility and stakeholder relations:** • Building a positive image as a good corporate citizen • Supporting designated charities, community projects, human rights groups and others, with money and marketing • Encouraging volunteering among employees, customers, suppliers, channel members • Communicating with stakeholders to understand their concerns and explain societal activities • Other objectives

FIGURE 5.5   Focus and purpose of societal objectives

To communicate their societal objectives, activities and results to stakeholders, some companies post social responsibility reports on their websites. For example, Royal Bank of Scotland explains its societal projects and plans via webcasts on its corporate site. As another example, Royal Dutch/Shell maintains an online chat room soliciting feedback about issues such as alternative energy sources and ecological protection. The company responds to every e-mailed comment and uses this input to shape its corporate social responsibility reports.[27] By engaging stakeholders in dialogue, considering their concerns and publicising relevant programmes and performance, Shell enhances its corporate reputation and paves the way for accomplishing both financial and marketing objectives. 'There is no other way to [operate] if you're going to have a sustainable business', comments Phil Watts, Shell's chairman.[28]

FROM OBJECTIVES TO MARKETING-MIX STRATEGY

The objectives you set during this stage of the marketing planning process are the targets to be achieved by implementing the marketing-mix strategies you develop in the next stage. This is the point at which your earlier work comes together: on the basis of your situational analysis, your market and customer research and your segmentation, targeting and positioning decisions, you will be creating product, place, price and promotion strategies and action programmes for the who, what, when, where and how of marketing. Your objectives will also guide the development of customer service and internal marketing strategies to support the marketing mix.

Chapters 6, 7, 8 and 9 discuss strategy for the four marketing-mix elements and Chapter 10 covers customer service and internal marketing.

 ## CHAPTER SUMMARY

1. *Explain how marketing plans are driven by direction and objectives.*
   Higher-level strategies and goals set the direction for marketing plans that outline objectives to be achieved through marketing strategies, tactics and programmes. The direction and objectives inform management decisions about marketing planning. Each objective, strategy and programme in the marketing plan must be consistent with the chosen direction as well as with higher-level strategies and goals.

2. *Describe the three broad directions that can shape a marketing plan.*
   Many organisations prepare marketing plans to move in the direction of growth through market penetration (offering existing products to existing markets), product development (offering new products or variations to existing markets), market development (offering existing products to new markets or segments) or diversification (offering new products to new markets or segments). Non-growth strategies include maintenance (to sustain current levels of revenues, share or profits) and retrenchment (to prepare for a turnaround into growth or to close down entirely).

3. *Discuss the characteristics of effective marketing plan objectives.*
   Objectives are effective for guiding marketing activities when they are relevant, specific, time-defined, measurable and realistic yet challenging. Marketing plan objectives should also be consistent with the current situation: the organisation's mission statement, its overall goals and strategy, its strengths and core competencies, market opportunities and external threats.

4. *Explain the distinctions and linkages between financial, marketing and societal objectives.*
Financial objectives are targets for attaining financial results such as profitability through marketing strategies and programmes. Marketing objectives, which are targets for achievements in marketing relationships and activities, directly support the organisation in attaining financial objectives. Societal objectives provide targets for social responsibility accomplishments in areas such as ecological protection and community development. Accomplishing these objectives indirectly supports the organisation's ability to achieve its financial and marketing objectives.

KEY TERM DEFINITIONS

Balanced Scorecard Broad organisational performance measures that seek to balance financial performance and performance affecting other stakeholders

cause-related marketing Marketing a brand or product through a connection to benefit a social cause or non-profit organisation

diversification strategy Growth strategy in which new products are offered in new markets or segments

financial objectives Targets for achieving financial results such as revenues and profits

maintenance strategy Non-growth strategy to sustain revenues, profits or market share at current levels or defend against deterioration

market development strategy Growth strategy in which existing products are offered in new markets and segments

market penetration strategy Growth strategy in which existing products are offered to customers in existing markets

marketing objectives Targets for achieving results in marketing relationships and activities

product development strategy Growth strategy in which new products or product variations are offered to customers in existing markets

retrenchment strategy Non-growth strategy to reduce operations by quitting markets, deleting products, downsizing marketing efforts, shrinking distribution or closing down

societal objectives Targets for achieving results in social responsibility areas

THE PRACTICAL MARKETER CHECKLIST NO. 5:
CHARACTERISTICS OF EFFECTIVE OBJECTIVES

Useful for guiding activities

Is the objective relevant to the organisation's direction, strategy and long-term goals?

Is the objective specific?

Is the objective time-defined?

Is the objective measurable?

Is the objective realistic?

Is the objective challenging?

Consistent with current situation

Is the objective consistent with the organisation's mission statement?

Is the objective consistent with the organisation's strengths and core competencies?

Is the objective appropriate for the market's opportunities and threats?

Is the objective in conflict with other objectives?

Source: After Marian Burk Wood, *The Marketing Plan: A Handbook* (Upper Saddle River, NJ: Prentice Hall, 2003), p. 70.

ONLINE RESOURCES

CORPORATE SOCIAL RESPONSIBILITY

- Business for Social Responsibility (www.bsr.org) – Explains and promotes corporate social responsibility, sustainability and ethical standards.

- Sustainability Reporter (www.sirisdata.com) – Posts data about sustainability and social responsibility activities of Australian corporations.

- Institute of Social and Ethical Accountability (www.accountability.org.uk/aa1000) – Maintains a voluntary framework for reporting on corporate social responsibility objectives, initiatives and results.

- Corporate Social Responsibility Newswire service (www.csrwire.com) – Posts business news releases about social responsibility programmes and performance.

QUESTIONS FOR DISCUSSION AND ANALYSIS

1. Should every organisation set societal objectives?

2. Under what circumstances would you, as a marketer, want to speak publicly about your marketing plan objectives?

3. What kinds of marketing and financial objectives might non-profit organisations set in their marketing plans, and why?

APPLY YOUR KNOWLEDGE

Research the direction, marketing, financial and societal objectives of a particular company by examining its website, news releases, products, advertising, packaging, financial disclosures, social responsibility reports and other aspects of its operation.

- Is the company pursuing a growth strategy, maintenance strategy or retrenchment strategy? How do you know?

- Does the company disclose specific objectives of any kind? If so, what are they and how do they relate to the company's direction?

- Identify one specific marketing, financial or societal objective this company has set and compare it to the characteristics in Checklist No. 5. What changes would you recommend to make this objective more effective as a target for performance?

- Look for clues about whether the objective you have identified was actually achieved (and if not, why).

- Prepare a brief oral or written report summarising your comments.

BUILD YOUR OWN MARKETING PLAN

Continue working on the marketing plan for a hypothetical organisation or an actual organisation you have chosen. Look at the organisation's current situation, environment, markets, customers, segmentation decisions and targeting coverage, and decide what is an appropriate direction for your marketing plan. What marketing, financial and societal objectives will you set to move in your chosen direction? Do any of these objectives conflict? Which should take priority? How will these objectives guide your marketing-mix strategies and programmes? What might cause you to rethink your objectives? Take a moment to consider how these ideas and decisions fit in with the information you have already entered in your marketing plan and how practical they are in terms of marketing implementation. Then record your thoughts and explain their implications in *Marketing Plan Pro* software or in a written marketing plan.

CLOSING CASE: LEGEND GROUP SEEKS LEGENDARY PERFORMANCE

Legend Group is China's largest computer maker, with a 25 per cent market share in desktops and a 17 per cent share in notebooks. Its success is due, in part, to pressure resulting from the government's desire to increase penetration of personal computers throughout China. As a result, Legend has kept domestic prices low, raising turnover and increasing market share but also dampening profit margins. Legend is therefore planning for international growth and seeking to 'improve gross margins by introducing more products and services', according to Alice Li, head of corporate marketing.[29]

Legend's main growth strategy is diversification. 'The marketing potential for [information technology] services in China is huge', says Li. 'Because there is currently no large-scale and well-established IT service company in China, we believe this presents a great opportunity for Legend to expand.'[30] The company recently acquired stakes in two information technology services firms and is boosting its research and development budget to support introductions of new computer-related services and equipment for consumers and business customers. In addition, it has marketing plans for expanding into mobile phones, personal digital assistants and digital cameras. It sold 810,000 mobile phone handsets during one recent year and, observing intense demand, set the ambitious objective of doubling unit sales during the following year.

New markets represent Legend's next marketing frontier. To this end, it has obtained trademark registration for the Lenovo brand for marketing personal computers in countries where the Legend brand is owned by others. Now the company is marketing products in Hong Kong and planning its next move into European and US markets, supported by extensive promotion. Yet it faces formidable threats: low brand awareness; unclear perceptions of quality; competition from Dell and other strong rivals; and lack of distribution. 'We don't want to establish Legend as a brand of cheaper, lower quality', explains the chief financial officer. 'Acquisition is one of the possibilities, and hopefully we can go through other people's distribution channels or [form] partnerships.'[31] The goal is to increase foreign revenues from 7 per cent of current annual turnover to 25 per cent or more by 2007.

Concurrent with this diversification strategy, Legend is using market penetration to drive domestic expansion outside China's major cities. Price is a key point of differentiation, but distribution plays a vital role as well. One marketing objective is a deadline to establish 1,000 distribution and service centres throughout the country; another is to increase sales to businesses by encouraging purchases of 'build-to-order' computers tailored to customers' specific needs. Can marketing help Legend build legendary performance over the long term?[32]

Case questions

1. How might Legend's market penetration strategy affect its ability to follow a profitable diversification strategy?

2. To set consistent and realistic yet challenging objectives, what internal and external factors should Legend's marketers consider?

ENDNOTES

1. Quoted in Shin Jung-Won, 'Financial Services: HSBC Takes Aim at Retail Market in South Korea', *Wall Street Journal*, 18 March 2003, p. D5.

2. Quoted in Leon Harris, 'HSBC Targets More Than 20 pc Growth', *Business Times*, 18 August 2003, n.p.

3. Quoted in 'Hong Kong Unit of HSBC to Focus on Wealthy Clients', *Wall Street Journal*, 19 August 2003, p. C9.

4. Quoted in Christina le Beau, 'HSBC's New Loan: 2,000 Environmentalists', *New York Times*, 20 October 2002, sec. 3, p. 6; also based on information from: 'Hong Kong Unit of HSBC to Focus on Wealthy Clients'; Harris, 'HSBC Targets More Than 20 pc Growth'; Parista Yuthamanop, 'HSBC Taps Rising Demand for Mortgages', *Bangkok*

Post, 11 July 2003, www.bangkokpost.com; Shin Jung-Won, 'Financial Services: HSBC Takes Aim at Retail Market in South Korea'; HSBC Holdings, www.hsbc.com.

5. Tim Ambler, 'Set Clear Goals and See Marketing Hit Its Target', *Financial Times*, 29 August 2002, p. 8.

6. Jo Johnson, 'Carrefour Raises Growth Target', *Financial Times*, 28 August 2003, www.ft.com; 'Carrefour Opens 11th Store in Indonesia', *Xinhua News Agency*, 17 July 2003, www.comtexnews.com; Elaine Sciolino, 'Once Again, the French Storm the Cash Registers', *New York Times*, 9 January 2003, p. A4; Leslie Chang, 'Western Stores Woo Chinese Wallets', *Wall Street Journal*, 26 November 2002, pp. B1ff.

7. H. Igor Ansoff, 'Strategies for Diversification', *Harvard Business Review*, September–October 1957, pp. 113–25; Philip Kotler, *Kotler on Marketing* (New York: Free Press, 1999), pp. 46–8.

8. Hiroyuki Kachi, 'Shiseido Swings to Net Profit on Cost Cuts and Strong Sales', *Wall Street Journal*, 7 May 2003, www.wsj.com.

9. Sian Harrington, 'Upside of Going Upside Down', *Grocer*, 21 June 2003, pp. 68ff.; Paul Lukas, 'Bottoms Up', *Fortune*, 21 July 2003, p. 32.

10. Matthew Boyle, 'Brand Killers', *Fortune*, 11 August 2003, pp. 89–100.

11. Abby Ellin, 'Building a Brand, One Brick at a Time', *New York Times*, 15 June 2003, sec. 3, p. 13; *Hoover's Handbook of World Business* (Austin, TX: Hoover's Business Press, 2002), pp. 252–3.

12. Quoted in Jeffrey A. Trachtenberg, 'Barnes & Noble Pushes Books from Ambitious Publisher: Itself', *Wall Street Journal*, 18 June 2003, pp. A1, A8; *see also*: Jim Milliot, 'Barnes & Noble Buys B'mann's B&N.com Stake', *Publisher's Weekly*, 4 August 2003, p. 9.

13. Quoted in Nicholas George, 'Brio's Toy Trains Hit the Buffers', *Financial Times*, 29 August 2003, www.ft.com; www.brio.net.

14. Tim Ambler, 'Awards Scheme Highlights the Need for Data-Driven Marketing', *Marketing*, 21 March 2002, p. 16.

15. Harris, 'HSBC Targets More Than 20 pc Growth'.

16. 'Nestlé: A Dedicated Enemy of Fashion', *The Economist*, 31 August 2002, pp. 47–8.

17. 'BT Mobile Sets Sights on Families', *Marketing*, 7 August 2003, p. 15.

18. Quoted in Ray Marcelo, 'Deccan Aspires to Soar Above Rivals', *Financial Times*, 12 September 2003, www.ft.com.

19. Marcelo, 'Deccan Aspires to Soar Above Rivals'; Rasheed Kappan, 'Air Deccan to Link "Unconnected" Towns in South', *The Hindu*, 13 August 2003, www.thehindu.com.

20. Neal E. Boudette and Joseph B. White, 'Car Sales Get Chilly at Altitudes of $150,000', *Wall Street Journal*, 11 September 2003, www.wsj.com.

21. *See* Sandy D. Jap and Erin Anderson, 'Testing the Life-Cycle Theory of Inter-Organisational Relations: Do Performance Outcomes Depend on the Path Taken?', *Insead Knowledge*, February 2003, www.knowledge.insead.edu.

22. Craig Smith, 'Marketers Still Lost in the Metrics', *Marketing*, 10 August 2000, p. 15.

23. Sarah Ellison, 'In Lean Times, Big Companies Make a Grab for Market Share', *Wall Street Journal*, 5 September 2003, pp. A1, A6.

24. Tom Pope, 'Fundraising Ideas from North of the Border', *The Non-profit Times*, 15 January 2003, pp. 1ff.

25. Quoted in 'Power Distributor Cited for Social Responsibility', *Business World*, 23 July 2003, n.p.

26. 'Krispy Kreme Plans UK Doughnut Stores Debut', *Marketing*, 15 May 2003, p. 6.

27. Howard Stock, 'U.K. Large Caps Hone Social Reporting Online', *Investor Relations Business*, 9 June 2003, n.p.

28. Quoted in Janet Guyon, 'From Green to Gold', *Fortune*, 10 November 2003, p. 226.

29. Quoted in Karen Cohn, 'Extending Legendary Success', *Electronic Business*, 15 May 2003, pp. 52ff.

30. Ibid.

31. Quoted in Keith Bradsher, 'Chinese Computer Maker Plans a Push Overseas', *New York Times*, 22 February 2003, pp. C1ff.

32. Based on information from: Bruce Einhorn and Dexter Roberts, 'A New Twist in Legend's Tale', *Business Week*, 23 June 2003, p. 50; Justine Lau, 'Legend Struggles to Hold Market Share', *Financial Times*, 28 May 2003, www.ft.com; Cohn, 'Extending Legendary Success'; Bradsher, 'Chinese Computer Maker Plans a Push Overseas'.

6

Developing product and brand strategy

Closing case: Building a brand named George

Endnotes

Comprehension outcomes

After studying this chapter, you will be able to:

- Explain the product mix and line decisions involved in product strategy
- Discuss the product life cycle and its role in product strategy
- Outline the steps in new product development
- Identify the various product attributes that can be used, in combination, to create and deliver customer value
- Define brand equity and describe the four levels leading to strong brand equity

Application outcomes

After studying this chapter, you will be able to:

- Analyse a product's position in the product mix and the life cycle
- Plan product strategy
- Plan brand strategy

OPENING CASE: SONY POLISHES ITS PRODUCT LINES

The Sony brand, associated with innovation and high quality, is stamped on a wide variety of consumer and industrial products sold worldwide. Over the years, Sony engineers and designers have gone beyond the basics by inventing new product categories (such as the portable Sony Walkman players), adding innovative features and making products more stylish or smaller (or both). The B2B side of the Japanese company sells microchips and other electronics components; the consumer side is the undisputed global leader in consumer electronics, especially dominant in camcorders and digital cameras. Yet the firm's product variety is both a strength and a weakness.

Until recently, Sony marketed an impressive group of more than 100 consumer electronics product lines. However, the company found that as technology matured and Matsushita, Samsung, Philips and other rivals stepped up competitive pressure, its prices and profit margins were moving downward. Moreover, Sony's share of the television market was falling from 55 per cent to 45 per cent. At one point, consumer electronics products made up 66 per cent of Sony's overall sales, but only 22 per cent of operating income. In contrast, video game products made up 13 per cent of overall sales and contributed a whopping 61 per cent of operating income.

To pursue higher growth and profitability, Sony's top management therefore decided to prune up to 10 per cent of the product lines, cut costs, shift resources to stronger product lines and accelerate new product development. Although they eliminated a number of products, such as selected Vaio computer models, they retained other products that indirectly support profitability. PlayStation consoles, for example, are modestly profitable at best – but they help sell many related, more profitable products such as video games and memory cards.

As another example, Sony created the Qualia line of state-of-the-art electronics primarily to reinforce its reputation for innovation, quality and high performance. These products carry decidedly upmarket prices: the tiny digital camera sells for about €3,000 and the home-theatre projector sells for about €20,000. Sony doesn't intend to mass-produce Qualia products for wide distribution; on the contrary, it will manufacture them only as customers place orders. Reinforcing Sony's image for leading-edge technology and design will pay off in sales for years to come, even if the Qualia line itself achieves modest volume. 'All of these are the kinds of products that wouldn't have been possible if we had worried about how many would sell', CEO Nobuyuki Idei said in introducing the first Qualia products.[1]

CHAPTER PREVIEW

Sony's experience illustrates the challenges and opportunities of seeking to achieve objectives through product and brand strategy, part of stage 5 in the marketing planning process. Multinational corporations with hundreds or thousands of products face more complex decisions when planning product strategy, but they still apply the same basic principles used by smaller organisations. The key is to coordinate product strategy with all other marketing decisions to move the organisation more effectively in the desired direction.

This chapter opens with a discussion of marketing planning decisions about the product mix, product lines and the product life cycle, and this is followed by an examination of new product development. Next, you will learn how to vary different attributes in devising a tangible good or intangible service that will meet your customers' needs, your organisational targets and the marketplace realities. The final section looks at how to build strong brand equity and encourage customer loyalty. *As you read, think about how you can apply this chapter's principles, along with concepts from earlier chapters, to develop a successful marketing plan for your product or brand.*

PLANNING PRODUCT STRATEGY

As a prerequisite to planning product strategy, review your research and conclusions about the current situation, analyse how customers respond to each of your current products and examine what each product means to the organisation in financial and marketing terms. If you are creating a marketing plan for a company, your product may be a physical item, a service or a combination of tangible and intangible elements. If you work for a non-profit organisation, your product may be an idea such as better health; if you are developing a marketing plan for a geographic region, your product may be a place such as a city being marketed as a tourist destination. Regardless of the specific product you are marketing, you will want to look closely at:

- the customer segment being targeted by each good or service

- the needs satisfied by each product and the value created

- product by product trends in pricing, unit sales, market share, revenues and profits

- the age of each product and performance over time, by segment, channel and geography

- the sales connections between products

- each product's competitive strengths and weaknesses
- the opportunities addressed (and unaddressed) by each product
- the current or potential threats each product faces
- each product's competitive position
- customers' perceptions of competing products.

The point of these analyses is to determine the value of each product to the market and to your organisation. As a visual summary, you can create a grid matching each product to the intended target market, detail the need each product satisfies and indicate the value delivered from the customer's and organisation's perspectives. Figure 6.1 shows, in simplified form, what such an analysis grid would contain; the actual number of columns and rows depends on each organisation's targeting strategy and product offerings. As an option, you may want to add information about the competitive position and strength of each product.

	Customer segment A (briefly describe)	Customer segment B (briefly describe)	Customer segment C (briefly describe)
Product 1 (identify)	Customer need: Value to customer: Value to organisation:	Customer need: Value to customer: Value to organisation:	Customer need: Value to customer: Value to organisation:
Product 2 (identify)	Customer need: Value to customer: Value to organisation:	Customer need: Value to customer: Value to organisation:	Customer need: Value to customer: Value to organisation:
Product 3 (identify)	Customer need: Value to customer: Value to organisation:	Customer need: Value to customer: Value to organisation:	Customer need: Value to customer: Value to organisation:

FIGURE 6.1 Product/segment analysis grid

Next you will set specific objectives for product strategy to be achieved through decisions about managing the product mix and product lines; the product life cycle; new product development; and product attributes including quality and performance, features and benefits, design, packaging, labelling and brand. Figure 6.2 shows these four categories of product strategy decisions.

Product mix and product lines
- Change product line length
- Change product line depth
- Change product mix width
- Manage cannibalisation

Product life cycle
- Locate product in cycle by segment and by market
- Change product progression through life cycle
- Balance life cycles of multiple products

New product development
- Open new product categories (widen mix)
- Extend existing lines or brands
- Manage steps in process
- Address ecological and ethical concerns

Product attributes
- Plan appropriate level of quality and performance
- Deliver valued customer benefits through product features
- Plan design for functionality and differentiation
- Create packaging and labelling
- Build brand equity

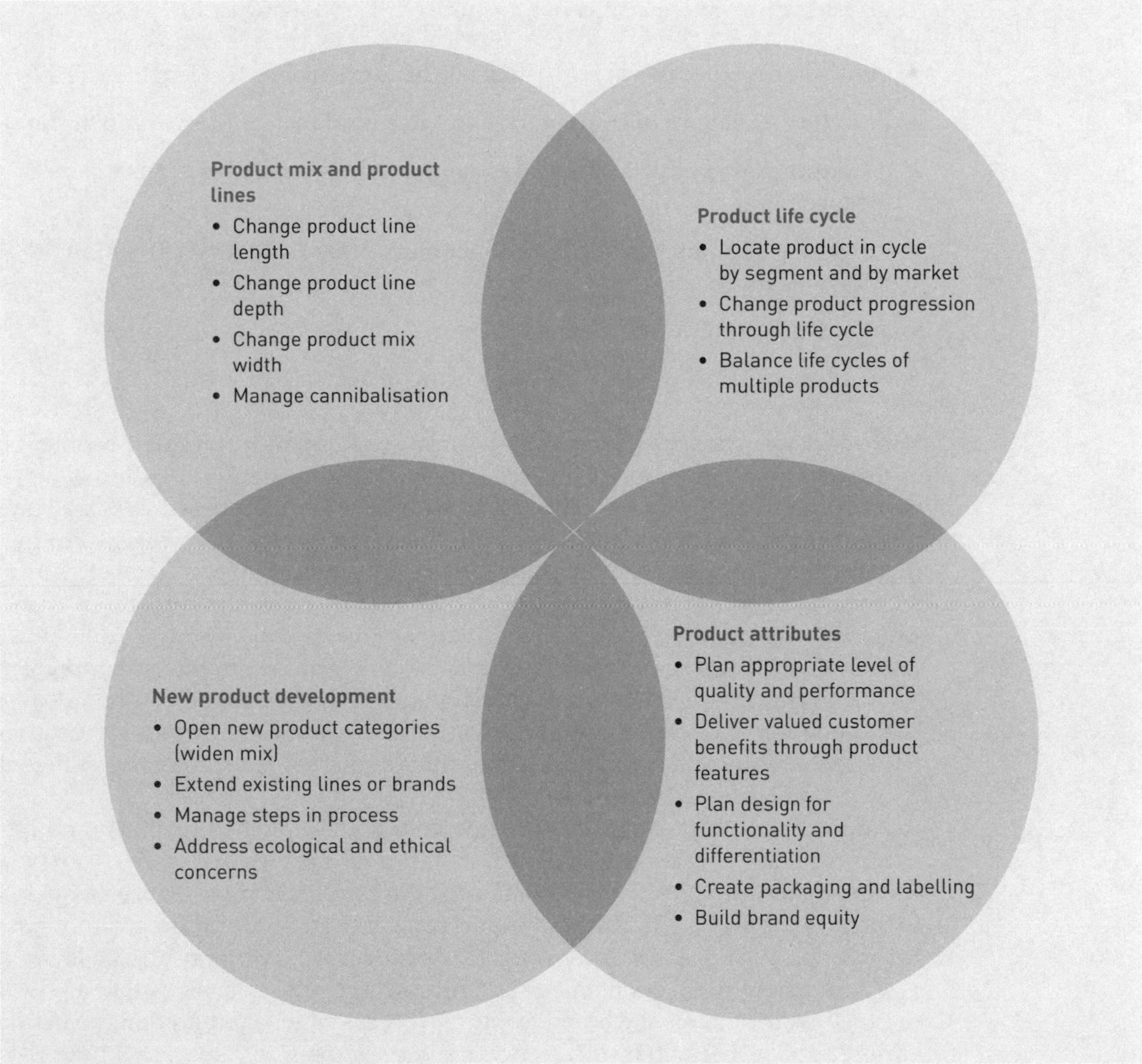

FIGURE 6.2   Product strategy decisions

Product mix and product line decisions

When planning for product strategy, you will face choices about managing the **product mix** (the assortment of product lines offered by an organisation), **product line length** (the number of individual items in each line of related products) and **product line depth** (the number of variations of each product within one line). Your marketing plan can cover one or more of the following actions:

- introduce new products in an existing line (**line extensions** that lengthen the line)
- introduce variations of existing products in a product line (deepening the line)
- introduce new products under an existing brand (**brand extensions** that widen the mix)
- introduce new lines in other product categories (**category extensions** that widen the mix)
- eliminate a product (shortening the line)
- eliminate or add a product line (narrowing or widening the mix).

Each decision changes the way you satisfy customers in targeted segments, address opportunities, avert threats, allocate marketing resources and achieve marketing objectives. For example, Beiersdorf, the German-based personal-care products company, recently changed product strategy by narrowing its product mix to a core group of 400 lines under ten brand names. With this change, its marketers could support a corporate growth strategy by concentrating attention and a €1.3 billion marketing budget on the strongest, most profitable lines under powerhouse brands such as Nivea.[2] Procter & Gamble is taking a different approach, adding variations to its toothpaste product lines as a way to capitalise on its Crest brand and wrest market share from rival Colgate-Palmolive. Some of the variations centre on new flavours like herbal mint and citrus; others feature different formulas and different size packages.[3]

Adding new products by extending a familiar, established line or brand can minimise the risk that customers and channel partners may perceive in trying something new. Because of this familiarity, the product's introductory campaign is likely to be more efficient and may even cost less than for an entirely new brand or product in a new category. Your development costs may also be lower if you base a new product on an existing product. Finally, extensions that are well received will reinforce the brand, capture new customers and accommodate the variety-seeking behaviour of current customers. Extensions are not without risk, however. If you extend a line or brand, customers or channel member may become confused about the different products you offer. Channel members may be reluctant to carry additional products, given space limitations. And if the product does not succeed, perceptions of the brand or the remaining products in the line may be affected.[4]

When planning this aspect of product strategy, look closely at whether you are spreading your resources too thinly and at how each product and line are expected to contribute to organisational objectives. You have to be ready to cut products or lines that do not perform as desired, as Heinz did by eliminating a line of unusually coloured and flavoured frozen chips – even as its green ketchup was gaining popularity. The company is also reducing the number of product variations offered in European markets to make better use of the shelf space stores allot to its brands.[5]

In addition, you should manage your products with an eye toward minimising **cannibalisation**, which occurs when one of your products takes sales from another of your products. A line extension may attract customers who previously purchased other products in the same line, for example. Still, marketers some-times decide they can attract new customers, retain current customers or achieve other objectives only by cannibalising their own products rather than risk having competitors lure customers away. Undoubtedly, Heinz's green ketchup canni-balised sales of the company's red ketchup. Yet the unexpected colour – intended to appeal to children – garnered considerable publicity, encouraged product trial, led to repeat purchasing and boosted the company's overall ketchup sales.

Product life-cycle decisions

As you develop product strategy, you must make decisions about how to manage the **product life cycle**, a product's movement through the market as it passes from introduction to growth, maturity and eventual decline. Although no individual product's life cycle is entirely predictable or even necessarily sequential, the typical life cycle pictured in Figure 6.3 shows how sales and profitability can change in each part of the cycle. Here, the products were released in the order: A, B, C; as Product A's sales and profitability drop, Product B's sales and profits are likely to be solid but levelling off and Product C's sales and profitability are likely to be increasing. A corporate giant such as Beiersdorf will have numerous products in targeted markets at one time, and each could very well be in a different part of its life cycle.

Analysing a product's life-cycle situation and using marketing strategy actively to manage the cycle can help you plan to take advantage of anticipated ups and downs. Where is the product within its life cycle, how quickly is it pro-gressing through each part of the cycle and what can marketers do either to alter the cycle or to get the most out of each part? As Figure 6.3 suggests, profitability is highest during the growth part of the life cycle and starts to drop with maturity. This is why many companies plan strategies to extend or at least reinvigorate product growth. Moreover, some products are reaching maturity much faster, compressing their life cycle. The DVD player, for instance, matured extremely quickly because of standardised components and technology; as more competitors entered the market and volume skyrocketed, the average price dropped to little more than 10 per cent of the introductory price in only six years. Now manufacturers are seeking to extend the life cycle by adding new features and improving the technology.[6]

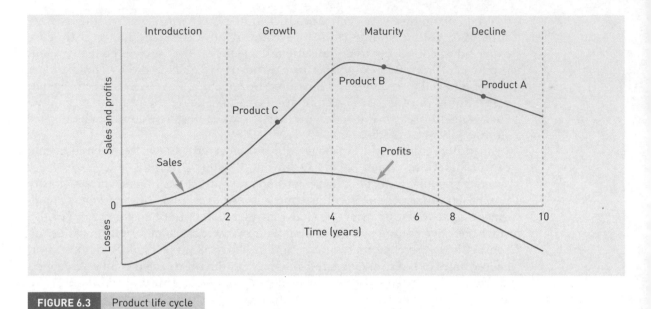

| **FIGURE 6.3** | Product life cycle |

Source: Sven Hollensen, *Marketing Management* (Harlow, Essex: Pearson Education, 2003), p. 279.

Be aware that product life cycle can vary by segment and by market. For instance, research shows that sales of new household products and foods tend to increase more rapidly and reach maturity earlier in the United Kingdom and the Netherlands than in France and Spain. Knowing this, marketers targeting UK and Dutch consumers would push for wide distribution by the launch date to build growth momentum early in a product's introduction stage.[7] On the other hand, home appliances and consumer electronics products tend to move into the growth stage earlier in Denmark, Norway and Sweden – in about four years – than in France, the UK and Greece, where accelerating growth takes more than six years. Based on this research, marketers should consider launching products in markets where faster growth is possible early in the life cycle, and expect to wait longer for rapid growth in other markets.[8]

MARKETING IN PRACTICE: CHINA MOBILE AND UTSTARCOM

China's market leader in mobile phone service is China Mobile, which serves more than 125 million subscribers. After years of rapid growth in subscriptions, however, its customer base is barely growing, signalling that this service is moving toward maturity within the domestic market. At this stage in the life cycle, China Mobile is experiencing more competition, which in turn puts downward pressure on prices and profits as industry players defend their share. One competitor challenging China Mobile is UTStarcom which offers a different technology and more favourable pricing to attract subscribers. Given the product's maturity, both UTStarcom and China Mobile will need solid strategies for increasing revenues from existing subscribers if they are to continue pursuing growth. Meanwhile, mobile phone service is nowhere near mature in India and Vietnam, which is why UTStarcom has begun operating in those markets.[9]

The previous example shows how mobile phone service providers in China are dealing with product life-cycle changes in their markets.

New product development decisions

Having discovered promising opportunities during earlier stages of the planning process and analysed the life cycle of current products, you may decide to change your product mix by developing new products for targeted customer segments. Some products may open up new product categories not previously addressed by your organisation; other products may extend existing lines or brands. Either way, you usually put the details of new product development decisions in an appendix or separate document, not in the main marketing plan. However, your marketing plan should outline the major decisions that have been made, provide supporting research or other evidence, highlight actions scheduled for the period covered by your plan and show the development schedule for each new product.

Here is an overview of the new product development process:

1. *Gather product ideas* from inside the organisation and from customers, sales representatives, channel partners, suppliers, competitive materials and other sources.

2. *Screen product ideas* to eliminate those that are inappropriate or not feasible, given the organisation's strengths, core competencies and resources.

3. *Research reaction* to find out whether customers (and perhaps influential channel members) perceive value in the remaining ideas and respond positively to the concepts.

4. *Analyse the business case* for introducing each new product, including associated marketing strategies, to gauge the contribution toward achieving organisational objectives.

5. *Develop the actual product* to see whether the concept is practical, cost-effective and capable of meeting customers' needs and expectations.

6. *Test market the product*, with associated marketing strategies, to assess the likelihood of market acceptance and success. This is the time to try different marketing activities, evaluate customer response, anticipate competitors' reactions and adjust the product (and its marketing) for maximum effectiveness.

7. *Launch the product commercially*, applying the lessons learned from test marketing and from previous product introductions.

8. *Monitor market response*, including the reactions of customers, channel members and competitors. If you see that the product is not selling as well as projected, you will want to change the product or other elements of the marketing mix as needed.

Research shows that the most successful new product innovations result from need identification, solution identification and marketing research. At the same time, the rate of new product failure is so high that you must carefully screen ideas to avoid investing in unpromising or unneeded products.[10] Needs-based product development is an integral part of the marketing plans at the US-based United Technologies, which makes and markets Otis brand lifts. Staff members research the needs and requirements of business customers by talking with architects, contractors, building owners and others who influence or make such purchases. Then engineers and designers work to perfect lift technology that will deliver customer-valued benefits such as avoiding breakdowns by detecting potential repairs for preventive maintenance. They test new lifts by simulating severe conditions such as earthquake tremors and sub-freezing temperatures.

Sometimes United Technologies gets ideas for quality and performance improvements from the experience of losing sales. After watching competitors win contracts in Japan for lifts in which passengers were unaware of the motion of the lift, the company developed a ride-control system that senses and minimises any bumps or vibrations as the lift moves. This feature helped the company sell lifts for skyscrapers in Japan and position itself to profit from other construction projects in Asia.[11]

As you plan new product development projects, you should give thought to both ecological and ethical considerations. Can eco-friendly supplies and processes be incorporated? Will the product's production or use adversely affect the natural environment? How will the new product serve your organisation's societal objectives? What ethical questions might arise (such as whether to test products on animals) and how can you address these in a satisfactory way?

Whether you are developing new products or improving existing ones, you will seek the optimal combination of quality and performance, features and benefits, design, packaging, labelling and brand (*see* Figure 6.4). The purpose is to make your product competitively distinctive, attractive and valuable to customers in the targeted segment and profitable for the organisation. To be at all competitive, your product may need certain features or quality; be sure that your product is competitively superior on an attribute that customers value and that the new product makes economic sense in terms of your financial objectives. At W.L. Gore, a US company known for innovation, top management assesses new product ideas by asking: 'Is the opportunity real? Is there really somebody out there that will buy this? Can we win? What do the economics look like? Can we make money doing this? Is it unique and valuable? Can we have a sustained advantage [such as a patent]?'[12]

	Product 1	Product 2	Product 3
Quality (customers' view) and **performance** (objective measures)			
Features (and benefits delivered to satisfy customer needs)			
Design (for performance differentiation)			
Packaging (protect, store, facilitate use) and **labelling** (information, marketing communication)			
Brand (identity, differentiation, provoke response)			

FIGURE 6.4   Planning product attributes

Quality and performance decisions

Quality means different things to different people; this is why you should define a product's **quality** in terms of how well it satisfies the needs of your customers. From this perspective, a high-quality product is one that does a better job of satisfying customer needs than a poor-quality product. You can certainly use objective performance measures to demonstrate a product's functionality, reliability, sturdiness and lack of defects. In the marketplace, however, consumers and business customers are the final judges of quality and decide for themselves what level of quality they want and how much they are willing to pay for it. Clearly, your decisions about product quality are related to your decisions about pricing and other marketing mix strategies.

Extremely affluent consumers may be satisfied only by the exceptionally high performance and quality of Sony's Qualia product line, for example. Or, as Hewlett-Packard found out, far superior quality may not be necessary.

MARKETING IN PRACTICE: HEWLETT-PACKARD

Hewlett-Packard, the US marketer of laser and inkjet printers and other computer-related equipment, routinely designed printers to exactingly high standards, even though this resulted in higher costs and higher initial prices. When its marketers saw lower-priced printers from competing firms capturing market share, however, they realised they were missing an important segment of customers who wanted reasonable quality at a reasonable price.

In response, the marketing staff collaborated with the product engineers to eliminate non-essential features, substitute smaller and lighter materials and develop more cost-effective printer technology. Customers liked Hewlett-Packard's new line of printers, and their acceptance increased the company's printer sales and its market share. From an internal perspective, the new line is 'much cheaper to make, much better in terms of image quality and speed, and it's half the size', according to the category manager.[13] Seeking to capture more of the consumer market and diversify beyond printer products, the company launched a new-product initiative and recently introduced 158 new consumer electronics products in only two months.[14]

Yet customers who expect or are willing to pay for superior quality, based on a brand's history of performance or on competitive comparisons, may not be satisfied with anything less. Mercedes recently faced this challenge. A few of its models slipped lower in US customer surveys of quality after years of top rankings, even as Toyota's Lexus and Nissan's Infiniti vehicles moved up; at the time, European customers continued to rank Mercedes at the top in terms of quality. The company has moved aggressively to reassure customers about vehicle quality in light of the potential threat posed by competition from Lexus in many markets.[15]

If you are in B2B marketing, you know that quality is essential to products such as computer chips, which are the heart of many technology products. Aware that business customers require consistently high performance, for example, Intel meticulously documents and controls its computer chip manufacturing process to maintain the same high quality whether chips are made in Ireland or Arizona.[16] Before you introduce or even begin developing a new product, you have to ensure that the entire organisation is capable of consistently delivering the expected quality, given the available resources and schedule. This, too, is part of the marketing planning process.

Feature and benefit decisions

Customers buy a product not only for the **features**, specific attributes that contribute to functionality, but also for the **benefits**, the need-satisfaction outcomes they want or expect. Hewlett-Packard's customers want quickly printed, clear documents; some may even quantify the benefits sought in terms of number of pages printed per minute. When they evaluate competing printers, customers look at whether each model has the features that provide the benefits they value. In practice, you should plan for features that deliver the benefits that you know your customers value (based on marketing research).

As Hewlett-Packard discovered, not all customers want or are willing to pay for the bundle of benefits provided by all the features of a particular product. In fact, different segments may have different needs and different perceptions of the value of the benefits delivered by product features. Figure 6.5 shows, in simplified form, how Groupe Michelin, the French tyre maker, matches features to benefits that satisfy the needs of specific segments of the consumer and business markets. In this way, Michelin adds value and differentiates its tyres from those of Goodyear and other competitors.[17] Creating this type of matrix can help you pinpoint the needs of each targeted segment and identify the product benefits that individual features will deliver to satisfy those needs.

Customer and need	Feature and benefit
Drivers of sport-utility vehicles who need different tyre pressure for highway and off-road conditions	On board Tire Intelligent Pressure Management system automatically checks and adjusts tyre inflation depending on driving conditions
Farmers who need to drive tractors over fields and in uneven terrain	Large, deep tyre patterns provide more secure road grip
Professional sports car drivers who seek winning performance	Special composition tyres for speed and handling

FIGURE 6.5 Matching features and benefits to customer needs

Features are as important for service businesses as for companies that market physical products. For example, Dangdang.com, China's largest Web-based bookseller, recognised that its customers wanted convenient access to more books than were available in local stores. To satisfy this need, the company created a searchable database of 200,000-plus titles – more than ten times the usual bookshop inventory – and began selling CDs and DVDs as well. Because credit cards are not yet widespread in China, Dangdang.com developed payment alternatives such as money orders and cash on delivery. These features have been so valuable that the retailer is receiving as many as 4,000 online orders every day and is doubling revenues yearly.[18]

Design decisions

Directly or indirectly, customers' perceptions and buying choices are influenced to some degree by design. Moreover, your design decisions can affect the ecology as well as product performance. Therefore, as with all other product strategy decisions, you should be sure that a product's design is consistent with your organisation's marketing, financial and societal objectives and that it fits with your other marketing mix decisions.

Your company may develop designs internally or hire outside design specialists. Denmark's Bang & Olufsen generates new product ideas and hires specialists to come up with designs that are aesthetically pleasing and technologically advanced as well as functional. 'If we have designers in-house, they tend to come too close to the technicians', explains the design and concepts director. 'That means they begin solving technical problems rather than focusing on the design.'[19]

Product design has become such a prime point of differentiation, especially for mature products like household appliances, that everyday products need not be ordinary-looking. The unusually sleek design lines of refrigerators made by China's Haier Group, for example, attract customers and help the company compete in the domestic market and internationally. In fact, the pressure of global competition has prompted many marketers to devote more time and resources to product design. As one example, Samsung Electronics, based in South Korea, has doubled the size of its design staff to 350 employees. These experts are responsible for giving Samsung's mobile phones, televisions and other products fashion appeal while enhancing functionality.[20]

Service providers such as airlines and even hospitals also make design decisions about the surroundings in which they operate. To illustrate, British Airways has designed comfortable and stylish airport clubs for the use of first-class passengers flying its transatlantic routes. And Long Island College Hospital, in New York City, recently redesigned its emergency room to be more comfortable and more efficient; this move reduced the waiting time for medical attention by half.[21] Design – specifically website design – is important for e-commerce businesses, as well. From the user's perspective, well-designed websites are easy to navigate, interesting to explore and helpful throughout the purchasing process. And e-commerce businesses such as Amazon.com often extend design decisions to the packaging and labelling of customers' purchases.

Packaging and labelling decisions

Good packaging protects tangible goods, makes their use or storage more convenient for customers and, ideally, serves societal objectives such as ecological protection. Consider Top Down Tomato Ketchup, marketed by Heinz on the basis of convenience. The unique lid-down packaging allows consumers to store and dispense ketchup without mess or waste. In addition to delivering benefits that customers find valuable, this packaging is recyclable. As another example, Nike is reducing excess packaging and shipping costs by packaging some of its trainers in moulded cardboard containers that exactly fit the shoes, rather than in uniform rectangular shoeboxes.[22]

When planning strategy for any product to be sold in a store, think carefully about how labelling can serve marketing functions. Labels are more than informative: they can capture the shopper's attention, describe how product features deliver benefits, differentiate the product from competing items and reinforce brand image. Here is how the UK grocery chain Somerfield's uses labelling for marketing purposes.

MARKETING IN PRACTICE: SOMERFIELD'S

Somerfield's, locked in a fierce competitive contest with Sainsbury and other supermarkets, has been redesigning packaging and labelling to differentiate its own products, attract shoppers and describe benefits. Not long ago, its marketers asked a design group to change the packaging and labelling for the store's own brand of pre-packaged fresh salads and vegetables. Instead of continuing to list ingredients in tiny type on the back label, the designers highlighted the ingredients on colourful graphics resembling plant labels prominently displayed on the front of the packet. The new label has an old-fashioned look that contrasts sharply with the more modern labels on competing supermarket brands. Carole Baker, a Somerfield brand manager, explains: 'Rather than keep it abstract, we felt it was important to convey to our customers information on all the different flavours and salad leaves'.[23] One of the designers adds, 'It's fun and functional and fits with Somerfield's mission statement, "good food made easy".'[24]

Marketing functions aside, your labels must meet applicable laws and regulations. Cigarette marketers in the European Union, for instance, are required to devote 30 per cent of the front label and 40 per cent of the back label to health warnings. Also, labelling cannot use terminology implying that one type of cigarette is safer than others.[25] In Canada's Quebec province, multilingual labels must include a French equivalent for every word, printed in type that is as big as or bigger than the type used for other languages. Cultural sensitivities are another factor. Spanish-language labels prepared for products sold in Spain may not be appropriate in South America, just as French-language labels for products sold in France may not be appropriate in Quebec.[26]

PLANNING BRAND STRATEGY

Branding is a pivotal aspect of product strategy because it provides identity and competitive differentiation to stimulate customer response. An unbranded product is just a commodity, indistinguishable from competing products except in terms of price. A branded product may have the same attributes as competitors yet be seen as distinctly different (and provoke a different customer response) because of the rational or emotional value the brand adds in satisfying the customer's needs and wants.[27]

In planning brand strategy, you should identify avenues to increasing **brand equity**, the extra value customers perceive in a brand that ultimately builds long-term loyalty. Higher brand equity contributes to sustained competitive advantage, attracts new channel partners and reinforces current channel relationships. It also enhances marketing power, allowing you to wring more productivity out of your marketing activities because customers (1) are aware of your brand and its identity, (2) know what the brand stands for, (3) respond to the brand and (4) want an ongoing relationship with it. The brand equity pyramid in Figure 6.6 illustrates these four levels leading to strong brand equity.

Be aware that customers in the targeted segment may know the brand, understand what it stands for and respond to it – but not want the kind of ongoing relationship that the organisation would like. Manchester United, for example, commissioned research to find out how its team brand was received in Asia, where football is increasingly popular. The study revealed that 20 million Asians consider themselves fans of the team (meaning they know the brand, know what it stands for and respond to it). That's not enough for Peter Draper, Man U's director of marketing. His team's merchandising reportedly brings in more than €30 million every year; by comparison, Real Madrid's annual merchandising sales are estimated at more than €90 million. To increase Man U's merchandise sales in Asian markets, Draper's plan is to convert 'committed fans into committed customers'.[28]

The ultimate objective of brand strategy is to move customers upward through the levels of brand equity and encourage them to remain at the top. This raises the customer's lifetime value to the organisation and helps achieve your objectives. It is important to remember that companies benefit financially from brand equity, but the identity, meaning, response and relationships all derive from customer interaction with the brand.[29]

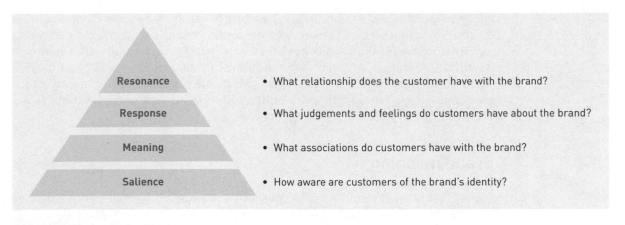

FIGURE 6.6 Brand equity pyramid

Source: After Kevin Lane Keller, *Strategic Brand Management*, 2nd edn (Upper Saddle River, NJ: Prentice Hall, 2003), p. 76.

Brand identity

Here, you want to make customers in the targeted segment aware of your brand's identity. A brand can consist of words, numbers, symbols and/or graphics to add salience, such as the Nike name combined with its swoosh symbol or the Nestlé name combined with the nesting bird logo. You can develop or license a brand using one or more of the following approaches:

- *Company brand*. The company name becomes the brand, such as Sony, Starbucks and Coca-Cola. This associates the company's image with the product. If the company's image suffers, however, the brand is likely to feel the effect.

- *Family or umbrella brand*. Each product in one or more lines or categories is identified as belonging to that particular brand family (or being under that brand umbrella). For example, Toyota puts the Lexus brand on a family of vehicles; Anheuser-Busch puts the Budweiser brand on a family of beers.

- *Individual brand*. A product is identified with a brand not shared by other products. The household lubricant WD-40 is a good example of an individual brand used only for that product.

- *Private label brand*. Retailers and other channel members frequently brand their own products for differentiation from manufacturers' branded products. The supermarket chain Tesco uses Finest as its private label brand; competitor Sainsbury uses Taste the Difference.

Bringing customers to this first level of brand equity involves decisions about the brand itself as well as other product attributes and marketing actions. For example, how can you use product packaging and labelling to convey a distinctive brand identity? Coca-Cola (ranked by some as the world's most valuable brand) uses hourglass bottles and red-and-white labelling to set its colas apart from other soft drinks. You can also build customers' awareness of the brand through advertising, in-store promotions, websites and other marketing activities that reinforce the differentiation. Customers who are unaware of a brand will not think of it when purchasing, which is why organisations often set marketing objectives for awareness. Establishing a brand identity and making customers aware of it is a prelude to creating brand meaning.

Brand meaning

The second level of brand equity is to shape the associations that customers have with your brand. What do you want the brand to stand for? What image or personality does the brand have, and is it the same as what you want to create? For instance, Philips Electronics, based in the Netherlands, has recently been rethinking its brand image to compete more effectively in the consumer market for home entertainment products and the business market for monitors and medical products. 'Philips already has an image of being reliable and trustworthy, and that gives us a great base on which to build', notes the head of global management. 'But we're not perceived as exciting or innovative in the minds of our consumers, even though we are constantly innovating. So we need to change that perception.'[30]

Once customers understand a brand's meaning, they come to rely on it as a shortcut when making buying choices, which expedites the buying process and reduces the perceived risk. You can mould brand meaning through positioning and through favourable associations backed up by product performance, features that deliver value through need satisfaction, distinctive design and so on. As with brand identity, other marketing activities are involved, as well.

Consider how Virgin manages its brand's meaning.

MARKETING IN PRACTICE: VIRGIN

What does the Virgin brand stand for? Ashley Stockwell, group brand marketing director, answers: 'Value for money – but that doesn't mean cheap – and great customer service. The Virgin brand is challenging convention in existing markets. And there's an element of simplicity, an element of fun and an element of innovation.'[31] Because the Virgin brand appears on so many products, including airlines, mobile phone service and retail stores, Stockwell coordinates the marketing efforts of all Virgin's business units, checks that customer service lives up to the brand meaning and enforces guidelines to protect the brand's identity. For instance, the Virgin brand logo used on promotional material and elsewhere must be presented in a consistent manner from unit to unit and product to product. Although some product lines have not performed up to expectations and customer service on Virgin Trains has been criticised from time to time, surveys confirm that the Virgin brand is as strong as ever.[32]

Brand response

The third level of brand equity relates to customer response. Once customers are aware of the brand's identity and understand its meaning, they can make up their minds about the brand. Ideally, you want your customers to believe in your brand, trust it and perceive it as embodying positive qualities. You also want customers to see the brand as competitively superior and, just as important, have an emotional connection to it. Virgin, for example, wants customers to see its brand as fun and a bit of a rebel, and respond accordingly. Determining customer response requires marketing research, followed up by action steps to either reinforce positive responses or to turn negative (or neutral) responses into positive ones through product and marketing strategy.

Marketers for Campbell's Soup recently faced the problem of less enthusiastic response to the company's condensed soups. Sales volume is sizeable but the brand dominates an ever-shrinking market as ready-to-serve tinned soups gain popularity. 'I've got millions of households every week buying the product, despite the fact that we've priced too aggressively, that we haven't innovated, that we've allowed the quality gap between ourselves and alternatives to shrink', says Campbell's CEO Douglas R. Conant.[33] So to reignite brand perceptions of quality and competitive superiority following the slogan 'It's not enough to be a legend', Conant and his marketing team have been devising new cooking methods and improved recipes for traditional soup favourites.[34]

Brand relationship

The fourth level of brand equity deals with customers' relationship to the brand. They know about the brand, know what it means to them and how they feel about it. But are they sufficiently attached to remain loyal buyers? You want to encourage strong and enduring brand relationships because loyal customers tend to buy more, resist switching to competing brands and be willing to pay a premium for the brand and recommend it to others.[35] The issue is therefore how you can use product strategy, along with other marketing-mix strategies, to reinforce customers' brand preference and loyalty.

One approach is to improve or at least maintain product quality and performance to avoid disappointing customers, tarnishing the brand and discouraging customer loyalty. Another is to add products or features that better satisfy current customers' needs. A third is to continue introducing innovative or upgraded product designs, packaging and labelling consistent with the brand image. Finally, your marketing plan should allow for marketing research to see how effective the product strategy is in moving customers up the brand equity pyramid toward sustained customer loyalty. See this chapter's online resources for websites about branding.

 **CHAPTER SUMMARY**

1. *Explain the product mix and line decisions involved in product strategy.*
   Product strategy entails decisions about the organisation's product mix (its assortment of product lines), product line length (the number of items in each line) and product line depth (the number of product variations within a line). By introducing or eliminating products, marketers can lengthen a product line (line extension), deepen a line, widen the mix (through brand extension and category extension), shorten a line and narrow or widen the mix. Another consideration is cannibalisation, the extent to which a product draws sales from the organisation's other products.

2. *Discuss the product life cycle and its role in product strategy.*
   The product life cycle is a product's market movement as it progresses from introduction to growth, maturity and decline. The life cycle can vary by segment and by market, as well as by product. Understanding each product's place in its life cycle alerts marketers to forthcoming changes in sales and allows for planning to slow down or speed up movement and maximise performance in each part.

3. *Outline the steps in new product development.*
   The eight steps in new product development are: (1) gather product ideas; (2) screen product ideas; (3) research customer reaction to ideas; (4) analyse the business case for each new product; (5) develop the actual product to determine practicality; (6) test market the product; (7) launch the product commercially; and (8) monitor market response.

4. *Identify the various product attributes that can be used, in combination, to create and deliver customer value.*
   When formulating product strategy, marketers make decisions about quality and performance; features and benefits; design; packaging and labelling; and branding. Quality should be seen in terms of how well a product satisfies customer needs. A product's features are attributes that contribute to functionality. They deliver benefits, the need-satisfaction outcomes that customers expect or want. Product design is especially important for differentiation. Packaging delivers the benefits of protecting products and facilitating their use or convenient storage while serving societal objectives. Labels provide information, grab attention, describe features and benefits, differentiate products and reinforce brand image. Branding identifies a product and differentiates it from competing products to stimulate customer response. All of these decisions must be coordinated with other marketing strategy decisions.

5. *Define brand equity and describe the four levels leading to strong brand equity.*
   Brand equity is defined as the extra value customers perceive in a brand that builds long-term loyalty. The four levels leading to strong brand equity are: (1)

making customers aware of the brand's identity; (2) clarifying the meaning of the brand; (3) encouraging customers to respond to the brand; and (4) encouraging customers to maintain an ongoing relationship with it.

 ## KEY TERM DEFINITIONS

benefits Need-satisfaction outcomes that a customer expects or wants from a product

brand equity Extra value that customers perceive in a brand, which builds long-term loyalty

brand extension Widening the product mix by introducing new products under an existing brand

branding Giving a product a distinct identity and supporting its competitive differentiation to stimulate customer response

cannibalisation Situation in which one product takes sales from another marketed by the same organisation

category extension Widening the mix by introducing product lines in new categories

features Specific attributes that contribute to a product's functionality

line extension Lengthening a product line by introducing new products

product life cycle Product's movement through the market as it passes from introduction to growth, maturity and decline

product line depth Number of variations of each product within one product line

product line length Number of individual products in each product line

product mix Assortment of product lines offered by an organisation

quality Extent to which a good or service satisfies the needs of customers

THE PRACTICAL MARKETER CHECKLIST NO. 6:
PLANNING PRODUCT AND BRAND STRATEGY

Product-related decisions

What is the current situation of each product in the context of its line and the overall product mix?

Would customers' needs and the organisation's interests be served by changing the product mix, product lines or line depth?

Where is each product in its life cycle and what are the implications for product strategy?

What new products can be developed to take advantage of promising opportunities in targeted segments?

How can cannibalisation be minimised following new product introductions?

What are the ecological and ethical considerations associated with each product?

What is the optimal combination of quality and performance, features and benefits, design, packaging, labelling and branding for each product?

Brand strategy and customers

Are customers aware of the brand?

What does the brand mean to customers?

What do customers think and feel about the brand?

What relationship do customers have or want with the brand?

Brand strategy and the organisation

How is the brand identified?

How is the brand positioned for differentiation?

How do product attributes support the brand?

How can brand awareness be expanded?

How can brand image be improved?

How can brand preference and loyalty be encouraged?

Source: Adapted from Kevin Lane Keller, *Strategic Brand Management*, 2nd edn (Upper Saddle River, NJ: Prentice Hall, 2003), Chapter 2.

 ## ONLINE RESOURCES

BRANDING

- Superbrands Council (www.superbrands.com.au) – Posts case studies of successful brands being marketed in Australia.

- American Brands Council (www.americasgreatestbrands.com) – Provides background on some of the best-known brands in the United States.

- Brandingasia (www.brandingasia.com) – Includes news, surveys and case studies about branding in Asian markets.

- Transdiffusion Network (www.transdiffusion.org/ident) – Contains brief articles about television network branding and history in the United Kingdom and elsewhere.

- Marketing Profs (www.marketingprofs.com) – A marketing site by marketing professionals and professors, with features about branding, products and more.

 ## QUESTIONS FOR DISCUSSION AND ANALYSIS

1. From the organisation's perspective, what are the advantages and disadvantages of line and brand extensions?

2. What types of products might reach maturity more quickly than other products? What are the implications for marketing planning?

3. How can you use research to support decisions about building brand equity?

APPLY YOUR KNOWLEDGE

Select an organisation offering a branded good or service with which you are familiar and research its product strategy.

- From a customer's perspective, how would you describe the product's quality and performance? Do you think this perception of value matches what the marketer intended?

- How do the product's features deliver benefits to satisfy needs of the targeted customer segments?

- How do design, packaging and labelling contribute to your reaction, as a customer, to this product?

- Where does this product appear to be in its life cycle? How do you know?

- How would you describe this product's brand? Are the organisation's branding decisions supported by its other product strategy decisions?

- Prepare a brief oral or written report summarising your comments.

BUILD YOUR OWN MARKETING PLAN

Proceed with the marketing plan you have been preparing. Are you formulating a product strategy for a tangible good or an intangible service? What level of quality is appropriate (and affordable) to meet the needs of the customer segments you are targeting? What needs do customers satisfy through products such as yours and what features must your product have to deliver the expected benefits? What decisions about design, packaging and labelling will help add value and differentiate your product? What brand image do you want to project? How do you want customers to feel about the brand and react toward it? What can you do with product strategy to encourage customer loyalty? Develop a product strategy for at least one product and record it in *Marketing Plan Pro* software or in a written marketing plan, ensuring that the decisions are consistent with decisions and information you entered earlier in the process.

CLOSING CASE: BUILDING A BRAND NAMED GEORGE

As a brand, George means 'affordable fashion and a phenomenal combination of design, quality and price', states Andy Bond.[36] Bond is MD of the George clothing brand, marketed by the UK retail chain Asda, and an expert on the hot topic of private label brands. With a team of 300 employees, he manages every aspect of George brand clothing, from procuring supplies and arranging production to transporting the right assortment of items to each Asda store.

Because of the expertise and global buying power of its owner Wal-Mart, Asda can continually lower its product costs and pass the savings on to its customers in the form of lower retail prices. 'We are now buying fabric at up to 60 per cent cheaper than we used to, and components at 15 per cent less', says Bond. Thanks to lower costs combined with supply chain improvements, 'in the last 12 months alone, our average selling price has dropped by over 20 per cent', he adds.[37]

Who would buy clothing in a food shop? Millions of people, as it turns out: of the 11 million weekly visitors to Asda stores, 30 per cent buy George clothing. And George is only one of Asda's private label brands. The retailer also offers supermarket merchandise under brands such as Extra Special, Value and Good For You. Catriona Land, Asda's director of private label, explains that ingredients, sizes and price positioning are varied to differentiate each of the chain's 8,000 private label products from competing products. 'Our advantage over the brand manufacturers is that we can afford to take more risks in terms of own brand development', she notes. 'Retailers' costs are much lower, and that means there are times when we can afford to fail.'[38]

Asda has such a strong commitment to private label branding that it encourages marketing managers to take risks in search of innovative products that will draw more customers. All marketing managers have completed a special training course on 'Asdaness' to stimulate new product thinking. Still, the most successful products, Andy Bond points out, are the result of listening to customers. 'All the colleagues that work with me at George all work on the shop floor', he says. 'I can't think of a better way of getting closer to our customers and our colleagues.'[39] Based on customer response, the George brand covers a wide variety of clothing products for teens, women, mothers-to-be, men, babies and children.

Now Asda is testing the brand's strength by opening stand-alone George stores south of London and in Yorkshire. The US department store chain Macy's did this with its Aeropostale private label brand. Ultimately, the Aeropostale stores were purchased by another company and expanded into a chain operating hundreds of branded outlets across the country. Will George be successful outside Asda stores and lead to a chain of branded stores?[40]

Case questions

1. What brand extensions would you suggest Asda consider for George – and why would they make sense for this brand?

2. How does customer contact help Asda's marketing managers to gauge the strength of George's brand equity?

 **ENDNOTES**

1. Quoted in Phred Dvorak, 'Home Theatre at Just $20,300? Sony Unveils Pricey Products', *Wall Street Journal*, 11 June 2003, p. D7; also based on information in: Irene M. Kunii, 'This Time, Sony Better Finish the Job', *Business Week*, 3 November 2003, p. 50; Phred Dvorak, 'Facing a Slump, Sony to Revamp Product Lines', *Wall Street Journal*, 12 September 2003, pp. B1, B4; Kevin J. Delaney, 'New Sony Videogame Camera Sells Well', *Wall Street Journal*, 29 August 2003, p. B6; Phred Dvorak, 'Sony Profit Drops Amid Price Cuts, Weak Demand', *Wall Street Journal*, 25 July 2003, p. A16; P.J. Huffstutter, 'Sony's Moment of Truth', *Los Angeles Times*, 20 June 2003, p. C1.

2. Edward Taylor, 'Beiersdorf Sharpens Its Brand Focus', *Wall Street Journal*, 23 July 2003, p. B5D.

3. Sarah Ellison, 'Crest Spices Up Toothpaste War with New Tastes', *Wall Street Journal*, 15 September 2003, pp. B1, B10.

4. Kevin Lane Keller, *Strategic Brand Management*, 2nd edn (Upper Saddle River, NJ: Prentice Hall, 2003), pp. 582–91.

5. Kevin O'Donnell, 'Green Ketchup Works, But Not on Blue Fries', *Brandweek*, 1 September 2003, p. 17; Sian Harrington, 'Sharper NPD at Heinz', *Grocer*, 21 June 2003, pp. 10ff.

6. Adam Lashinsky, 'Shootout in Gadget Land', *Fortune*, 10 November 2003, pp. 74ff.

7. Caroline Parry, 'New! Nouveau! Nieuw!', *Marketing Week*, 19 June 2003, p. 30.

8. 'When Will It Fly?', *The Economist*, 9 August 2003, p. 51.

9. Peter Burrows, 'Ringing Off the Hook in China', *Business Week*, 9 June 2003, pp. 80, 82; Mure Dickie, 'China Groups' Subscriptions Slow Down', *Financial Times*, 20 May 2003, www.ft.com.

10. 'Expect the Unexpected', *The Economist*, 6 September 2003, p. 5.

11. J. Lynn Lunsford, 'United Technologies' Formula', *Wall Street Journal*, 2 July 2003, pp. A1, A6.

12. Ann Harrington, 'Who's Afraid of a New Product?', *Fortune*, 10 November 2003, pp. 189ff.

13. Quoted in Noshua Watson, 'What's Wrong with This Printer?', *Fortune*, 17 February 2003, pp. 120C–120H.

14. Lashinsky, 'Shootout in Gadget Land'.

15. Gail Edmondson, 'Mercedes' Head-On Collision with a Quality Survey', *Business Week*, 21 July 2003, p. 27.

16. Eric Pfeiffer, 'Chip off the Old Block', *Business 2.0*, July 2003, pp. 54–5.

17. Ian Morton, 'Michelin System Will Check, Inflate Tyres', *Automotive News*, 21 July 2003, p. 22; 'Keeping Michelin on a Roll', *Business Week*, 7 July 2003, p. 46.

18. 'China's Amazon', *The Economist*, 23 August 2003, pp. 52–3.

19. Quoted in Poul Funder Larsen, 'Better Is . . . Better', *Wall Street Journal*, 22 September 2003, pp. R6, R11.

20. Frederick Balfour, 'China's Dream Team', *Business Week*, 1 September 2003, pp. 50–1; Moon Ihlwan, 'Pink-Haired Designers, Red Cell Phones – Ka-Ching!', *Business Week*, 16 June 2003, pp. 60–1.

21. Larry Selden and Geoffrey Colvin, 'What Customers Want', *Fortune*, 7 July 2003, pp. 122–7; Peter Landers, 'Hospital Chic: the ER Gets a Makeover', *Wall Street Journal*, 8 July 2003, pp. D1, D3.

22. Nancy Einhart, 'Are Your Competitors Packing?', *Business 2.0*, July 2003, p. 52.

23. Quoted in 'Somerfield Hails Taxi Salad Refresh', *Design Week*, 20 February 2003, p. 6.

24. Quoted in Liz Farrelly, 'Shelf Raising', *Design Week*, 19 June 2003, pp. 16ff.

25. 'EU's Tobacco Clamp Upheld', *Grocer*, 14 December 2002, p. 9.

26. Pan Demetrakakes, 'Multilingual Labelling Broadens Product Appeal', *Food & Drug Packaging*, July 2003, pp. 38ff.

27. This section draws on Keller, *Strategic Brand Management*, Chapters 1 and 2.

28. Quoted in Henry C. Jackson, 'Europe's Soccer Clubs Make Asia Pitch', *Wall Street Journal*, 13 August 2003, p. B5A; other sources: Emma Daly, 'Soccer Team of Century Enters Age of Marketing', *New York Times*, 15 August 2003, p. W1; Stanley Holmes, 'Can Man U Score in America?', *Business Week*, 23 June 2003, pp. 108–9.

29. Don E. Schultz, 'Branding Geometry', *Marketing Management*, September–October 2003, pp. 8–9.

30. Quoted in Rina Chandran, 'Philips to Rework Brand Positioning', *Asia Africa Intelligence Wire*, 23 August 2003, n.p.

31. Quoted in Lucy Barrett, 'Protecting the Purity of the Virgin Brand', *Marketing Week*, 25 July 2002, p. 22.

32. Terry Keenan, 'Virgin Group Chairman – Interview', *The America's Intelligence Wire*, 6 July 2003, n.p. 'Profile: Policing Growth', *Marketing*, 25 July 2002, p. 18; Jeremy Lee, 'Close-up: Newsmaker Ashley Stockwell', *Campaign*, 26 July 2002, p. 15; Barrett, 'Protecting the Purity of the Virgin Brand'.

33. Quoted in Sarah Ellison, 'Inside Campbell's Big Bet: Heating Up Condensed Soup', *Wall Street Journal*, 31 July 2003, pp. B1–B2.

34. Ellison, 'Inside Campbell's Big Bet: Heating Up Condensed Soup'.

35. 'New Customer Research on Customer Referrals, Commitment, Loyalty', *Report on Customer Relationship Management*, August 2003, pp. 2ff.

36. Quoted in David Moin, 'George's Fashion Democracy', *WWD*, 18 November 2002, pp. 20ff.

37. Quoted in Moin, 'George's Fashion Democracy'.

38. Quoted in 'Analysis: Supermarkets Harness the Brand', *Marketing*, 1 August 2002, pp. 15ff.

39. Quoted in Moin, 'George's Fashion Democracy'.

40. Based on information in 'Asda Trains Staff to Boost Own-Brand', *Marketing*, 31 July 2003, p. 4; '"George" Goes Solo at Wal-Mart's Asda', *Chain Store Age Executive Fax*, 13 June 2003, p. 1; 'Analysis: Supermarkets Harness the Brand'; Moin, 'George's Fashion Democracy'.

7 Developing channel and logistics strategy

Closing case: Wal-Mart masters the details of logistics

Endnotes

Comprehension outcomes

After studying this chapter, you will be able to:

- Discuss the functions of the value chain, marketing channels and logistics
- Describe direct channels, indirect channels and the three types of intermediaries
- Contrast exclusive, selective and intensive distribution
- Identify the main functions involved in logistics strategy and explain the need to balance costs and customer service

Application outcomes

After studying this chapter, you will be able to:

- Analyse the value chain for a good or service
- Determine the number of channel levels and members to meet customers' and organisational needs
- Develop an appropriate strategy for logistics

OPENING CASE: GETTING NOKIA'S PHONES INTO THE WORLD'S HANDS

How can the world's largest manufacturer of mobile phones get its products to consumers and business customers in more than 100 countries? For Finland's Nokia, the answer is savvy channel arrangements. Dealing individually with each of the planet's one billion mobile phone users would be impractical and expensive, of course. Instead, Nokia relies on a country by country coterie of mobile phone service providers, wholesalers and electronics stores to market its handsets based on network compatibility and customer needs. Its marketers also gather customer data from these channel members for use in marketing planning.

Nokia is a dominant industry player in Europe but wants sales growth everywhere, especially in the United States, Japan, China and South Korea. To do this, the company is forging closer ties to market handsets through mobile phone service providers. In the United Kingdom, for example, Nokia has added a special button to handsets sold through Vodafone so those subscribers can quickly access the proprietary Vodafone Live! Data service. In the United States, Nokia has re-established ties with Sprint PCS, a service provider that sells handsets and accessories to subscribers. After selling no Nokia phones for three years, Sprint was very successful with one of Nokia's less expensive phones. Shortly afterwards, Nokia expanded its distribution by marketing a model through Sprint's rival, Verizon Wireless. In addition, customers can order handsets designed to work with most US networks directly from Nokia's website.

Inventory management is a critical factor in this fast-moving industry. When demand is strong, manufacturers boost output and channel members stock up; as sales growth slows, however, the risk of being caught with quantities of soon-to-be-outdated products increases. Nokia has become expert at inventory management: it maintains stock to cover less than one month's worth of channel orders. Contrast this to the recent industry overstock situation in China, where an estimated 20 million handsets languished in warehouses, assembly plants and stores – enough to fulfil market demand for four months.

Supplementing its mobile phone business, Nokia markets network equipment directly to service providers such as Orange and tech-compatible mobile systems to corporations. Looking ahead, Nokia will be doing more marketing in nations where mobile phone service is in its infancy. 'There is extraordinary potential in the number of people currently without mobile service', observes CEO Jorma Ollila. 'We expect that for an increasing number of these people, a mobile will be their first and only phone, and within a few years there will be a large number of mobile users who have never seen a fixed telephone.'[1] And if the company's marketing plans work out, many of those people will be talking on Nokia handsets.[2]

CHAPTER PREVIEW

'Place' strategy is all about convenience: enabling customers to take possession of a product in a convenient place and time, in a convenient form and quantity and at an acceptable price. As basic as this may sound, channel strategy and logistics are actually complex because they must coordinate with other marketing mix strategies, meet customers' needs and satisfy organisational objectives. For instance, Nokia offers customers many ways to obtain its products: it makes network-ready handsets available directly to customers, through mobile phone service providers, through retail chains like Carphone Warehouse and through wholesalers that sell to smaller stores. These arrangements ensure that customers can buy where, when and how they prefer. Nokia must also allow for details such getting the right assortment and quantity of handsets to each outlet (or directly to customers) and maintaining sufficient inventory to despatch orders on schedule – a delicate balance of cost and customer service.

This chapter opens with an overview of the value chain for goods and services, the starting point for place strategy. Next is a discussion of the flows and responsibilities within the value chain and this is followed by sections exploring decisions about direct and indirect channels, number of channel levels, number of channel members, selection of channel members and the difference between push and pull strategies. The closing section examines the development of logistics strategy, including the trade-off between cost and customer service and decisions about storage, inventory, transportation, order processing and order fulfilment. *To ensure consistency, your channel and logistics strategies should be coordinated with the other marketing-mix strategies and earlier decisions documented in your marketing plan.*

ANALYSING THE VALUE CHAIN

The **value chain**, also known as the **supply chain**, is the succession of inter-related, value-added functions undertaken by the marketer with suppliers, wholesalers, retailers and other participants to source supplies and ultimately deliver a product that fulfils customers' needs. Figure 7.1 shows the basic decisions involved in developing a value chain. Analysing this sequence is important if you are to understand how each participant in the chain adds value to the final good or service that your customers buy and use. In Nokia's situation, the company derives value from buying plastics for handsets from suppliers, avoiding the need to manufacture those materials itself. Nokia does, however, add value by designing its own computer chips for certain mobile phone products, even though competitors use chips designed by others. After the handsets are assembled, mobile phone service providers and retailers add value by giving customers in local markets access to a selection of handsets.

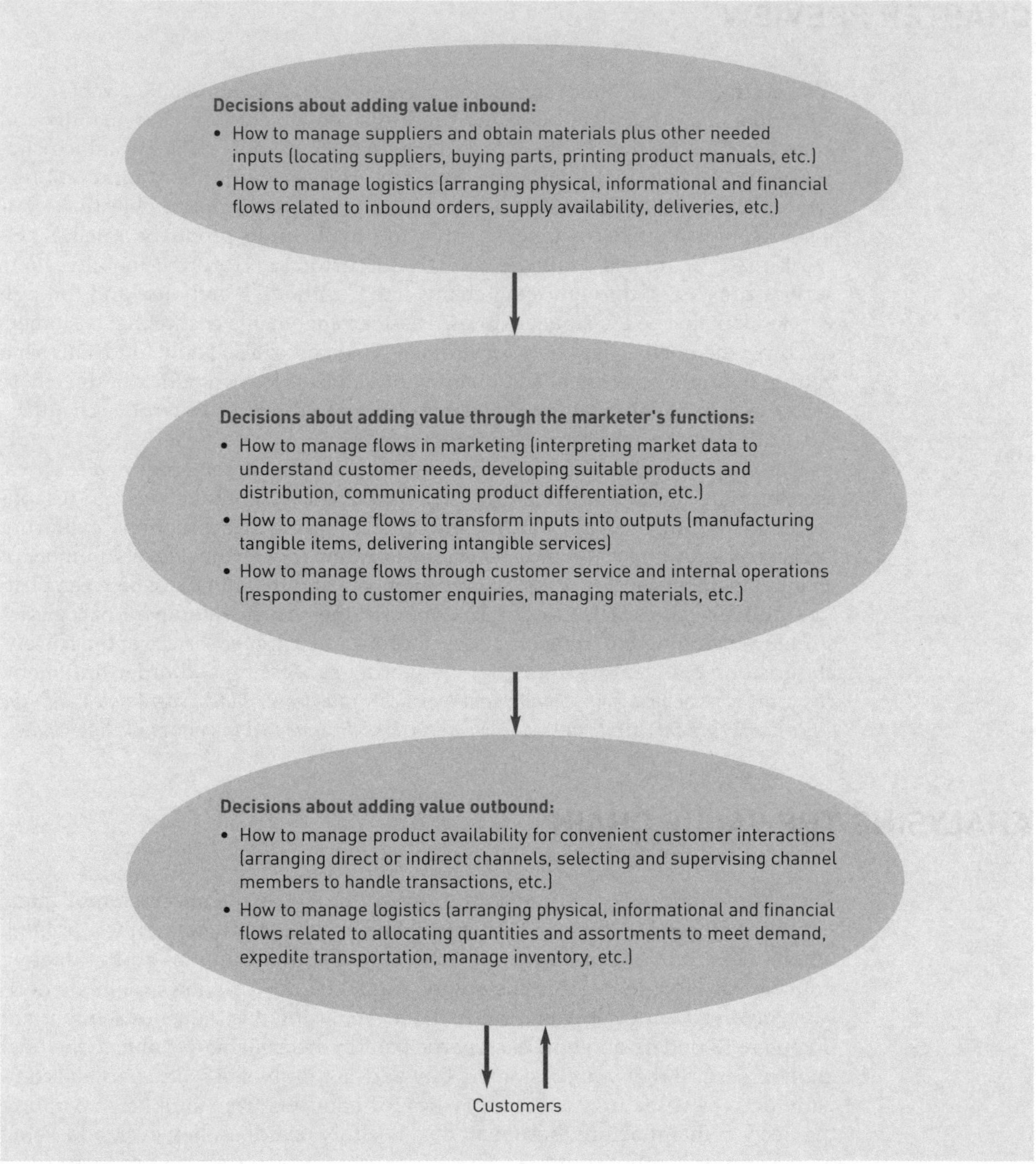

Decisions about adding value inbound:

- How to manage suppliers and obtain materials plus other needed inputs (locating suppliers, buying parts, printing product manuals, etc.)
- How to manage logistics (arranging physical, informational and financial flows related to inbound orders, supply availability, deliveries, etc.)

Decisions about adding value through the marketer's functions:

- How to manage flows in marketing (interpreting market data to understand customer needs, developing suitable products and distribution, communicating product differentiation, etc.)
- How to manage flows to transform inputs into outputs (manufacturing tangible items, delivering intangible services)
- How to manage flows through customer service and internal operations (responding to customer enquiries, managing materials, etc.)

Decisions about adding value outbound:

- How to manage product availability for convenient customer interactions (arranging direct or indirect channels, selecting and supervising channel members to handle transactions, etc.)
- How to manage logistics (arranging physical, informational and financial flows related to allocating quantities and assortments to meet demand, expedite transportation, manage inventory, etc.)

Customers

FIGURE 7.1   Simplified value chain

Your organisation, which is the central link of the value chain, is responsible for coordinating the transformation of inputs into outputs as well as inbound functions that occur upstream and outbound functions that occur downstream. The value added downstream occurs within a **marketing channel**, also known as a **distribution channel**, the set of functions performed by the producer or intermediaries to make a particular good or service available to customers. The flow of products, information and payments inbound, through the central link and outbound is accomplished through **logistics**. One or more parties must handle inbound transportation of raw materials and components so you can produce the good or service; maintain inventory, track production quantities and despatch finished goods outbound; and manage downstream customer transactions, for example.

In developing channel and logistics strategies, you should take into account the needs and behaviour of targeted customer segments; your organisation's strengths, weaknesses and competitive situation; your product's positioning; and your marketing plan objectives. Then consider which functions in the value chain must be accomplished and which participants should be responsible for each. These decisions lay the groundwork for achieving objectives for channel and logistics efficiency – adding meaningful value at acceptable cost to customer and organisation – and for effectiveness – meeting customers' needs and contributing to the organisation's success. You may propose a number of alternatives for channel and logistics, look at how each might achieve the set objectives and think about threats that could limit success before settling on specific strategies for your marketing plan.

The value chain for services

Value chains for services also follow the flows inbound, through the service process and then outbound for customer access. Inbound functions cover supplies, information and payments related to providing the service; in the central link, the marketing organisation's functions cover service operations and delivery; and outbound functions cover service availability and associated information and payments. Production in the central link is highly visible to customers because they are generally present when services are rendered; logistics are more concerned with having the right supplies (and people) in the right place rather than warehousing and shipping goods. Moreover, because services are perishable – they cannot be stored for future sale or consumption – you must carefully manage all flows to balance supply and demand.

Travel websites such as that of Expedia.co.uk add value (and generate revenue) by making the services of airlines, hotels, ferries and car-hire companies conveniently available online. Expedia groups some services into holiday packages and sells others one by one, to satisfy the different needs of different segments. Expedia is responsible for the logistics of fast and easy order and payment processing, arranging for sufficient travel offers to meet demand, notifying providers when their services are purchased and getting any travel documents to customers – organisational costs that affect the final price customers pay for their purchases. Services can also be made available through retail stores. In Japan, convenience stores such as Lawson sell tickets for a wide range of services, including theme park passes, concert tickets and holiday travel packages.[3]

Flows and responsibilities in the value chain

The traditional view of the value chain is that all flows move from upstream supplier sources to the marketer in the central link, then downstream to channel members and ultimately to customers. Today, however, many marketers include a **reverse channel** in the marketing plan, to return goods for service or when worn out and to reclaim products, parts or packaging for recycling. Scottish & Newcastle, for example, has arranged a reverse channel to return its Bass ale kegs from US markets to the UK brewery.[4]

In addition, you may want to look beyond immediate value-chain functions to see whether your suppliers' suppliers are providing the required quality or ecologically safe materials and, in B2B situations, to see how your customers' customers use the final product. Lori L. Kress, a specialist at General Electric Aircraft Engines, has helped solve difficult maintenance problems facing US airline customers, such as Southwest Airlines. 'The more successful our customers are, the more successful we will be', she says.[5] In essence, this means examining the demand side as well as the supply side, with the customer's needs and expectations guiding decisions and relationships throughout the value chain. The North American paper manufacturer Boise Cascade, for example, stopped buying wood from endangered forests after losing some corporate and academic customers over the issue. And Boise Cascade has begun pressing its own suppliers to keep inbound supplies as green as possible. 'We decided we ought to make sure what we are doing is aligned with what our customers are doing', commented one company official.[6]

A growing number of companies are revising their strategies to realign responsibilities for specific channel and logistics functions. The relationship between the US department store chain J.C. Penney and its private label shirt maker, TAL Apparel, is a good example (see page 177).

This example shows that participants in the value chain do not have to continue handling the same inbound and outbound functions forever. Penney's managers were open to new strategies in which TAL expanded its supplier role by adding value through logistics. Customers' needs were met, Penney's needs were met and the value-chain activities were completed on time and at acceptable cost to all parties. As another example of adjusting responsibilities, look at Superquinn, a supermarket chain in Ireland that has taken over some functions on the supply side. The grocer established a 140-acre farm and prepared it for certification by the Irish Organic Trust. 'Having our own dedicated organic farm will give us locally produced organic fruit and vegetables and reduce our dependence on imports', explains deputy chairman Eamonn Quinn.[7]

MARKETING IN PRACTICE: J.C. PENNEY

Through 1,040 stores in North America, J.C. Penney retails famous brand names like Levi's and private label brands such as Stafford and Crazy Horse. Its marketers are so concerned about matching supply and demand that they sometimes stockpile merchandise in quantity to avoid empty shelves. At one point, Penney's warehouses had a six months' supply of private label men's shirts made by TAL Apparel of Hong Kong – and its stores had another three months' supply.

Then Harry Lee, managing director of TAL, suggested that his company plan and despatch the right assortment and quantity of shirt styles, sizes and colours for each Penney store. This change would add value for the retailer by boosting efficiency: TAL could sort orders at less cost and eliminate the need for high inventory levels. Penney's management agreed and provided data to help TAL build a computerised stock replenishment plan. For its part, the supplier rearranged fabric orders, production schedules and shipments according to the new replenishment plans. TAL also said it would absorb the cost of despatching shirts by air (instead of sending them on container ships) if the replenishment plan left a Penney store with insufficient stock. Knowing that shirts can arrive so quickly reassures Penney's marketers that store shelves will never be empty.[8]

You face difficult trade-offs between value added and cost when making decisions about channel strategy and logistics. Having a wide variety of products immediately available at all times in all locations (or ready to be despatched quickly on demand) is the most desirable situation but often too costly for your organisation and for your customer. On the other hand, your customers will not be satisfied – and will turn to competitors – if the organisation has too few products available; the wrong quantities or models available; or slow transactions and delivery. Penney's previous strategy of maintaining high inventory levels ensured that customers would find shirts on the shelves, but it tied up money that could be used in other ways. Now the expanded relationship with TAL saves money while keeping shelves stocked, which in turn satisfies customers and improves Penney's profit margin on private label shirts.

This relationship also illustrates a growing trend toward strengthening long-term relationships with value chain partners for mutual benefit. To illustrate, the Swedish furniture company IKEA Group forges long-term connections with its suppliers to ensure a steady stream of products designed to its specifications and cost guidelines. The company teaches suppliers to negotiate with their suppliers for the best price, quality materials and delivery schedules. 'When we buy fabric, for example, we have to compare the price from many, many suppliers', says a manager at the Binh Thanh Textile Factory in Vietnam, one of IKEA's suppliers.[9]

Another consideration during the planning process is whether thinning your supplier ranks will cut costs. Manufacturers such as Sony and Matsushita are saving money by sourcing from a dramatically smaller number of suppliers. Sony is doing this by slashing the number of parts used in its electronics products and reducing its supplier base from 4,700 to approximately 1,000.[10]

Finally, the J.C. Penney example shows the dual role of retailers that offer private label products and also are intermediaries in the channel strategy of other marketing organisations. The next section examines the development of channel strategy.

PLANNING CHANNEL STRATEGY

Depending on your organisation's situation and channel objectives, you can choose a strategy calling for direct channels or for indirect channels. In **direct channels**, you make products available directly to customers. In **indirect channels**, you work through **intermediaries**, outside businesses or individuals that specialise in helping producers make goods or services available to customers. Figure 7.2 shows how goods or services would reach customers through direct and indirect channels. It also shows the three major types of intermediaries, each of which adds value in a particular way:

- **Wholesalers** are B2B companies that buy from producers, sort and store the products they buy, create smaller lots for buyer convenience and then resell to other channel members (such as retailers) or to business customers. Some wholesalers add extra value by undertaking responsibilities normally handled elsewhere in the value chain, such as monitoring a customer's inventory or generating automatic reorders.

- **Retailers** are B2C companies such as IKEA and Tesco that make their own products or buy from producers or wholesalers, then resell to consumers. Retailers add value by giving consumers easy access to an array of products and by completing purchase transaction functions.

- **Representatives, brokers and agents** (such as travel agents and insurance agents) bring producers together with consumer or business customers but generally do not take ownership of the products being marketed. These intermediaries add value through their knowledge of the market, customers' needs and product offerings. Some also take on specialised roles such as arranging for import or export.

As you plan channel strategy, you have to decide about the number of intermediary levels you want to use for each product – the length of the channel.

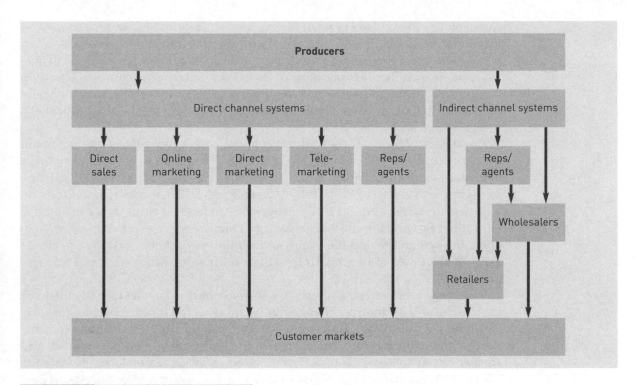

FIGURE 7.2   Alternative channel systems

Source: Adapted, with permission, from Roger J. Best, *Market-Based Management*, 2nd edn (Upper Saddle River, NJ: Prentice Hall, 2000), p. 199.

Channel length decisions

Longer channels have more intermediary levels separating the producer and its customers; shorter channels have fewer intermediaries. A direct channel is the shortest because there are no intermediaries and the producer deals directly with its customers through any or all of the methods shown at the left in Figure 7.2. This is appropriate when you want as much control as possible over dealings with customers and your organisation can handle all outbound functions. If your markets and segments are not well defined or you lack the resources and knowledge to work directly with customers, however, using a direct channel can be inefficient at best and ineffective at worst.

Direct and short channels

The zero-level channel can work well for both B2B and consumer marketers, despite differences in products, customers, prices and markets. Nippon Steel, one of the world's largest steel producers, uses direct channels to sell steel plates, sheets and related products to construction companies, carmakers and other businesses in its home country of Japan and in Europe, the Americas and other markets. The company has a good idea of what businesses are likely to buy, when and how, so it can make contact directly. Organisations targeting consumers have also effectively used direct channels. To illustrate, the airline Ryanair uses a direct channel to reach air travellers, selling most of its tickets online. This choice is based on economics – dealing directly and electronically with air travellers dramatically reduces distribution costs – and on an understanding of the target market's Internet behaviour.

Royal Bank of Scotland uses a direct channel, with a twist, for marketing financial services through 22 different banking units. The Edinburgh-based bank owns National Westminster Bank, Citizens Financial and other banks as well as being co-owner, with Tesco supermarkets, of Tesco Personal Finance. Each banking unit has its own identity but, in many geographic markets, competes for customers with other Royal Bank units. The parent company reaps economies of scale in operating systems behind the scenes and profits every time a customer opens an account with any of its units rather than with some other financial services provider.[11]

Some organisations use a direct channel for certain segments (usually business customers) and an indirect channel with one level for other segments (usually consumers). This allows more control over the typically large-volume transactions with businesses and delegates responsibility for the higher number and smaller size of consumer transactions to intermediaries. Carmakers, for instance, use a direct channel when selling to government agencies and businesses so they can negotiate specifications, pricing and delivery, but design a separate single-level indirect channel of dealers to sell to consumers. Here is a glimpse of Renault's short channel strategy.

MARKETING IN PRACTICE: RENAULT

Renault, like other vehicle manufacturers, selects dealers to hold franchises for selling its vehicles in each market. Recently the French carmaker also tested a strategy of awarding 'premier' status to certain of its UK dealerships and marketing the more expensive Avantime, Vel Satis and Espace models only through those dealers. The purpose was to add more value by pampering buyers with specially trained staff members, plush showrooms and upmarket loan cars while buyers' cars were being serviced. Although the Espace was selling well, sales of the Avantime and Vel Satis models did not meet the company's expectations. This prompted a return to the traditional single-level channel. 'We are still selling the Avantime and Vel Satis, but in fewer numbers than we hoped for', said Philippe Talou-Derible, Renault UK's managing director. 'The cars are now available through all of our dealers.'[12] Renault continues to deal directly with fleet customers such as German Post through company-owned dedicated business centres.[13]

Long channels

Longer channels, such as the two- and three-level indirect channels illustrated at the right of Figure 7.2, send products through a series of representatives or agents, wholesalers or retailers before they reach the final customer. Such channel arrangements allow intermediaries to add value when your company is targeting multiple or geographically dispersed markets; you have limited resources or little customer knowledge; your customers have specialised needs; or your products require training, customisation or service. Although the price paid by customers reflects a profit for intermediaries at all levels and covers the value they add, you may find that long channels are the best way to make certain products available.

For instance, Reckitt Benckiser, based in the United Kingdom, markets dish-washing detergent stain remover and other household products under various brands. The company uses indirect channels to get its products to millions of consumers across Europe, North America and other regions. Supermarkets have long been an important retail channel for Reckitt Benckiser's products because customers in targeted segments value one-stop shopping convenience. Now drug-store chains have become a key channel for new products in the United States – so much so that the company has downsized its product packaging specifically for that channel. According to Mike Murray, vice president of sales, 'when you really have a unique item, a new concept, drug is very quick to adopt that concept'. For this reason, he says, 'We're very conscious of package size and how important space is to the drug channel.'[14] However, the company does not aggressively pursue retail channel members in rural Africa, India or China because, says CEO Bart Becht, 'our products are uniquely unsuited for low-disposable income, rural areas'.[15]

Within a long indirect channel, wholesalers add value in different ways. Consider DCS, which specialises in reselling cosmetics and household products to Bestway, TM Retail, Bewise, Woolworth's and other retailers across the United Kingdom and beyond. Customers expect to see branded toiletries from Unilever, Gillette and other manufacturers on store shelves, but these products rarely turn over as quickly as foods. DCS adds value on the logistics side because of its deal with Taylors of Martley to ship all orders within 24 hours. Not only can channel members get orders quickly, they buy from DCS because 'we can provide [retail] customers with a price that they could not get direct from the manufacturer without having to buy in truckloads', explains Denys Shortt, who has expanded the company into the largest UK wholesaler of its kind.[16]

Channel member decisions

Once you have decided to work with at least one level of intermediary, the next decision is how many and what type of channel members to use at each level in each market. Your decisions about channel members depend on the market, the product and its life cycle, customer needs and behaviour, product pricing and product positioning. Figure 7.3 summarises the three broad choices in number of channel members.

If you use **exclusive distribution**, one intermediary will handle your product in a particular area. If you use **selective distribution**, you will have a fairly small number of intermediaries selling your product in the area. If you use **intensive distribution**, you will arrange for as many intermediaries as possible to handle your product in the area. How do you choose? If you are marketing upmarket or specialised goods and services, you can enhance the luxury image by using exclusive distribution. New products that require extensive customer education may be sold in exclusive or selective distribution. Also, products that require some expert sales support or for which customers shop around are often marketed through selective distribution. Finally, consider intensive distribution for inexpensive, everyday products – especially items that customers buy on impulse – because of the opportunity to achieve higher sales volumes.

	Exclusive distribution	Selective distribution	Intensive distribution
Value added for customer	• Individual attention • Knowledgeable sales help • Availability of training, other services	• Choice of outlets in each area • Some services available	• Convenient availability in many outlets • Competition among outlets may lower price
Value added for producer	• Positioning of expensive or technical product reinforced • Closer cooperation and exchange of information • More control over service quality, other aspects	• Ability to cover more of the market • Less dependent on a small number of channel members	• Higher unit sales • Ability to cover an area completely • Lower cost per unit
Concerns for producer	• Higher cost per unit • Potentially reach fewer customers	• Medium costs, medium control	• Less control over service quality, other aspects • More difficult to surpervise • Possible conflict among channel members

FIGURE 7.3　Exclusive, selective and intensive distribution

The more channel members you work with, the more complex your planning and coordination. It is important to note that you may experience some cannibalisation of sales among channel members if you use intensive distribution. At Starbucks, the US-based coffee bar chain, a new outlet may cannibalise up to 30 per cent of the sales of the company's area outlets. Its marketers accept this situation because new outlets still draw new customers, reduce the waiting time for customers at all stores and make local delivery of supplies that much more efficient.[17]

Once you have determined an appropriate number of channel members to cover your markets, you choose specific intermediaries for each channel. In a marketing plan for an existing product or a new entry in an existing line, you may want to reassess the value each member is providing; add more channel members to expand market coverage if needed; and replace ineffective or inefficient members as necessary. As coverage increases, however, so does the possibility for conflict among channel members over customers, market coverage, pricing and other issues. When preparing a marketing plan for a new or existing product, allow for educating channel members about the product's benefits and inducing them actively to promote it.

As you decide whether to do business with a particular wholesaler, retailer, representative or agent in a targeted market, consider whether the intermediary:

- has an image or reputation that is compatible with the brand and product
- is convenient for your customer segment
- has a capable sales or support staff
- is equipped to store, process or display sufficient quantities and varieties of the product
- is financially strong
- will be a strong partner in marketing the product (and possibly later products).

Sometimes marketers decide against using certain channel members. For example, online retailer Amazon.com is known for selling products at discount prices. This is why Callaway Golf, which makes upmarket golf clubs and equipment, does not want its goods sold on Amazon. 'Our concern is for the brand', comments Callaway's director of worldwide sales. 'We try to convey a premium brand image.'[18] Similarly, a Nike spokesperson says Amazon is 'not a venue that we think is appropriate for our brand now'.[19] Summarise your decisions and explain the criteria for choosing channel members when you draft your marketing plan.

Push and pull in the channel

As part of your channel strategy, you may decide to use intermediaries to move or *push* your product through the outbound connections of the value chain to customers, an approach known as a **push strategy**. The point is to encourage retailers, wholesalers, reps and agents to carry the product and make it readily available to customers. Marketers using a push strategy typically stir channel interest through sales and communication programmes targeting intermediaries.

An alternate channel approach is the **pull strategy**, which relies on customers requesting the product from channel members until intermediaries agree to carry it. This *pulls* the product through the channel from producer to customer, because intermediaries generally strive to satisfy their customers by selling what is requested. Some marketers successfully use this approach to build distribution in targeted areas: they place advertisements or otherwise communicate with customers, who in turn are motivated to contact local retailers or distributors and ask for the products (*see* Chapter 9 for more about marketing communication).

In terms of marketing planning, pull strategy can mean a better match between demand and supply. The car manufacturer Jaguar, for example, has shifted from push to pull and changed its supply chain and delivery schedules accordingly.[20] BMW uses a pull strategy it calls 'customer oriented sales and production' to manufacture and despatch vehicles equipped as ordered by customers from local dealers. Manfred Stoeger, vice president of logistics and information technology, says this allows better response to demand but requires supply chain flexibility to meet the needs of customers.[21] Nonetheless, marketers introducing new consumer goods frequently do so using push strategies.

PLANNING LOGISTICS STRATEGY

A good logistics strategy can help you compete by serving customers more effectively or by saving money. But details count. For example, Wal-Mart has built a highly profitable retail empire based on driving logistics costs ever lower, as highlighted in the closing case in this chapter. Whatever your strategy, you will need clear-cut, non-conflicting objectives. If your objective is to make more products available or get them to customers more quickly, expect your costs to be higher. If your objective is to cut the total cost of logistics, expect customers to notice the difference because products will be available more slowly or in more limited amounts because of lower inventory levels. In setting logistics objectives, therefore, you must strike a balance between your customers' needs and your organisation's financial and marketing objectives.

Ethical issues also may come into play, as with RFID tags.

MARKETING IN PRACTICE: LOGISTICS AND PRIVACY

Campaigners for privacy rights are raising concerns about marketers using radio frequency identification tags – RFID for short – to monitor and control the flow of supplies and products through the supply chain. Each RFID tag attached to a package or product contains a computer chip, a tiny antenna and a unique identification number. The tags automatically send radio signals to indicate where they (and the items they identify) are located, whether on a warehouse or store shelf, a loading dock or an assembly line. Companies use the tags to improve accuracy and efficiency, eliminate hand-counting and minimise theft. Procter & Gamble estimates that using RFID to maintain in-stock positions in retail stores could increase its annual turnover by €450 million or more.

For example, the UK retail chain Marks & Spencer uses RFID to track more than three million refillable trays of fresh foods as they are transported from distribution centres to stores. Being able to read the tags electronically – and from a distance – helps the retailer speed foods to the right stores and leads to less spoilage. As another example, the brewer Scottish & Newcastle uses RFID tags to monitor each keg's progress as it is filled with beer, despatched, delivered and returned for refill. Through lower handling costs and lower theft rates, the brewer enjoys substantial annual savings from its use of RFID.

RFID technology is more than 50 years old, but ethical questions are being raised as the tags come into wider use by retailers. Will RFID be used to check on what individuals buy, how products are used or how long products remain in a home or office? In response to some opposition due to privacy concerns, Benetton halted a plan for putting RFID labels on its clothing; Tesco and other retailers are proceeding with tests. Wal-Mart is proceeding to track warehouse inventory via RFID – but not stock in its stores, as yet.[22]

Once you have determined your logistics objectives, you implement them using decisions about pre- and post-production inventory, storage, transportation, order processing and fulfilment (*see* Figure 7.4).

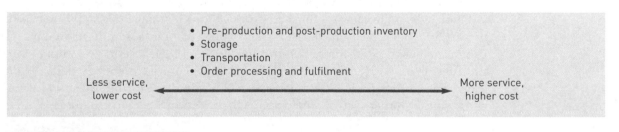

- Pre-production and post-production inventory
- Storage
- Transportation
- Order processing and fulfilment

Less service, lower cost ⟵⟶ More service, higher cost

FIGURE 7.4   Logistics strategy

Inventory decisions

Your decisions about inventory must be made even before the first product moves into the channel. Pre-production, you should identify the inventory level of parts and supplies required for the planned output. Post-production, think about how much inventory of a particular product is needed outbound to meet customer demand, balanced with organisational constraints of budgets, production and storage capacity. If your inventories are too low, customers will not find products when and where they want and your channel members will lose sales; if your inventories are too high, the organisation's investment is tied up and you risk having some products go out of style, spoil or become obsolete. As an example, Wholesaler Stock Building Supply keeps inventory low in its 240 US outlets by filling orders from the outlet closest to the point of customer delivery, regardless of where the order was placed.[23]

Increasingly, producers, suppliers and channel members are collaborating to forecast demand and have the right amount of inventory in the right part of the value chain when needed. Arrow Electronics, which wholesales electronics parts, has developed an automated system for forecasting what each industrial customer is likely to need, based on the individual business, order history and recent shipments.[24] The ideal is just-in-time stock replenishment, with inventory arriving when production is set to begin or customers are ready to buy. Consider the decision by Maxtor, a computer disk drive manufacturer, to outsource some inventory functions to logistics expert Exel. This makes Exel responsible for delivering drives to computer manufacturers' plants in Asia and the United States within 48 hours or less. Exel also manages just-in-time parts deliveries for Volkswagen and Nokia, enabling these producers to keep minimal inventory on hand.[25]

Storage decisions

Where will you store materials before production and where will you store finished products until needed to fill intermediary or customer orders? How long will you store materials and finished products? Such storage decisions are based, in part, on your inventory decisions and your customers' requirements. If you promise a business customer just-in-time stock replenishment, you might store products in a nearby warehouse or distribution centre for speedy delivery on schedule. Also examine how much space is needed for storing inventory at the site where customers actually gain access to the product, as Mikasa does.

MARKETING IN PRACTICE: MIKASA

Mikasa, which makes kitchen glassware and china, recently realised that its central distribution centre was operating at full capacity and its 170-plus North American stores had limited storage space for stock. Thus, the company – which is owned by France's Arc International – could neither make larger shipments to each store nor retain additional stock in the distribution centre for store replenishment. Faced with this dilemma, Mikasa's logistics experts devised a new system: the distribution centre loads giant trailers with replenishment lots in store-by-store order and has the trailers transported to a 'pool point' where orders for each store are separated and secured for safe shipment by outside freight hauliers who deliver the orders to the designated stores. Mikasa's system permits more frequent store deliveries and minimises the storage space needed at both ends. Just as important, it helps the company keep its logistics costs down.[26]

Also look at the product itself and typical variations in demand when planning for product storage. Is your product perishable? Is it especially large (or small) or fragile? Does it have other physical characteristics that affect storage? Are large quantities needed quickly during periods of peak demand? Is demand erratic or steady?

Transportation decisions

Mikasa's experience is another example of how one logistics decision affects other logistics decisions. When storage space was tight, the company solved the problem through transportation. Instead of assembling all store orders in final form at the distribution centre, the company handles part of the task outside the distribution centre and relies on outside freight hauliers to make store deliveries from there.

In the course of planning inbound and outbound logistics, you have to choose the transportation modes that are appropriate for your product, your budget and your customers' needs. Choices include road transport by lorry (convenient for door-to-door shipments), rail transport (for bulky or heavy items), air transport (when time is a factor and budgets allow), water transport (when time is not a factor but cost is) and pipeline transport (for liquids and natural gases). Often products are despatched by more than one mode of transportation, such as lorry to water, rail or air and back to lorry. Global trade is leading to more transportation choices, such as sending products on enormous cargo ships that can each carry 8,000 containers of goods from Asian factories to Western ports.[27] Figure 7.5 shows some of the key questions to ask when making transportation decisions.

Question	Transportation choices
How quickly must products be at their destination?	Air is speediest; water is slowest
Is steady, predictable receipt of products desirable?	Pipeline allows for fairly steady transport of liquids and gases; water is least predictable
What level of transportation cost is acceptable to customers and organisation?	Pipeline and water are least expensive; air is most expensive
Is transportation available from the point of despatch directly to the point of delivery?	Road transport offers the most convenient door-to-door delivery
What capacity is needed to transport this product?	Water and rail easily accommodate large, bulky products

FIGURE 7.5   Questions to ask when making transportation decisions

Your flexibility in transportation choices depends, in part, on legal and regulatory rules governing competition in pricing and schedules; in many areas, transportation companies differentiate themselves through special product handling and convenience. As one example, rail companies in some areas are adding equipment, increasing train frequency, improving on-time performance and boosting train speed. Now freight space on Canadian National Railway trains between the eastern provinces and Toronto is in such demand that businesses must schedule shipments in advance. In the United States, United Parcel Service has changed from lorries to rail for cross-country deliveries. Still, you might have to rely on road transportation if customers want immediate delivery or products must receive special handling.[28]

Order processing and fulfilment decisions

A growing number of organisations are planning better customer service through reduced order cycle time. This means your customers (whether consumers or businesses) will have as short a wait as possible between placing an order and receiving delivery. Order processing and fulfilment covers decisions about the method and timing of:

- accepting orders
- confirmation of order and available inventory

- picking products for despatch

- packing products for despatch

- documenting and tracking the contents of shipments

- billing of purchases

- handling returns, errors and damaged goods.

Your organisation's technological capabilities have a lot to do with your order processing and fulfilment choices. The Montreal distribution centre of Avon Canada, for instance, receives more than one million cosmetics orders every year – up to 5,000 orders every day – from the company's independent sales representatives. Once an order enters the warehouse system, it is usually fulfilled within 24 hours, thanks to cutting-edge technology. At one time, warehouse workers made one error per 1,000 products picked during order fulfilment; with a new picking procedure, workers make only one error per 3,000 products picked. And new technology ensures that inbound deliveries are unpacked and stored more quickly so inventory is available to fulfil orders. Soon Avon's order fulfilment system will be able not only to signal when an order has too many or too few items but also to determine which specific item has been left out if the order is incomplete. The result: Avon reps receive complete orders more quickly and can make personal deliveries to satisfy their customers.[29]

 ## CHAPTER SUMMARY

1. *Discuss the functions of the value chain, marketing channels and logistics.*
   The value (or supply) chain is the succession of interrelated, value-added functions that enable a producer to source supplies and ultimately deliver a product that fulfils customers' needs through connections with suppliers, wholesalers, retailers and other participants. Each participant, including the producer as the central link, adds some value to the product that is meaningful to customers. Marketing (or distribution) channels are the set of functions performed by the producer or by wholesalers, retailers, or agents and representatives in making a product available to customers. Marketing channels are outbound functions that are considered downstream in the value chain, closer to the customer. Logistics refers to the flow of products, information and payments inbound, through the central link and outbound. These flows must occur for the value chain to operate effectively and efficiently.

2. *Describe direct channels, indirect channels and the three types of intermediaries.*
   Channel strategies can employ direct channels – in which the organisation deals directly with customers – and/or indirect channels – in which the organisation

works through other businesses or individuals (intermediaries) in making products available to customers. The three major types of intermediaries are: (1) wholesalers, B2B companies that resell producer's goods or services to other intermediaries or to businesses; (2) retailers, B2C companies that buy from producers or wholesalers – and sometimes make their own products – and sell to consumers; (3) representatives, brokers and agents, who match buyers and sellers but generally take no ownership stake in the products they market.

3. *Contrast exclusive, selective and intensive distribution.*
With exclusive distribution, the producer uses only one intermediary in a particular geographic area. With selective distribution, the producer chooses a relatively small number of intermediaries to handle the product in a particular area. With intensive distribution, the producer works with as many intermediaries as possible within a given area, to make the product more widely available.

4. *Identify the main functions involved in logistics strategy and explain the need to balance costs and customer service.*
The main functions involved in logistics strategy are: pre- and post-production inventory; storage; transportation; order processing and fulfilment. Using logistics to raise customer service levels (through faster delivery, more available inventory and other approaches) generally raises costs; lowering the cost of logistics generally reduces the level of customer service. Thus, logistics strategy should be guided by clear objectives to balance organisational cost with acceptable customer service.

 ## KEY TERM DEFINITIONS

direct channel Marketing channel used by an organisation to make its products available directly to customers

exclusive distribution Channel arrangement where one intermediary distributes the product in an area

indirect channel Marketing channel in which intermediaries help producers make their products available to customers

intensive distribution Channel arrangement in which as many intermediaries as possible distribute the product in an area

intermediaries Businesses or individuals that specialise in distribution functions

logistics Flow of products, associated information and payments through the value chain

marketing or distribution channel Set of functions performed by the producer or participating intermediaries in making a product available to customers

pull strategy Approach to channel strategy that emphasises customer demand pulling products through the value chain

push strategy Approach to channel strategy that emphasises pushing (moving) the product through intermediaries in the value chain to customers

retailers Intermediaries that buy from producers or wholesalers and resell to consumers

reverse channel Channel that allows for returning goods, parts or packaging

selective distribution Channel arrangement in which a relatively small number of intermediaries distribute a product within an area

value or supply chain Sequence of interrelated, value-added actions undertaken by marketers with suppliers, channel members and other participants to create and deliver products that fulfil customer needs

wholesalers Intermediaries that buy from producers and resell to other channel members or business customers

THE PRACTICAL MARKETER CHECKLIST NO. 7: PLANNING CHANNELS AND LOGISTICS

From the customer's perspective

How do customers in the target market prefer to gain access to the good or service?

What channels are best suited to the product, positioning and brand image?

Do channel and logistics decisions result in the product form and quality customers expect?

Are the right assortment of products available at the right time and in the right quantities?

Are support services such as installation available (directly or from channel members) as needed?

Do logistics help customers to obtain products quickly, easily and conveniently?

How can channels and logistics cost-effectively add more value by boosting customer benefits or decreasing customer costs?

From the organisation's perspective

How much control does the organisation want over channel functions?

How efficient and effective are the organisation's current channel and logistics strategies?

How can channel strategy be used to manage the product life cycle?

What legal and regulatory considerations affect channel and logistics decisions?

What geographical considerations affect channel and logistics decisions?

What ecological considerations affect channel and logistics decisions?

How do internal strengths and resources affect channel and logistics decisions?

How can channels and logistics be used for competitive advantage?

How can channels and logistics be used to reinforce positioning?

How can channels and logistics deliver organisational benefits or reduce organisational costs?

What is the optimal balance of logistics costs and customer service?

ONLINE RESOURCES

Logistics

- Logistics Europe (www.logisticse.com/) – Offers white papers and information about supply chain management, relations among participants.

- Council of Logistics Management (www.clm1.org) – Posts definitions of logistics terms, resources and links to other logistics sites.

- Food Chain Centre (www.foodchaincentre.com) – Shows ideas about managing the value chain for foods from farms to stores, with customers in mind.

- Heriot-Watt University's Logistics and Freight Transport Research site (www.sml.hw.ac.uk/logistics) – Makes available studies revealing insights into logistics issues and transport efficiency.

- Materials Handling Industry of America (www.mhia.org) – Presents case studies, technical literature and benchmarking tools for materials management and logistics.

- Log Link (http://loglink.com) – Offers dozens of categorised links to transportation and logistics providers and associations.

QUESTIONS FOR DISCUSSION AND ANALYSIS

1. What are the advantages and disadvantages of using both direct and indirect channels in one market?

2. From the customer's perspective, how might a long channel be beneficial?

3. Why is a good logistics strategy especially vital for foods and high-tech products?

APPLY YOUR KNOWLEDGE

Select a common consumer product, then research and analyse its value chain and its channel strategy.

- Draw a diagram to show a simplified value chain for this product. Is a reverse channel necessary or desirable? Why?

- Is this product available through direct channels such as by mail or from the producer's website? How does this channel arrangement benefit customers and the organisation?

- Is the product available through indirect channels such as retailers? Why is this appropriate for the product, the market and the targeted customers?

- Is the product available through exclusive distribution? Through intensive distribution? Do you agree with this decision?

- Prepare a brief oral or written report summarising your comments.

BUILD YOUR OWN MARKETING PLAN

Continue developing your marketing plan by planning your product's channel arrangements and logistics. Should you market this product directly to customers? Is a combination of direct and indirect channels appropriate? How long should your channel be, and what value do you expect each level to add? Will you use intensive, selective or exclusive distribution? What kinds of channel members would be most appropriate? How does the product life cycle affect your channel decisions? Do you plan to use a push or pull strategy? Does your product require any special transportation or storage? How quickly will customers expect to receive their products after ordering? What other customer needs should you take into account? How will you balance the cost of logistics with the level of customer service you will provide? Will reverse channels and logistics be needed? How do these decisions and ideas fit in with previously documented information in your marketing plan? Record your decisions and explain their implications in *Marketing Plan Pro* software or in a written marketing plan.

CLOSING CASE: WAL-MART MASTERS THE DETAILS OF LOGISTICS

How did Wal-Mart grow to become the largest retailer on the planet? The chain has several core competencies but perhaps the most important is its mastery of logistics. Think of the complexities of having the right merchandise in the right place to satisfy the 138 million shoppers who visit Wal-Mart's 5,000 European, Asian and American stores every week. Behind the scenes, the company maintains more than 150 distribution centres globally and uses extremely sophisticated technology to plan store inventory, receive and transfer merchandise quickly and – its hallmark – keep logistics costs down so retail prices are low.

Every new distribution centre represents an opportunity to hone efficiency by reducing the distance that merchandise must be transported inbound and outbound. With replenishment stock so close at hand – and one or more deliveries scheduled every day – Wal-Mart stores can carry lower inventory levels. Moreover, if a product unexpectedly sells out, it can be restocked in one day or even sooner. Inventory turns over so quickly that more than two-thirds of Wal-Mart's products are purchased by customers before the company is scheduled to pay the suppliers.

In fact, supplier collaboration is a critical component of Wal-Mart's logistics strategy. The retailer works directly with its major suppliers to forecast demand months in advance and plan inbound orders that will meet the needed inventory levels and merchandise assortments on a store by store basis. Because of this collaboration, suppliers are able to plan their production to meet Wal-Mart's specifications and arrange efficient despatch schedules. Sometimes Wal-Mart despatches its own fleet of lorries to fetch merchandise from volume suppliers and plans deliveries so precisely that some products never make it to distribution centre shelves. Instead, cartons of merchandise may move non-stop from inbound lorries to outbound lorries and onward to stores without being unloaded in a distribution centre.

Although Wal-Mart is always looking to minimise costs, its logistics experts have been known to choose more expensive transportation options for the sake of speed. As one example, when bringing merchandise from China by ship, the retailer arranges for some shipments to travel by the most direct route, which may not be the most economical route but gets merchandise to its destination more quickly. In this way, Wal-Mart successfully minimises inventory carrying charges yet has merchandise in each store when and where it is needed.[30]

Case questions

1. What effect would you expect an economic recession to have on Wal-Mart's logistics decisions about seasonal products?

2. From a supplier's standpoint, what are the advantages and disadvantages of dealing directly with Wal-Mart rather than through a wholesaler?

 ENDNOTES

1. Quoted in Robb M. Stewart, 'Nokia Targets New Markets', *Wall Street Journal*, 28 August 2003, p. 1.

2. Based on information from 'Orange Divides UMTS Network Contract Between Alcatel, Nokia and Nortel', *Europe Intelligence Wire*, 18 September 2003, n.p.; Antony Savvas, 'Mobile: Nokia to Help Firms Integrate Mobile IT', *Computer Weekly*, 16 September 2003, p. 6; Evan Ramstad, 'China Has Cellphone Hangover', *Wall Street Journal*, 2 September 2003, p. B10; Stewart, 'Nokia Targets New Markets'; David Pringle, 'Nokia's New Phones Spur U.S. Comeback', *Wall Street Journal*, 10 July 2003, p. B4; Rob Budden, 'Mobile Networks Start Pushing Own Brands', *Financial Times*, 9 June 2003, www.ft.com.

3. Philip Sidel, 'The Luxury of Convenience', *Kansai Time Out*, November 2002, www.japanfile.com.

4. Satellite Logistics Group, 'Satellite Logistics Group', *Traffic World*, 15 September 2003, p. 26.

5. Quoted in Diane Brady, 'Will Jeff Immelt's New Push Pay Off for GE?', *Business Week*, 13 October 2003, pp. 94–8.

6. Quoted in Jim Carlton, "Boise Cascade Turns Green", *Wall Street Journal*, 3 September 2003, p. B6.

7. Quoted in 'Superquinn Gets Growing Its Own', *Grocer*, 31 May 2003, p. 13.

8. Gabriel Kahn, 'Invisible Supplier Has Penney's Shirts All Buttoned Up', *Wall Street Journal*, 11 September 2003, pp. A1, A9; William Armbruster, 'SARS War Not Hurting JC Penney Shipping', *Journal of Commerce Online*, 3 April 2003.

9. Quoted in Margo Cohen, 'IKEA Expects Vietnam Business, with Its Cheap Supplies, to Surge', *Wall Street Journal*, 24 September 2003, p. B13E.

10. Kanji Ishibashi, 'Sony Will Slash Parts List, in Bid to Boost Margins', *Wall Street Journal*, 7 October 2003, p. B5; Bolaji Ojo, 'Sony, Matsushita Slash Supply Base to Cut Costs', *EBN*, 25 August 2003, p. 1.

11. Erik Portanger, 'Royal Bank's Road to Riches: Stay Divided, Conquer', *Wall Street Journal*, 23 September 2003, pp. A1, A10.

12. Quoted in Chris Wright, 'Renault Kills Plan for Premier Dealers', *Automotive News Europe*, 30 June 2003, p. 5.

13. 'Imports Are Landing German Fleet Sales', *Automotive News Europe*, 25 August 2003, p. 8; Wright, 'Renault Kills Plan for Premier Dealers'.

14. Quoted in 'Reckitt Benckiser Does "Right Thing" for Chains', *Chain Drug Review*, 7 April 2003, pp. 9ff.

15. Susan Kitchens, 'New Life in the Labels', *Forbes Global*, 21 July 2003, p. 49.

16. Quoted in Elaine Watson, 'Small Drops, Big Money', *Grocer*, 19 July 2003, pp. 45ff.

17. Cora Daniels, 'Mr. Coffee', *Fortune*, 14 April 2003, pp. 139–40.

18. Quoted in Nick Wingfield, 'A Web Giant Tries to Boost Profits by Taking on Tenants', *Wall Street Journal*, 24 September 2003, pp. A1, A10.

19. Quoted in Wingfield, 'A Web Giant Tries to Boost Profits by Taking on Tenants'.

20. Brent Haight, 'The Perils of Supply Chain Management', *Automotive Industries*, August 2003, pp. 24+.

21. David Maloney, 'What Drives BMW', *Modern Materials Handling*, August 2003, pp. 20ff.

22. Matthew Boyle, 'Wal-Mart Keeps the Change', *Fortune*, 10 November 2003, p. 46; Lucien Joppen, 'Getting Results with Tags', *Food Engineering & Ingredients*, August 2003, pp. 36ff; James Covert and Christina Cheddar Berk, 'Tracking Chips Stir Privacy Concerns', *Wall Street Journal*, 29 July 2003, pp. 1ff.; Gerry Khermouch and Heather Green, 'Bar Codes Better Watch Their Backs', *Business Week*, 14 July 2003, p. 42.

23. 'Distributors Look to "Crystal Balls"', *Information Week*, 22 September 2003, n.p.

24. Ibid.

25. 'A Moving Story', *The Economist*, 7 December 2002, pp. 65–6.

26. Henry C. Calhoun, 'D/C Growing Pains', *World Trade*, September 2003, pp. 26ff.

27. Moon Ihlwan, 'Monsters on the High Seas', *Business Week*, 13 October 2003, p. 58.

28. Daniel Machalaba and Christopher J. Chipello, 'Back on Track: Left for Dead, Railroads Revive by Watching Clock', *Wall Street Journal*, 25 July 2003, pp. A1, A16.

29. Bob Trebilcock, 'Makeover Story', *Modern Materials Handling*, November 2002, pp. 16ff.

30. Based on information from Anthony Bianco and Wendy Zellner, 'Is Wal-Mart Too Powerful?' *Business Week*, 6 October 2003, pp. 102–10; Mike Troy, 'Logistics Still Cornerstone of Competitive Advantage', *DSN Retailing Today*, 9 June 2003, pp. 209ff.; Michael Garry and Sarah Mulholland, 'Master of Its Supply Chain', *Supermarket News*, 2 December 2002, pp. 55ff.; Jerry Useem, 'One Nation Under Wal-Mart', *Fortune*, 3 March 2003, pp. 63–76.

8

Developing price strategy

Comprehension outcomes

After studying this chapter, you will be able to:

- Explain how customers' perceptions of value affect price decisions
- Identify the external and internal influences on price strategy
- Contrast the two approaches to new product pricing
- Discuss how marketers can adapt prices

Application outcomes

After studying this chapter, you will be able to:

- Understand a product's value from the customer's perspective
- Identify and analyse applicable influences on price strategy
- Set appropriate pricing objectives
- Make planning decisions about the pricing of new and existing products

OPENING CASE: PRICE BATTLE BREWING IN BEER

Pricing has become a prime marketing-mix strategy for beer industry giants SABMiller, Heineken and Interbrew as they contend for market share and fend off challenges from other alcoholic beverages and from speciality beers. In the United Kingdom, for example, the four largest brewing companies account for 80 per cent of the market's beer sales. The overall market is growing, but slowly, so breweries see price discounting as a way to quickly capture share from competitors and build sales volume.

Channel strategy is another factor affecting beer pricing. Many retailers like to price beer low to attract shoppers, especially during peak sales periods such as the year-end holiday season. As a result, customers are paying less for the most popular beer brands, which in turn squeezes margins for channel members and producers alike. Not long ago, Andy Carling, Somerfield's beer buyer, explained that the grocery retailer felt compelled to reduce its pre-Christmas price on a 24-pack of Carlsberg beer because other retailers featured low prices on competing brands. 'We are always being criticised for this type of pricing activity but in my opinion criticism should be shared by the brewers', he noted.[1] 'We are in a market where you have to be ultra competitive to sell beer and it's down to the leading brands to cap their sales forecasts and say that they don't want the volume.'[2]

What do the brewers think? The managing director of Scottish Courage Brands has called for more price stability over the long term. An Interbrew manager says, 'You can't demonise promotions because they are part of the retail mix, but the balance is wrong at the moment.'[3] And what do customers think? Research indicates that about half of the consumers who buy beer, wine and liquor base their decisions on bargain prices; yet when a store has no more stock of a brand being promoted, most consumers will buy another brand.

Pricing for speciality beers, however, works differently. 'Consumers have positive perceptions of speciality brews', observes Interbrew's marketing manager for speciality brews. Therefore, she says, these beers 'are never sold on promotion because they are seen as value, premium products'. Sainsbury's category buyer for beer agrees, saying that the grocery chain 'won't have speciality beers on promotion because the category's not really about price'.[4] A bottle of a speciality beer such as Duvel, made by Belgium's Duvel Moortgat, can sell for twice the price of more mainstream beers – and return a handsome profit margin, as well.[5]

CHAPTER PREVIEW

As the opening case shows, price can be used to achieve such marketing objectives as increasing market share, attracting shoppers, supporting differentiation and strengthening competitive position. It is also the key to achieving financial objectives such as sales and profitability targets. The organisation spends money on other parts of the marketing mix but actually brings in money on the price of a good or service. Nonetheless, ultimately it is the consumer or business customer who determines whether the price of an offer represents real value. Beer connoisseurs discern a difference between speciality beers and the larger-volume mainstream brands – and they value the difference enough to pay more for the speciality beers.

This chapter begins with a discussion of how customers perceive value and the difference between pricing based on cost and pricing based on value. Then you will learn about the external influences on price strategy, including customers, market and demand, competition, channel members and legal, regulatory and ethical considerations. Next comes an examination of internal influences on pricing, which include objectives, costs, targeting and positioning, product decisions and life cycle and other marketing mix decisions. The last section discusses specific pricing decisions, including the use of pricing objectives, pricing new products, pricing multiple products and adapting prices. *As you read, think about how these pricing principles and activities can be combined with other strategies and decisions to achieve your marketing plan's objectives and satisfy your customers.*

UNDERSTANDING PRICE AND VALUE

Whether the price is a pound sterling, a euro or a litre of milk, customers will buy only when they perceive value – when a product's perceived benefits in meeting their needs outweigh the perceived price. Even when the price is collected in barter, customers will not complete a transaction if they perceive insufficient value. Customers in a village near Delhi have little cash but perceive enough value in making a mobile phone call that they pay in milk, wheat or other commodities.[6]

As shown in the opening case, the people who buy Duvel beer perceive its value in delivering tangible benefits such as superior taste and intangible benefits such as status. Could the company sell more beer by lowering the price? Perhaps, but this would change the way people perceive the brand's status and change the value they attach to the product's total benefits. Thus, you cannot develop an effective price strategy without a clear understanding of how your customers perceive your product's value.

Perceptions of value

Customers perceive value in a product according to the total package of benefits they receive. An individual customer may consider one benefit more important than the others, but the combination of all benefits is what delivers value.

Moreover, customers form perceptions in the context of competing or substitute products that might meet their needs. Even if customers perceive that Duvel beer provides the benefit of status, for example, they may not buy it if they perceive that another brand tastes significantly better.

In general, customers perceive value on the basis of benefits such as:

- *Performance*. Does the product perform as it should in meeting the customer's needs? Does the product enable customers to complete certain tasks more effectively or efficiently? Does it perform better than competing products?

- *Features*. Does the product have all the features expected or desired to meet the customer's needs? How do the features compare with those of competing products? Are the features suitable for meeting future needs or unspoken needs as well as current needs?

- *Quality*. Is the product free from defects? Is it reliable and durable? Is it made better than competing products? Does it deliver more benefits than competing products?

- *Service*. Does the service meet customers' expectations? Is it faster, more convenient or more personalised than that offered by competitors?

- *Personal benefits*. Does the product deliver personal benefits such as status or self-expression? Does it do so more effectively than competing products?

- *Availability*. Is the product available whenever needed? Does the price change according to availability? How does this compare with that of competing products?

Against the total perceived benefits, customers weigh the total perceived costs (time and money) associated with the product, including:

- *Initial purchase price*. What must the customer spend in time and money to obtain the product initially? How does this initial purchase price compare with that of competing products?

- *Maintenance and repair costs*. What is the estimated cost of maintenance during the first year? How often is maintenance or repair generally required and what is the total estimated cost over the life of the product? How much time or money might the customer lose in waiting for repairs or maintenance?

- *Ongoing fees*. Does the good or service require an annual usage charge or other fees that apply after the initial purchase? Does the customer have to pay a tax periodically to continue using or possessing the product?

- *Installation*. Does the product require installation? What is the cost in time and money for installing this product compared with competing products?

- *Training*. Do customers need training to use the product properly? What is the cost in time and money for this product's training compared with that for competing products?

- *Ancillary products*. Does the product require the purchase of ancillary products, and at what cost? How does this compare with competing products?

- *Financing*. If applicable, what is the total cost of financing the purchase of this product, what is the monthly payment (if any) and how do finance costs compare with those of competing products?

Pricing based on value

Through research, you can determine how customers in the targeted segment perceive the value of your product's total benefits and costs and the value of competing products. Then you can use this understanding of the customer's perspective to formulate price strategy and influence product cost and design (*see* Figure 8.1a). This is not the way marketers have traditionally formulated price strategy. In the past, most started with the product and its cost, developed a price strategy to cover costs and then looked for ways to communicate value to customer (*see* Figure 8.1b).[7]

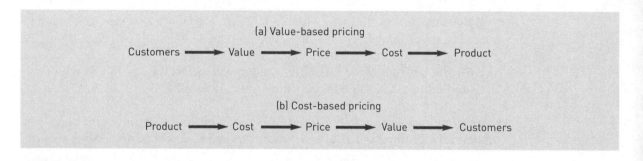

| FIGURE 8.1 | Value-based pricing compared with cost-based pricing |

Source: Adapted from Thomas T. Nagle and Reed K. Holden, *The Strategy and Tactics of Pricing*, 3rd edn (Upper Saddle River, NJ: Prentice Hall, 2002), p. 4.

Customers' perceptions of value influence their buying behaviour – and these perceptions are not always in line with the way you have positioned your product or view its benefits. If your customers believe your product is not worth the price – or believe that a competing product offers more value – they will buy something else unless you lower your price or enhance the product's benefits. Consider the pricing experiences of marketers at Hindustan Lever, a Unilever unit in India.

MARKETING IN PRACTICE: HINDUSTAN LEVER

Concerned about pricing levels for their products, marketers for Hindustan Lever set out to study their customers' needs and value perceptions. They also researched what rivals were charging for competing products. On the basis of this research, the marketers reworked their prices, costs and products in line with the value that research showed customers expected. Not only did Hindustan Lever introduce smaller packages of branded products such as Sunsilk shampoo (containing just enough product for one use or a few uses), it set correspondingly small prices. Customers responded enthusiastically, and soon these products were contributing half of the company's revenues in India.

Even though the prices were lower because the packages were smaller, Hindustan Lever was able to price at a premium because customers perceived its branded products as delivering higher value. Over time, the company made more product improvements to lower costs and prices, as when it applied new technology to manufacture Breeze soap more efficiently. Other improvements increased benefits, as when the company developed the low-sudsing detergent Surf Excel. In some categories, however, the price premium over local brands became so pronounced that Hindustan Lever's marketers re-examined customers' value perceptions and then decided to cut prices on selected products to retain market share. Hindustan Lever's director of finance observed, 'We are here to sustain a brand and a relationship with our consumers for the long term.'[8]

Illustrating the trend toward value-based pricing, the furniture retailer IKEA starts by identifying a customer problem, such as the need for affordable, stylish, smaller-size furniture suitable for entertaining visitors in the kitchen. After studying what competitors are doing, its marketers set a target price lower than rivals and establishes general costs and product specifications in line with the target price. Next, they consult with the suppliers who make the furniture and come to agreement on costs. Finally, they meticulously design the product, send the design to suppliers for manufacture, then pack and ship the furniture to stores as inexpensively and expeditiously as possible.[9]

ANALYSING INFLUENCES ON PRICE STRATEGY

Notice that marketers at IKEA and Hindustan Lever thought about a variety of external and internal factors as they priced their products. IKEA looked closely at customer needs and the competition (external influences) as well as costs (internal). Hindustan Lever examined customers' perceptions of value, the market and demand, and competitive pressure (external influences) plus costs, marketing plan objectives and product decisions (internal influences). The next sections explain the major external and internal influences that you should consider when developing price strategy (see Figure 8.2).

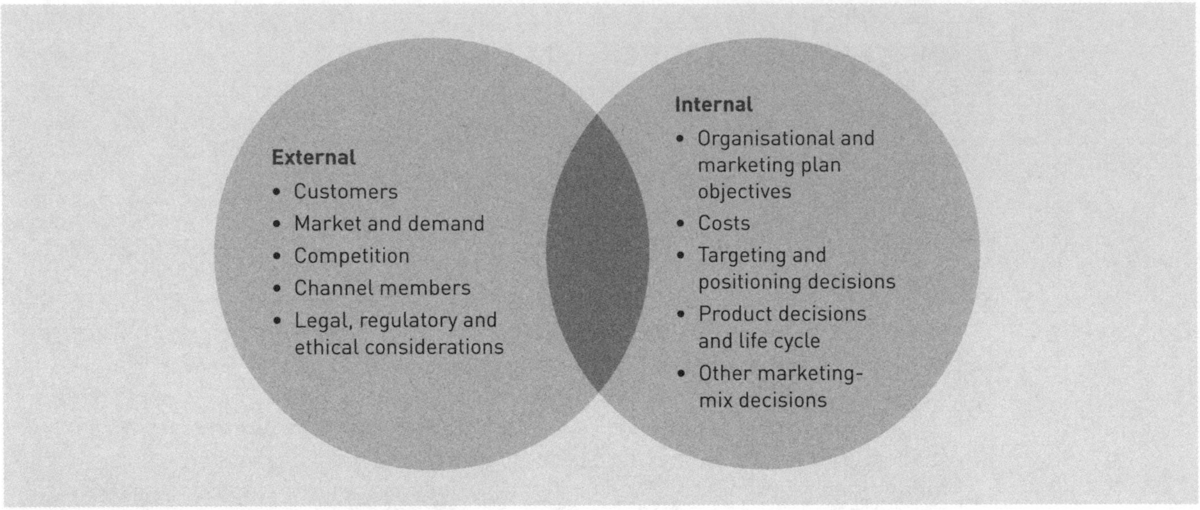

External
- Customers
- Market and demand
- Competition
- Channel members
- Legal, regulatory and ethical considerations

Internal
- Organisational and marketing plan objectives
- Costs
- Targeting and positioning decisions
- Product decisions and life cycle
- Other marketing-mix decisions

FIGURE 8.2 Influences on pricing strategy

External influences

The five major external influences on pricing include: (1) customers; (2) market and demand; (3) competition; (4) channel members; and (5) legal, regulatory and ethical considerations.

Customers

During the marketing planning process, you have to analyse how pricing affects customer behaviour. Not all customers can or want to compare prices; not all customers are interested in buying the lowest-priced alternative. Research shows that consumers will accept a price if it is within what they consider to be an acceptable range for that good or service.[10] Customers may decide against buying a product that is priced unusually low because they suspect poor quality yet be willing to spend more if a product appears to offer value-added benefits, such as a prestige brand or special service.

Business buyers in particular may feel great pressure to acquire raw materials, components or services at the lowest possible prices, which in turn affects their suppliers' pricing strategies. Some business buyers and consumers constantly switch brands or suppliers in search of perceived bargains, especially as it is now very quick and easy to compare prices using Internet sources. Your challenge as a marketer is to communicate your product's benefits so customers recognise the differentiation compared with competing products and perceive the value in relation to the price. Look at Glaxo's initial pricing for its anti-ulcer drug Zantac, introduced to compete with the highly successful Tagamet (then marketed by SmithKline Beecham). Glaxo's marketers decided to price the drug much higher than Tagamet and implemented a plan to communicate that not only was Zantac effective, but it resulted in fewer side-effects. Because doctors and patients perceived higher value in Zantac and were willing to pay more for it, Zantac soon became the market-leading anti-ulcer drug.[11]

If your product is particularly innovative or meets unspoken customer needs, you may have to go against long-established traditions of pricing and service levels. For example, Kuniyoshi Konishi, founder of Japan's QB Net barbershops, was accustomed to paying 3,000 yen or more for a traditional hour-long haircut with personal service. In a hurry during one such haircut, he wondered how many other men shared his need for speed. So he undertook marketing research to answer one question: 'Would you be interested in using a barbershop that provided only haircuts in 10 minutes for 1,000 yen?'[12] Customers responded so positively to the perceived value that Konishi opened a barbershop and, within seven years, was operating a chain of 200 shops serving more than 3.5 million customers annually. Now he is bringing the QB concept to Singapore and other parts of Asia.[13]

Market and demand

You also need to research the **demand** for your product in the target market – how many units are likely to be sold at different prices – and the effect of price sensitivity, or the **elasticity of demand**. When your research reveals **elastic demand**, a small percentage change in price will usually produce a large change in quantity demanded. On the other hand, if your research reveals **inelastic demand**, a small percentage change in price will usually produce a small percentage change in quantity demanded (*see* Figure 8.3). Note that you can actually maintain or increase revenues by raising the price when demand is inelastic or by cutting the price when demand is elastic. Still, if you price a product excessively high you risk reducing demand; price it too low and you may spark strong demand that you cannot profitably satisfy. Yet it can be difficult to research the exact elasticity of demand for a particular product, even though you can conduct pricing experiments and analyse previous sales history to get data for estimating the elasticity of demand.

Pricing decision	Inelastic demand	Elastic demand
Small decrease	Small increase in demand	Larger increase in demand
Small increase	Small decrease in demand	Larger decrease in demand

FIGURE 8.3 Pricing and elasticity of demand

Elasticity of demand can vary widely from one segment to another and one market to another. This means a pricing strategy that is effective in one segment may produce entirely different results in another. Although many marketers are wary of price-sensitive customers, some organisations successfully target this segment. The UK car-hire company easyCar, for example, sets a low daily rate to stimulate higher demand for rentals reserved far in advance. As the date and time of rental approaches and demand increases, however, the company raises its rates for rentals booked just before the rental period. Customers have limited choices (only two types of car for hire) and pay more for reservations made by phone. Even so, easyCar's prices are very competitive and its cars are on hire more than 90 per cent of the time, a productive use of company assets.[14]

Competition

Whether the product is car-hire services, beer or furniture, competition exerts a strong influence on price strategy. Customers are apt to look at the costs and benefits of competing products when thinking about value, so marketers need to be aware of what competitors are charging. And remember that it can be risky simply to imitate another organisation's price strategy for competitive reasons, because your organisation probably has very different costs, objectives and resources from those of your rival.

Should you become involved in a price war, your profit margins and prices will fall lower and lower. As an example, Colgate-Palmolive felt compelled to react when its competitor Hindustan Lever changed its price strategy in India. Hindustan Lever lowered the price of its Close-up toothpaste, introduced two smaller packages with correspondingly lower prices and introduced two smaller, low-priced packages of Pepsodent toothpaste. Colgate responded by lowering the price of several sizes of its toothpaste brands. As the price war escalated, competitors sought to keep their brand-loyal customers and attract new price-sensitive customers by offering free toothbrushes and other extras with each toothpaste purchase.[15]

Global competition is transforming pricing in a number of industries and countries. In China, Gzitic Hualing Holdings, a local appliance manufacturer, was faced with increased competition from foreign manufacturers marketing air conditioners and refrigerators at lower prices. After watching domestic prices of air conditioners and refrigerators fall by 10 per cent or more in a year and seeing the company's profit margin cut nearly in half, Gzitic Hualing's management put more emphasis on exporting appliances to fuel sales and profits.[16] The lesson: look at pricing from an industry perspective and on a market by market basis.

Not competing on price carries its own risks. For example, the German software company SAP resisted entering an industry price war even though it said it lost some orders to competitors offering lower prices. Instead, SAP is emphasising its position as the global leader in business software and its long-term stability – an important consideration for businesses installing sophisticated software – to counter price competition.[17] SAP management wants to reinforce the idea that its software is not a commodity to be bought on the basis of price alone but a clearly differentiated product with distinct benefits and value. This may or may not work for your product, however.

Your product may face price competition from products that meet customers' needs in different ways, as when travellers can choose between air travel and train travel. To illustrate, Iberia Lineas Aereas de España knows it is competing against full-price airline rivals and no-frills carriers plus high-speed train services linking Spanish cities with other destinations. Because Iberia has experience competing against bargain-priced charter flights, it knows how to communicate the benefits and the value its pricing represents. And the threat of train travel as a substitute for air travel is prompting some airlines to change the way they price flights. SkyTeam, an alliance of six airlines, is competing with the Eurail Pass by offering flat prices for travel within five specific European zones.[18] What substitutes might your customers choose to meet their needs, and how do these choices affect your pricing decisions?

Channel members

When making channel arrangements, you must ensure that wholesalers and retailers can buy at a price that will allow profitable resale to business customers or consumers. Channel members have to be able to cover the costs they incur in processing customer orders, repackaging bulk shipment lots into customer-size lots, product storage and other operations. To make this work, you have to think carefully about the costs and profit margins of all channel participants, along with the price perceptions of the targeted customer segment, when setting your product's price.

Even your choice of intermediaries depends on your product's price. If you market high-quality, high-priced products, you will have difficulty reaching your targeted segment through intermediaries known for stocking low-quality, low-priced products. If you market lower-quality, low-priced products, upmarket channel members will not stock your products because of the mismatch with their target market. In short, carefully coordinate your channel decisions with your price decisions.

Legal, regulatory and ethical considerations

You will have to abide by local, national and regional laws and regulations when pricing your products. Among the issues are:

- *Price controls and price fixing.* Some countries control the prices of products such as prescription drugs, which limits pricing choices. Some areas also forbid the use of price fixing and other actions considered anti-competitive. For example, the European Commission recently announced that a German company and three Japanese companies would be fined for price fixing of food preservatives.[19]

- *Resale maintenance*. Companies in the United Kingdom, the United States and some other nations are generally not allowed to insist that channel members maintain a certain minimum price on their products. This paves the way for more competition and reinforces the need to consider pricing throughout the channel.

- *Industry regulation*. Government regulators can affect pricing in some industries by allowing or blocking the sale of certain products or product bundles, as Taiwan has the power to do in the cable television industry.[20]

- *Government requirements*. Legal and regulatory actions can affect pricing by mandating product standards, tests or labelling; these requirements add to the costs that you will seek to recoup through product pricing.

- *Taxes and tariffs*. Prices for products sold in certain countries must include value-added tax (VAT) or sales taxes, which vary from nation to nation. In addition, import tariffs also raise the price that customers pay for some products. As a result, imported products may not be as competitively priced as domestic products, or customers may be inclined to seek lower prices by buying in another country.

Going beyond legal and regulatory guidelines, marketers must look at the ethical implications of their pricing decisions. For example, is an airline or bank acting ethically when it promotes a special price without fully and prominently explaining any restrictions and extra fees? Is a pharmaceutical manufacturer acting ethically when it sets high prices for a life-saving drug that patients in some areas cannot afford? As challenging as such issues may be, building a reputation for ethical pricing ultimately enhances your brand's image and reinforces long-term customer loyalty.

Internal influences

Your pricing decisions will be affected by five major internal influences: (1) organisational and marketing plan objectives; (2) costs; (3) targeting and positioning; (4) product decisions and life cycle; and (5) other marketing-mix decisions.

Organisational and marketing plan objectives

Price and every other marketing-mix strategy must tie back to the objectives of the organisation and the marketing plan. Because price generates revenue, it is a particularly important ingredient for achieving sales and profitability targets. Price also brings in money for meeting societal objectives and, in some cases, may directly incorporate a charitable donation. If growth and market share are your key objectives, you might lower the product's price and reduce its perceived benefits or develop an entirely new product with fewer benefits that can be marketed at a lower price. Or you might develop a new product designed to sell for less as a way of meeting customer needs, as Nokia management did by creating basic handsets for first-time mobile phone customers in India and other markets.[21] Figure 8.4 shows eight pricing options that can help balance market share, revenue and profitability objectives.

Strategic options	Reasoning	Consequences
1. Maintain price and perceived quality Engage in selective customer pruning	Firm has higher customer loyalty. It is willing to lose poorer customers to competitors	Smaller market share. Lowered profitability
2. Raise price and perceived quality	Raise price to cover rising costs Improve quality to justify higher prices	Smaller market share. Maintained profitability
3. Maintain price and raise perceived quality	It is cheaper to maintain price and raise perceived quality	Smaller market share. Short-term decline in profitability. Long-term increase in profitability
4. Cut price partly and raise perceived quality	Must give customers some price reduction but stress higher value of offer	Maintained market share. Short-term decline in profitability. Long-term maintained profitability
5. Cut price fully and maintain perceived quality	Discipline and discourage price competition	Maintained market share. Short-term decline in profitability
6. Cut price fully and reduce perceived quality	Discipline and discourage price competition and maintain profit margin	Maintained market share. Maintained margin. Reduced long-term profitability
7. Maintain price and reduce perceived quality	Cut marketing expense to combat rising costs	Smaller market share. Maintained margin. Reduced long-term profitability
8. Introduce an economy model	Give the market what it wants	Some cannibalisation but higher total volume

FIGURE 8.4   Options for pricing to balance objectives

Source: Philip Kotler, *Marketing Management*, 11th edn (Upper Saddle River, NJ: Prentice Hall, 2003), p. 496.

Sometimes you are obliged to give a particular objective more weight when establishing price strategy. Consider the situation in which profitability is your organisation's top priority, yet you cannot raise prices because of competitive or economic pressures. Some companies deal with this by reducing the amount of product in a way that effectively raises the price and yields the same or better profit margin. When the US unit of Danone, for example, reduced the amount of yoghurt in some of its containers by 25 per cent, it relabelled the packaging accordingly and cut the price by only 19 per cent. Explaining this change, the company said that 'most people prefer a 6-oz. cup of yoghurt'.[22] Can or should you do this?

Costs

Most companies price their products to at least cover costs over the long run. In the short term, however, you may be willing to price for little or no profit when establishing a new product, competing with aggressive rivals or seeking to achieve another objective. General Motors Japan, for example, has created its HydroGen3 car to gain more experience building cars that run on ecologically friendly fuel-cell energy. Being among the first to introduce such cars – initially in small numbers – entails higher costs for research and production but fulfils another objective, according to GM Japan's CEO: 'Japan is a key area for developing and positioning fuel-cell cars for commercialisation.'[23]

When you have limited control over the **variable costs** that vary with production and sales, such as the cost of raw materials and parts, you will find pricing for profit even more challenging. For example, the sweets manufacturer Hershey recently experienced an increase in cocoa costs. Although the company had not raised the price of its chocolate candy bars for years, it finally decided on an 11 per cent increase. To pave the way for customer reception of this increase, the company promoted special 'limited edition' versions of Kit-Kat and several other candy bars. The strategy worked: sales increased 3 per cent during the three months following the price hike.[24]

If you compete primarily on the basis of price, you will be particularly concerned with managing variable costs and **fixed costs** (such as rent, insurance and other business expenses, which do not vary with production and sales). This keeps prices low and protects profit margins, as illustrated by Colruyt.

Although you may have difficulty determining a product's exact costs – especially if it has not yet been launched in the marketplace – you need cost information to calculate the **breakeven point**. This is the point at which a product's revenues and costs are equal and beyond which the organisation earns more profit as more units are sold. Unless you make some change in price (which will affect demand) or variable cost, your product will not become profitable until unit volume reaches the breakeven point. The equation for this calculation is:

MARKETING IN PRACTICE: COLRUYT

Franz Colruyt, the Belgian discount food chain, looks for every possible way to min-imise costs so it can keep grocery prices low. Its 165 stores have no fancy decorations, background music or shopping bags for customers to use. Instead of spending heavily on television or newspaper advertising, Colruyt invites customers to sign up to receive notices of forthcoming sales by post. Despite already low cost levels, staff members are constantly studying procedures to improve efficiency and increase the chain's profits. Not long ago, for example, an employee found that stores could complete transactions five seconds faster if customers pay at a separate counter after their groceries are scanned. Even five seconds per shopper adds up to much higher productivity when multiplied by thousands of shoppers every week.

To ensure that its grocery prices are competitive, 15 Colruyt employees check prices at rival food stores every day. The chain also publicises a special hot-line number for customers to call if they find an item sold elsewhere for less. This reassures shoppers that Colruyt's prices are the lowest, encouraging loyalty and helping the chain meet its sales and profitability objectives.[25]

$$\text{breakeven point} = \frac{\text{total fixed costs}}{\text{unit price} - \text{variable costs per unit}}$$

If, for example, a product's total fixed costs are €100,000, and one unit's variable costs are €2, the breakeven point at a unit price of €6 is:

$$\frac{\text{€}100,000}{\text{€}6 - \text{€}2} = 25,000 \text{ units}$$

Using this breakeven point, the organisation will incur losses if it sells fewer than 25,000 units priced at €6. Above 25,000 units, however, the company can cover both variable and fixed costs and increase its profits as it sells a higher quantity. Figure 8.5 is a graphical depiction of breakeven analysis, which does not take into account any changes in demand; how competitors might respond; how customers perceive the product's value; or other external influences on pricing. Nor does breakeven analysis reflect how the cost per unit is likely to drop as you produce higher quantities, gain economies of scale and learn how to be more efficient. Still, it provides a rough approximation of the unit sales volume that you must achieve to cover costs and begin producing profit.

If you source materials from other countries or despatch to customers across national borders, you must also be aware of how currency fluctuations affect prices and costs. Heineken, for example, considers currency exchange rates when looking at the price it will charge in other markets and its costs for producing and shipping beer from the Netherlands to other countries; when exchange rates are unfavourable, Heineken's profits suffer.[26]

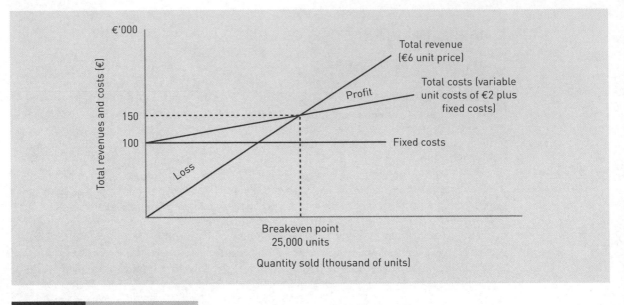

FIGURE 8.5 Breakeven analysis

Targeting and positioning

Any pricing strategy should be consistent with the targeting and positioning decisions you make during the planning process. easyCar, for example, is positioned as a low-price, no-frills car-hire company; it therefore uses a low-price strategy in targeting price-sensitive segments of the consumer and business market. Aldi, the second-largest grocery chain in Europe, also targets price-conscious consumers but positions itself as marketing good-quality products for less. In line with this targeting and positioning, the retailer sets low prices and adjusts all its activities to keep costs as low as possible.[27]

Of course, if you decide to target non-price-sensitive customer segments and position your products on the basis of high status or exceptional service you will formulate a different price strategy. To illustrate, watch companies such as Patek Philippe and Rolex differentiate their products according to high-quality and status, supported by prices that are higher than those of lower-quality watches. As another example, the UK window manufacturer Boulton & Paul targets architects, municipal housing associations and other business buyers with a positioning of high quality and durability. Every timber window is manufactured to the customer's specifications and is guaranteed for at least ten years. Buyers are therefore encouraged to look beyond the initial price of a Boulton & Paul window – which is higher than that of a non-timber window – and focus on the value compared with the total cost, including maintenance, over the window's life.[28]

Product decisions and life cycle

As you can see in Figure 8.1a, price strategy is closely intertwined with product strategy. More companies are developing new products after they have determined customers' perceptions of value, set target costs and set a target price, rather than starting the pricing process after initiating production. You may be able to demonstrate value and sell a top-quality product or one backed by a premium brand at a premium price; conversely, customers will perceive low-quality products or those under bargain brands as having less value and therefore you will be unable to sell them at high prices. Of course your pricing decisions will change during the product life cycle. As discussed below, you may start with either skim pricing or penetration pricing when launching a new product and then make changes in other stages. (See this chapter's practical marketer checklist for questions to ask in pricing during different stages in the product life cycle.)

By the time your product reaches the growth stage, where competition is increasing, you should choose pricing strategies that support more differentiation in targeted segments or pricing strategies geared to stimulating higher demand for more economies of scale and lower costs (or a combination of both).[29] As one example, BMW's Mini Cooper car remains so well differentiated in its growth stage that the company does not have to use the pricing-lowering tactics that many other carmakers employ to attract buyers in a highly competitive industry.[30]

Sales of a product in maturity will grow less rapidly even as more competitors are vying for the attention of customers, which necessitates another change in pricing strategy. Figure 8.6 shows five options, suggested by Nagle and Holden, to consider for profitable pricing in the mature stage of the life cycle. For instance, when Vodafone's Japanese subsidiary faced a mature market for mobile phone services, it sought to attract more price-sensitive customers with a steep rate cut for weekend and holiday calls between subscribers (while maintaining regular rates for weekday calls).[31] If you have a product in decline, you may have to set a low price to draw customers away from competitors or to continue improving economies of scale in an effort to lower costs and boost profits. If your competitors are already leaving the market and supplies of this type of product are particularly scarce, you might be able to maintain or raise your price in the short term.

Pricing alternatives	Purpose
Unbundle products and price individually	Compete by pricing to sell more individual products rather than fewer bundled products
Re-examine customer price sensitivity and change price accordingly	Maintain or improve revenue and profits
Set prices based on better understanding of costs and capacity	Reflect realistic costs and yield profit when demand outstrips capacity
Add related products	Leverage success of an existing product to introduce related goods or services at a profit
Change channel pricing	Expand channel coverage while reducing channel margins

FIGURE 8.6   Pricing mature products

Source: Adapted from Thomas T. Nagle and Reed K. Holden, *The Strategy and Tactics of Pricing*, 3rd edn (Upper Saddle River, NJ: Prentice Hall, 2002), pp. 189–92.

Other marketing-mix decisions

In addition to product decisions and channel arrangements, pricing is influenced by (and influences) promotion decisions. Obviously, many producers and channel members feature pricing in their promotions to attract customer attention and compete with direct rivals. The opening case in this chapter illustrated how breweries and retailers are using beer prices to attract or defend market share and to combat competitors. Discount retailers such as Asda and many online retailers rely on promotions based on price as a primary competitive strategy. Although marketers of luxury products may not make price as visible a part of the promotion strategy, their pricing strategy will be affected by the benefits and value they choose to communicate in promotions.

Coordinating pricing in the context of personal selling could be particularly challenging when you allow sales representatives to negotiate with customers. To prevent erosion of profit margins, companies such as Roche, the Swiss pharmaceutical firm, have given representatives sophisticated pricing models so they can quote prices that are within acceptable profitability levels.[32] Thus, you must look closely at the interaction of all marketing-mix strategies and coordinate carefully when making decisions about how to price a product.

MAKING PRICING DECISIONS

Once you understand the external and internal influences on pricing, you then set pricing objectives for the period covered by the marketing plan. If your product is new, you will decide between skim pricing and penetration pricing. As your product line expands, you will face decisions about pricing multiple products. If appropriate, you may plan to adapt your product's price in some way or participate in auction pricing.

Setting pricing objectives

Your objectives for pricing strategy will be based on your organisation's objectives and those of the marketing plan. There are three categories of pricing objectives:

- *Financial objectives for pricing*. You may seek to maintain or improve profits; maintain or improve revenues; reach the breakeven point by a certain date; support another product's revenues and profitability; or achieve a certain return. An example of an objective in this category might be: Through pricing, to achieve a gross profit margin of 15 per cent on full-year sales of Product A.

- *Marketing objectives for pricing*. Here, you set relationship targets for pricing that will attract or retain customers; build or defend market share; build or change channel relations; or build brand image, awareness and loyalty. An example of an objective in this category might be: Through pricing, to attract 10 per cent more customers for Product B during the first quarter.

- *Societal objectives for pricing*. In this category, you may set targets for covering the cost of using ecologically friendly materials and processes; providing reverse channels for recycling; generating cash for charitable contributions or worthy causes; or achieving non-business objectives. 'Fair trade' coffee certified by the Rainforest Alliance, for instance, is priced slightly higher to return more profit to small coffee growers using sustainable farming methods.[33] One example of a societal objective for pricing might be: Through pricing, to generate €50,000 within six months for donation to humanitarian causes.

A growing number of cities are setting the societal objective of pricing to manage traffic congestion.

MARKETING IN ACTION: PRICING FOR ROAD ACCESS

Pricing for road access has become a successful strategy for cities that want to reduce traffic jams and pollution. Central London roads, for example, were clogged with cars until the city set a pricing objective of reducing congestion and implemented it by levying a £5 fee for entering the financial and entertainment districts during weekdays. Local residents receive a 90 per cent discount, and certain vehicles (such as ambulances and taxis) pay nothing. The fee was high enough to cut traffic by 20 per cent, increase the average speed during peak times and pay for public transportation improvements.

Trondheim, Norway, and San Diego, California, have the same objective but different strategies. By varying its road charges by time of day, Trondheim has reduced traffic by almost 10 per cent. San Diego allows vehicles carrying two or people to travel in fast lanes for free but varies its fee for single-occupancy cars according to current traffic conditions. Drivers who take the San Diego fast lanes are willing to pay the price to cut an average of eight minutes from their journey to the city centre. Other cities are experimenting with road access pricing to unchoke crowded highways or manage city-centre traffic during peak periods, as well.[34]

Many companies use pricing for the marketing objective of building a certain brand image. Vertu, a division of Nokia, sells a line of expensive mobile phone handsets that are both chic and functional. The handsets are positioned as upmarket fashion accessories for celebrities and other wealthy customers, with a special service component. Users can reach Vertu's concierge staff with one button and request help (in five languages) with restaurant reservations, airline tickets and other arrangements anywhere in the world. Vertu prices the handsets high (at €3,000 and up) to enhance the brand image. Similarly, when Ferrari targets the niche segment of sports car collectors, it reinforces the image of exclusivity with pricing as well as through performance and limited production.[35]

Pricing new products

A new product presents a special pricing challenge because you must decide whether to use **penetration pricing** and price relatively low for rapid acquisition of market share or use **skim pricing**, setting a relatively high price to make an upmarket impression on selected customer segments that are less price-sensitive and value innovation. With penetration pricing, you are seeking to penetrate the market and build sales as quickly as possible. Telekomunikasi Indonesia recently used penetration pricing to introduce new international calling plans based on Internet technology. The first plan was priced 60 per cent below that of its main rival, but customers did not sign up as quickly as expected because they had to grapple with dialling a long access code for each call. When the company introduced a second plan requiring only a three-digit code – at a price that was 40 per cent lower than the rival plan – customers signed up much more quickly.[36]

When you introduce a product with penetration pricing, the price may be so low that the product is unprofitable and/or priced lower than competing products. Yet such pricing may be effective in the long run, if you are determined to boost volume and gain efficiencies that will lower costs as a foundation for future profitability. Toyota, for example, introduced its Yaris subcompact car in Europe using penetration pricing. To build sales, the carmaker packed the car with extra features that enhance value perceptions and accepted smaller profit margins than it earns on luxury cars under the company's Lexus brand.[37]

However, penetration pricing is not appropriate for every product, which is where internal and external influences come into play. Your customers may perceive less value in a luxury product that is launched with penetration pricing, for example. Also, penetration pricing may be inappropriate for the kinds of channel members you need to use to reach targeted customer segments. Finally, such pricing may not be consistent with your promotion strategy.

You can consider skim pricing for innovative or top-quality products. This strategy 'skims' the maximum amount of revenue from each segment or market through high prices that reflect a perception of high value. Skim pricing is common with products employing new technology such as digital radio receivers, for example, and handheld global positioning system units, which were introduced at high prices that gradually dropped. Not only do you take in more money to help cover costs with skim pricing, you have the flexibility to lower prices as you monitor competitive response, attain volumes that yield economies of scale and shift to targeting more price-sensitive segments. On the other hand, if your initial price is too high, you may set customer expectations too high, slow initial sales and lower repeat sales if the product does not fulfil those expectations.

Pricing multiple products

Your pricing strategy should take into account more than one product in the line or mix, any optional or complementary products and any product bundles. The way you price each product sets it apart from other products in your mix, reflecting or reinforcing customer perceptions of each product's value. You can then balance prices within the product line or mix to reach your total revenue or profit objectives. As an example, price competition among lower-priced models of car may produce slimmer profits for a carmaker even as prices on upmarket vehicles boost profit margins for those products.[38] In services, a hotel company may market deluxe hotels, convention hotels and modestly priced tourist hotels, each with its own target market, pricing objectives and room rates in line with the perceived value.

You also have the choice of pricing one product to stimulate sales of optional or complementary products. The cruise company Carnival attracts passengers with low cruise prices and boosts revenues through the sale of optional goods and services such as T-shirts, golf lessons and hair styling. Higher passenger loads mean more people buying these profitable extras.[39]

As another example, Gillette, the global leader in razors, invests millions in researching shaving technology and launches a new type of razor every eight years. Promoted as providing an improved shave, each razor is priced higher than older models and its replaceable razor cartridges are priced higher as well. Knowing that users of older models may be initially not keen to trade up, Gillette slowly raises the price of cartridges for older models until the differential seems so minimal that customers have no reason not to buy the newer model. This pricing strategy enables the company to profit from purchases of both razors and replacement blades. Note that shaving products represent about 40 per cent of Gillette's annual turnover but contribute more than 70 per cent of operating profit. Sales of new razor models and blades are pushing the company's earnings ahead quarter by quarter, despite strong competition from its rival Schick.[40]

Finally, if you offer goods or services bundled into one product you must determine how to price that bundle, given the competition and customers' perceptions of the bundle's value. To illustrate, Carnival prices its cruises – including cabins and meals – as a bundle but offers extras that customers can purchase separately. Sometimes it bundles air travel from certain areas, boosting the value because the overall price is lower than buying the cruise and the airline ticket separately. One advantage of this pricing strategy is that competitors will have difficulty duplicating every aspect of a unique, specially priced bundle. If customers do not want everything in your bundle at the price set, however, they may buy fewer products individually or look at competitive bundles. And later in a product's life cycle, you may get more benefit by unbundling and pricing each part separately.

Adapting prices

Your price strategy should allow for adapting prices when appropriate, either by increasing perceived value or by reducing perceived cost. Depending on local laws and regulations – and the other marketing-mix strategies in the marketing plan – some ways in which you can adapt prices include:

- *Discounts*. You can plan special discounts for customers who buy in large quantities or during non-peak periods; pay in cash; or assume logistical functions such as picking up products that would otherwise be delivered.

- *Allowances*. You can invite customers to trade-in older products and receive credit toward purchases of newer products; you may also offer customers refunds or rebates for buying during promotional periods.

- *Extra value*. To encourage intermediaries to carry your products, you may offer small quantities free when resellers place orders during a promotional period. For consumers, you may temporarily increase the amount of product without increasing the price.

- *Periodic mark-downs*. Retailers, in particular, plan to mark down merchandise periodically, at the end of a selling season, to attract or reward shoppers or to stimulate new product trial. Mark-downs can help revenues and profits if planned carefully. The clothing chain Gap, for example, has improved its profit margins by using software to determine when certain items should be reduced in price and by how much.[41]

- *Segment pricing*. Depending on your segmentation decisions, your pricing can be adapted for customers of different ages (such as lower prices for children and older customers); members and non-members (such as lower prices for professional association members); different purchase locations (such as lower prices for products bought and picked up at the main plant); and time of purchase (such as lower prices for mobile phone service during non-peak periods).

Internal or external influences may prompt you to raise or lower a product's price. For example, you can use a price cut to stimulate higher demand or defend against competitive price reductions. You may want to use a price increase to deal with rising costs or product improvements that raise perceived quality and value. Whether such price adaptations achieve their objectives will depend on customer and competitor reaction.

Although you will usually fix most prices, the final price for a product is some times reached by negotiation with customers, as in the way consumers buy cars or airlines buy jet planes. And more organisations and consumers are allowing prices to be set through online auctions and reverse auctions. In most online (English) auctions, prospective buyers compete by submitting higher and higher bids as the auction continues; at the end, the highest bidder makes the purchase at that price. QXL.com operates online auctions for a wide variety of consumer and business products, from electronics to real estate; Thistle Hotels invite bids for hotel deals around the United Kingdom. In online reverse auctions, consumers or organisations post prices for products they wish to purchase and suppliers have the choice of selling at those prices. Why set prices via auctions? It can be a good way to market excess or out-of-date stock to price-sensitive customers without affecting the fixed price set for other segments.

CHAPTER SUMMARY

1. *Explain how customers' perceptions of value affect price decisions.*
   Customers perceive a product's value according to the total benefits they receive weighed against the total costs and in the context of competitive products and prices. Marketers must therefore research how customers perceive the value of their product and the value of competing products. With this knowledge of customer perceptions, marketers can work backward from the perceived value to make price, cost and product decisions.

2. *Identify the external and internal influences on price strategy.*
   External influences on pricing are: customers; market and demand; competition; channel members; and legal, regulatory and ethical considerations. Internal influences on pricing are: organisational and marketing plan objectives; costs; targeting and positioning; product decisions and life cycle; and other marketing-mix decisions.

3. *Contrast the two approaches to new product pricing.*
   One approach to pricing a new product is penetration pricing. With this strategy, the product is priced relatively low to penetrate the market and rapidly acquire market share. A second approach is skim pricing, which entails setting a relatively high price to make an upmarket impression on customers who are less price-sensitive and who value innovation. Market share builds more slowly with this strategy but marketers have flexibility to lower the price for competitive reasons, to build volume and to target progressively more price-sensitive segments.

4. *Discuss how marketers can adapt prices.*
   Depending on local laws and regulations, marketers can adapt prices using discounts, allowances, extra value, periodic mark-downs or segment pricing. They can also raise or lower prices according to internal or external influences; negotiate prices; or use online or reverse auctions to price products.

KEY TERM DEFINITIONS

breakeven point Point at which a product's revenues and costs are equal and beyond which the product earns increasingly higher levels of profit as more units are sold

demand How many units of a particular product will be sold at certain prices

elastic demand Relationship between change in quantity demanded and change in price, in which a small percentage change in price produces a large percentage change in demand

elasticity of demand How demand changes when a product's price changes

fixed costs Business costs such as rent and insurance that do not vary with production and sales

inelastic demand Relationship between change in quantity demanded and change in price, in which a small percentage change in price produces a small percentage change in demand

penetration pricing New product pricing strategy that aims for rapid acquisition of market share

skim pricing New product pricing strategy that aims to make an upmarket impression on certain customer segments that are less price-sensitive and value innovative products

variable costs Costs for supplies and other materials, which vary with production and sales

THE PRACTICAL MARKETER CHECKLIST NO. 8: PRICING THROUGH THE PRODUCT LIFE CYCLE

During introduction

How can pricing be used to encourage channel acceptance of a new product?

What pricing approach will stimulate product trial among targeted customers?

What pricing approach will encourage repeat purchasing?

What balance of price, quality and service will appeal to customers while yielding long-term financial returns?

How can pricing be used to support other marketing-mix decisions?

How can pricing be used to manage initial supply and demand?

During growth

How can pricing be used to compete with rival products entering the market?

What pricing approach will recoup costs, achieve breakeven and lead to profitability?

How can price changes and adjustments be used to keep sales growing and achieve higher market share?

During maturity

How can pricing be used to reinforce customer loyalty?

How can pricing be used to defend market share?

How can pricing be applied to unbundled parts of the product or to related products?

What pricing approach will achieve sustained profitability and other financial objectives?

What pricing approach will support a channel strategy of expanded product availability?

What changes in quality or service will add customer value or lower organisational costs?

During decline

What pricing approach can be used to slow or possibly reverse a product's decline?

How can pricing be used to increase market share profitably as competitors withdraw?

How can pricing be used to wring more profit from or minimise the profit-eroding effect of lower unit sales?

How can pricing be used to support the removal of a product from the market?

Source: Adapted from Thomas T. Nagle and Reed K. Holden, *The Strategy and Tactics of Pricing*, 3rd edn (Upper Saddle River, NJ: Prentice Hall, 2002), Chapter 7; Philip Kotler, *Marketing Management*, 11th edn (Upper Saddle River, NJ: Prentice Hall, 2002), Chapter 16.

ONLINE RESOURCES

Pricing

- European Commission Urban Transport Pricing (www.transport-pricing.net) – Provides information about the financial, political and social issues of road pricing projects being studied in Europe.

- Biz/Ed (www.bized.ac.uk/virtual/vla) – From the Institute for Learning and Research Technology at University of Bristol, presents a variety of simulations to show the effect of different assumptions and conditions on pricing.

- Freeserve (http://auctions.freeserve.com/Scripts/glossary.asp) and eBay (http://pages.ebay.co.uk/help/basics/g-index.html) – Feature glossaries with definitions of online auction terms, plus links to information about these popular auction sites.

QUESTIONS FOR DISCUSSION AND ANALYSIS

1. Under what circumstances might penetration pricing hurt a product's long-term sales?

2. Should an organisation always post the prices of its products on its publicly available website?

3. Why would an organisation agree to a price proposed in a reverse auction conducted by a large manufacturer, rather than set a fixed price?

APPLY YOUR KNOWLEDGE

Choose a particular business product (such as a tractor or specialised software) and research the marketer's price strategy.

- What benefits does this product appear to offer to business customers?

- What initial and ongoing costs would business customers perceive in connection with buying and maintaining this product?

- If the product is new, what pricing strategy is the company using to launch it? Why is this pricing approach appropriate for the product?

- How does the price reflect the product's positioning and other marketing-mix decisions?

- How does the price of one competing or substitute product appear to reflect that product's value (from the customer's perspective)? If you were a customer, would you place a higher value on this competing product than on the product you have been researching? Why?

- Prepare a brief oral or written report summarising your comments.

BUILD YOUR OWN MARKETING PLAN

Continue developing your marketing plan by making pricing decisions about a new or existing product. What pricing objectives will you set for this product? If the product is new, will you use skim pricing or penetration pricing – and why? Which external influences are most important to the pricing of this product? How do internal influences affect your pricing decision for this product? If you are setting a breakeven objective, use the charting function in spreadsheet software or *Marketing Plan Pro* to portray graphically the approximate breakeven point for your product. What price will you set for this one product and in what situations would you consider adapting the price? Consider how these pricing decisions fit in with earlier decisions and with your objectives, then document them in *Marketing Plan Pro* software or in a written marketing plan.

CLOSING CASE: AMAZON.COM'S APPROACH TO PRICING

When customers can compare prices with a few clicks of the mouse, must a Web-based retailer always offer the best prices? When Amazon.com started selling books online in the United States, low prices were the major reason that shoppers tried the site and then became loyal customers. Many of its products are still priced as low as or lower than at competitive websites or traditional stores. Yet despite intense competition from online and bricks-and-mortar retailers alike, Amazon has successfully implemented some price increases over the years. According to one academic study, the company experiences a net revenue gain of 0.5 per cent when it raises prices by 1 per cent. By comparison, its arch-rival BarnesandNoble.com experiences a sales loss of 4 per cent if it raises prices by 1 per cent.

Now that Amazon's international sites (in the United Kingdom, France, Germany, Japan and Canada) carry a broader range of goods and services, its customers perceive value in the wider merchandise assortment and in the convenience of easy, quick transactions. They also benefit from Amazon's personalised product recommendations, customer reviews and links to related or complementary products. One of the biggest pricing decisions Amazon has made is to offer free delivery on the purchase of selected products that total at least £25 (on the UK site), €20 (on the French site) or $25 (on the US site). Although customers wait a little longer for orders that come with free delivery, many of the site's 33 million customers are willing to put up with the delay in order to save money.

Amazon likes to promote sizeable discounts on highly visible products. In anticipation of the US release of *Harry Potter and the Order of the Phoenix*, for example, the retailer promoted a 40 per cent discount on the book's price and special pricing for overnight deliveries. Setting a sales record, Amazon took orders for 1.4 million copies – and broke even on the price promotion.

These days, Amazon also makes money by acting as a channel partner for businesses and consumers that want to sell their wares online. The company provides links to some featured 'store' pages on its site and also displays the prices offered by participating retailers and sellers when customers search the site for a particular product. This is such a promising opportunity that Amazon has formed a business unit to provide more e-commerce services to other businesses and is developing a shopping search function for comparing products and prices online. Watch for more revenue growth ahead as Amazon enhances the value that its e-commerce customers and retail customers perceive in the company's products and pricing.[42]

Case questions

1. How would you explain the academic study's finding that a 1 per cent price increase yields Amazon a small revenue gain even though BarnesandNoble.com loses sales?

2. As a profit-seeking enterprise, why would Amazon settle for merely breaking even on a big price promotion?

 ENDNOTES

1. Quoted in Rosie Davenport, 'Somerfield Says Brewers Must Share Flak', *Grocer*, 18 January 2003, pp. 64ff.

2. Quoted in Rosie Davenport, 'Why Beer Is Pulling its Punches', *Grocer*, 12 July 2003, pp. 43ff.

3. Quoted in Davenport, 'Somerfield Says Brewers Must Share Flak'.

4. Preceding quotes in 'Great Escape from Pricing Pressures', *Grocer*, 12 July 2003, p. 46.

5. Based on information from Steve de Bonvoisinj, 'Loyal Customers Boost Duvel Profits', *Wall Street Journal*, 1 October 2003, p. B6B; 'Great Escape from Pricing Pressures'; Davenport, 'Why Beer Is Pulling its Punches'; Edward Kuehnle, 'In Beer, Wine and Liquor, Pricing Is Only Part of the Puzzle', *MMR*, 21 April 2003, p. 36; Davenport, 'Somerfield Says Brewers Must Share Flak'.

6. Rajendra Bajpai, 'Culture', *Fortune*, 15 April 2002, p. 56.

7. This section draws on concepts in Thomas T. Nagle and Reed K. Holden, *The Strategy and Tactics of Pricing*, 3rd edn (Upper Saddle River, NJ: Prentice Hall, 2002).

8. Quoted in Aarati Krishnan and Latha Venkatraman, '"The Slowdown Is a Transient Phenomenon"', *Asia Africa Intelligence Wire*, 29 June 2003, n.p.; other sources: 'Lever-Aging Price: HLL', *Asia Africa Intelligence Wire*, 6 May 2003, n.p.; 'HLL Patents Low-Cost Knowhow', *Asia Africa Intelligence Wire*, 28 April 2003, n.p.; Manjeet Kripalani and Pete Engardio, 'Small Is Profitable', *Business Week*, 26 August 2002, pp. 112–14.

9. Lisa Margonelli, 'How Ikea Designs Its Sexy Price Tags', *Business 2.0*, October 2002, pp. 106–12.

10. Wayne D. Hoyer and Deborah J. MacInnis, *Consumer Behaviour*, 3rd edn (Boston: Houghton Mifflin, 2004), p. 262.

11. Simon London, 'The Real Value in Setting the Right Price', *Financial Times*, 10 September 2003, www.ft.com.

12. Quoted in Jim Hawe, 'A New Style', *Wall Street Journal*, 22 September 2003, pp. R3, R7.

13. Hawe, 'A New Style'.

14. David Kirkpatrick, 'How to Erase the Middleman in One Easy Lesson', *Fortune*, 17 March 2003, p. 122; Scott Kirsner, 'Stelios Makes Growth Look Easy', *Fast Company*, November 2002, pp. 98ff.

15. 'Price War Rages: HLL Acts, Colgate Reacts', *Asia Africa Intelligence Wire*, 7 May 2003, n.p.

16. 'Gzitic Hualing Sinks into the Red as Price War Rages', *Asia Africa Intelligence Wire*, 17 April 2003, n.p.

17. 'SAP Faces Fierce Price Competition', *Europe Intelligence Wire*, 30 September 2003, n.p.

18. Mark Beresford, 'Trains, Low-Cost Airlines Likely to Put Squeeze on Iberia's Profit', *Wall Street Journal*, 3 September 2003, p. 1; 'Air Cheapo in Europe', *Business Week*, 26 May 2003, p. 107.

19. Mary Watkins, 'Celanese Warns of Loss Following Hoechst Fine', *Financial Times*, 6 October 2003, www.ft.com.

20. 'GIO Gives MSOs a Nasty Surprise on Premium Pricing', *Asiacom*, 21 January 2003, p. 2.

21. Leo Magno, 'Nokia Launches Entry-Level Phones for New Growth Markets', *Asia Africa Intelligence Wire*, 1 September 2003, n.p.

22. Sora Song, 'The Shrink Rap', *Time*, 2 June 2003, p. 81.

23. Irene M. Kunii, 'Japan's Power Play', *Business Week*, 13 October 2003, p. 90.

24. Michael V. Copeland, 'Hits & Misses: Lemons to "Limited Edition" Lemonade', *Business 2.0*, September 2003, p. 92.

25. Dan Bilefsky, 'Making the Cuts', *Wall Street Journal*, 22 September 2003, pp. R3, R7.

26. Dan Bilefsky, 'Heineken Brews Plans for Comeback in U.S.', *Wall Street Journal*, 27 May 2003, www.wsj.com.

27. David McHugh, 'German Chain Gives Wal-Mart a Rough Ride', *News-Times* (Danbury, CT), 14 August 2002, p. D5.

28. Stephen Powney, 'Striving for the Perfect Finish', *Timber & Wood Products*, 3 May 2003, pp. S8ff.

29. This section draws on concepts in Thomas T. Nagle and Reed K. Holden, *The Strategy and Tactics of Pricing*, 3rd edn (Upper Saddle River, NJ: Prentice Hall, 2002).

30. John Tagliabue, 'A Tale of 2 Carmakers and 2 Countries', *New York Times*, 16 May 2003, pp. W1ff.

31. Michiyo Nakamoto, 'J-Phone Rings Changes to Keep Callers Engaged', *Financial Times*, 20 September 2003, www.ft.com.

32. 'The Price Is Wrong', *The Economist*, 25 May 2002, pp. 59–60.

33. 'Kraft Foods to Sell Fair-Trade Coffee in Boon to Growers', *Wall Street Journal*, 8 October 2003, p. B2.

34. 'London Traffic Starts to See Benefits of Toll Levied on Motorists', *Wall Street Journal*, 6 May 2003, p. 1; 'Ken Livingstone's Gamble', *The Economist*, 15 February 2003, pp. 51–3.

35. 'The Origins of Vertu', *The Economist*, 22 February 2003, pp. 62–3; Dan Neil, 'Ferrari's Latest Toy Goes for a Cool $675,000', *New York Times*, 26 January 2003, sec. 3, p. 10.

36. Michael Shari, 'Telkom: Reaching Out Over the Net', *Business Week*, 23 June 2003, p. 85.

37. 'The Asian Invasion Picks Up Speed', *Business Week*, 6 October 2003, pp. 62–4.

38. Gail Edmondson, 'Classy Cars', *Business Week*, 24 March 2003, pp. 62–6.

39. Julia Boorstin, 'Cruising for a Bruising?', *Fortune*, 9 June 2003, pp. 142–50.

40. 'Gillette Hits Mach 4', *Business Week*, 17 November 2003, p. 52; Charles Forelle, 'Schick Puts a Nick in Gillette's Razor Cycle', *Wall Street Journal*, 3 October 2003, p. B7; Claudia H. Deutsch, 'For Mighty Gillette, There Are the Faces of War', *New York Times*, 12 October 2003, sec. 3, pp. 1, 11.

41. London, 'The Real Value in Setting the Right Price'.

42. Based on information from 'Jeff Bezos, Amazon.com', *Business Week*, 29 September 2003, p. 118; Matt Marshall, 'Amazon Builds Shopping Search Company', *San Jose Mercury News*, 26 September 2003, www.mercurynews.com; Virginia Postrel, 'When It Comes to Books, Internet Selling Has Not Led to Uniformly Low Prices', *New York Times*, 11 September 2003, p. C2; Dan Scheraga, 'Partnerships Pay Off', *Chain Store Age*, August 2003, p. 94; Ariana Eunjuna Cha, 'Amazon Narrows Loss, and Investors Respond', *Washington Post*, 23 July 2003, p. E4; Pauala L. Stepankowsky, 'Amazon's CEO Lauds Free Shipping', *Wall Street Journal*, 29 May 2003, p. B6.

9

Developing integrated marketing communication strategy

Comprehension outcomes

After studying this chapter, you will be able to:

- Explain the purpose of integrated marketing communication (IMC)

- Outline the process of planning IMC

- Discuss planning for the five major IMC tools

Application outcomes

After studying this chapter, you will be able to:

- Follow the steps in developing an IMC campaign

- Plan the use of appropriate IMC tools

OPENING CASE: ORANGE CALLS AUDIENCES USING MULTIPLE MEDIA

Using television, radio, the cinema, *The Times*, in-store promotions, online advertisements and outdoor posters, Orange is calling mobile phone customers through multiple media. Orange, owned by France Télécom, is the third-largest mobile phone service provider in Europe, a market where competitors are fighting hard for their share. Basic mobile phone services are reaching maturity and margins are dropping as rivals add pricing pressure, although higher-priced sophisticated services are still in the growth stage. Orange's CEO has set aggressive growth objectives for the coming years and is using carefully coordinated marketing communication programmes to support those objectives by retaining current subscribers, encouraging them to spend more with the company and targeting new subscribers from selected segments.

Orange often uses television advertising to reach large, diverse audiences in its target market. For example, its humorous 'Learn' television campaign (supported by newspaper advertising, outdoor posters, in-store assistance and direct mail) featured a teenager teaching adults to use mobile phone features. With the objective of encouraging current subscribers to sign up for more services, the campaign offered a three-month free trial of the data services package. According to Jeremy Dale, vice president of marketing, this campaign was 'all about demonstrating in a fun and practical way just how committed Orange and the phone trainers are to helping people get the most out of phones'.[1] After several months, research showed that a sizeable number of UK consumers were aware of the campaign; just as important, Orange stores were attracting more customers than during the same period in the previous year – and usage of the data services promoted had quadrupled.

In a break with tradition, Orange used no television during an August campaign aimed at communicating the overall value of its offer. First, Orange's agency purchased all advertising space in a Friday edition of *The Times*, an unusual move that attracted the notice of customers and the media. Next, the company put up thousands of posters outdoors and in London Underground sites to bring the value message to commuters and travellers. After two weeks, the posters were changed to show a new message, reinforced by 40-second radio advertisements on FM stations. An account director for Orange's media planning agency explained that all the messages, 'when taken together, show that Orange is the fairest network and demonstrate what it gives to its customers. It's good, it's full of impact and it has a highly PR-able use of media'.[2]

CHAPTER PREVIEW

Decisions about product, place and price ultimately must be communicated to customers and channel members. Orange's marketing plan combines advertising, free trials, mail offers, in-store sales and publicity about its campaigns. Although the television advertisements are the most visible, the company also orchestrates messages in other media and uses other promotion tools. For example, it has sent mailings offering 1,000 free text messages per year to budget-conscious teenagers who like to use SMS. To reach businesspeople, Orange has sent mailings emphasising how its services enhance productivity, a benefit valued by that audience. The company's online advertisements target travellers with messages about using the Orange phone service in other countries. Orange trains the salespeople in its stores to explain and sell both handsets and service, surrounded by promotional displays and literature echoing the theme of the latest advertising campaign. Orange is even at the cinema, using the 60-second space just before the film begins to promote its brand and remind filmgoers to turn their mobiles off.[3]

You may not want to reach millions of people or have the resources to place so many messages in so many media, but you should understand integrated marketing communication (IMC) and the five main IMC tools. First you will learn about the planning of a campaign, including: identifying the target audience; defining the objectives and the budget; considering legal, regulatory, social and ethical issues; choosing IMC tools, messages and media; and preparing for pretests and post-implementation analysis. The remaining sections in this chapter cover the highlights of planning for each IMC tool. *Reminder: your decisions about integrated marketing communication should fit in with the decisions you made earlier in the marketing planning process and the objectives you have set.*

PLANNING FOR INTEGRATED MARKETING COMMUNICATION

Integrated marketing communication (IMC) involves coordinating content and delivery of all the marketing messages in all media for an organisation, product or brand to ensure consistency and support the positioning and objectives. As a marketer, this means you have to pay careful attention to:

- *Coordinating content.* Are the words and meaning of the messages consistent with each other, with the brand image and with the product's main differentiating points? Does any message contradict any other or introduce confusion? Are the messages and media consistent with other marketing-mix strategies and with customer service?

- *Coordinating delivery.* Are messages delivered to the targeted segments in media that reach customers when and where they are receptive? Are media choices designed to foster customer receptivity, attention and interest? Is message delivery timed to increase the likelihood that customers will take the desired action? Is your organisation ready to respond when messages are delivered?

- *Supporting positioning and objectives*. Do the messages and media work together toward meeting marketing plan objectives? What specific marketing plan objectives do they support? Do any work against the positioning or the objectives to be achieved? How can results be measured to determine whether IMC programmes are working as planned?

In the opening case of this chapter, Orange had to be sure that all the messages in its 'Learn' campaign made sense separately and in combination, were consistent with the brand's image, were delivered as scheduled and supported other marketing-mix strategies. Otherwise, customers might misunderstand what Orange wanted to communicate or even be irritated by perceived contradictions. And Orange would be wasting its money if poor communication hampered its ability to pursue designated objectives.

It is important to remember that, regardless of the chosen tools, messages or media, your IMC strategy should fit in with your other marketing-mix strategies to ensure consistency and a sense of unity throughout your entire marketing plan.

Understanding IMC tools

You can plan campaigns using one or more of five major IMC tools: advertising, sales promotion, personal selling, direct marketing and public relations. These tools are briefly described here (and *see* Figure 9.1) and examined in more detail later in the chapter.

Advertising

Advertising is non-personal promotion paid for by an identified sponsor. You can use advertising as a cost-effective way to inform large numbers of customers or channel members about your brand or product; persuade customers or channel members about your brand's or product's merits and encourage purchase or support; and remind customers or channel members about your brand or product to encourage continued purchasing or support. If you work for a non-profit organisation, you may not always pay for advertising (or you may receive reduced rates), but you still control promotion content and are identified as the sponsor. The National Society for Prevention of Cruelty to Children, for instance, spends £5 million annually on television commercials and other advertising.[4] For planning purposes, note that advertising often does not allow for two-way communication between the organisation and its target audience.

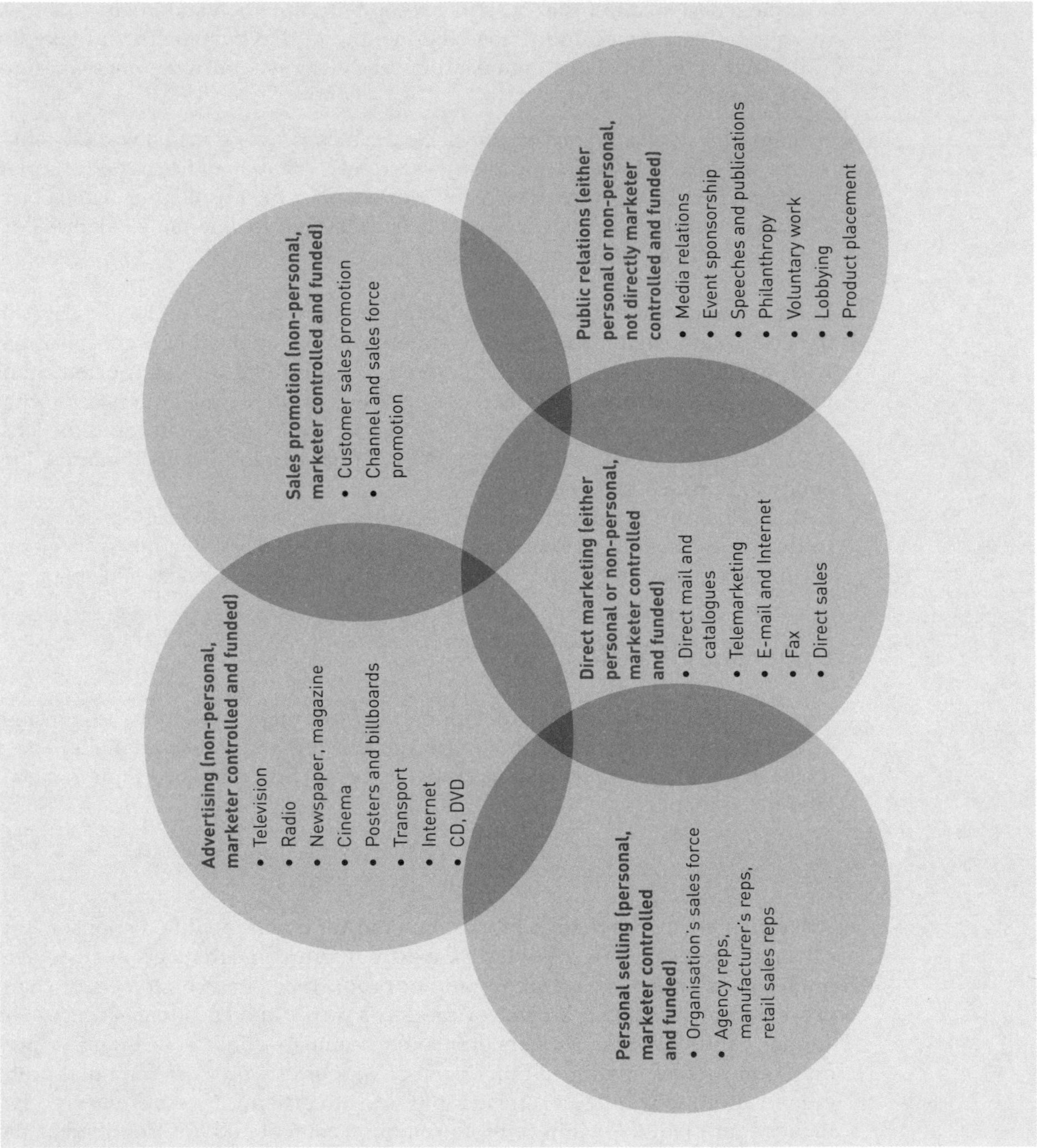

FIGURE 9.1 IMC tools

Advertising (non-personal, marketer controlled and funded)
- Television
- Radio
- Newspaper, magazine
- Cinema
- Posters and billboards
- Transport
- Internet
- CD, DVD

Sales promotion (non-personal, marketer controlled and funded)
- Customer sales promotion
- Channel and sales force promotion

Public relations (either personal or non-personal, not directly marketer controlled and funded)
- Media relations
- Event sponsorship
- Speeches and publications
- Philanthropy
- Voluntary work
- Lobbying
- Product placement

Direct marketing (either personal or non-personal, marketer controlled and funded)
- Direct mail and catalogues
- Telemarketing
- E-mail and Internet
- Fax
- Direct sales

Personal selling (personal, marketer controlled and funded)
- Organisation's sales force
- Agency reps, manufacturer's reps, retail sales reps

Sales promotion

When your marketing plan includes advertising, you may also plan for **sales promotions**. These are incentives designed to enhance a product's short-term value and stimulate faster response from the target audience. Although advertising is an excellent way to build brand image and awareness and even bring the target audience to the brink of action, sales promotions provide impetus to take action right away. If you choose a pull strategy, you can use sales promotions to induce customers to request a certain product from channel members; in a push strategy, you can use sales promotions to encourage channel members to stock and sell the product. You can easily measure the results of most sales promotions by counting the number of coupons redeemed, for instance, or the number of entries submitted for a draw.

Personal selling

Personal selling – especially useful for two-way communication – can take many forms, including: traditional in-person sales, Internet sales (using text, voice or Webcam communication) and telemarketing. Your budget is a major factor in personal selling decisions because sending a sales representative to call on customers is extremely costly, whereas personal selling in most retail, telemarketing and Internet settings can be less expensive. Still, B2B companies marketing costly or complicated products frequently depend on sales reps to identify or qualify customers, learn about their specific needs, recommend appropriate solutions, explain features and benefits, demonstrate product use, complete sales transactions, install products after purchase and, at times, offer training. Sales reps are also key players in building trust with customers and maintaining strong, satisfying relationships.[5] Good sales people serve as customer advocates within the organisation, advising on new product ideas and ensuring that customer orders are fulfilled correctly and on time. And they gather valuable data about market feedback, competitive moves, new opportunities and new threats.

Direct marketing

With **direct marketing**, you use two-way communication to interact with targeted customers and stimulate direct responses that ultimately lead to an ongoing relationship. You may plan communication through direct mail packages and catalogues, television, radio, e-mail, Web advertising, newspaper advertisements, telemarketing, fax, mobile e-commerce (m-commerce) or personal selling. The objective for an initial direct marketing contact might be to have a customer ask for product information, request a price quote or simply agree to receive further messages, for example. You can build on these responses to launch a dialogue that, in time, is designed to culminate in a purchase and set the stage for future contacts and more responses. One of the advantages of direct marketing is the ability to measure results precisely and immediately.

Public relations

No marketer can entirely control **public relations (PR)**, the promotion of a dialogue to build understanding and foster positive attitudes between the organisation and its stakeholders. Some PR is personal, as when a managing director addresses a community group or is interviewed by a reporter; some is impersonal, as when newspapers print articles about an organisation or a special event features a sponsor's logo. Because your organisation does not directly control or pay for media mentions, PR has more credibility than the advertising and sales promotion activities you do control. And yet, because of this lack of control, you cannot be sure that information you want to convey will reach the intended audience in the preferred form or at the preferred time – if at all. Proper PR planning allows for an exchange of views between your organisation and its stakeholders: you learn more about their attitudes and, in turn, use this input to shape and communicate your perspective and response.

Defining the target audience

As you can see in Figure 9.2, your first decision when planning an IMC campaign is to define the audience that you will target. This may be customers in a certain segment; people who influence buyers or users; people who are currently competitors' customers; current or potential channel members; members of the general public; media people; government officials or regulators; or other stakeholders. In a pull strategy, for example, you will primarily target customers as a way of stimulating demand; in a push strategy, you will primarily target channel members.

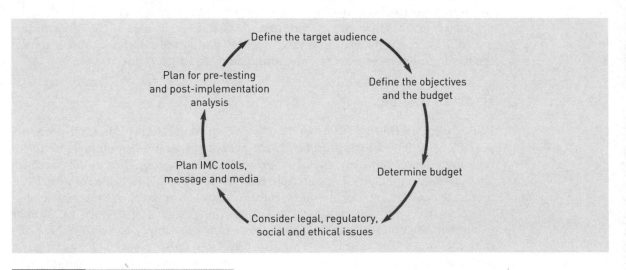

FIGURE 9.2 Planning an IMC campaign

The point here is to define clearly who each IMC programme will target and, using research, find out what audience members think or feel about the brand, product, organisation or idea; their attitudes and behaviour toward competitors; what kind of message, appeal, delivery and timing would be most effective; what the message should contain and how it should be conveyed. Going beyond generalities, you should research and profile the typical audience member in great detail and consider how people of different cultures in your targeted audience might respond to a particular IMC tool, message or medium.

Defining the objectives and the budget

Your IMC programmes will aim to achieve marketing objectives that move the target audience (particularly customers) through a hierarchy of cognitive, affective and behavioural responses. A **cognitive response** refers to a customer's mental reaction, including awareness of a brand and knowledge of a product's features and benefits. An **affective response** is a customer's emotional reaction, such as being interested in or liking a product. A **behavioural response** is how the customer acts, such as seeking out or buying a product. Customers move through these responses in different order, depending on how involved they are in making that type of purchase; the product differentiation in that category; and the influence of consumption experience (*see* Figure 9.3).

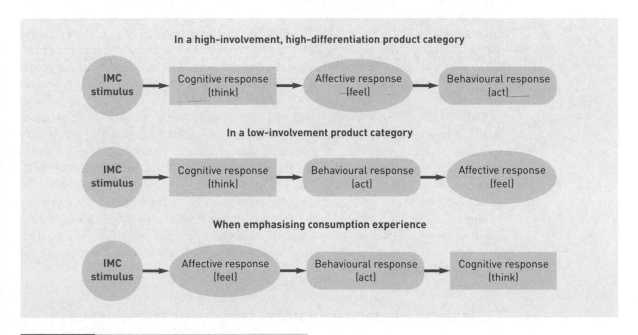

FIGURE 9.3   Using IMC to provoke audience response

Source: After Michael R. Solomon, *Consumer Behavior*, 5th edn (Upper Saddle River, NJ: Prentice Hall, 2002), pp. 200–02.

Usually your IMC objectives will relate to building long-term relationships by attracting customers' attention, communicating about the product or brand, persuading customers to seek out and buy the product once, supporting a positive attitude leading to repeat purchases and ultimately loyalty. Specific advertising objectives may then be to complement or support objectives for personal selling, direct marketing or other IMC tools used in the strategy. You may also set sales or profit objectives for IMC, particularly when you can measure and attribute the results to a particular campaign or message. Note that you may plan some IMC programmes to build your organisation's image or keep your brand in front of the audience, without specific financial objectives. Marketers for a non-profit organisation might want the target audience to adopt a certain behaviour, such as donating to a cause or volunteering; or want the audience to change behaviour, such as recycling more materials. (Review Chapter 5 for more about setting effective objectives.)

The IMC budget is developed and allocated in the context of your organisation's overall marketing budgeting process and budget approval process, which may be driven from the floor up or the top down (or a combination).[6] One floor-up option, frequently used in organisations with larger budgets, is to allocate funding according to the IMC objectives and the cost of the tasks to be completed in achieving those objectives. The advantage is a more direct tie between tasks and objectives and better accountability in terms of whether your budgeted tasks actually achieved the objectives. However, this method may lead to budget requests that are financially unrealistic, given the organisation's resources. It also presents complex planning challenges due to the difficulty of precisely linking particular tasks to specific objectives and the need to balance short-term objectives with larger, longer-term goals. Some organisations look at potential pay-back by insisting that IMC expenditures achieve a minimum return on investment.

Other budgeting methods include the affordability method (a top-down method based on how much the organisation can afford to spend), percentage-of-sales method (spending a certain percentage of previous annual sales revenue, future annual sales revenue or average industry percentage), competitive parity (setting the same IMC budget as main rivals, or a higher one). In practice, you may use a combination of methods to construct a preliminary budget, look realistically at these costs and at the market situation, consider both long-term and short-term objectives, think about appropriate IMC tools and then fine-tune these decisions to arrive at a reasonable budget. (*See* Chapter 11 for more on budgeting.)

Considering legal, regulatory, social and ethical issues

When planning IMC programmes, you need to be aware of a wide range of legal, regulatory, social and ethical issues. On the most basic legal and ethical level, your promotions should not be deceptive, distort facts or falsify product benefits. Some countries also outlaw certain types of promotions, such as comparative advertising, televised tobacco and alcohol advertisements or messages targeting children; others place restrictions on particular activities. For example, Brazil does not permit point-of-purchase promotions in store aisles, although they can be displayed in areas that customers pass through after paying for their purchases.[7] The United Kingdom forbids product placement on commercial television, although it allows sponsorship announcements; US consumer advocates have called for investigations of such 'embedded advertising' because these are not clearly labelled as commercial advertising.[8]

In some nations, companies must adhere to regulatory guidelines when using phrases such as 'low-fat' in their promotions.[9] Industry associations typically publish voluntary standards to assist marketers in developing campaigns that are both legal and ethical. Such standards cover details regarding how prices can be presented, how the word 'free' can be used, how draws, games and contests should be conducted, and so on. Investigate these limitations and guidelines and be sure your IMC programmes are in compliance.

Privacy is an increasingly important legal, social and ethical issue in the planning of IMC programmes. The European Union has strict rules about what personal data companies may collect and under what circumstances they are allowed to exchange such information. Retailers must first obtain permission before gathering customer data, sharing or selling it and using it for store marketing purposes. Also, companies must delete personal data after a set period, and they are forbidden to send personal data collected in the European Union to countries without equally strong privacy laws.[10] And privacy concerns have been raised over unsolicited messages delivered via e-mail, fax and mobile phone.[11] Such concerns about collection, storage, use and disclosure of personal data continue to make privacy a hot issue for marketers.

Choosing IMC tools, message and media

Most marketing plans employ more than one IMC tool to achieve their objectives. Your exact choices depend on your earlier decisions about target audience, objectives, budget and legal, regulatory, social and ethical considerations. They also depend on message and media strategy and, in a broader sense, your other marketing-mix decisions. To illustrate, television advertising is generally more expensive than print advertising, so if you have a small IMC budget or want to reach highly targeted audiences you may avoid television or use it sparingly. If your message involves an actual product demonstration to provoke cognitive response, you will probably find radio inappropriate.

Moreover, you have to consider the type of product or market and the product's stage in its life cycle. If you are planning a push strategy for a new product – targeting channel members – and the message discusses profit opportunities to prompt the behavioural response of placing orders, you are likely to find personal selling to be effective. You may also find personal selling effective for promoting expensive goods or services to business buyers, often supported by sales promotion and other tools. If you are launching a new consumer product you may use pull strategies heavily weighted toward advertising and sales promotion. (The use of each IMC tool is discussed more fully later in this chapter.)

Note that an unusually innovative or appealing IMC programme can start a groundswell of **word of mouth** – people telling other people about the message, the product or another aspect of the marketing. Word of mouth has more credibility because it is not marketer controlled and it reflects what people in the market think, feel and do. Yet as word of mouth spreads, people may not get a complete or accurate message, and many outside the target audience may get the message (while some inside the target audience may not). You can certainly try to initiate positive word of mouth but you cannot control whether your audience picks up on the message and passes it along. If word of mouth does get going, it can spread especially quickly on the Internet, as Honda learned when it aired a unique television commercial.

MARKETING IN PRACTICE: HONDA

Thanks to word of mouth, millions of people worldwide have seen a Honda television advertisement entitled 'Cog', which originally was broadcast on British television. The phenomenon started when Honda UK's advertising agency devised the idea of filming a carefully choreographed chain reaction involving Honda Accord parts. In the commercial, one cog hits a second cog, which taps a third cog that rolls into a bolt, which nudges a pipe . . . and on and on, with a total of 86 parts involved. The agency needed 606 takes to make this two-minute commercial in one shot, not digitally manipulated or edited to piece frames together.

The imaginative commercial immediately captivated UK viewers and newspaper reporters. Spurred by widespread press coverage and personal recommendations, Web surfers book-marked the commercial on Honda's website. Within two months, two million people had downloaded the advertisement and continued circulating it for months afterward in e-mails passed around the world. As the buzz continued, one survey named 'Cog' as the year's 'coolest' advertisement. Honda was pleased by the outcome: 'We think this campaign has managed to reposition Honda more toward the quality and sophistication of the European makers', summarises Nigel Bobs, a Honda UK marketing official. 'We certainly had no idea it would take off like this.'[12]

Planning for pre-testing and post-implementation analysis

To get the information you need for making better IMC decisions, you should plan time and money for research to pre-test messages, creative approaches and use of media. The purpose is to gauge the target audience's response and have the opportunity to make changes, possibly pre-test additional elements and then launch the programme fully. For example, you can conduct pre-tests to measure recognition (does a sample of the audience recognise what is being promoted?), recall (does the sample remember the message and what it communicated?), affective reaction (does the sample like the promotion and have more positive attitudes toward the product or brand?) and behavioural intentions (are people in the sample likely to buy the product or take some other action on the basis of the promotion?).

You should also plan for measuring and evaluating the results after full implementation. Where you have set cognitive objectives such as raising brand awareness or affective objectives such as increasing brand liking, you can plan for research to determine pre-programme levels and post-programme levels. Similarly, where you have set behavioural objectives such as achieving certain unit or monetary sales levels, you can check results by totalling orders, counting inventory, checking sales through services that link to grocery scanner systems or other methods. If results fall far short of expectations, you will need contingency plans for making changes in message or media or both.

Beyond comparing results to the plan's specific objectives, plan to dig deeper and obtain post-implementation audience feedback by researching:

- whether the message or media failed to reach the target audience at times, and why

- how well the audience understood the message and how the message can be clarified if needed

- what the audience thought and felt about the product or brand, message and media

- which messages and media were especially effective in provoking the desired audience response

- how well the IMC tools, messages and media are supporting the overall positioning and image and working with other marketing-mix strategies.

PLANNING ADVERTISING

When you plan for advertising you follow the general IMC planning pattern, starting with defining the target audience, setting specific objectives, determining the budget and considering legal, regulatory, social and ethical issues. Next comes planning for message and media decisions, both critical in planning advertising that integrates with other IMC tools and other parts of the marketing mix. As shown in Figure 9.1, you can convey a message using a number of advertising media. The key is properly to match message and media. Here's how British Airways effectively communicated a message using selected media.

MARKETING IN PRACTICE: BRITISH AIRWAYS

British Airways wanted to attract more business-class passengers for its international routes during an economic slowdown that lowered demand for air travel. Knowing that this segment values comfort, BA planned an unusual online advertisement to convey the idea that its business-class passengers can sleep during long flights because seats recline fully to serve as beds. The message began, 'Enjoy a revolutionary view from business class', then went on to link a sales promotion to membership in BA's frequent flyer programme. The visual was a passenger sleeping in the seat laid flat – with the twist that the online advertisement appeared sideways on the screen (reinforcing the horizontal position of the sleeper seat) and then turned upright before dissolving. While this advertisement ran on the *New York Times* website, BA placed banner ads on other websites and sent business travellers e-mails about the offer. Within ten weeks, BA had enrolled 12,000 new frequent flyer members – 40 per cent more than the objective – at a lower than average acquisition cost per member.

The sleeper seat has been the centrepiece of additional BA campaigns. One UK television commercial showed a business traveller getting into bed one night in New York City's busy Times Square and waking up the next morning in the middle of London's Piccadilly Circus. As the airline expanded installation of sleeper seats, its television, newspaper, billboard and online messages added the line 'More beds, more places, more often' to highlight the differentiation. 'There's a whole raft of competitors with beds that are not truly flat or products which are not there yet', explained BA's general manager of marketing for the United Kingdom and Ireland.[13]

Note that you will generally wait to make detailed advertising decisions until after your marketing plan has been approved and is being implemented. Still, you have to plan the general direction of both message and media in order to allocate the overall IMC budget among advertising programmes and coordinate all other IMC decisions.

Planning messages

What will the message actually say? What will it look (and/or sound) like? Broadly speaking, these are the two main decisions in planning message strategy. Some messages follow a 'hard-sell' approach to induce the target audience to respond now; others take a more 'soft-sell' approach, persuading without seeming to do so. You can use **rational appeals** that communicate logically on the basis of quality, features and benefits, solution to a problem, performance, price, competitive superiority or other points. Instead, or in addition, you may employ **emotional appeals** to touch the audience's feelings, as US-based Western Union Financial Services did in a recent global campaign.

MARKETING IN PRACTICE: WESTERN UNION

When people use Western Union to transfer funds to family or friends in other countries, the company wants to reinforce the idea of 'uniting people with possibilities' rather than simply providing 'the fastest way to send money'. As the worldwide market leader in funds transfer, Western Union is defending its dominance against competitors such as Travelers Express/MoneyGram and others that target the segment of people (especially immigrants) who use non-bank services to transfer money to recipients in other countries. A recent Western Union multinational advertising campaign relied mainly on the emotional appeal of what money transfer means to sender and recipient. The US commercial, broadcast in English and Spanish, showed a yellow bird launched by a Latino café owner to reach a young woman – apparently his daughter – as she moves into a new house, highlighting the emotional intent rather than the transactional nature of the money transfer.

The company has expanded the 'possibilities' appeal to other countries and interpreted it in billboard and print media, adding a human quality to a service used by millions. In conjunction with the campaign, Western Union provided its 150,000 agents worldwide with complementary point-of-purchase displays in local languages. The campaign kicked off in the United States, India and China before being launched in other countries. Summarising the international potential of this emotional appeal, Western Union's chief marketing officer said: 'We can adopt it without losing the overall message.'[14]

Organisations use a variety of emotional appeals in their advertising: fear avoidance (avoiding negative consequences such as drug abuse, for example); status (focusing on how a product enhances a person's image); sex (implying that a product may enhance a person's attractiveness); anger (focusing on why a person should vote against a certain proposal or candidate); aspiration (focusing on what a product can help someone become or achieve); humour (attracting attention and creating a positive atmosphere for the message).

Your message planning is inseparable from your media planning because the copy in the advertisement, the design and the creativity of its execution depend on media choice. A creative decision to show the product in action, for instance, can be executed through a visual medium such as television or the Web. Other design decisions include layout; size and type of advertisement; copy and graphics (or length of radio/television commercial); use of colour; shape; sound; and movement. Again, your decision details need not be finalised until the marketing plan is actually implemented – but you should have some idea of message and media strategy so you can plan IMC budgets, timing and marketing-mix coordination.

Planning media

Media planning has become more complex due to the multiplicity of media choices and vehicles and the resulting smaller audience sizes for each – **audience fragmentation**. You will always have budget constraints and yet need to find the best balance of reach and frequency. **Reach** refers to the number or percentage of people in the target audience exposed to an advertisement in a particular media vehicle during a certain period. Higher reach means the message gets to more people, but this usually comes at a cost. **Frequency** is the number of times those in the target audience are exposed to an advertisement in a particular media vehicle during a certain period. Higher frequency means you expose more people to your message on more occasions, again at a cost.

Should you spend more on reach or more on frequency? And with audience fragmentation, what combination of media and vehicles will get your message to the right number of people at the right time and in the desired frequency?

If your target segment is large, you may be able to use mass media. Orange did this by playing on the popularity of the television show *Big Brother* and buying the entire three-and-a-half-minute commercial period immediately before the episode revealing the year's winner.[15] B2B marketers are also adding television to their IMC mix as another way to reach buyers and purchase influencers. Cisco Systems, which makes networking equipment, started a television advertising campaign not long ago. 'You want to present a cohesive message, but not the same message', Cisco's vice president of worldwide marketing communications explained. 'You want your target consumer to learn more every time they come across your brand in an advertising medium.'[16]

Yet the clutter of competing messages bombarding audiences from all directions is a growing concern. To attract attention, some marketers are experimenting with non-traditional messages in non-traditional media. BMW has been successful with short Web-based films prominently featuring its cars in chase scenes or other action sequences. Its first five films drew hundreds of thousands of viewers and brought in 41,000 customer enquiries about BMW cars.[17] The CNX digital channel and FHM magazine have both tested an unusual medium: having their logos displayed on the foreheads of UK college students.[18] Another approach is to attract attention by enhancing the impact of a traditional medium. Adidas has done this in Tokyo by staging ten-minute live football matches between two players suspended from the top of a giant billboard bearing its logo. This helped Adidas cut through the clutter of billboards in urban Japan.[19]

An alternative to paying for high reach that may deliver your message to many people outside the target audience (which may happen with television commercials, for example) is to use more precisely targeted media. The UK supermarket chain Safeway has done this by concentrating on people in each store's trading area. 'Three years ago, the national advertising budget was redirected to a local level with the majority of spend focused on door-to-door distribution of our weekly deals flyer', says a Safeway official.[20] Using flyers to deliver the message was a cost-effective decision: the chain has attracted one million new shoppers since the switch. Now door-to-door delivery of advertising leaflets is becoming increasingly popular across Europe.[21] This chapter's practical marketer checklist summarises considerations in planning for media.

PLANNING SALES PROMOTIONS

You can plan sales promotions to stimulate faster response from consumers and business customers, channel members (sometimes called *the trade*) and the sales force. Although such promotions are designed to add value for only a limited time, some marketers use them as part of a longer-term strategy to strengthen relationships with members of the target audience. Sales promotion spending now exceeds advertising spending in a number of industries, reflecting increased competitive pressure and the need to produce immediate results.

However, because many sales promotions add value by reducing perceived cost – lowering the product's price, in effect – over-use may heighten price sensitivity among customers, diminish brand strength and hurt profitability. Moreover, says promotion specialist Stephen Callender, 'Promotions that go wrong make a brand's strategies appear ill-thought out. That leads to insidious damage to the brand's credibility.'[22] Thus, you should set clear objectives, understand applicable laws and regulations, choose your techniques carefully, monitor implementation and evaluate results to make your sales promotions successful.

Planning for customer sales promotions

Figure 9.4 shows a variety of common sales promotion techniques you can use, depending on your objectives and your IMC strategy. Consider using sales promotions targeting consumers or business customers when you want to:

- *Encourage product trial.* Potential customers have to try a product at least once before they can form a definite opinion and decide to buy it again (and again). Sales promotion is therefore commonly used in the introduction stage of a product's life cycle and to stimulate higher sales during the maturity stage. L'Oréal, for example, encouraged trial not long ago by giving away one million samples of its Garnier Fructis Anti-Dandruff Shampoo through health and fitness clubs.[23]

- *Reinforce advertising for a product or brand.* An exciting sales promotion can help customers notice and remember your advertising messages. One February, Müller supplemented its Müllerlove yoghurt advertising campaign with a sales promotion offering London customers St Valentine's Day prizes such as romantic weekend getaways and bouquets of flowers. The company also sent its Müllerlove bus into London with samples to draw new customers.[24]

- *Attract more shoppers or interest.* Simply getting customers to visit a channel member or contact a manufacturer about a product can be a challenge. Some marketers use coupons, samples or other techniques in an attempt to get customers to take the first step. In B2B markets, organisations may offer free consultations, free design assistance or even limited-period trials of goods or services.

- *Encourage purchase of multiple products.* Depending on your product mix, you can use sales promotion to stimulate customer purchases of two, three or even more products. The Nestlé example, below, shows how this can be done quite effectively for a family of products.

Technique	Description
Sample	Free trial of a good or service
Coupon	Certificate redeemable for money off a product's price
Premium	A free or low-priced item offered to induce purchase of a product
Sweepstake or draw, contest, game	Chance to win cash or prizes through luck, knowledge or skill
Refund, rebate	Returning part or all of a product's price to the customer
Price pack	Special price marked by producer on the package or for multiple products bought together
Loyalty reward	Opportunity to earn gifts or cash for continuing to buy a certain product or from a certain company
Point-of purchase display or demonstration	In-store materials promoting a product or in-store product demonstration
Branded speciality	Everyday item such as a calendar or T-shirt bearing the product name or brand, for reminder purposes

FIGURE 9.4 Sales promotion techniques targeting customers

- *Encourage continued product purchase and usage.* Here, you want to prevent customers from switching to other brands or products and build loyalty, which leads to higher sales and lower customer acquisition costs. Airlines do this with their frequent flyer programmes; supermarkets do this with their frequent shopper programmes.

MARKETING IN PRACTICE: NESTLÉ ARGENTINA

Nestlé faced a difficult market situation in Argentina. For years, companies had successfully courted Argentine customers with price-related sales promotions. Then economic problems caused both consumers and marketers to slow their spending. To make a big impression for its full family of food products, Nestlé planned a major sweepstake preceded by radio and television advertisements advising customers to 'get ready to collect Nestlé proofs of purchase because a huge promotion is coming'.[25] At the start of the promotion, television, print, billboard and online advertisements invited customers to submit proofs of purchase for any four Nestlé products and be eligible for weekly prize draws.

During each week of the seven-week promotion, the company gave away a grand prize of a house plus many other gifts. Customers responded enthusiastically: Nestlé received more than 800,000 entries and its sales increased as much as 20 per cent in some product categories. A Nestlé Argentina official observed that 'our primary objective was not just to increase sales, but to get consumers to recognise that our products represent a variety of different categories, including foods, beverages, breakfast cereals, chocolate, ice cream, pet foods and mineral waters'.[26]

Field marketing is becoming more popular as companies work with outside agencies to bring sales promotions to (and sometimes take orders from) customers 'in the field' – in stores, shopping districts and office locations. Canon Europa, for example, has contracted with a London agency to promote its digital cameras and printers by demonstrating these products outside stores that sell Canon merchandise. As another example, the cosmetics firm Maybelline New York recently hired an agency to conduct makeovers of women in UK offices, night spots and shopping centres, as a demonstration of its beauty products.[27] Consider whether some form of field marketing will help you reach your IMC objectives.

Planning for channel and sales force promotions

Particularly when using a push strategy, you may find sales promotions effective in enlisting the support of channel members and motivating sales representatives. Specifically, you can use channel and sales force promotions to:

- *Build channel commitment to a new product.* So many new products are introduced every year that channel members rarely have the space (or the money) to carry them all. Channel promotions can focus attention on a new product, encourage intermediaries to buy it, motivate the sales force to sell it and provide rewards according to results.

- *Encourage more immediate results.* As with customer sales promotions, channel promotions and sales force promotions offer inducements to take action during a specific time period.

- *Build relationships with channel members.* Keeping the ongoing support of major retail or wholesale businesses takes time and effort. Channel promotions help the process along and offer opportunities for interactions that benefit the producer and its channel members.

- *Improve product knowledge.* To market a product, channel members and sales representatives need to understand its features and benefits. You can support your other marketing efforts by offering training and information through channel and sales force promotions.

Sales force promotions include contests (with cash or prizes as rewards), sales meetings (for training and motivation) and special promotional material (to supplement personal sales efforts). In planning a channel promotion, you may use monetary allowances (either discounts or payments for stocking or displaying a product); limited-time discounts (for buying early in the selling season or during other specified periods); free merchandise (extra quantities provided for buying a minimum quantity or a certain product); cooperative advertising (sharing costs when a channel member advertises a particular brand or product); or trade shows (setting up a booth or room at a convention centre to demonstrate products, offer samples and otherwise interact with potential channel members or business buyers).

Trade shows are good opportunities to showcase products for new channel members, connect with current channel members and gather valuable market information. In North America, for example, children's retailers visit the ENK International Children's Club trade show to view and order fashions offered by Diesel, Liberty of London, Young Versace and other clothing manufacturers. Another big trade show is the Fancy Food Show, where speciality foods stores and Web retailers sample and order foods from around the world. 'I consider this an extraordinary learning experience', comments the owner of A Touch of Italy, a food store in Florida, about the Fancy Food Show. And a biscuit manufacturer notes, 'It's a chance to really meet and talk to customers, to show them what's new, to hear what's doing well and what's not.'[28] Plan carefully because you rarely can afford to participate in every industry trade show in every market. Also look into virtual trade shows staged on the Web, where buyers can log on to view displays posted by sellers like your organisation.[29]

PLANNING PERSONAL SELLING

One of the most compelling reasons to include personal selling in a marketing plan is to establish solid relationships with new customers and maintain good relationships with the current customer base. Personal attention can make all the difference when your customers have unique problems, require customised solutions or place very large orders. In the pharmaceutical industry, for example, personal selling is more common than advertising. Thousands of sales representatives are on the road visiting doctors' offices to announce new prescription drugs, explaining their use and, frequently, leaving samples or customer coupons. Gift giving is not unheard of in this competitive industry, which is why Italy and other countries put a limit on their value. Still, doctors have less time than ever to meet with reps in person; therefore companies such as Eli Lilly encourage doctors to telephone company call centres with questions.[30]

Your marketing plan can provide guidance for each step of the personal selling process, as shown in Figure 9.5. In some organisations, the sales force reports to the top marketing executive; in others, reps report to a sales executive who is a peer of the marketing executive. Regardless of the organisational structure, you must coordinate personal selling activities with all other marketing plan strategies in order to achieve the desired results. In addition, stress to your sales force the importance of building long-term relationships rather than merely completing individual sales transactions. Even organisations that have not traditionally emphasised personal selling are now recognising its benefits. The UK Royal Mail Group has trained post office personnel to sell an ever-wider range of products, including travel insurance and other financial services products.[31]

When planning for personal selling, consider:

- *Need*. Should your company maintain its own sales force or sell through retailers, agents or manufacturers' representatives? Can field marketing agencies you hire accept orders from customers?

- *Organisation*. Will you organise reps according to geographic market, product, type of customer, size of customer or some other structure?

- *Size*. How many sales reps should you have, based on your objectives and current sales levels?

- *Compensation*. How will you determine sales force compensation?

- *Management*. How will you recruit, train, supervise, motivate and evaluate sales reps? How will sales reps be educated about legal, regulatory and ethical guidelines?

- *Process*. How will you generate leads for sales reps? How will reps and managers access information about prospects and customers before, during and after transactions? What logistical activities must be coordinated with sales transactions, and who will be responsible?

Step in personal selling process	Marketing planning input
Identify and qualify prospects	Marketing plan objectives, segmentation and targeting decisions
Plan sales approach (before sales contact)	Data from market and customer analysis
Approach the prospect	Data about customer needs
Present the product	Data about product features and benefits, positioning
Handle objections	Knowledge of product, customer needs and competitive strengths
Close the sale	Knowledge of pricing decisions and policies, order fulfilment and other logistics
Follow up to maintain relationship	Customer service strategy, relationship building strategy

FIGURE 9.5 How marketing planning guides the personal selling process

PLANNING DIRECT MARKETING

Although mail order and telemarketing are hardly new, a growing number of organisations now include these and other direct marketing techniques in their IMC plans because of the ability to use sophisticated software and databases to target audiences more precisely, adjust messages and timing according to the audience's needs and build relationships cost-effectively. Direct marketing costs more than advertising in mass media, yet its interactive quality, selectivity and customisation potential may add enough flexibility to make the difference worthwhile. Just as important, you can easily measure customer response and modify the offer or the communication again and again to move customers in the desired direction and achieve programme objectives.

Planning objectives and response

In planning direct marketing, first decide what response you want to elicit from the target audience(s), in accordance with your objectives. Many B2B marketers use direct marketing to generate leads for sales representatives; the desired response is to have a potential customer indicate interest in the product by calling, e-mailing or sending a reply by post. Credit card companies, banks and mobile phone companies frequently use direct marketing – especially mailings – to attract new customers, bring former customers back and encourage current customers to open additional accounts or sign up for more services.

Car manufacturers are using direct marketing to encourage people to visit a local dealer showroom. Fiat, for example, has supplemented its media advertising with direct mail packages offering incentives such as a discounted hotel stay to consumers who test-drive one of the featured models at a local dealership.[32] Direct e-marketing is becoming more common. The UK supermarket chain Tesco has found that 20 per cent of the sales for Tesco Personal Finance, a joint venture with the Royal Bank of Scotland, come through the Tesco.com website.[33]

If you work for a non-profit organisation, you should investigate direct marketing to reach targeted audiences and generate contributions. The charity Oxfam, for instance, has found Web advertising effective for disseminating information about disasters and soliciting online donations from concerned contributors.[34] Beaumont Hospital Foundation, which raises money for Dublin's Beaumont Hospital, maintains a website encouraging donations and operating online charity auctions. Visitors to the site can sign up for the foundation's newsletter, as well. The site helps the foundation raise thousands of pounds every year to benefit the hospital.[35]

Planning media and offer

Once you have set response objectives for each target audience, you are ready to select appropriate media and formulate an appropriate offer, based on research into the target audience's media and buying patterns. Different audiences and markets require different media and offers. According to one specialist, Australian consumers are not as accustomed to catalogue shopping as US consumers, for example; another specialist observes that television is just gaining popularity as a direct marketing medium in Japan.[36]

Before putting your full resources behind a direct marketing programme, be sure it is consistent with the chosen positioning and allow time in the marketing plan schedule for testing the offer's creative, message and product components. Also test that the mechanisms for response (such as a freephone number, URL or postage-paid envelope) fit with customer preferences and behaviour. By measuring the response to each test and to the entire programme, you can see what actually works and use the results to plan future direct marketing programmes.

PLANNING PUBLIC RELATIONS

At one time or another, nearly every organisation has prepared news releases, called news conferences and answered questions from reporters. Yet media contact is only one aspect of this flexible and powerful IMC tool. You can use public relations not just to convey the organisation's messages but also to build mutual understanding and maintain an ongoing dialogue between your organisation and key members of the 'public'. Moreover, your message has more credibility when conveyed by media representatives than when communicated directly by your organisation, as noted earlier.

Defining the 'public'

The 'public' in public relations may refer to people in any number of target audiences, depending on your organisation and IMC strategy (*see* Figure 9.6). Each of these audiences is a stakeholder that can affect your plan's success and performance, but not all will be addressed in the same way within one marketing plan.

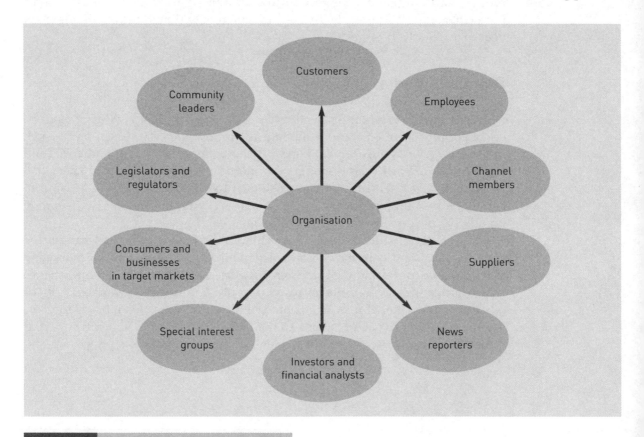

| FIGURE 9.6 | Target audiences for public relations |

In general, you can use PR to achieve one or more of the following objectives:

- *Identify and understand stakeholder concerns*. Through PR contacts such as community meetings, surveys and other methods, you can learn what your stakeholders think and feel about important issues such as your products, image, ecological record and so on. Kingfisher, a UK-based home products retailer, seeks out public opinion and government views on social and ecological issues such as buying timber sourced from endangered forests. The idea is to see how public concern is growing so the company can phase in changes over time.[37]

- *Convey the organisation's viewpoint or important information*. Knowing your target audience's views, you can reconsider your organisational position on an issue and adapt it if appropriate. At the very least, you can use PR to explain your management's viewpoint, especially vital in the midst of a crisis. PR is also useful for educating your public about pressing issues. For example, World Vision recently asked Miss Scotland to participate in a media tour of the charity's projects in West Africa. Scottish media representatives went along and sent back reports that reached 12 million people, doubling the charity's awareness among potential contributors and educating the public about the dangers of children living in poverty.[38]

- *Correct misperceptions*. If one or more target audiences have misperceptions about some aspect of your organisation – such as the quality of its products – you can use PR to counteract the inaccuracies by providing more information, answering questions and allowing for periodic updates. This is vital during a crisis if you want to protect your reputation and maintain good relations with customers, channel members and others. The marketing planning process is the right time to make policy decisions about crisis communication, not when the emergency is in progress.

- *Enhance the organisation's image*. Many organisations apply PR techniques to enhance their public image. Consider the goodwill created when the US hamburger chain Hardee's announced a donation of one million beef patties to hunger-relief charities before it introduced a new, improved burger.[39] If an organisation has recently been embroiled in controversy, PR can show what management is doing to improve and emphasise situations in which the organisation has gone beyond minimum requirements to satisfy stakeholders.

- *Promote products and brands*. You can use PR to communicate the features, benefits and value of your products and promote your brands. To introduce the Porsche Cayenne, Norden Autohaus in Edmonton, Canada, reserved a 2,000-seat IMAX theatre, screened a 45-minute film about the SUV, served refreshments to invited guests and then brought the SUV onstage with a flash of smoke, laser lights and upbeat music. Thanks to this PR event, the dealership sold five Cayennes within just a few weeks to people who had attended the event.[40]

Planning PR techniques

As you can see, you may include a variety of PR techniques within your marketing plan, although you need not specify every detail until implementation is about to begin. One of the most commonly used PR techniques is the news release, written and distributed to media representatives. Your release can be provided in a printed document, an e-mail, a Web link or page or a video. For more significant news, you may want to call a news conference, let media reps hear management speak and hold a question-and-answer session. If appropriate, you can incorporate new product demonstrations as part of a news conference.

Consider whether you should seek PR attention by sponsoring some event. Many companies now sponsor football or basketball games, concerts, children's festivals or other events. China Kejian, which makes mobile phones, sponsors an English Premier League football team; the Japanese clothing company Narumiya International sponsors teen fashion shows featuring its latest clothing and accessories, for example.[41] Where it is legal to do so, some companies arrange to have brands or products placed in films, television shows or in other surroundings. The US mobile phone company AT&T Wireless hired entertainers to perform on the streets of Boston, New York, San Francisco and Chicago, singing familiar pop songs with lyrics adapted to the company's services. With this programme, AT&T Wireless was able to communicate with customers in everyday surroundings – and garner some media attention for its unusual approach.[42] Such PR programmes require advance planning to ensure adequate budget support and coordination with other IMC tools and marketing-mix strategies.

CHAPTER SUMMARY

1. *Explain the purpose of integrated marketing communication.*
   The purpose of integrated marketing communication (IMC) is to ensure that content and delivery of all the marketing messages in all media are coordinated and consistent and support the positioning and objectives of the product, brand or organisation.

2. *Outline the process of planning integrated marketing communication.*
   The first decision in IMC planning is to define the target audience. Next, you define IMC objectives, generally set according to a hierarchy of cognitive, affective and behavioural responses that the programmes are intended to provoke from the target audience. Then you determine an appropriate budget, using one or a combination of methods. You also take into account any applicable legal, regulatory, social and ethical issues that can affect messages, media or other aspects of IMC strategy. This sets the stage for choosing IMC tools, mes-

sage and media, pre-testing, and then implementation and analysis of results. IMC strategy should be planned in the context of other marketing-mix strategies.

3. *Discuss planning for the five major IMC tools.*
In planning advertising, marketers consider message appeal, creativity and appropriateness for media, and balance reach and frequency in the context of the budget. In planning sales promotions, marketers distinguish between programmes targeting customers (consumers or business customers) and those targeting channel members or the sales force. Sales promotions are designed to stimulate faster response by adding value (or reducing perceived cost) for a limited time to encourage trial, reinforce advertising, attract more interest, encourage purchasing of multiple products or encourage continued product purchasing. Personal selling, more common in business marketing than in consumer marketing, can take the form of in-person sales, Internet sales or telemarketing. Planning issues include: need for a dedicated sales force; organisation, size, compensation and management of the sales force; and planning for the sales process itself. Direct marketing allows marketers to target audiences more precisely; test and change messages, offer and timing; build relationships cost-effectively; and measure response compared with objectives. Marketers use public relations to increase mutual understanding and maintain an ongoing dialogue between management and key stakeholder publics. Marketers plan PR to identify and understand stakeholder concerns; convey the organisation's viewpoint or key information; correct misperceptions; enhance the organisation's image; and promote products.

KEY TERM DEFINITIONS

advertising Non-personal promotion paid for by an identified sponsor

affective response Customer's emotional reaction, such as being interested in or liking a product

audience fragmentation Trend toward smaller audience sizes due to the multiplicity of media choices and vehicles

behavioural response How the customer acts in responding to an IMC stimulus, such as seeking or buying a product

cognitive response Customer's mental reaction, such as awareness of a brand or knowledge of a product's features and benefits

direct marketing The use of two-way communication to engage targeted customers and stimulate a direct response that leads to a sale and an ongoing relationship

emotional appeal Appeal in an advertising message intended to touch the audience's feelings.

field marketing Working with outside agencies on sales promotions that take place in stores, shopping districts and office locations

frequency The number of times people in the target audience are exposed to an advertisement in a particular media vehicle during a certain period

integrated marketing communication (IMC) Coordinating content and delivery of all marketing messages in all media to ensure consistency and to support the chosen positioning and objectives

public relations (PR) Promoting a dialogue to build understanding and foster positive attitudes between the organisation and its stakeholders

rational appeal Appeal in an advertising message based on logic

reach The number or percentage of people in the target audience exposed to an advertisement in a particular media vehicle during a certain period

word of mouth People telling other people about a product, advertisement or some other aspect of an organisation's marketing

THE PRACTICAL MARKETER CHECKLIST NO. 9:
PLANNING FOR MEDIA

Audience considerations

What media do people in the targeted segment use and prefer?

What media will help the message be understood and remembered?

What media are available in the geographic market being targeted?

What research is available about each medium and vehicle's audience?

Can the media reach the right number of people in the targeted segment?

How will certain media and vehicles fit with other marketing-mix strategies?

What media are being used by competitors to reach this target audience?

Will the audience consider some media excessively intrusive or annoying?

Timing considerations

When should the message be available to coincide with the buying cycle?

For how long will the message be available to the audience?

What media will most effectively capture attention and interest when the audience is receptive?

Should media be used to deliver the message continuously, intermittently or seasonally?

Can a message be scheduled at short notice?

Can the message be delivered at the desired frequency level?

Creative and production considerations

How much creative flexibility does each medium offer?

Will the medium's creative characteristics allow product demonstration?

What are the production requirements of each medium?

Financial considerations

What is the cost for the desired reach and frequency?

What is the cost of developing and producing messages for the medium?

How will projected media costs fit with other costs in the IMC plan and the marketing plan budget?

What is the expected payback based on audience reaction?

 **ONLINE RESOURCES**

Integrated marketing communication

- MediaGuardian (http://media.guardian.co.uk/advertising) – Displays news, special reports and analyses of advertising, public relations, media and promotion activities.

- Institute of Public Relations news centre (www.ipr.org.uk/news/index.htm) – Offers links to news stories about public relations, marketing and media.

- Advertising Association (www.adassoc.org.uk) – See, especially, the Food Advertising Unit, with information about regulations and advertising to children.

- History of Advertising Trust (www.hatads.org.uk) – Archive of advertisements that have appeared in the UK, including those of Selfridges, the Dairy Council and Heinz UK.

- Committee of Advertising Practice (www.cap.org.uk) – Provides information about the British Code of Advertising, Sales Promotion and Direct Marketing.

- World of Events.net (www.worldofevents.net) – Offers links and information about special events, exhibitions and related promotional techniques.

- Connected in Marketing (www.connectedinmarketing.com) – From the Chartered Institute of Marketing, news and research about advertising and promotion.

- Direct Marketing Association (UK) (www.dma.org.uk) – Access to resources such as direct marketing guidelines and codes of practice plus case studies of successful programmes.

QUESTIONS FOR DISCUSSION AND ANALYSIS

1. Should the concept of IMC apply to all the programmes undertaken by a multinational corporation in different countries? Why or why not?

2. Why would a marketer set cognitive and affective response objectives but not behavioural response objectives for an IMC programme?

3. What is the benefit of pre-testing an advertisement, sales promotion or direct marketing offer?

APPLY YOUR KNOWLEDGE

Choose a particular product or cause; find two or more advertisements, promotions or other communications in which it is featured; and analyse the organisation's IMC strategy.

- What target audience do you think these communications are designed to reach?

- What cognitive, affective or behavioural response(s) might these communications provoke?

- What objectives do you think the organisation has set for these communications and how would you recommend that it measure results?

- What legal, regulatory, social or ethical considerations are likely to shape this organisation's IMC strategy?

- Do these communications appear to follow IMC principles and reflect consistency?

- Prepare a brief oral or written report summarising your comments.

BUILD YOUR OWN MARKETING PLAN

Plan your IMC strategy as you continue developing your marketing plan. Who constitutes each target audience that you want to reach? What objectives will you set for IMC programmes targeting each audience? What is an appropriate IMC budget, given the available resources, reach and frequency preferences and the tools you want to use? Identify any legal, regulatory, social or ethical issues that would affect your IMC decisions. Will you use advertising, sales promotion, personal selling, direct marketing and/or public relations – and why? What message and media choices are most appropriate for your target audience and objectives? Outline at least one IMC programme, indicating objectives, target audience, general message and media decisions, approximate budget and how results will be measured. Finally, document your ideas in *Marketing Plan Pro* software or in a written marketing plan, being sure that your decisions are consistent with earlier decisions and will help achieve the objectives you have set.

CLOSING CASE: COCA-COLA REACHES OUT TO THE WORLD

One of the world's most recognisable brands is reaching out to world audiences in new and different ways. Coca-Cola still promotes its venerable soft drink brand through television commercials, neon signs and point-of-purchase displays. Given increased competition and product maturity, however, the company is exploring new ways of creating synergy from its messages and media.

Many Coca-Cola commercials rely on emotional appeals to win the hearts of customers. For example, a cola commercial broadcast in China depicted a young boy handing a Coke bottle to the Chinese football team heading to South Korea to play in the World Cup. Instead of fizzy drink, the bottle held soil from China, symbolic of taking the home-ground advantage with the team. Entertainment is a growing part of the equation, as well. To support its national television campaign in China, Coca-Cola sent football teams to rural areas with instructions to give away samples and promote its beverages in an entertaining way. 'Road shows give people a much stronger impact and connection with our brand', explains Brenda Lee, Coca-Cola's director of external affairs for China. The stakes are particularly high in non-urban areas of China: 'Imagine if we have 500 million people in the countryside', she says. 'If we can get each of them to buy just two more drinks, maybe at festivals, that will be a billion beverages.'[43]

The company is constantly alert for opportunities to adapt its successful campaigns for additional markets. For example, it has transferred to the UK a television commercial that was first popular in Spain (showing a busker singing 'Chihuahua' on a train). Consumer response was so strong that the music became an integral part of Coca-Cola's pan-European marketing for months. 'Not only do we need to think of how we can provide entertainment, but we have to realise that consumers are actively looking to us to entertain them', explains Coca-Cola's strategic marketing director of core brands for Europe and the Middle East.[44] Coca-Cola now features new performers in commercials broadcast in some markets instead of using only established stars, as a way of broadening the entertainment element. And it is even beaming sales promotions directly to mobile phone users in Tokyo, offering a free download of advertising music for customers who buy from Coca-Cola vending machines that day – a promotion that increased sales by 50 per cent among recipients.

Although the company usually focuses each message on one of its products or brands, it recently featured its entire product mix in a campaign addressing rising public concerns about obesity by demonstrating that the company sells a wide range of beverages, including healthier alternatives like fruit juices and bottled water. The company has also used PR to respond to criticism that it (and rival PepsiCo) are commercially exploiting students by paying school districts for the exclusive right to place branded beverage vending machines in US schools. Coca-Cola has begun distributing educational booklets about healthy food and exercise decisions; it is also promoting a new line of milk-based beverages, some to be sold only in schools. Finally, it is using advertising for societal objectives, as in South American campaigns explaining a recent change to recyclable glass bottles.[45]

Case questions

1. What kind of response (cognitive, affective or behavioural) do you think Coca-Cola wanted to elicit with the campaign featuring its entire product mix – and why?

2. What are the advantages and disadvantages of using mobile phone messages for customer sales promotions?

 **ENDNOTES**

1. Quoted in 'Orange Trains Users to Improve Phone Ability', *Campaign*, 16 May 2003, p. 12.

2. Quoted in Glen Mutel, 'Media: Strategy of the Week – Orange', *Campaign*, 8 August 2003, pp. 12ff.; also based on information from David Pringle and Kevin J. Delaney, 'Orange Chief Will Stick to His Strategy', *Wall Street Journal*, 28 October 2003, p. B4; 'Direct Mail Showcase', *Marketing*, 17 July 2003, p. 25; Lucy Barrett, 'Dale's Action Hints at Orange Disorder', *Marketing Week*, 10 July 2003, pp. 19ff; 'Orange Trains Users to Improve Phone Ability, p. 12; 'Direct Choice: Orange Bright Business', *Marketing*, 8 May 2003, p. 10.

3. 'Orange Unveils Summer Work', *Campaign*, 18 July 2003, p. 6; '£10m Spend for Orange's Learn Project', *Marketing Week*, 15 May 2003, p. 10; 'Direct: Orange Seeks to Lure Teen Texters in DM Campaign', *Marketing*, 5 December 2002, p. 10; 'Orange Cinema Spots Use Hollywood Names', *Campaign*, 23 May 2003, p. 4.

4. 'NSPCC Initiates Agency Talks for Pounds 5M Account', *Campaign*, 14 March 2003, p. 5.

5. See Sandy D. Jap and Erin Anderson, 'Testing the Life-Cycle Theory of Inter-Organisational Relations: Do Performance Outcomes Depend on the Path Taken?', *Insead Knowledge*, February 2003, www.knowledge.insead.edu.

6. See Nigel F. Piercy, 'The Marketing Budgeting Process: Marketing Management Implications', *Journal of Marketing*, October 1987, pp. 45–59.

7. Arundhati Parmar, 'POP Goes the World', *Marketing News*, 11 November 2002, p. 13.

8. Erin White, 'U.K. TV Can Pose Tricky Hurdles', *Wall Street Journal*, 27 June 2003, p. B7; Virginia Rohan, 'All Those Brand Names on TV Are No Coincidence', *The Record* (New Jersey), 19 October 2003, pp. A1, A14.

9. Lexie Williamson, 'Healthcare: Consumer Health', *PR Week* (UK), 19 September 2003, p. 14.

10. David Scheer, 'Europe's New High-Tech Role: Playing Privacy Cop to the World', *Wall Street Journal*, 10 October 2003, pp. A1, A16.

11. 'Direct Marketers Worried by Overuse of Spam SMS', *New Media Age*, 4 September 2003, p. 16.

12. Quoted in John Battelle, 'Downloading the Future of TV Advertising', *Business 2.0*, July 2003, p. 46; also: 'Honda "Cog" Ad Tops Cool League', *Marketing*, 21 August 2003, p. 2; Devin Gordon and Emily Flynn, 'For Want of a Nail, the Car Commercial Rocked', *Newsweek*, 30 June 2003, p. 14.

13. Quoted in 'BA Backs Club World with Flat Bed Ads', *Marketing*, 11 September 2003, p. 2; other sources: Stephanie Clifford, 'Most Bang for the Buck', *Business 2.0*, May

2002, p. 102; 'BA Woos the Business Market with Pounds 3M Ads', *Campaign*, 14 February 2003, p. 8.

14. Quoted in Brian Steinberg, 'Western Union Ads to Centre on Emotions for Immigrants', *Wall Street Journal*, 2 May 2003, www.wsj.com; other sources: 'Western Union P2P Case Study: Romania', *Europe Intelligence Wire*, 31 August 2003, n.p.; Kate MacArthur, 'Western Union Sets Global Effort to Protect Its Turf', *Advertising Age*, 24 March 2003, p. 16.

15. 'Media Brief: Orange Ambushes mmO2', *Marketing*, 31 July 2003, p. 7.

16. Quoted in Keith Regan, 'New and Improved Guerrilla Marketing Tactics for High Tech', *E-Commerce Times*, 14 March 2003, www.ecommercetimes.com.

17. Donna Fuscaldo, ' . . . Create a Buzz for Your Product', *Wall Street Journal*, 15 September 2003, pp. R6, R12.

18. Arundhati Parmar, 'Maximum Exposure: Advertisers Use Bodies as Billboards to Up Brand Visibility', *Marketing News*, 15 September 2003, pp. 6, 8.

19. Geoffrey A. Fowler and Sebastian Moffett, 'Adidas's Billboard Ads Give a Kick to Japanese Pedestrians', *Wall Street Journal*, 29 August 2003, pp. B1, B4.

20. Quoted in Rachel Miller, 'Door-to-Door: Delivering High Response Rates', *Marketing*, 30 January 2003, pp. 31ff.

21. Ibid.

22. Quoted in Belinda Gannaway, 'Hidden Danger of Sales Promotions', *Marketing*, 20 February 2003, pp. 31ff.; other sources: Liz Hamson, 'Measured Approach: There Is a Trade-Off Between Promotions and Profits and, Contrary to UK Marketers' Views, It Can Be Measured', *Grocer*, 19 April 2003, p. 38; Philip Kotler, *A Framework for Marketing Management*, 2nd edn (Upper Saddle River, NJ: Prentice Hall, 2003), pp. 318–19.

23. Dareth Miller, 'Fair Exchange', *Promo*, 1 September 2003, n.p.

24. 'Muller Turns the Love Up Louder for St Valentine's Day', *Grocer*, 8 February 2003, p. 48.

25. Quoted in Amie Smith Hughes, 'Home Improvement', *Promo*, 1 September 2003, n.p.

26. Quoted in Hughes, 'Home Improvement'.

27. 'Field Marketing: Once More into the Field', *Marketing Event*, 10 June 2003, p. 37.

28. Quotes in Suzanne Hamlin, 'A National Stage for Puff Pastry and Duck Jerky', *New York Times*, 6 July 2003, sec. 3, p. 4; other source: 'Trade Show Update', *Children's Business*, August 2003, pp. 52ff.

29. Jennifer Saranow, 'The Show Goes On', *Wall Street Journal*, 28 April 2003, pp. R4, R7.

30. 'Pharmaceuticals: Pushing Pills', *The Economist*, 15 February 2003, p. 61; Scott Hensley, 'More Than Ads, Drug Makers Rely on Sales Reps', *Wall Street Journal*, 14 March 2002, pp. B1, B6.

31. 'Post Office Trains Staff to Cross-Sell Products', *Marketing*, 7 August 2003, p. 4.

32. Ken Gofton, 'Direct Mail Showcase', *Marketing*, 18 September 2003, p. 25.

33. 'Net Viable for More Than Just Grocery Sales', *MMR*, 26 May 2003, p. 22.

34. Chris Dillabough, 'Monitoring Advances Lead to First Paid-For Oxfam Campaign', *New Media Age*, 14 June 2001, p. 13.

35. Arundhati Parmar, 'Sláinte!', *Marketing News*, 17 March 2003, pp. 6ff.

36. Doug McPherson, 'Riding the Wave of Opportunity', *Response*, November 2002, pp. 34ff.

37. Erin White, 'PR Firms Advise Corporations on Social-Responsibility Issues', *Wall Street Journal*, 13 November 2002, p. B10.

38. 'Campaigns: World Vision Raises Profile Among Scots – Charity PR', *PR Week* (UK), 23 May 2003, p. 13.

39. 'Hardee's Giving 1 Million Patties in Menu Switch', *Nation's Restaurant News*, 18 August 2003, p. 112.

40. Arlena Sawyers, 'It's Showtime!' *Automotive News*, 1 September 2003, p. 13.

41. Frederik Balfour, 'It's Time for a New Playbook', *Business Week*, 15 September 2003, p. 56; Yuji Utsunomiya, 'Apparel Firm Teaches Teenagers to Like Its Fashions', *Japan Times*, 1 July 2003, p. 12.

42. Brian Steinberg and Nick Wingfield, '"You Can't Always Answer Your Phone . . ."', *Wall Street Journal*, 18 July 2003, p. B1.

43. Quoted in Craig Simons, 'Marketers Woo China's Real Masses', *Wall Street Journal*, 29 August 2003, p. A6.

44. Quoted in 'Let Me Entertain You', *Marketing*, 11 September 2003, p. 20.

45. Based on information from Miriam Jordan, 'Coke Brings Glass Out of Retirement', *Wall Street Journal*, 15 October 2003, p. B2I; Chad Terhune and Gabriel Kahn, 'Coke Lures Japanese Customers with Cellphone Come-Ons', *Wall Street Journal*, 8 September 2003, pp. B1, B4; Sherri Day, 'Coke Moves with Caution to Remain in Schools', *New York Times*, 3 September 2003, p. C1; Brian Steinberg, 'Coke's New Marketing Message: Not Just Soda', *Wall Street Journal*, 28 August 2003, p. B5; 'Let Me Entertain You'; Simons, 'Marketers Woo China's Real Masses'.

10 Supporting the marketing mix

Comprehension outcomes

After studying this chapter, you will be able to:

- Explain why a marketing plan should include customer service and internal marketing strategies
- Discuss the decisions involved in planning for customer service
- Describe what an internal marketing strategy should cover

Application outcomes

After studying this chapter, you will be able to:

- Make appropriate decisions to develop a customer service strategy
- Plan internal marketing to support the marketing plan

OPENING CASE: SERVICE FIRST AT RITZ-CARLTON HOTELS

The motto, 'We are ladies and gentlemen serving ladies and gentlemen', sums up the service strategy of the 54 luxury Ritz-Carlton hotels and resorts. Each of the company's 23,000 employees in Europe, Asia, the Middle East and the Americas carries a pocket-sized card with this motto, plus the 'employee promise' and a succinct list of service basics. Ritz-Carlton hotels and resorts are elegantly decorated, impeccably maintained and offer the finest accommodation, food and amenities. But it is the company's attention to personalised service that has earned it numerous awards and – more important – traveller and travel agent loyalty.

Employees learn guests' names, note their preferences (such as room type and wake-up calls) and look for opportunities to be of service. Not only do employees respond to direct requests, they strive to anticipate what guests will want and act before being asked. If problems arise, employees are empowered to do 'whatever they think is appropriate to complete their work and serve our guests', notes company vice president Mark Lettenbichler.[1]

In addition to building strong relationships with travellers, the company has a separate strategy for working with travel agents, who are critically important channel members. A designated representative of each Ritz-Carlton property works directly with travel agents to answer questions and book rooms for clients. Some of the hotels arrange briefings during which agents can experience at first hand the service for which the company is acclaimed. This is also a time for agents to meet the staff who will, says Ritz-Carlton vice president Georgia Kirsner, 'handle their clients and fulfil their promises'.[2]

To deliver such a high level of customer service, Ritz-Carlton managers start with hiring, continue with training and devise rewards for performance. Experience counts, but attitude and motivation are also major factors in employee selection. After staff members are hired for the opening of new Ritz-Carlton properties, they receive rigorous training, including talks by executives such as Simon Cooper, the company president, about the significance of quality customer service. Cooper distinguishes between elements of the product offering that guests can buy (such as booking a room, paying for a meal, arranging for sightseeing) and those that cannot be bought (such as service in anticipation of a guest's request and good memories of the hotel stay). The list of elements that cannot be purchased, Cooper says, 'is what creates value and loyalty for the Ritz-Carlton guest. What guests can't pay for is what they value the most'.[3]

The company's service is so renowned that it now sells seminars teaching managers from other industries how to plan for service excellence. Director of training Rob George tells those attending these seminars: 'When it comes to pleasing guests, there are no wrong decisions – some are just much more expensive than others.'[4]

CHAPTER PREVIEW

Customers expect good service from any organisation, but great service is an especially compelling point of differentiation in the hotel industry. Ritz-Carlton's reputation depends on every employee delivering a high level of service to every guest at every property, consistent with the elegant surroundings, room rates and upmarket advertising. Great service attracts new customers, encourages repeat business, generates word-of-mouth referrals, draws positive publicity, smoothes the way for travel agents to sell to guests and confers a competitive edge. Yet great service does not simply happen – it requires careful planning and marketing to internal audiences.

This chapter covers planning for the customer service and internal marketing strategies used to support your marketing-mix strategies. The first section explains the vital role of customer service and internal marketing in any marketing plan. The second section discusses some of the decisions you must make in planning customer service strategy, including those about process and outcome; service levels; service before, during and after the purchase; and service recovery. The final section looks at the decisions involved in developing internal marketing strategy. *As you read this chapter, think about how the principles can be applied to create a cohesive, practical marketing plan that will achieve its objectives and satisfy customers, given the organisation's capabilities.*

THE ROLE OF CUSTOMER SERVICE AND INTERNAL MARKETING

Even in organisations that maintain a designated service department, customer service is actually every employee's responsibility. This is because customers judge service quality by their interaction at every point of contact, not just when they are making a purchase or complaining about a problem. From the customer's perspective, service is an integral part of the experience of dealing with a product or brand. Thus, if your company does not respond to a request for information or your non-profit organisation does not acknowledge a monetary contribution, the customer perceives these lapses as poor customer service.

Poor and inconsistent customer service quality can hinder your ability to achieve marketing plan objectives, even if you have the most meticulously researched targeting and positioning or the most carefully planned marketing-mix strategies. Just as bad, many dissatisfied customers tell others about their experiences, generating negative word of mouth that can hurt your product or brand's image.[5] It is important to see complaints not as annoyances but as excellent opportunities to identify areas for improvement and give the complaining customers tangible reasons to continue the relationship.

As Figure 10.1 indicates, the customer service strategy supports the marketing effort outside the organisation and is, in turn, implemented with the support of the internal marketing strategy, which focuses on people and processes inside the organisation.

FIGURE 10.1 Customer service and internal marketing

Marketing applications of customer service

Good customer service can make a highly positive contribution to your marketing plan. You can use it to help in the following areas:

- *Attract new customers.* Even manufactured goods such as industrial rubber hoses cannot be marketed without customer service these days. 'Our business is increasingly a service business', observes the president of Summers Rubber Co., a US manufacturer.[6] Company engineers not only match hose design to each customer's particular use, but are available to diagnose any hose problems that might occur. Good customer service can therefore attract new customers through added value. Medical centres are also using good customer service to attract patients. One group of US hospitals guarantees that a nurse will look at each accident and emergency patient within 15 minutes of arrival and a doctor will be involved within 30 minutes – or the visit is free.[7]

- *Retain current customers.* If your current customers remain loyal, you will need fewer or less expensive customer acquisition programmes to meet your objectives. According to John Girard, general manager of the Marco Polo Hongkong Hotel, 'Repeat business saves us 10 times the cost and effort of getting new business.' This makes initial customer service contacts even more important: 'Guests judge us immediately. They will not come again if we deliver mediocre service', he says.[8]

- *Build image for competitive advantage.* You can leverage a good customer service image as a competitive strength. In the B2B market, Saint-Gobain Abrasives uses customer service to support its global reputation as a provider of high-quality industrial abrasives. Technical sales representatives and application engineers from the UK manufacturing plant visit customers, learn about their needs, recommend suitable abrasive products such as grinding wheels and then follow up to answer customers' technical questions after the purchase.[9]

- *Achieve objectives.* If you deliver good customer service that satisfies customers the first time, you save time and money, contributing to the achievement of both financial and marketing objectives. Marten Transport, a family-run freight company, takes great care with deliveries because its refrigerated lorries carry perishable items such as frozen foods and fresh vegetables. The company uses a satellite tracking system to follow every aspect of every pick-up, transport and delivery, then shares the information with customers so they can work together to improve efficiency. Although some freight companies are having financial difficulties, Marten Transport is reaping profits and strengthening customer relationships. 'The success of our business is in the details', says the chairman.[10]

Marketing applications of internal marketing

Good customer service – and, in fact, effective implementation of the entire marketing plan – depends on **internal marketing**, a carefully coordinated set of policies and activities designed to build internal employee relationships and reinforce and reward internal commitment to the marketing effort and to good customer service. You need to do more than give notice of a forthcoming television campaign for your internal audiences. Internal marketing strategy covers decisions about hiring and training managers and employees, motivating and rewarding them for working to satisfy customers and communicating with them about marketing plans and performance. In short, robust internal marketing lays the foundation for implementing all your marketing activities and delivering good, consistent customer service according to your strategy.

You can use internal marketing to help in the following areas:

- *Focus on the customer.* Some employees in functions with little customer contact – such as finance or human resources – may get caught up in the daily pressures of work and lose their customer focus. Internal marketing is a good way to refocus on the customer and remind employees that their performance is essential for implementing plans that serve and satisfy customers.

- *Build employee knowledge.* Be sure employees throughout the hierarchy know at least the general outline of the marketing effort, are informed about the needs and expectations of targeted customers and understand what you want to achieve. This knowledge gives them the background they need to serve customers and solve any service problems. The Ritz-Carlton chain hires people who have a good attitude about delivering high-quality service; offers training and management support as well as a pocket-sized reminder of service basics to build employee knowledge; and then rewards those who perform.

- *Encourage organisation-wide cooperation with and commitment to the plan.* Success really is in the details, as the head of Marten Transport observed. If your organisation's employees do not understand the plan or resent it, they may not give details the proper attention, let alone implement every tactic to full effect. Remember that marketing is not the only function affected by the marketing plan; manufacturing, finance and all the other departments must cooperate to achieve the objectives and you need senior management's support. Use internal marketing to build relations inside the organisation and encourage commitment among those responsible for approving the plan and making it succeed through implementation.

- *Boost pride in performance.* Internal marketing can increase employees' sense of involvement and boost their pride in performing over and above expectations. For example, the Marco Polo Hongkong Hotel gives widespread internal recognition to employees who deliver outstanding service, based on guest comments. Such feedback shows employees that the organisation and its customers appreciate good customer service.

The next two sections highlight how you can plan for customer service and for internal marketing in the course of preparing a marketing plan. Many of the examples in the following pages are from service businesses but the customer service ideas can be adapted for many situations.

PLANNING CUSTOMER SERVICE STRATEGY

Knowing what your customers want and value, you face process decisions about how to make the customer service experience as pleasant as possible. You also face outcome decisions related to whether the customer service is delivered on time, as promised and in a satisfactory manner. Your customers will be dissatisfied if they receive the promised quality of service but find the experience of arranging for it tedious or inconvenient. On the other hand, customers who are satisfied with both the process and the outcomes are likely to become loyal. The following example shows how Auto Europe delivers good customer service.

In this example, the process includes inviting travel agents to place orders in the way that is most convenient for them; establishing a 24-hour free hot-line for fast, personal service; and ensuring that staff members are always available to respond to questions and deal with problems. One decision Khalidi has made to influence service outcomes is to guarantee that any caller who waits on 'hold' for more than a minute will receive a future discount. Auto Europe gives few discounts because its employees actually do answer and react quickly, making the process as smooth as possible for callers and providing good customer service outcomes. The specific process and outcome decisions that you will make depend on your objectives, marketing strategies, resources and capabilities.

MARKETING IN PRACTICE: AUTO EUROPE

Auto Europe specialises in arranging car-hire services for US travellers visiting Europe, Australia, New Zealand, South Africa and other countries. CEO Imad Khalidi is personally involved in building strong relationships with travel agents, who provide 90 per cent of the company's business. He visits agents and guarantees that Auto Europe offers the best car-hire rates. He also sets his agency apart by offering sports cars and luxury cars such as Alfa Romeo and Jaguar as well as chauffeured cars with multilingual drivers. However, agents stay loyal because of the company's top-quality customer service, which enables them to satisfy travellers' needs. Agents can phone or use Auto Europe's online reservation system to check car availability, place orders and receive immediate confirmations.

Khalidi and his staff are ready to resolve any problem at any time. The company maintains a 24-hour free hot-line for emergency calls so car-hire customers can get assistance whenever needed. The CEO sets a good example by working closely with his team to solve problems, even if a call comes in what is the middle of the night at Auto Europe's headquarters. Says the president of one agency: 'They listen, they act and they do it fast. It's really comforting to deal with a company that can offer that level of personal attention.' For his part, the CEO understands that good customer service is vital to building long-term loyalty. 'If you lose a travel agency, you lose hundreds of bookings', Khalidi stresses. 'This is why we are on our toes with service.' Auto Europe has been successful because 'You cannot find this level of service at other car rental firms', he says.[11]

You must also consider what level of customer service you will promise and be able to deliver; the type of customer service you will offer before, during and after a purchase; and the process you will follow to recover from any customer service lapses (*see* Figure 10.2).

Decisions	Purpose
Process	To create a satisfactory experience for customers who arrange for service delivery
Outcomes	To deliver service on time, as promised and with the expected result for customer satisfaction
Timing	To provide needed service before, during or after a purchase
Service recovery	To handle complaints, fix lapses in customer service delivery and identify areas of improvement

FIGURE 10.2   Key customer service strategy decisions

Levels of service

Few companies can afford the highest level of customer service, with completely personalised attention immediately available on request, but then again, not every customer in every segment can afford (or will expect) such service. For example, many carriers in the airline industry are eliminating extras, cutting costs and reducing ticket prices to compete with no-frills, low-fare airlines. Bangkok Airways is going against this trend: It pampers its passengers – tourists visiting Thailand – and charges accordingly. Passengers waiting to board its planes in Thai airports can eat snacks, surf the Net, examine museum-quality ceramics or relax with garden views, all included in the fare; on-board customer service is also gracious. Although Bangkok Airways is small, its high level of customer service is attracting more passengers and yielding profits.[12]

The level of customer service you plan should be consistent with the following elements:

- *Customer needs and expectations*. What do targeted customers want, need and expect in terms of customer service? Passengers who fly Bangkok Airways expect nothing less than a high level of customer service. Compare their expectations to those of Asda shoppers, who pay discount prices and do not expect a high level of customer service. In fact, Asda stores in the United Kingdom are experimenting with self-service checkout tills, with the result that shoppers would perform services previously handled by cashiers at the point of sale.[13] Use marketing research to identify the service levels that would satisfy customers in each targeted segment; uncover trends in customer turnover; and determine whether customers are defecting because of poor customer service. The US store chain Federated Department Stores found through research that shoppers care more about fast, convenient shopping and uncomplicated pricing than about being waited on by sales staff.[14] If you segment your market according to service usage and expectations, you may find promising opportunities and steer the organisation away from unprofitable segments.[15]

- *Positioning and competitive strategies*. What level of service is consistent with your product's or brand's positioning? What level of service would help the product or brand compete more effectively? Commonwealth Bank in Australia understands that good customer service is an important point of differentiation in the highly competitive financial services industry. Its managers therefore redesigned service processes to produce better service outcomes. As one example, they eliminated redundant bank procedures, rearranged branch layouts and changed staffing (process), aiming to reduce queue times to five minutes or less (outcome).[16]

- *Other marketing-mix decisions*. Is the product new or complicated? To provide service for customers who buy its high-end plasma television screens, for example, Philips India has opened a series of Star Service Centres that stock parts and diagnose product problems.[17] How is pricing likely to influence customers' expectations of customer service? Do the product's promotions promise or imply a high level of customer service? What level of customer service can your channel members deliver? How will a certain level of customer service fit in with the strategies and objectives in your marketing plan?

- *Organisational resources and strengths.* What level of customer service fits in with your organisation's financial and human resources? Is technology available to support or substitute for customer service delivery? Is good customer service delivery a particular strength? Can or should customer service be outsourced? To improve response times and in-stock situations, Japan's Fujitsu Technology Solutions outsources its North American post-purchase services to United Parcel Services. Under this contract, UPS plans parts inventory, distributes parts and manages returns for Fujitsu's technology products.[18] In deciding about customer service levels, you should carefully analyse the cost–benefit trade-offs for each targeted segment.[19]

You may need new customer service strategies if you notice changes in competitive activity, buying behaviour or customer needs. Meiji Dairies in Japan decided to re-emphasise its home delivery service after years of declining participation because customers were buying milk in supermarkets. With less time to shop, customers were placing more value on convenience. Now Meiji has signed up more than 2.6 million households to receive fresh milk, yoghurt and other dairy items at their doors each morning. For these customers, it is worth paying a slightly higher price for the convenience.[20]

Pre-purchase service

Depending on your product and market, customers may have questions and require service assistance before they buy. Business buyers in particular may need help with product specifications or configuration, installation options and warranty or repair information. If you market directly to customers, you must be prepared to provide at least some service before a purchase transaction. If you market through intermediaries, you will be relying on channel members to answer customers' questions and demonstrate features.

You want to be sure customers get the service they need at this point in the buying process because otherwise they may choose another company's product or forego the purchase entirely. Harley-Davidson, for example, offers motorcycle riding lessons and safety tips to help prospective buyers pass the riding test so they feel qualified to buy and ride its powerful bikes.[21] To encourage non-tech-oriented consumers to buy new electronic products and related software, Hewlett-Packard and Microsoft have partnered to open demonstration centres in retail stores. Employees answer questions and show how to use products in combination, such as the easiest way to move images from a digital camera to a printer. Why make a point of demonstrating products before the sale? 'Would you buy a car without a test drive?', asks a Hewlett-Packard executive.[22]

Matsushita, the Japanese maker of electronics and appliances, also gives its channel members extra support so they can provide good pre- and post-purchase customer service. In the Philippines, for instance, the company holds periodic seminars to introduce dealers and repair technicians to new products and the latest technical features. This attention to customer service has helped Matsushita maintain a strong competitive position in the Philippine market.[23]

Point-of-purchase service

At the time or place of the purchase, your customers may want help in: testing a product; completing the paperwork for a transaction; arranging for delivery or pick-up; arranging payment method or terms; taking advantage of promotions connected with purchasing; or other purchase-related service tasks. If your customer service falls short here, customers may not complete the purchase; conversely, if you deliver good customer service during the purchase transaction, you will build customer satisfaction and encourage repeat purchasing.

W.W. Grainger, the US-based distributor of industrial parts and supplies, provides point-of-purchase customer service on behalf of all the manufacturers whose products it sells. When customers visit one of Grainger's 600 branch outlets, they get personal attention from staff members. 'You won't find a customer here who waits more than a couple of minutes', says the manager of one Grainger outlet. 'We stay focused on the customer and make sure they leave here with their problem solved', says another Grainger manager.[24]

Post-purchase service

To encourage repeat business and strengthen customer relations, you will probably have to deliver some sort of customer service after the purchase. This may include: training buyers in product use; explaining maintenance or repair procedures; exchanging defective products; returning products for refunds; installing replacement parts; or other post-purchase services. Some companies are using technology to detect the need for post-purchase service even before customers notice any problems. As one example, Carrier can equip its air conditioners with software and Internet links to signal service technicians the moment any fault develops, preventing any serious difficulties.[25]

Whether your organisation has a physical presence or operates only on the Web, post-purchase service should be part of the planning process. For instance, Mothercare, the UK maternity and children's clothing chain, invites customers to return items purchased online by mail or in a local store. Should a child's pushchair purchased at Mothercare need repair, the customer can borrow a pushchair free.[26] Although many retailers allow in-store refunds of merchandise purchased online, recent research shows that the customer service process is sometimes cumbersome and time-consuming; the study also cited as good customer service the ability to return online purchases to stores.[27]

Service recovery

Because customer service may not be delivered perfectly every time, you should plan for **service recovery**, how your organisation will recover from a service lapse and satisfy customers. Service recovery offers an excellent opportunity to demonstrate understanding of customers' expectations and needs and – equally important – rebuild ties with customers by implementing a speedy and satisfactory resolution. According to one study, at least 70 per cent of dissatisfied customers will keep buying from a company if their complaints are resolved satisfactorily. If you please these customers you can turn them from potential defectors into advocates for your organisation – a good way to stimulate positive word of mouth.[28]

Internal marketing is vital for service recovery, because employees must have the commitment, skills and authority to clarify the extent and nature of a service lapse, offer a suitable response and see that it is implemented as promised. For instance, rather than refer a guest to someone else or write a report for later action, any Ritz-Carlton employee who receives a complaint is responsible for satisfying the guest.

As you plan for service recovery, focus on both process and outcome (*see* Figure 10.3). Customers will be more dissatisfied if you provide no convenient method for receiving complaints or fail to resolve their complaints satisfactorily. Sometimes customers only want to express their dissatisfaction and receive an apology. The director of customer relations for a regional airline observes: 'Things do go wrong but you have to try to recover. You have to listen and try to find out what the customer needs.'[29]

Be sure to seek the input of staff members who deal directly with customers when determining what tools and support you need to correct service mistakes. Also solicit suggestions from these employees for practical ways to improve delivery and prevent service lapses.[30] And try to involve top management in service recovery, as doing so will go a long way toward proving your organisation's commitment to satisfaction and to keeping the customer relationship alive. The head of Citizens Trust Bank in Atlanta makes a point of listening and responding to service problems. 'Customers are always pleasantly surprised that they can talk directly to me, the president of the bank, when they have a complaint', he says.[31]

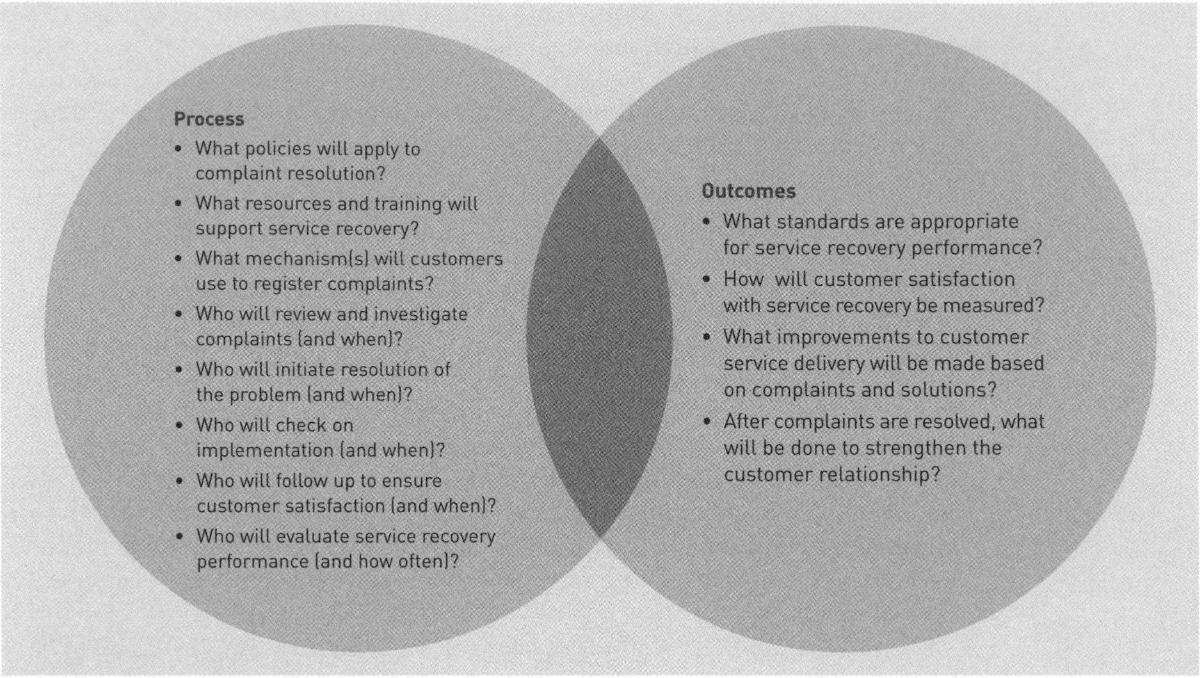

Process

- What policies will apply to complaint resolution?
- What resources and training will support service recovery?
- What mechanism(s) will customers use to register complaints?
- Who will review and investigate complaints (and when)?
- Who will initiate resolution of the problem (and when)?
- Who will check on implementation (and when)?
- Who will follow up to ensure customer satisfaction (and when)?
- Who will evaluate service recovery performance (and how often)?

Outcomes

- What standards are appropriate for service recovery performance?
- How will customer satisfaction with service recovery be measured?
- What improvements to customer service delivery will be made based on complaints and solutions?
- After complaints are resolved, what will be done to strengthen the customer relationship?

FIGURE 10.3 Planning service recovery process and outcomes

PLANNING INTERNAL MARKETING STRATEGY

Ideally, you want your internal marketing strategy to engage the hearts and minds of managers and employees at every organisational level – the internal equivalent of what good external marketing seeks to achieve. First, of course, you will 'market' the marketing plan to gain senior management approval and support. Then, for the approved plan to succeed, you need internal marketing to build enthusiastic commitment among the organisation's middle managers, front-line managers and employees.[32] This means going beyond a catchy slogan or one-time special event to develop an ongoing internal marketing strategy that you can adapt as the situation changes.

Although the specifics of internal marketing strategy will differ from organisation to organisation, most touch on the following:

- *Hiring and training*. Even when you are not directly involved in personnel decisions, you can influence hiring procedures to ensure that new employees have a positive attitude toward customer service. You should also influence or participate in training to build the staff's knowledge of the customer and of the marketing effort.

- *Standards*. What, exactly, constitutes performance in implementing marketing programmes? Ritz-Carlton employees are expected to learn guests' names, record and respond to guests' preferences and completely resolve any guest complaints they may receive. Auto Europe expects employees to handle phone calls promptly and avoid putting callers on hold for more than one minute. Your marketing performance standards should be consistent with the marketing plan's (and the organisation's) objectives, with other job-related standards, with what customers want and with what you are promising and promoting.

- *Communication*. This is essential for reinforcing objectives and standards; co-ordinating programmes and implementation responsibilities; keeping employees informed; and keeping them interested and connected. You use any number of communication techniques, from printed newsletters and voice-mail messages to internal websites and teleconferences. For instance, the Marco Polo Hongkong Hotel has condensed its service basics into five succinct messages introduced at a company party, repeated at staff meetings and printed on pocket calendars for employees to check daily. The hotel also circulates the results of customer service studies and compliments submitted by guests.

- *Participation*. Inviting participation in the marketing planning process can encourage stronger support and commitment among those who are charged with implementation. Customer contact personnel, in particular, may be able to suggest how your proposed programmes can be improved. In other words, view internal marketing communication as a two-way, relationship-building dialogue, with information flowing to you and from you, as Disney does.

MARKETING IN PRACTICE: WALT DISNEY

'Our goal is to treat one another the way we treat our guests', says Scott Milligan, Walt Disney's manager of performance/training.[33] The company gives every employee at every level some training in 'Disney Traditions', which includes learning about service quality standards and participating in team-building exercises to build internal cooperation. During peak periods, managers get out from behind their desks and work alongside theme park employees in restaurants, on rides or wherever needed, gaining first-hand knowledge of what customers want and how the company is doing.

Disney relies on internal communication to support internal marketing activities. Managers hold daily staff meetings to keep employees ('cast members') updated; the company also distributes a newsletter in multiple languages every other week to keep everyone fully informed about new initiatives and ongoing activities. Employees can access the Disney intranet for more detail and they are asked to complete a yearly survey about how well the organisation and its managers are communicating. Cast members who deliver excellent service performance earn rewards for their performance. Milligan notes that Disney receives hundreds of letters from customers ('guests') every day, describing 'how one or another member of our cast helped make their vacation special'.[34]

- *Monitoring and rewards.* Are employees performing up to the standards that have been set and cooperating for smooth implementation of marketing programmes? If not, what needs improvement? If so, how should you reinforce and reward good performance? Your internal marketing reward system must be consistent with the organisation's overall system of motivation, performance evaluation and rewards.

Walt Disney, the US entertainment company, puts great emphasis on internal marketing, including all of these areas.

See Chapter 12 for more about controlling marketing plan implementation.

CHAPTER SUMMARY

1. *Explain why a marketing plan should include customer service and internal marketing strategies.*

   The customer service strategy supports the external marketing effort. In turn, implementation of the customer service strategy and all marketing-mix strategies in the marketing plan must be supported by a suitable internal marketing strategy focusing on people and processes inside the organisation. Customer service can help the organisation attract new customers, retain current customers, build image for competitive advantage and achieve its objectives. Internal marketing can help the organisation focus on customers, increase employee knowledge, encourage internal cooperation and commitment to marketing and boost pride in performance.

2. *Discuss the decisions involved in planning for customer service.*

   Marketers face decisions about process (the experience customers will have in arranging for customer service) and outcomes (delivering service on time, as promised and to the customer's satisfaction). They also face decisions about the appropriate level of customer service to be promised and delivered; the delivery of customer service before, during and after a purchase; and the process of recovering from any customer service lapses.

3. *Describe what an internal marketing strategy should cover.*

   In addition to gaining top management approval and support, internal marketing generally covers involvement in hiring and training; performance standards; communication; participation; performance monitoring and rewards.

KEY TERM DEFINITIONS

internal marketing Coordinated set of activities and policies designed to build employee relationships within the organisation and reinforce internal commitment to the marketing plan and to good customer service

service recovery How the organisation recovers from a service lapse and satisfies the customer

THE PRACTICAL MARKETER CHECKLIST NO. 10:
CUSTOMER SERVICE STRATEGY

External considerations

What level of service do targeted customers need, expect and prefer?

What level of service fits with the positioning and value as perceived by customers?

Do customers need service support before the purchase? During the purchase? After the purchase?

How will you resolve complaints and satisfy customers?

What competitive, industry and market considerations might affect customer service strategy?

What legal, regulatory, ecological, technological, social or ethical issues might affect customer service strategy?

Internal considerations

What customer service level is practical, based on organisational resources and objectives?

Will other organisations be involved with service support before, during or after the purchase?

How will you train and reward employees and channel members for delivering the proper level of customer service?

What service recovery plans and policies do you need?

How will your customer service strategy fit in with the personal selling strategy and other decisions about marketing?

ONLINE RESOURCES

CUSTOMER SERVICE

- International Customer Service Association (www.icsa.com) – Offers access to case studies and white papers about customer service trends and successes.

- Institute of Customer Service (www.instituteofcustomerservice.com) – Presents glossary of customer service terms, information about service delivery and links to additional sites.

- EFQM (www.efqm.org) – Provides benchmarks for customer service excellence, publishers service studies and offers educational programmes to help organisations deliver good customer service.

QUESTIONS FOR DISCUSSION AND ANALYSIS

1. What might non-profit organisations and government agencies do to plan for service recovery?

2. Is customer service more important in B2B marketing than in consumer marketing?

3. Should internal marketing be tied only to the period covered by each marketing plan?

APPLY YOUR KNOWLEDGE

Select a retailer with a nearby store location and an online presence. Visit one store, browse the website and then analyse this retailer's customer service strategy.

- Where on the website does the retailer place its customer service policies? Where in the store are such policies displayed? Are the policies practical and easy to understand?

- How would you describe the level of service in the store? How is this consistent with the retailer's positioning and competitive situation, its pricing and other strategies as implemented in the store?

- What pre-purchase, point-of-purchase and post-purchase services are offered online? Does the website invite shoppers to interact with service representatives via e-mail, online chat, telephone or some other method?

- What pre-purchase, point-of-purchase and post-purchase customer services are offered in the store? How do these differ (if at all) from the online customer service offerings?

- What changes in customer service strategy would you suggest for this retailer?

- Prepare a brief oral or written report summarising your analysis.

 **BUILD YOUR OWN MARKETING PLAN**

Continue developing your marketing plan by making decisions about customer service and internal marketing strategies. First, what do you think is an appropriate level of customer service to support the positioning and marketing-mix decisions made earlier in the planning process? How does this level of service fit in with customers' needs and expectations? How does it compare with the level of customer service offered by competitors? What pre-purchase, point-of-purchase and post-purchase customer service will you plan to offer? Will you have the resources to support the level and types of service you envision? How will you use internal marketing to describe the marketing plan and build commitment inside the company? Outline one or more customer service programmes and internal marketing programmes, based on your budget and on earlier marketing plan decisions, and note how these will help achieve your objectives and fulfil customers' needs. Finally, document your ideas in *Marketing Plan Pro* software or in a written marketing plan.

CLOSING CASE: DRIVING QUALITY AND CUSTOMER SERVICE AT MERCEDES-BENZ

'Quality is part of our heritage, one of our core values', stresses Mercedes-Benz boss Jürgen Hubbert.[35] This reputation for quality brings people into showrooms to buy, where good customer service keeps them coming back for post-purchase maintenance and encourages repeat purchasing. If customers have complaints about quality, however, they expect their local dealers to come up with solutions.

For years, Mercedes-Benz ranked at the top of an influential US survey of car quality; then the company slid below number 20, on the basis of customers' reports of car problems after three years of ownership. Mercedes fell out of the top rankings in a European survey of customer satisfaction, as well. Hubbert says the main problem is the sophisticated electronics systems Mercedes incorporates into new models. Therefore the company is having its US dealers expand their service facilities and train new technicians to diagnose and fix ever-more complex components. Joachim Schmidt, who heads worldwide sales and marketing, points out that the dealers are successfully addressing nearly every customer complaint. This is confirmed by a recent Customer Service Index survey, which shows that Mercedes has improved capacity for timely servicing of new cars.

'We have customers that have high expectations', Schmidt observes.[36] Mercedes' service recovery strategy is therefore focused on doing what is right for the customer. Consider what happened when 2,000 buyers ordered and paid for E-class Mercedes vehicles equipped with an optional navigation system. Dealers told customers that delays in receiving supplies of the navigation system would result in dealer installation rather than factory installation. But once the navigation system became available a few months later, Mercedes decided against dealer installation. 'The retrofit is very complex and time-consuming', a spokesperson explained. 'Our feeling is that the customers would be better served if we could simply move them into vehicles which have already been produced with a new navigation system.'[37] Mercedes offered new E-class cars to all 2,000 buyers (and sold the cars received in exchange as used vehicles).

Post-purchase service not only generates revenue for dealers, but influences customer satisfaction and brand loyalty. This is why Mercedes dealers like Atlanta Classic Cars are adding new amenities and finding innovative ways to boost customer service levels. For example, Atlanta Classic Cars will drive customers to a local shopping centre (and bring them back) if they want to browse while waiting for their Mercedes cars to be serviced. The dealer invites customers to enjoy the on-site nature reserve, use the putting green and driving range or watch through a huge garage window as their cars are serviced.

Good customer service is important regardless of whether the economy is up or down, because 'people will service their cars even if they're not buying', notes the dealership's president, Cathy Ellis. She acknowledges that customers' time is valuable. 'If you come out here for an oil change, you can hit a bucket of [golf] balls. You won't be totally wasting your time', she observes.[38]

Case questions

1. Why would a Mercedes dealership install a huge window so customers – and anyone who visits the showroom – can watch technicians servicing vehicles?

2. What can Cathy Ellis do to determine whether her service strategy is having an effect on the behaviour of Atlanta Classic Cars' customers?

 **ENDNOTES**

1. Quoted in Wendy Ng, 'The Ritz-Carlton Refers to Its Employees as Its "Ladies and Gentlemen"', *Asia Africa Intelligence Wire*, 24 April 2003, n.p.

2. Quoted in Erin F. Sternthal, 'Designs on the Future', *Travel Agent*, 10 March 2003, pp. 32ff.

3. Ibid.

4. Quoted in Mary Sisson, 'Dose of Hospitality', *Crain's New York Business*, 14 April 2003, p. 3; also based on information from Wendy Ng, 'The Ritz-Carlton Refers to Its Employees as Its "Ladies and Gentlemen"'; Erin F. Sternthal, 'Designs on the Future'; and www.ritzcarlton.com.

5. Jane Spencer, 'Cases of "Customer Rage" Mount as Bad Service Prompts Venting', *Wall Street Journal*, 17 September 2003, pp. D4ff.

6. Quoted in Clare Ansberry, 'Manufacturers Find Themselves Increasingly in the Service Sector', *Wall Street Journal*, 10 February 2003, p. A2.

7. Sisson, 'Dose of Hospitality'.

8. Quoted in Wendy Ng, 'Guests Help Hotel to Raise Levels of Service Excellence', *Asia Africa Intelligence Wire*, 29 March 2003, n.p.

9. 'Delivering Manufacturing Excellence', *Foundry Trade Journal*, April 2003, pp. 26ff.

10. 'Trucker Rewards Customers for Good Behavior', *Wall Street Journal*, September 9, 2003, p. B4.

11. All quotes in James Olearchik, 'On the Fast Track with Agents', *Travel Agent*, 5 August 2002, pp. 50+.

12. 'Rolling Out the Red Carpet', *The Economist*, 7 September 2002, p. 58.

13. 'Self-Service Trials', *Grocer*, 9 August 2003, p. 4.

14. Shelly Branch, 'Forget "May I Help You?"', *Wall Street Journal*, 8 July 2003, pp. B1ff.

15. See Russell G. Bundschuh and Theodore M. Dezvane, 'How to Make After-Sales Services Pay Off', *McKinsey Quarterly*, no. 4, 2003, www.mckinseyquarterly.com.

16. 'Harley Focuses on the Service Experience', *Australian Banking & Finance*, 15 July 2003, p. 11.

17. 'Philips Now for Star Service at Premium End', *Asia Africa Intelligence Wire*, 28 July 2003, n.p.

18. 'Fujitsu Chooses UPS for Post-Sales Service', *Journal of Commerce Online*, 29 September 2003, n.p.

19. See Simon Glynn and Ewan Jones, 'The Satisfaction Payoff', *Marketing Management*, September–October 2003, pp. 26ff.

20. Taiga Uranaka, 'Got Milk Delivery? Doorstep Service Doubles in Last 10 Years', *Japan Times*, 24 July 2003, p. 8.

21. Joseph Weber, 'Hurdles on the Road to Hog Heaven', *Business Week*, 10 November 2003, pp. 96–8.

22. Adam Lashinsky, 'Shootout in Gadget Land', *Fortune*, 10 November 2003, pp. 74ff.

23. 'Matsushita Electric Corp. Strengthens Customer Service', *Asia Africa Intelligence Wire*, 1 August 2003, n.p.

24. Quoted in Nancy Syverson, 'Inside Grainger', *Industrial Maintenance & Plant Operation*, November 2002, pp. 20ff.

25. Jaikumar Vijayan, 'IBM Service Follows Products After Delivery', *Computerworld*, 9 July 2001, p. 14.

26. www.mothercare.com.

27. Valerie Seckler, 'Shopping Woes Deter Retailers from Web', *WWD*, 29 August 2003, p. 13.

28. Rod Stiefbold, 'Dissatisfied Customers Require Recovery Plans', *Marketing News*, 27 October 2003, pp. 44–6.

29. Don Oldenburg, 'Seller Beware', *Washington Post*, 9 September 2003, p. C10.

30. Ron Zemke, 'The Customer Revolution', *Training*, July 2002, pp. 44–48.

31. Quoted in Charles Haddad, 'Eyes on the $1 Billion Prize', *Business Week*, 7 April 2003, p. 72.

32. See 'Internal Comms Failing to Capture Hearts and Minds', *PR Week* (UK), 11 July 2003, p. 2.

33. Quoted in 'Working Their Magic: Disney Culture Molds Happy Employees', *Employee Benefit News*, 1 September 2003, www.benefitnews.com.

34. Ibid.

35. Quoted in Alex Taylor III, 'Mercedes Hits a Pothole', *Fortune*, 27 October 2003, pp. 140–6.

36. 'Mercedes Reviews Tech Leadership', *Automotive News Europe*, 22 September 2003, pp. 1ff.

37. Quoted in Lee Hawkins Jr, 'Mercedes Offers New Cars to 2,000 Customers', *Wall Street Journal*, 22 July 2003, p. D4.

38. Quoted in Greg Bluestein, 'Atlanta Mercedes Dealer Piles on Service Amenities', *Atlanta Journal-Constitution*, 15 July 2003, www.ajc.com; also based on information from 'Mercedes Reviews Tech Leadership'; Taylor, 'Mercedes Hits a Pothole'; Hawkins, 'Mercedes Offers New Cars to 2,000 Customers'; Ann Keeton, 'Car Dealers' Customer Service Is Losing Ground, Study Finds', *Wall Street Journal*, 24 July 2003, p. D4.

Closing case: Forecasting and scheduling for success at Zara

Endotes

Comprehension outcomes

After studying this chapter, you will be able to:

- Describe how and why marketers plan with forecasts, budgets, schedules and metrics
- Identify the types of forecasts and forecasting approaches available to support marketing planning
- Discuss budgeting methods and types of budgets used in marketing planning
- Explain how and why marketers select and apply metrics for tracking progress

Application outcomes

After studying this chapter, you will be able to:

- Prepare for forecasting, budgeting and scheduling during the planning process
- Select metrics to measure interim progress after marketing plan implementation

OPENING CASE: MEASURING THE NATURE CONSERVANCY'S PERFORMANCE

Non-profit organisations, like their business counterparts, need to measure marketing and organisational performance on a regular basis. In five decades of operation, the non-profit Nature Conservancy has preserved more than 93 million acres of land and raised money to protect plants and animals in 29 nations. Despite this impressive performance, its senior managers were concerned not long ago about whether the organisation was, in fact, moving toward fulfilling its mission: 'to preserve the plants, animals and natural communities that represent the diversity of life on Earth by protecting the lands and waters they need to survive'.[1]

Traditionally, the Nature Conservancy had measured yearly marketing performance in terms of the amount of money raised, the number of members and membership fees income. Year after year, these numbers had moved ever higher, with global membership now well over one million. The organisation was measuring long-term performance in terms of the number of acres preserved country by country – numbers that have also increased dramatically since the organisation was founded in 1946.

However, Nature Conservancy executives realised that these performance measures did not directly relate to the part of the mission dealing with preserving 'diversity of life on Earth'. They therefore set out to develop measures for tracking progress toward fulfilling the entire mission and reaching long-term goals through marketing, preservation activities and resource allocation. After considerable deliberation, they decided on a 'family of measures' covering three categories: impact measures (to determine progress toward the mission and keep the organisation focused on long-term goals); activity measures (to determine progress in implementing programmes that protect land and biodiversity); and capacity measures (to determine progress toward building resources that enable the organisation to implement effective programmes).

Applying these measures to the organisation's performance, management weeded out activities that were inconsistent with the mission and reordered marketing priorities in accordance with pre-set objectives. As one example, the Nature Conservancy's ambitious Yunnan Great Rivers Project in China – initiated with an investment of less than €2,000 – now operates on a five-year plan to preserve endangered habitats, discourage polluting activities and encourage ecologically friendly activities, working with the provincial government. To be sure this project moves ahead as planned, management regularly measures interim progress toward the five-year objectives, compares actual resource use against projected use and checks completion dates against scheduled deadlines.[2]

CHAPTER PREVIEW

The purpose of measuring marketing progress and performance is to determine whether your plan is having the intended effect. As the opening example showed, the Nature Conservancy decided on a family of measures to use in checking that its various initiatives were moving the organisation in the direction of fulfilling its entire mission, not just one or two parts of it. The time to plan for measuring progress and performance is before you implement your marketing plan, so you can establish standards and checkpoints in advance for measuring outcomes at specific intervals. Then, by monitoring your results after implementation, you can assess progress in the context of previous results, industry performance, overall market conditions and other factors. These analyses show when and where performance is not meeting projections and help you diagnose the need for marketing control, as covered in Chapter 12.

This chapter opens with an overview of the four types of tools used to measure marketing progress: forecasts, budgets, schedules and metrics. Next you will learn about the various types of forecasts, and sources of information and methods for devising forecasts. The third section examines different budgeting methods and specific marketing plan budgets, and then discusses schedules for implementation. The chapter closes by exploring how to select and apply metrics for measuring marketing outcomes and activities. *Consider how you can use the techniques in this chapter to prepare for measuring marketing progress after you implement your plan.*

TOOLS FOR MEASURING MARKETING PROGRESS

In Stage 6 of the marketing planning process, you will decide on measures to track progress and performance toward meeting the marketing, financial and societal objectives you previously set (*see* Chapter 5). Every programme and every tactic in your marketing plan should contribute, if only in a small way, toward achieving these targets and, ultimately, your organisation's goals. You can apply four tools to measure your marketing plan's progress, as summarised in Figure 11.1:

- *Forecasts* project the estimated level of sales (for example, by product or market) and costs (for example, by product or channel) for the specific period covered by the marketing plan. By comparing actual sales and costs with forecast levels, you can spot deviations and prepare to adjust your assumptions or your activities as trends develop.

- *Budgets* are time-defined allotments of financial resources for specific programmes, activities and products. As an example, you may prepare one overall budget for advertising and allocate it across specific campaigns, programmes, products or geographic areas. After you implement the marketing plan, you can check whether actual expenditures are above, below or at the budgeted level.

- *Schedules* are time-defined plans for coordinating and accomplishing tasks related to a specific programme or activity, such as new product development. You will prepare individual schedules showing starting and ending dates as well as responsibilities for the major tasks within a programme plus an overall schedule reflecting the key tasks and target dates for implementing marketing plan programmes.

- *Metrics* are specific numerical standards used on a regular basis to measure selected performance-related activities and outcomes. The point is to examine interim results by applying metrics measurements at set intervals and analyse progress toward meeting marketing plan objectives. Ambler stresses that the financial and non-financial metrics monitored by top management should be vital to the business, precise, consistent and comprehensive.[3]

Tool	Description	Use	Example
Forecast	Forward-looking estimate expressed in unit or monetary terms	Projected level of sales or costs against which to measure actual results	Forcast of product sales
Budget	Funding allotment for specific programme or activity	Guideline for spending against which to measure actual expenditures	Budget for advertising
Schedule	Series of target dates for tasks related to a particular programme or activity	Guideline for anticipated timing against which to measure actual timing	Schedule for launching new product
Metric	Specific numerical standard measuring an outcome that contributes to performance	Target for interim achievement against which to measure actual outcome	Metric for customer retention

FIGURE 11.1 Measuring marketing plan progress

To be meaningful, your measures of marketing progress and performance must link back to your mission, direction and objectives. For example, Bristol Myers Squibb's Health, Safety and Environment division assesses progress toward the direction of growth and its objective of higher sales by monitoring product sales monthly, quarterly and annually (measured in monetary and unit terms) and comparing these measures with the forecast levels. To gauge progress toward societal objectives, it uses metrics that measure customer perceptions of the company's citizenship image. For new pharmaceutical products, Bristol Myers uses detailed market introduction schedules – adjusted for any delays in government approvals – to track progress toward successful implementation.[4]

If you achieve the expected results day after day, you will move ever closer to accomplishing both short-term objectives and long-term goals. However, avoid overemphasising short-term measurements because of the risk that you might lose sight of what your customers really want and what your organisation is striving to achieve. Instead, try for a balanced perspective as you apply the forecasting, budgeting, scheduling and metrics discussed in the remainder of this chapter.

FORECASTING AND THE PLANNING PROCESS

The purpose of forecasting is to project future sales and costs so you can make marketing decisions and coordinate internal decisions about manufacturing, finance, human resources and other functions. (Depending on the coming year's forecasts, your organisation may need to expand or reduce manufacturing capacity; change inventory levels; reallocate budgets; and increase or reduce the workforce.) Forecasting is particularly challenging because of the dynamic business environment, unpredictable competitive moves, changeable customer demand and other uncertainties that can affect marketing performance.

Moreover, your product forecasts must take into account the interrelationships between products in the marketplace. For business markets, apply the principle of **derived demand**: the demand you forecast for a business product is based on (derived from) the demand forecast for a related consumer product. When industry analysts forecast higher consumer sales of digital cameras, for example, personal computer manufacturers raise their own forecasts knowing that many camera buyers will use computers to view, store and alter images. In turn, higher forecasts for computer sales prompt manufacturers of semiconductors, disk drives and other computer components to raise their sales forecasts, and so on through the upstream supply chain.[5]

Forecasts are, at best, only informed estimates, even when based on statistical data and carefully adjusted for the effect of external influences such as market growth, economic conditions, technological developments and industry trends. Despite the imperfect nature of predictions, you should make your forecasts as accurate as possible to improve the quality of information supporting the decision-making process. To illustrate, here is how BabyBoom Consumer Products handles forecasting.

MARKETING IN PRACTICE: BABYBOOM CONSUMER PRODUCTS

This US manufacturer of baby clothes and related products forecasts sales for every item in its product mix by channel member and by market. 'Each retailer has different needs, structures, requirements, lines of communications and expectations', notes Chris Cassidy, director of planning. 'Some are similar, but none are the same'. BabyBoom personnel discuss their sales forecasts and plans in detail with each retailer's buyers, which 'greatly improves communications and provides different perspectives from which to make decisions', Cassidy says.[6]

In addition to consulting channel members, BabyBoom's marketers look at the past sales history of each item; its influence on sales of other items in the same line; the age of each product in each line; each item's profit margin; and average inventory levels. They also correlate historical sales results with consumer demographics such as household size, household income and consumer age to track trends and incorporate population changes into future forecasts. With these forecasts, BabyBoom's marketers can better plan and measure store by store merchandise assortments, design products and make other marketing decisions.[7]

You may want to develop forecasts for the most optimistic situation, the most pessimistic situation and the most likely situation you will face, then – if possible – statistically estimate the probability of each. This helps you think about the diverse ways in which your product, industry, competition and market may develop. *Harvard Business Review* magazine creates multiple sales forecasts: 'We prepare three sets of numbers and then we try to come up with what we think is going to be the consensus', explains Jefferson Flanders, vice president of consumer marketing.[8] Once the marketing plan is implemented, the magazine uses sophisticated software to analyse actual monthly subscription and retail sales. On the basis of these results, Flanders and his marketing staff fine-tune the sales forecasts for the remainder of the year. More companies are, in fact, reforecasting future sales and costs using actual monthly or quarterly results throughout the planning period.[9]

Types of forecasts

What forecasts do you need for your marketing plan? Most organisations start at the macro level by forecasting industry sales by market and segment, then move to the micro level by forecasting sales for their company; sales by product; sales costs by product; and sales and costs by channel. With these forecasts in hand, you can estimate future changes in sales and costs to examine trends by product and by channel. Such analyses will show the magnitude of projected sales increases or decreases for your market, segment and individual products as well as the expected rate of change over time for sales and costs.

Market and segment sales forecasts

The first step is to project the level of overall industry sales in each market and segment for the coming months and years, using the external audit and the market analysis completed earlier in the planning process. Here you will forecast sales in the qualified available market and in your targeted segment of this market, adjusted for external influences such as expected legal restrictions and the economic outlook. Car manufacturers project industry sales five years in advance (and often further into the future) because of the lead time needed to design new vehicles, build or retrofit assembly facilities and plan for other operational activities. Over time, they regularly adjust these market forecasts in accordance with the latest economic indicators and other external influences.

For example, Toyota forecasts car sales on a global level, for specific regions and for specific national markets.

MARKETING IN PRACTICE: TOYOTA

Economic conditions are a major influence on carmaker Toyota's global and market by market sales forecasts. Not long ago, Toyota's president Fujio Cho observed that car sales in the home market of Japan had contracted considerably in the past decade because of a sluggish economy. Since then, company marketers have forecast higher industry sales as Japan recovers economic strength; they have also forecast higher sales in China, North America, Africa, Southeast Asia and other markets because of economic growth and population growth.

In addition to forecasting industry-wide sales years ahead, Toyota's marketers reforecast sales for each market as actual sales figures become available. This enables the company to plan ahead for new factories in markets where sales are expected to grow, contributing to the president's objective of achieving a 15 per cent share of the global car market by 2010. To boost productivity, Cho has also set the objective of finding ways to cut the cost of many parts for new Toyota models by 30 per cent. Although Toyota's profits are already higher than those of its main Japanese and North American competitors, Cho continues to cut costs and reduce the number of hours needed to assemble each vehicle in his drive to gain profits market by market and worldwide.[10]

Aircraft manufacturers need so much lead time for product design and testing that they look ahead decades when forecasting industry sales. Toulouse-based Airbus, for example, recently forecast that 1,500 large-capacity commercial jets would be sold during the next 20 years. Its US rival, Boeing, had a different view: believing that airlines will be buying smaller jets for direct point-to-point flights, it projected that only 320 large-capacity jets would be sold.[11]

Once you have forecast the size of the market, you can forecast the share you aim to achieve with your marketing plan, as well as estimating the future share for each of your competitors. Then bring industry sales forecasts down to the segment level to support your targeting and strategy decisions. The next step is to project sales for your company and for each product.

Company and product sales forecasts

Use your market and segment forecasts, your market and customer analyses and your knowledge of the current situation to develop sales forecasts at the company and product levels. Also factor in earlier decisions about direction, strategy and objectives when thinking about future company sales. To illustrate, marketers at Avon Products looking at the Chinese market for cosmetics products recently set an industry-wide forecast of €2.6 billion for annual sales and forecast a minimum of €120 million in annual company cosmetics. By comparison, the company's actual sales in China topped €102 million during the previous year, so its marketers' forecasts were reasonable given historical results and continued market growth. Avon is currently selling through retail channels but will certainly raise its company and product sales forecasts after China eliminates its ban on direct-to-consumer sales within the next few years.[12]

Most marketers prepare month by month sales forecasts for the coming year, although some firms prefer week by week forecasting and some project sales 15–18 months ahead. Marketers at Krispy Kreme Doughnuts prepare monthly sales forecasts one year ahead, on the basis of top-down and floor-up input, so they can plan production facilities accordingly. Involving value chain partners not only may improve accuracy but also gives your suppliers the data they need for better forecasting to meet your needs. To illustrate, Chapter 7 discussed the J.C. Penney department store's concerns about accurately forecasting product sales. To avoid running out of private label men's shirts, marketers kept a six months' supply in the warehouse and another three months' supply in the stores. Once they helped shirt supplier TAL Apparel build a software model for forecasting sales and planning store inventory, they could more effectively meet demand, satisfy customers and cut costs.[13]

If your marketing plan covers at least one new product introduction, you will want to forecast those sales separately so that you may more easily measure results and track progress toward financial and marketing objectives. Also consider the effect that other value-chain participants could have on your product forecasts. For instance, Microsoft's sales forecasts (and schedules) were affected when T-Mobile had to postpone introducing a mobile phone handset incorporating Microsoft software. Orange and other mobile phone service operators feature the company's software but Microsoft is still racing to capture market share from Nokia, which dominates mobile phone software as well as handset sales.[14]

Cost of sales forecasts

Now you are ready to forecast the total costs you can expect to incur for the forecast sales levels and project when these costs will occur. This gives you an opportunity to consider the financial impact of your forecasts and revise them if necessary. For instance, the German electronics company Siemens recently set an annual forecast for mobile phones sales that was 20 per cent higher than in the previous year, on the basis of continued demand and plans to introduce a large number of new handsets. At the same time, Siemens had to forecast higher sales costs because of the added new product expenditures and full-capacity factory operations.[15]

Your forecasts will be more realistic if you discuss cost figures with line managers or others who are knowledgeable about the products and markets. Hendrick Motorsports, a car racing company, assigns its racing team crew chiefs to forecast costs and provide company management with support in forecasting. 'I've got to believe that the more people we get involved, the more accurate the forecasts will be', says the chief financial officer.[16] Be aware that you may need to adjust your overall cost forecasts after the marketing plan is implemented. Nonetheless, estimating these costs during the planning process helps you allocate funding to individual programmes and products.

Channel forecasts

Like BabyBoom, companies that work with multiple channels and channel members often forecast sales and costs for each, including the cost of logistics. In addition to providing benchmarks against which to measure actual channel results and costs, these forecasts give you an opportunity to reconsider your channel and logistics decisions if the costs seem too high (or surprisingly low). Even companies that own their own stores can use channel forecasts to project sales on a store by store basis. Ideally, you will want to forecast unit and monetary sales by product and by channel (perhaps by store as well) so you can track progress after implementation and make changes if actual performance varies significantly from forecasts.

Forecasting approaches and data sources

There are a number of approaches to forecasting sales and costs, as shown in Figure 11.2. Some rely on statistical analysis or modelling, whereas others rely on expert judgement. Note that for a forecast developed with a time series or causal analysis to be at all accurate, you must have sufficient historical sales data. Also note that judgemental forecasting approaches such as the jury of executive opinion can be very valuable if applied in a systematic way.[17] To avoid overemphasising an internal focus during the forecasting process, take care to incorporate external information and expertise. In the end, you may do better using both statistical and judgemental approaches to arrive at forecasts.

Technique	Description	Benefits/limitations
Sales force composite estimate	Judgemental approach in which sales personnel are asked to estimate future sales	Can provide valuable insights from customer-contact personnel but may introduce bias
Jury of executive opinion	Judgemental approach in which managers (and sometimes channel members or suppliers) are asked to estimate future sales	Combines informed judgement of many but may give too much weight to some individuals' estimates
Delphi method	Judgemental approach, in which outside experts participate in successive rounds of input, that leads to a consensus forecast	Minimises possibility of bias or over-weighting one individual's estimates but is time-consuming and accuracy depends on choice of experts
Survey of buyer intentions	Research-based approach in which buyers in a given market are asked about their purchasing intentions	Solicits market input but the resulting forecast may not be indicative of customers' actual behaviour
New product test marketing	Research-based approach in which a new product's sales performance in limited markets is tested and the results used to forecast future sales	Reflects actual customer behaviour but may be affected by competition or other factors
Time series analyses	Statistical approaches in which the patterns of historical data are analysed to predict future sales; examples: moving averages, exponential smoothing	Uses actual purchase data to produce forecast estimates quickly but assumes that similar buying trends will continue in future
Causal analyses	Methods that statistically determine the relationship between demand and the factors that affect it; examples: regression analysis, neural networks	Provides insights into relationships between factors that affect long-term demand but requires sufficient data for analysis

FIGURE 11.2   Selected approaches to forecasting

The Old Navy division of the Gap clothing stores, for example, applies multiple forecasting methods and combines top-down with floor-up forecasts. Corporate planners prepare product forecasts on the basis of economic trends and other big-picture influences; merchandise managers prepare product forecasts on the basis of style trends, offers of complementary products and other factors. Then the two groups meet to discuss their forecasts and agree on a final set – which is more accurate because of the diverse methods and in-depth discussion of influences.[18] For a final 'reality check', compare your forecasts with the actual figures from recent periods to identify major anomalies.

As background in preparing forecasts, access the online resources listed in Chapters 2, 3, 4 and 7 for information about markets, customers, channels and costs. Also consult industry associations, government information and financial analysts' reports when estimating future sales and costs, especially at the macro level. Finally, carefully check the source, methodology, credibility, completeness and timeliness of any secondary data used to construct forecasts.

For instance, Nokia, Samsung and other manufacturers of mobile phone handsets sold in China typically rely on statistics compiled by the government's Ministry of Information Industry when determining market size and market share. But industry analyst Sean Debow has challenged the accuracy of these statistics because the ministry counts chip cards (installed for use with a particular service provider) as a proxy for handsets. Travelling in Shanghai, he observed people replacing chip cards to switch mobile phone services and avoid higher 'roaming' charges in outlying areas. After investigating, Debow estimated that the Chinese mobile phone market was only two-thirds the size indicated by official figures – and he therefore forecast much higher handset sales growth for the next two years due to additional growth potential.[19]

PREPARING BUDGETS AND SCHEDULES

With sales and cost forecasts complete, you can develop an overall marketing budget and, within that budget, estimate spending for specific programmes and activities in line with your marketing plan objectives. Every marketer must make hard choices because marketing budgets (and other resources) are never unlimited. As with forecasts, some marketers budget for the most optimistic, most pessimistic and most likely scenarios so they are prepared to tackle threats and opportunities.

Your organisation may set budget requirements for return on investment; limit the amount or percentage of funding that can be allocated to certain activities or products; set specific assumptions; cap cost increases; or prefer a particular budget method or format. For example, every autumn, the chief financial officer of the magazine *Cook's Illustrated* provides marketing management with a spreadsheet template complete with assumptions for planning the coming year's budget. After department heads estimate their budget needs, they meet several times to agree on allocations, formalising the next year's plans and budgets by December. After plans are implemented, all departments keep their spending within the agreed budget, even though the chief financial officer tracks ongoing expenditures and reforecasts costs and sales as interim results become available.[20]

Threats and opportunities can prompt marketers to alter their budgets even after implementation. Consider what happened to Procter & Gamble in Argentina.

MARKETING IN PRACTICE: PROCTER & GAMBLE IN ARGENTINA

This corporate giant maintains an annual worldwide marketing budget in excess of €3 billion for its detergents, toothpastes, nappies and other consumer products. Despite P&G's careful budgeting process, its marketing managers sometimes are confronted with unexpected circumstances that warrant speedy budget adjustments. In Argentina, the company's laundry detergent brands compete with Unilever brands – and the competition can become quite heated. When Unilever suddenly slashed its detergent prices by 30 per cent to stimulate sales at a time when the local economy was struggling, P&G's marketers had to act quickly to protect their market share.

Assisted by colleagues from manufacturing, engineering and logistics, they came up with software to spot waste in the budget and free up money for promoting their Ariel brand detergent more aggressively. P&G marketers ultimately reallocated more than €3 million for extended advertising and sampling of Ariel. The software proved so valuable that P&G has used it in other markets and for other products. And the company has made dramatic budget changes to help other products rebuild market share, such as doubling the marketing budget for Mr. Clean household cleaner during one recent year.[21]

Budgeting methods

Budgets may originate in the marketing department and move upward for review (floor up); at the top management level and move downward for specific allocations (top down); or be constructed through a combination of floor-up and top down methods (*see* Figure 11.3). The **objective and task budget method**, a floor-up option common in large organisations, allocates overall marketing funding according to the total cost of the tasks to be accomplished in achieving marketing plan objectives. If you can relate specific tasks to specific objectives, this method offers good accountability; however, the combined cost may result in too high a budget, given your organisation's resources. For this reason, a growing number of corporations are using the **econometric modelling method** to calculate programme or activity budgets using formulas that take into account anticipated customer response, budget constraints, product profitability, competitive spending and other relevant variables.[22]

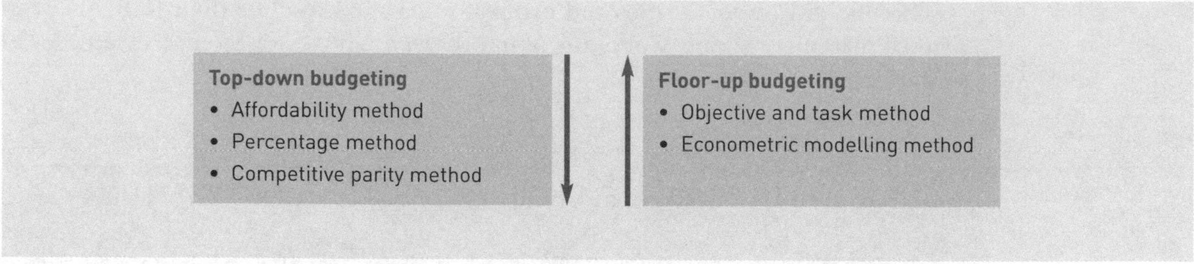

Top-down budgeting
- Affordability method
- Percentage method
- Competitive parity method

Floor-up budgeting
- Objective and task method
- Econometric modelling method

FIGURE 11.3 Top-down and floor-up budgeting methods

On the other hand, your organisation may use one of the top-down budgeting methods. With the **affordability budget method**, senior managers set the amount of the marketing budget on the basis of how much the organisation can afford (or will be able to afford during the period covered by the plan). Although simple, this method has no connection with market conditions, opportunities, potential profits or other factors. With the **percentage budget method**, senior managers set the overall marketing budget on the basis of a percentage of the previous year's annual turnover; next year's expected turnover; the product's price; or an average industry percentage. However, as with the affordability method, the percentage method ignores the market situation. With **the competitive parity budget method**, senior managers establish a total marketing budget at least equal to that of competitors. The problem with the competitive parity method is that no two organisations are exactly alike, and mimicking another organisation's budget may be disastrous for yours.

The top-down budgeting methods are relatively easy to apply, but they fail to relate costs to objectives. Compared with the affordability method, Piercy stresses, the objective and task budgeting is more sophisticated; results in larger marketing budgets; and is related to better profitability.[23] In practice, most marketing budgets are developed through a combination of top-down and floor-up methods, guided by higher-level strategic planning and product or brand-level input relative to objectives and costs. This is analogous to the three-level strategy planning process (*see* Chapter 1) in which marketing strategy incorporates floor-up knowledge of customers and markets balanced by top-down development, direction and fine-tuning of organisational and business strategies.

Budgets within budgets

At this point, you are ready to create separate budgets for specific marketing activities and programmes, schedule planned expenditures and fix responsibilities for spending. This allows you to compare the actual outlays with the budgeted outlays after the marketing plan has been implemented. You will want to prepare budgets (for annual, monthly and perhaps weekly costs) covering individual marketing-mix programmes matched with appropriate objectives (such as projected profit or return on investment).

In addition, you can establish budgets within your overall budget reflecting planned expenditures by market, segment, region, business unit, product or line/category, brand, activity or responsibility. For example, marketers for the Dollar-Thrifty car-hire service create budgets within budgets for different advertising media. They recently increased the percentage of the advertising budget allocated to online advertisements (and decreased the percentage allocated to traditional media) because of the positive customer response and because they can easily measure the results.[24]

Global banks such as Citigroup typically budget by country, market, product and specific customer segments, including subcultures they are targeting within larger markets. This allows examination of segment by segment performance in the context of planned expenditures and helps management reconsider budget priorities depending on results.[25] Another example is Sara Lee, well known for its food products, which budgets by brand to concentrate funding on those it forecasts will experience the highest growth during the coming five years. Brands forecast for slower growth are to receive correspondingly smaller budgets than those with high-growth forecasts.[26]

Planning schedules for implementation

When planning schedules for implementation, you will estimate the timing and deadlines for each programme or task to coordinate concurrent activities, prevent conflicts, obtain needed resources and track progress toward completion. Although you may not have to include detailed programme schedules when documenting your marketing plan for management review, you should present a schedule summarising the timing and responsibilities for major programmes. Then, if tasks do not start or finish on schedule, you can determine the effect on other tasks, work to regain the expected timing and get back on track toward results. In most cases, returning to schedule will have consequences for other activities and costs, so review the new timing with management and communicate with the major customers and suppliers who would be affected.

As with budgeting and forecasting, you may want to develop schedules for the most optimistic, most pessimistic and most likely situations – and be ready to make changes in response to emerging opportunities, threats or other factors. When the UK travel company TUI Thompson was planning a new online division, Budget Holidays, its marketers originally scheduled advertising and other promotions to support a springtime launch. However, because holiday travel sales were dropping off, they postponed some of the activities, continued monitoring the environment and then rescheduled a number of promotions for summer months.[27]

MEASURING PROGRESS WITH METRICS

After implementation, how will you know whether you are making progress toward achieving your marketing plan's objectives? Metrics allow you to measure the outcomes and activities that really contribute to performance. But you will need clear objectives and baseline measures against which to compare interim results and ultimate performance. Here is how Holiday Inn UK used metrics to measure the results of an important promotion.

> **MARKETING IN PRACTICE:** HOLIDAY INN UK
>
> After Holiday Inn bought the UK hotel chain Posthouse, its marketing managers planned a promotion they called 'Under the Pillow' to boost sales quickly by 20 per cent. They also set objectives for increasing online reservations, expanding the chain's loyalty club membership, raising brand awareness and earning a solid return on the programme's investment. Targeting the segment of UK businesspeople who travel midweek, the marketers arranged for each Holiday Inn guest to find a prize notice (such as winning cash or loyalty club points) beneath the pillow. Guests could pick up their prizes after they joined the chain's loyalty club. The 'Under the Pillow' theme not only described the prize scheme, but reinforced the idea that guests sleep better at Holiday Inns because they have a choice of pillows.
>
> This campaign was implemented through radio and newspaper advertising, direct mail, online advertisements, digital newsletters and in-hotel displays. During the campaign and at its end, Holiday Inn's marketers measured performance using metrics directly related to the financial and marketing objectives: percentage change in sales, percentage change in loyalty club membership, percentage change in online reservations and percentage change in target segment awareness. The results: sales increased by 25 per cent (well over the 20 per cent target), loyalty club membership rose by 223 per cent, online reservations rose by 90 per cent and awareness improved from 44 per cent to 52 per cent among targeted business travellers. Just as important, the actual return on investment was four times the planned level – making this a hugely successful programme for the hotel chain.[28]

Note that Holiday Inn had baseline measures for sales, loyalty club membership, hotel brand awareness and online reservation volume so it could track changes in these metrics. Yet just because you *can* measure something does not mean you *should* measure it – nor should you measure everything. The key is to identify the specific metrics that apply to the most significant activities and results affecting marketing performance. Best suggests four categories of metrics to measure progress toward objectives: internal in-process, external in-process, internal performance (end-result) and external performance (end-result) metrics (*see* Figure 11.4 for examples).[29]

Measurement perspective	Time of measurement	
	In-process metrics	End-result metrics
Internal (in-company)	Product defects Late deliveries Billing errors Accounts receivable Inventory turnover	Net profit/earnings Return on sales Profit margin per unit Return on assets Asset turnover
External (in-market)	Customer satisfaction Relative product quality Relative service quality Intentions to purchase Product awareness	Market share Customer retention Relative new product sales Revenue per customer Market growth rate

FIGURE 11.4   Categories of process and performance metrics

Source: Adapted from Roger J. Best, *Market-Based Management*, 2nd edn (Upper Saddle River, NJ: Prentice Hall, 2000), p. 32.

Achieving in-process market metrics paves the way for achieving marketing and financial objectives. For example, the metric of product awareness (used by Holiday Inn) measures progress toward the marketing objective of strengthening and expanding customer relationships: the higher the awareness, the higher the probability that prospects will become customers. In contrast, internal and external performance metrics measure results that more directly contribute to specific financial and marketing objectives. Holiday Inn marketers knew they had achieved their financial objectives for the 'Under the Pillow' promotion because they could measure and compare the change in sales, online reservations, awareness and other metrics before, during and after programme implementation.

Selecting metrics

Holiday Inn's metrics covered not only short-term results (measuring immediate sales) but also longer-term objectives (encouraging customer loyalty by building awareness and expanding loyalty club membership). Select metrics that will help you evaluate progress throughout the course of each programme and into a new marketing plan period, so you can determine ongoing progress and compare results. Thus, when selecting metrics:

- *Match metrics to programme and marketing plan objectives*. Be sure your metrics are relevant to your objectives. A company seeking 10 per cent higher sales in the coming year would check performance by regularly measuring unit or monetary sales and market share. However, if it measures the number of sales leads generated but has no metric for conversion rates, it will not know the ultimate outcome of lead generation, which directly influences sales objectives. The UK financial services firm Bradford & Bingley, which offers mortgages and savings accounts, uses metrics to measure customer profitability by segment as well as to track customer defection and retention. By looking at these and other customer-related metrics, the firm can track monthly progress toward meeting yearly financial and marketing objectives.[30]

- *Measure activities or outcomes that show progress toward fulfilling the organisation's mission and moving in the desired direction*. Your metrics should track results that are consistent with your mission and direction. Andersen Corp., which makes timber windows, uses metrics to monitor relationships with dealers and the construction trade, two channels that directly affect the company's turnover and connections with consumers. Among the metrics measured are the channel members' willingness to recommend Andersen windows; willingness to carry more Andersen products; and willingness to make Andersen their sole window supplier.[31] As another example, Holiday Inn UK had just expanded through acquisition in pursuit of more aggressive growth, so its metrics were chosen in line with growth measures (such as sales increases).

- *Measure the non-financial and financial outcomes that can be quantified and that matter to customers*. Supported by marketing research, you can select and measure metrics for changes in customers' perceptions of company image, product quality and value, all of which affect customers' attitudes and behaviour. You cannot measure the process customers use in deciding to switch brands but you can use metrics to track the number of defectors, percentage change and reason for defections. To follow the development of customer relationships, you can track your progress in attracting new customers, selling additional products to current customers, retaining customers over time, reactivating dormant relationships and re-establishing relations with defectors. And you can select metrics to track profit per customer and acquisition costs in line with your objectives, giving you data on which to base future targeting and marketing decisions.[32]

- *Measure appropriate internal metrics*. By tracking internal performance using metrics such as measuring order fulfilment accuracy or on-time shipping, you can quickly identify areas for improvement in processes and procedures that affect customer satisfaction and loyalty. Digex, an information technology company, uses metrics measuring the responsiveness of its billing and technical support staff, knowing that these have a significant bearing on customer satisfaction.[33]

- *Use metrics to reinforce ongoing priorities.* You can use metrics to track the proportion of sales made to more profitable customers compared with those made to less profitable customers as a way to reinforce marketing priorities for long-term success. As another example, using metrics to track the ratio of new product sales to existing product sales can show the extent to which new product innovation is fuelling growth.[34]

Type of objective	Sample metrics
Financial objectives	• To increase sales: performance metrics measuring results by product, region, channel, customer segment or company • To increase profitability: performance metrics measuring annual gross or net margin by product, region, channel, customer segment or company • To achieve return on investment levels: performance metrics measuring the return by programme, product or activity • To improve cash flow by reducing the time between billing and receiving payment: in-process metrics constantly measuring the age and status of accounts receivable by customer segment, product, region or manager
Marketing objectives	• To acquire new customers: performance metrics measuring the annual number or percentage of new customers added; in-process metrics measuring customer awareness, attitudes and buying intentions at designated intervals • To retain existing customers: performance metrics measuring the number or percentage of customers who continue purchasing; performance metrics measuring the number or percentage of customers who defect during the period; performance metrics measuring size and frequency of repeat purchases by existing customers • To increase speed of new product development: in-process metrics measuring the time for each step from idea generation to product launch and the total time needed to introduce a product
Societal objectives	• To improve public image: in-process metrics measuring stakeholders' attitudes at certain intervals • To reduce waste: performance metrics measuring amount of waste generated by or resulting from products and processes at certain intervals; performance metric measuring level of recycling at certain intervals

FIGURE 11.5   Sample in-process and performance metrics

Source: After Marian Burk Wood, *The Marketing Plan: A Handbook* (Upper Saddle River, NJ: Prentice Hall, 2003), p. 115–16.

The specific metrics selected depend on your organisation, its mission and objectives, your marketing plan objectives and the programmes you will implement. Most companies select metrics to measure profitability and profit margins, sales, product awareness and number of new products, among others – with profitability and sales metrics seen as the most valuable in assessing progress.[35] Rather than simply replicate the metrics common to your industry, select metrics that pertain to your organisation's particular situation. Figure 11.5 presents sample in-process and performance metrics for some of the financial, marketing and societal objectives shown in Figures 5.3, 5.4 and 5.5. You can also select narrowly defined metrics to track progress toward particularly crucial outcomes or activities, such as the number of new products in development, a key metric for pharmaceutical firms because it directly affects achievement of sales and profit objectives.

Applying metrics

You will need pre-implementation numbers for every metric so you can track progress from that point forward. If possible, obtain benchmark metrics (from your industry or from the best-in-class organisations) against which to compare your progress and objectives. E-commerce companies, for instance, strive to beat the typical 1–2 per cent conversion rates measuring percentage of website visitors who actually buy – in addition to measuring progress toward specific objectives for each programme.[36]

Depending on your organisation, objectives and technology, you may apply selected metrics weekly, monthly, quarterly or yearly. In especially volatile markets, you may check metrics daily or even hourly. Be sure to analyse the direction and rate of change in measurements taken at different intervals as well as the total progress from pre-implementation levels. This will show how quickly you are moving toward your objectives (and reveal problem areas for attention). Check your previous results to see the progress measured in comparable pre-implementation periods as a way of identifying unusual trends. By documenting your measurements, you will have historical data for comparison with future results. Also analyse your metrics in the context of competitive results whenever possible – an especially important point with measures such as market share, profitability and quality perceptions. Remember that the metrics you apply today may not be as useful tomorrow because of environmental shifts; new competition; changes in organisational strategy; or evolving customer attitudes and behaviour. Finally, keep the use of metrics in perspective: such measures are only one input in decisions about adjusting marketing programmes because interim results do not meet expected results, as discussed in Chapter 12.

CHAPTER SUMMARY

1. *Describe how and why marketers plan with forecasts, budgets, schedules and metrics.*
   Marketers use forecasts to project the estimated level of sales and costs for the marketing plan period so they can compare actual results with forecast levels and identify deviations. They use budgets to allot financial resources during certain periods to programmes, activities and products. Comparing actual expenditures to budget figures will reveal deviations from expected spending patterns. Marketers use schedules to define the timing of tasks to be accomplished in completing programmes and activities. As with budgets, comparing actual task initiation and completion dates will show deviations from the planned timing. Marketers use metrics to measure selected performance-related activities and outcomes numerically and on a regular basis. The point is to examine interim results at set intervals and track progress toward meeting marketing plan objectives.

2. *Identify the types of forecasts and forecasting approaches available to support marketing planning.*
   Marketers use forecasts at the macro level to project industry sales by market and segment and at the micro level to project company and product sales; cost of sales; and sales and costs by channel. Some marketers prepare forecasts for the most optimistic, most pessimistic and most likely situation they will face. Among the most common approaches to forecasting are expert judgement methods (sales force composite estimate, jury of executive opinion, Delphi method); research-based approaches (survey of buyer intentions, new product test marketing); and statistical approaches (time series analysis, causal analysis).

3. *Discuss budgeting methods and types of budgets used in marketing planning.*
   Budgets may be developed using floor-up methods (objective and task, econometric modelling) and top-down methods (affordability, percentage budget, competitive parity). In practice, most marketing budgets are developed through a combination of these methods. Marketers may develop separate budgets for each programme, showing the annual, monthly and perhaps weekly estimated expenditures. They also may prepare time-defined budgets for each market, customer segment, geographic region, business unit, product or product line/category, brand, activity or responsibility.

4. *Explain how and why marketers select and apply metrics for tracking progress.*
   Metrics are used to measure outcomes and activities that contribute toward achieving short-term objectives, long-term objectives and the organisation's mission. These include internal in-process metrics, external in-process metrics, internal performance (end-result) metrics and external performance (end-result) metrics. Marketers select metrics according to programme and marketing plan objectives; measurement of activities and outcomes consistent

with mission and strategic direction; financial and non-financial outcomes that are quantifiable and relevant to customers; internal measures of processes and procedures that affect customer satisfaction and loyalty; and reinforcement of priorities for success.

 ## KEY TERM DEFINITIONS

affordability budget method Method in which senior managers set the total marketing budget on the basis of how much the organisation can afford or will be able to afford during the period covered by the plan

budget Time-defined allotment of financial resources for a specific programme, activity or product

competitive parity budget method Method in which senior managers establish a total marketing budget at least equal to that of competitors

derived demand Principle that the demand forecast for a business product ultimately derives from the demand forecast for a consumer product

econometric modelling method Use of sophisticated econometric models incorporating anticipated customer response and other variables to determine marketing budgets

forecast Projection of the estimated level of sales and costs during the months or years covered by a marketing plan

metric Numerical standard used to measure a performance-related marketing activity or outcome

objective and task budget method Method in which money is allocated according to the total cost of the tasks to be accomplished in achieving marketing plan objectives

percentage budget method Method in which senior managers set the overall marketing budget on the basis of a percentage of the previous year's annual turnover, next year's expected turnover, the product's price or an average industry percentage

schedule Time-defined plan for coordinating and accomplishing tasks connected to a specific programme or activity

THE PRACTICAL MARKETER CHECKLIST NO. 11:
PLANNING PROGRESS AND PERFORMANCE METRICS

Measuring long-term marketing performance

What marketing results will help the organisation move toward achieving its mission and long-term objectives, and what measurements can track progress toward these results over time?

What measures can be used to track marketing outcomes that contribute to managing the life cycle of a customer relationship?

What measures can be used to monitor marketing outcomes that contribute to long-term customer retention and loyalty?

Measuring short-term marketing progress and performance

What metrics can be used to measure the progress and outcome of marketing activities that are most important for achieving the marketing plan's financial, marketing and societal objectives?

What metrics can be used to track the progress and performance of marketing-mix programmes toward achieving their objectives?

What measures can be used to assess interim marketing results in the context of the previous marketing results, competitors' results, market conditions and other factors?

How often should interim results be measured by each metric?

What internal processes and procedures that influence customer satisfaction and loyalty should be measured by metrics?

Source: Adapted from Marian Burk Wood, *The Marketing Plan: A Handbook* (Upper Saddle River, NJ: Prentice Hall, 2003), p. 114.

ONLINE RESOURCES

Forecasting

- Principles of forecasting (www.forecastingprinciples.com) – Maintained by the Marketing Department of the Wharton School, the site features a glossary of forecasting terms and informative explanations of forecasting principles.

- Econometrics Journal Online (http://econometriclinks.com) – Displays journal articles, research papers and links to detailed information about econometrics and forecasting.

- Time-critical decision-making for economics and finance (http://ubmail.ubalt.edu/~harsham/stat-data/opre330Forecast.htm) – By Dr Arsham of the University of Baltimore, this presents background and principles of sophisticated forecasting methods.

QUESTIONS FOR DISCUSSION AND ANALYSIS

1. What are the advantages and disadvantages of judgemental approaches to forecasting, and why is judgement needed for every forecast?

2. Under what circumstances might you use the affordability budgeting method?

3. Why should a company not replicate the metrics used by a direct competitor?

APPLY YOUR KNOWLEDGE

Review your work researching a company's marketing, financial and societal objectives in the 'Apply your knowledge' exercise in Chapter 5 to answer the following questions about measuring progress and performance:

- Has the company revealed any of its forecasts or budgets? If so, what are they based on and how do they relate to its objectives?

- What secondary data sources would you consult if you were preparing a forecast for one of this company's products? Be specific.

- Has the company discussed any schedules for marketing activities, such as launching a new product or starting a new advertising campaign? If so, what connection do you see between the schedules and forecasts or budgets?

- Does the company explain any metrics used to measure interim progress and performance? What metrics would you recommend, given your knowledge of this company and its objectives?

- Prepare a brief oral or written report summarising your analysis.

BUILD YOUR OWN MARKETING PLAN

Move ahead with your marketing plan by researching and estimating sales and costs, starting with forecasting at the macro level and moving to the micro level with forecasts for company and product sales; cost of sales; and sales and costs by channel. What sources will you use? Do your forecasts represent the most optimistic, most pessimistic or most likely situation you will face? Are they appropriate for your product and plan, given your knowledge of the market, the industry and the current situation? Next, develop an overall marketing budget using the objective and task method. If possible, prepare at least one budget for a specific programme or activity (such as advertising), indicating expected expenditures by month. List any factors that would affect your budgets for the most optimistic, most pessimistic and most likely situations. Now select internal in-process metrics, external in-process metrics, internal performance metrics and external performance metrics based on your objectives and mission. Discuss how, when and why you will apply these metrics to measure progress in achieving your marketing plan's objectives and to satisfy your customers. Document your decisions in *Marketing Plan Pro* software or in a written marketing plan.

CLOSING CASE: FORECASTING AND SCHEDULING FOR SUCCESS AT ZARA

Filling nearly 600 stores with the right fashions at the right time and in the right quantities is a major forecasting challenge – but Zara meets the challenge by careful scheduling, forecasting and reforecasting. Owned by the Spanish retailer Industria de Diseño Textil (Inditex), Zara operates women's clothing stores in Europe, Asia, the Middle East and North and South America. Its marketers need not forecast product by product sales a year or more ahead, which many retailers do, because the company is vertically integrated and works on a tight schedule to respond quickly when sales trends emerge.

Zara manufactures about 75 per cent of the products sold in its stores; its state-of-the-art distribution centres can sort and pack 80,000 garments per hour. The company also plans for a 48-hour delivery schedule to get merchandise from the distribution centre to the stores. Thus, Zara is not hampered by suppliers' constraints or other upstream problems that can add weeks to the restocking period – time that makes all the difference between having a fashion when it's in style and receiving a shipment just after the fad fades. 'We don't want to miss out on the latest trend, which means a fast response to the demands of our customer and the market', explains Zara official Raul Estravera. 'Having our own factories allows us this flexibility – 15 days from product decision to delivery and twice-weekly shipments of fresh merchandise – and there is less chance of error.'[37]

Zara's marketers and designers scout many sources for fashion ideas; they need about one month to develop a new product line and another week to have it manufactured. In all, they market 11,000 clothing items every year and use sales projections to determine which stores should receive which products and in what quantities. They also forecast sales and manufacture items on the basis of customer comments. If customers in one store are asking for a particular fashion (or want a variation of one already on the rack), Zara projects short-term sales, makes the item and ships it to that outlet in less than two weeks.

Once products reach the stores, marketing personnel statistically analyse the first sales results to identify the fastest selling items and re-order immediately so they can meet the demand for each outlet. This early-and-often reforecasting method is essential because the company makes only what will sell and despatches only what stores need. Zara's Carmen Melon says: 'There is no stock that doesn't move; we have no extra inventory.'[38]

Inditex applies its winning schedule and forecast processes to its other chains, among them Bershka teen fashion stores, Oysho lingerie stores and Massimo Dutti men's wear stores. In all, the parent company maintains about 1,400 stores in 41 nations and plans dozens of new store openings every year, although Zara constitutes the largest share of Inditex's revenues. Watch for ever-faster response as Zara's marketers use their scheduling and forecasting skills to compete with H&M, Benetton and other global clothing chains.[39]

Case questions

1. Would Zara's forecast/reforecast method work for retailers that are not vertically integrated? Explain.

2. Which types of forecasts do you think Zara's marketers prepare – and why?

ENDNOTES

1. Quoted in Bill Birchard, 'Landed Manager: Steven McCormick's Goal for The Nature Conservancy', *Chief Executive* (USA), December 2002, pp. 46ff.

2. Based on information from 'Rose Niu: China Program Director, The Nature Conservancy, China', *Business Week*, 9 June 2003, p. 58; Steven J. McCormick, 'Balancing The Nature Conservancy Story', *Washington Post*, 13 May 2003, p. A19; Birchard, 'Landed Manager'; John Sawhill and David Williamson, 'Measuring What Matters in Nonprofits', *McKinsey Quarterly*, no. 2, 2001, www.mckinseyquarterly.com.

3. Tim Ambler, *Marketing and the Bottom Line* (London: Financial Times Prentice Hall, 2000), p. 5.

4. See Francesco G.G. Zingales and Kai Hockerts, 'Balanced Scorecard and Sustainability: Examples from Literature and Practice', in S. Schaltegger and T. Dyllick, *Nachhaltig managen mit der Balanced Scorecard* (Wiesbaden: Gabler, 2002), pp. 151–66; www.knowledge.insead.edu; also: Peter Landers, 'Bristol-Myers 3rd-Quarter Net More Than Doubled', *Wall Street Journal*, 24 October 2003, p. A10.

5. Jim Kerstetter, 'PCs: The Elves Are Working Overtime', *Business Week*, 10 November 2003, p. 50.

6. Quoted in Tracy Haisley, 'Survival of the Forecasting and Planning Fittest', *Apparel*, July 2003, pp. 42ff.

7. Haisley, 'Survival of the Forecasting and Planning Fittest'.

8. Quoted in Leslie Brokaw, 'Eraser Heads', *Folio*, 1 March 2003, n.p.

9. See Richard Barrett, 'From Fast Close to Fast Forward', *Strategic Finance*, January 2003, pp. 24ff.

10. Brian Bremner and Chester Dawson, 'Can Anything Stop Toyota?', *Business Week*, 17 November 2003, pp. 114–22; Yuzo Yamaguchi, 'Upbeat Toyota Revises Forecast for Global Sales', *Automotive News*, 28 July 2003, p. 18; Michele Yamada, 'Toyota Raises Global Forecast for Sales, Output', *Wall Street Journal*, 23 July 2003, p. B2.

11. Carol Matlack, 'Mega Plane', *Business Week*, 10 November 2003, pp. 88–92.

12. Leslie Chang, 'Avon, Seeing China's Potential, Sets Aggressive Plan for Growth', *Wall Street Journal*, 23 October 2003, pp. 1ff.

13. Gabriel Kahn, 'Invisible Supplier Has Penney's Shirts All Buttoned Up', *Wall Street Journal*, 11 September 2003, pp. A1, A9.

14. David Pringle, 'T-Mobile Delays Microsoft Phone', *Wall Street Journal*, 16 May 2003, www.wsj.com.

15. 'Technology Brief: Siemens AG', *Wall Street Journal*, 2 September 2003, p. C13.

16. Quoted in Rick Whiting, 'Gain the Financial Edge', *InformationWeek*, 2 June 2003, pp. 52ff.

17. Gary L. Lilien and Arvind Rangaswamy, *Marketing Engineering*, 2nd edn (Upper Saddle River, NJ: Prentice Hall, 2003), pp. 174–5.

18. Marshall L. Fisher, Ananth Raman and Anna Sheen McClelland, 'Rocket Science Retailing', *Harvard Business School Working Knowledge*, 7 August 2000, http://hbsworkingknowledge.hbs.edu.

19. Evan Ramstad, 'China's Cellphone Market Has Even More Room to Grow', *Wall Street Journal*, 29 October 2003, p. B7.

20. Brokaw, 'Eraser Heads'.

21. Jack Neff, 'Employing Actuaries' System: P&G Tests Risk Model', *Advertising Age*, 2 December 2002, p. 54; Jack Neff, 'Mr. Clean Gets $50M Push', *Advertising Age*, 18 August 2003, p. 3.

22. Lilien and Rangaswamy, *Marketing Engineering*, 2nd edn, pp. 312–15.

23. Nigel Piercy, 'The Marketing Budgeting Process: Marketing Management Implications', *Journal of Marketing*, October 1987, pp. 45–59.

24. Jean Halliday, 'Car Renters Flock to Internet', *Advertising Age*, 27 October 2003, p. 44.

25. 'Banks to Raise Ethnic Marketing Budgets', *Europe Intelligence Wire*, 29 September 2003, n.p.

26. Stephanie Thompson, 'Sara Lee Strategy on Budget and Ad Agencies', *Advertising Age*, 15 September 2003, p. 4.

27. 'TUI Launches "Modern" Budget Holiday Brand', *Marketing*, 6 March 2003, p. 3; 'TUI Backs Online Budget Holidays with Pounds 2M Activity', *Marketing*, 3 July 2003, p. 4.

28. 'Best Group Marketing Campaign; Holiday Inn', *Caterer and Hotelkeeper*, 3 July 2003, p. 25.

29. Roger J. Best, *Market-Based Management*, 2nd edn (Upper Saddle River, NJ: Prentice Hall, 2000), pp. 30–2.

30. Ambler, *Marketing and the Bottom Line*, pp. 28–9.

31. Lawrence A. Crosby and Sheree L. Johnson, 'Do Your Metrics Reflect Your Market Strategy?', *Marketing Management*, September–October 2003, pp. 10–11.

32. See Werner Reinartz, Manfred Krafft and Wayne D. Hoyer, 'Measuring the Customer Relationship Management Construct and Linking It to Performance Outcomes', *Insead*, January 2003, www.knowledge.insead.edu.

33. Deborah L. Vence, 'Do It Right', *Marketing News*, 27 October 2003, p. 39.

34. See June Lee Risser, 'Customers Come First', *Marketing Management*, November–December 2003, pp. 22ff.

35. Ambler, *Marketing and the Bottom Line*, p. 163.

36. Nick Evans, 'How Palm, Coca-Cola and Crutchfield Excel at Online Customer Relationship Management', *InternetWeek*, 29 September 2003, n.p.

37. Quoted in Barbara Barker, 'Inside the Inditex Empire', *WWD*, 30 July 2002, p. 10.

38. Ibid.

39. Based on information from Robert Murphy, 'Inditex Profits Rise 21% in Half', *WWD*, 22 September 2003, p. 2; John Tagliabue, 'A Rival to Gap That Operates Like Dell', *New York Times*, 30 May 2003, pp. W1, W7; Robert Murphy, 'The Far Reaches of Fast Fashion', *WWD*, 4 February 2003, pp. 16ff.; Barker, 'Inside the Inditex Empire'; Carlta Vitzthum, 'Just-in-Time Fashion', *Wall Street Journal*, 18 May 2001, pp. B1ff.; Marshall L. Fisher, Ananth Raman and Anna Sheen McClelland, 'Rocket Science Retailing', *Harvard Business School Working Knowledge*, 7 August 2000, http://hbsworkingknowledge.hbs.edu.

12

Controlling marketing and implementation

Comprehension outcomes

After studying this chapter, you will be able to:

- Outline the marketing control process and explain its purpose
- Identify the levels of marketing control that an organisation may apply
- Explain the four types of marketing control and how they are used

Application outcomes

After studying this chapter, you will be able to:

- Follow the marketing control process at different levels
- Diagnose interim results and plan corrective action
- Use annual, financial, productivity and strategic control to assess performance
- Prepare for contingency planning

OPENING CASE: DUCATI'S RACE FOR SALES AND PROFITS

One of the world's best-known motorcycle racing brands is running a never-ending race toward sales and profit targets. Ducati, which has its headquarters in Bologna, has built a reputation for speed, engineering and style, supported by its repeated success in the World Superbike Championships. Its marketing plans focus on translating these strengths into euros, pounds, dollars and yen through sales of four Ducati product lines in Europe, North America, Japan and other countries. However, to achieve its objectives, the company must overcome competition from other motorcycle manufacturers, sluggish economic conditions and channel inefficiencies.

As a public company, Ducati announces quarterly and yearly sales and profits, and coordinates its marketing forecasts and budgets with this schedule. For instance, Ducati sold nearly 5,000 Multistrada dual-purpose sport/touring bikes in the product's first six months by targeting buyers who ride under varying weather and road conditions. These results were so far ahead of plan that marketers increased the model's full-year sales objective. Ducati has also taken the opposite approach, making limited edition bikes more appealing to buyers by strictly capping sales. When the company offered a special motorcycle exclusively on the Web, its first year's production sold out in a scant 31 minutes.

Nonetheless, Ducati has made a number of changes to its marketing plans after measuring interim progress and assessing the external environment. Its US dealers had more than a 12-month inventory supply at one point – much higher than the 4.5-month average that Ducati would like to see and higher than the inventory levels of rivals' dealers. Because short-term forecasts projected minimal sales growth, Ducati concentrated on reducing inventory levels by cutting prices and giving away free helmets as buying incentives. Within a year, inventory levels were down to the six-month level and continuing to drop, making way for newer models and freeing up resources for other marketing activities.

Some of Ducati's key metrics are percentage change in net sales and gross profit; percentage change in number of motorcycles produced and sold; and percentage change in its motorcycle registrations by market. Its marketers monitor changes in these measurements every month, quarter and year to determine progress toward objectives and identify problems that require further investigation and attention. They know their marketing plans are succeeding when they see Ducati motorcycle sales rising faster than registrations – and faster than production levels.[1]

CHAPTER PREVIEW

The final stage in the marketing planning process is to implement, control and evaluate the plan. Ducati's marketers established a variety of metrics to determine whether their plans and implementation were working as intended. As measurements came in, they analysed what was happening and made changes (such as discounting certain bikes) to bring the results closer to the desired performance. Ducati and other marketers know that even the best plan will be ineffective without proper implementation from start to finish; even the worst plan will not be improved by superb implementation. Thus, as you implement your own marketing plan, think about what to measure and when; how to interpret your measurements of interim progress; and what to do with your analysis.

This chapter examines the purpose and process of marketing control, starting with a discussion of its importance and the steps involved. The next section describes the levels of marketing control, and this is followed by an explanation of annual control, financial control, productivity control and strategic control. These types of control not only help you adjust your current marketing activities, projections and assumptions but also yield important information for the next marketing plan you develop. The final section touches on contingency planning for marketing. *Think about how you can apply the principles of marketing control described in this chapter when planning to measure post-implementation results.*

PLANNING FOR MARKETING CONTROL

Marketing control is the process of setting standards and measurement intervals to gauge marketing progress, measuring interim results after implementation, diagnosing any deviations from standards and making adjustments if needed to achieve the planned performance. Without marketing control, you will be unable to determine whether your strategies and programmes are leading to the marketing performance you expect. With marketing control, you can see exactly where and when results fall short of or exceed expectations – and come to a decision about the action you will take. Figure 12.1 illustrates how marketing control works.

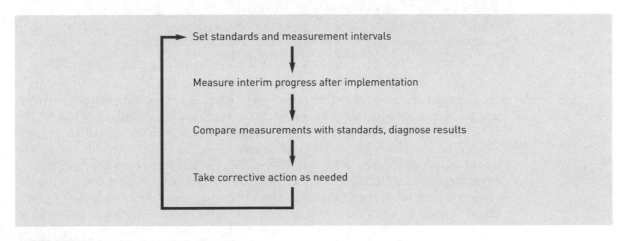

Set standards and measurement intervals

Measure interim progress after implementation

Compare measurements with standards, diagnose results

Take corrective action as needed

FIGURE 12.1 Applying marketing control

The use of marketing control assumes that the organisation is willing and able to make changes after implementing the marketing plan. If Ducati had not decided to offer discounts and free helmets to boost short-term sales and reduce dealer inventory, it might not have been able to move as many motorcycles through the channel to free up resources. Marketing control is intended to help you identify the warning signs of an emerging problem early enough to take corrective action. This may entail a small change or a major decision such as discontinuing a product, as in the case of S.C. Johnson.

MARKETING IN ACTION: S.C. JOHNSON

When S.C. Johnson introduced a line of plastic plates and cups under the Ziploc TableTops brand, it supported the product launch with a promotional budget of more than €50 million. The blue plastic dishes were more substantial than flimsier disposable plates, giving customers the choice of using them once and throwing them away or washing them to save for re-use. Rather than have TableTops displayed alongside ordinary dishes or plastic storage containers, S.C. Johnson paid slotting fees to have retailers display the products next to other disposable tableware items, and set initial prices in line with those of the least expensive non-disposable items.

After seven months of sales, some retailers were so disappointed by the results that a number were quoted as saying they planned to 'delist' the line – even though S.C. Johnson was willing to halve the wholesale price. As disposable products, TableTops were simply not living up to these retailers' sales forecasts; according to one store official, 'There are no repeat purchases. The things last forever.'[2] Meanwhile, in addition to competition from Dixie Rinse & ReUse and Hefty Elegantware, S.C. Johnson faced a new threat when Clorox launched a line of premium disposable dishes at a lower price than TableTops. S.C. Johnson's marketers closely monitored the situation, and, a year after introduction, they made the difficult decision to discontinue the line. TableTop's resources were invested in a new group of product introductions as marketers pursued financial objectives and – a top management priority – enhanced the corporation's image as an innovator.[3]

S.C. Johnson and its channel members were applying marketing control to measure interim progress toward their objectives; finding that actual measured results were not up to pre-set standards, they diagnosed the problem and devised solutions. The retailers believed that consumers found TableTops durable enough to avoid buying replacements and, therefore, the line's sales were unlikely to improve substantially. Their solution was to stop carrying the line and devote the shelf space to other merchandise. After examining product sales and weighing channel reaction, S.C. Johnson ultimately concluded that the line's progress toward objectives did not merit continued investment; its solution was to discontinue the line after approximately one year on the market.

The use of marketing control also raises several ethical questions. Will marketers set less stringent standards or lower short-term sales forecasts in order to qualify for bonuses or promotions? Will they honestly and adequately explain deviations from expectations and amend or reverse their earlier decisions if necessary? Will marketers apply marketing control laxly or inconsistently if they feel pressured by senior managers to produce ever-higher quarterly results? This can lead to myopic concentration on short-term progress to the detriment of long-term objectives and, as in several highly publicised instances, decisions to make current sales or profits look better than they actually are.

The marketing control process

The marketing control process starts with the objectives you have already set and the detailed forecasts, budgets, schedules and metrics you have developed to track post-implementation progress toward objectives. Next, determine exactly which standards must be met to show progress at each interval of measurement. Suppose your forecast calls for selling 500 units of a product in June; your financial metrics specify an average gross profit margin of 30 per cent; and your advertising budget for June totals £3,000. During June you can get early indicators of progress by measuring actual results weekly; at the end of June you can measure full-month results and see if you are meeting your forecast, metrics and budget standards.

The standards and measurement intervals used for marketing control will vary from organisation to organisation. Supermarket chains such as Tesco can measure store and product sales by day, week, month, quarter and year; some track store sales by the hour for staffing purposes as much as for marketing purposes. Fashion retailers like Zara measure product sales daily or at even shorter intervals so they can identify fast-selling merchandise for immediate reorder, determine which items are slow sellers and see the effect of pricing and other decisions.

Whatever standards and intervals you choose should provide sufficient information and time to recognise an emerging problem and be able to diagnose it. You do this by comparing actual interim results with pre-set standards, examining the magnitude and direction of variations and calculating the rate of change from the previous period's results. Assume that your non-profit organisation actually receives £2,000 in contributions during November, although your monthly forecast standard is £2,500. Your actual results are 20 per cent lower than the standard, which is a sizeable variation. However, sharply lower November results would signal an even more problematic trend if your October contributions were 10 per cent lower than the standard and your September contributions were 5 per cent lower.

How can you diagnose the cause and significance of any deviations from standards? Examine your actual results and recent trends in the context of your marketing activities, previous results and overall industry results. Use internal and external audits to identify and analyse changes that may have affected your progress. Internally, you might find staffing shortages, budget cuts or operational difficulties contributed to worse-than-expected results. Externally, you might find that better-than-expected results were due, in part, to a competitor's troubles or reduced unemployment in targeted markets. B2B marketers have to look for answers both upstream and downstream in the value chain: on the supply side, production may depend on just-in-time deliveries; on the demand side, sales may depend on demand for certain consumer products. Marketers should also look for answers by researching customer behaviour, perceptions, attitudes and relationships.

If measurements show no deviations, you can continue implementation as planned. You may do this even if you find deviations, to allow more time for a definite trend to develop and avoid acting prematurely. If you decide to respond to a deviation, you can take one of three corrective actions: (1) adjust marketing programmes, schedules or budgets; (2) adjust the standards or measurement intervals; or (3) change the assumptions factored into your marketing plan, such as the prevailing economic climate or increased price competition. In turn, changing a key assumption may cause you to change your objectives or other aspects of the marketing plan. Finally, if interim results are much better than expected, you can use your diagnosis to maintain these outstanding results and enhance the implementation of other programmes (*see* Figure 12.2).

Action	Description
Continue with implementation	Leave programmes, timing, expenditures, responsibilities, standards and measurement intervals as planned
Adjust implementation to solve a problem	Change marketing programmes, timing, expenditures, responsibilities as suggested by diagnosis of deviation
Adjust standards or measurement intervals	Make changes that will allow more accurate or timely identification of emerging problems
Adjust marketing plan assumptions	Change relevant assumptions on which strategies and programmes are based to fine-tune planning and implementation
Act to maintain outstanding results and enhance implementation	Use the diagnosis to find ways of sustaining superior results and enhancing the implementation of other programmes

FIGURE 12.2　Responding to the diagnosis of interim results

Levels of marketing control

During plan implementation, you can apply marketing control at a number of different levels, as your organisation chooses. These levels include:

- *Business unit*. Is the marketing plan of a particular business unit achieving interim results as expected? How do these results compare with the results of the company's other units and with the industry in general?

- *Marketing-mix strategies*. Are the planned product, channel, pricing and IMC strategies achieving the desired results? Is each product meeting sales targets and other interim standards? Are sales through each channel (and channel member) up to expectations? Are advertising campaigns achieving their awareness and response objectives? Are price changes stimulating sales to the desired degree?

- *Programme*. How is each programme performing relative to the standards for interim results? Which programmes are yielding better results and which are yielding disappointing results?

- *Product or line*. Are individual products (or the entire line) meeting standards for interim progress toward objectives? Are the products or line moving toward market share targets?

- *Segment*. What are the interim results for each customer segment being targeted?

- *Geography*. What do interim results look like for each branch or region? The temporary staffing services firm Manpower requires 800 branch offices to input actual revenue and expense data on a month-to-month basis so headquarters executives can track results against forecasts and use the information in preparing the next year's marketing plan.[4]

- *Manager*. For accountability, what is the status of each manager's results compared with agreed-upon standards?

- *Brand*. Is each brand performing up to the pre-set standards, in financial and marketing terms? How do interim results compare with those of other brands in the portfolio and with those of competing brands?

Organisations usually apply marketing control at multiple levels, both macro and micro. Zara and other fashion retailers give special emphasis to marketing control at the product and store level; consumer packaged-goods marketers such as Unilever look closely at the business unit, region, product line and brand levels. Do not depend only on one or two levels; if you do, you will get an incomplete or distorted picture of interim results and might therefore take action inappropriately. Remember, forecasts and schedules are just targets; your actual results may be slightly higher or lower at each measurement interval as you move toward achieving full-year performance. When applying marketing control, you want to act soon enough to make a difference in the final outcome of your marketing plan without overreacting.

Types of marketing control

To determine the overall effectiveness of your marketing plan at its conclusion and to gauge progress while it is being implemented, you will use annual control, financial control, productivity control and strategic control, applied at the various levels you have chosen. Figure 12.3 summarises these four types of marketing control, which are discussed in more detail in the following sections.

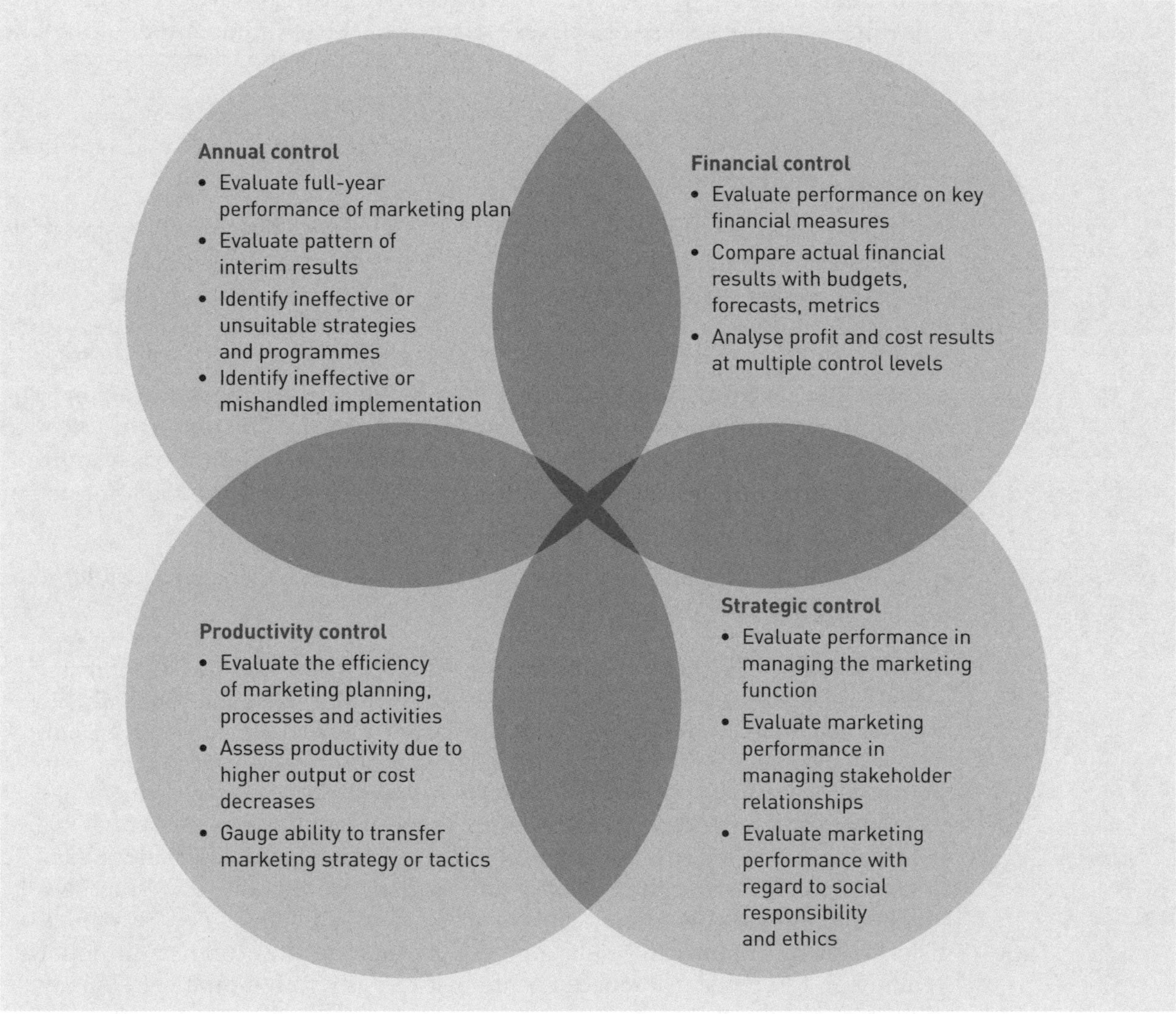

Annual control
- Evaluate full-year performance of marketing plan
- Evaluate pattern of interim results
- Identify ineffective or unsuitable strategies and programmes
- Identify ineffective or mishandled implementation

Financial control
- Evaluate performance on key financial measures
- Compare actual financial results with budgets, forecasts, metrics
- Analyse profit and cost results at multiple control levels

Productivity control
- Evaluate the efficiency of marketing planning, processes and activities
- Assess productivity due to higher output or cost decreases
- Gauge ability to transfer marketing strategy or tactics

Strategic control
- Evaluate performance in managing the marketing function
- Evaluate marketing performance in managing stakeholder relationships
- Evaluate marketing performance with regard to social responsibility and ethics

FIGURE 12.3   Annual, financial, productivity and strategic control

Annual control

Annual control allows you to evaluate the current marketing plan's performance in preparation for developing next year's marketing plan. This annual control process provides an important check of what your plan has achieved and where improvements can be made, feeding back to the environmental scanning and analysis for next year. Start with a broad overview of the plan's performance. How do the full-year results match up with the primary marketing, financial and societal objectives such as increasing sales and profits, strengthening customer loyalty or improving corporate image?

Looking at performance measured by a few vital objectives can suggest strengths and weaknesses to be further investigated through internal analysis. For example, Porsche compares full-year sales and profit performance with objectives and examines each individual model's contribution to performance. In one recent year, its marketers determined that the Cayenne sport-utility vehicle and Carrera GT were especially instrumental in achieving a ninth consecutive year of high profits; the Cayenne's sales alone accounted for 15 per cent of annual revenues.[5]

Now look at whether other marketing plan objectives were achieved, and by what margin. Using these targets, was full-year performance below expectations, at the expected level or above expectations? At the micro level, how did each programme and marketing-mix strategy perform relative to its objectives? What can you learn from the pattern of interim progress measurements throughout the year that will help in next year's forecasting and implementation? Can line managers and others responsible for implementation and customer contact offer constructive feedback about the programmes, objectives, activities or anything else connected with the marketing plan?

MARKETING IN ACTION: TUPPERWARE

The US manufacturer Tupperware has traditionally marketed its plastic storage containers through a direct channel; its independent sales reps hold product parties, show samples and take customer orders. As part of a recently implemented overall growth strategy, the company decided to add a channel and began distributing its products through the 1,100-store Target discount chain. However, only eight months after implementation, marketing managers discovered that this indirect channel strategy was yielding unexpectedly higher-than-forecast sales.

Tupperware found that as long as consumers were able to buy its products in a local store, they were less interested in attending product parties. Therefore, the good response actually posed a threat to the company's direct channel, 'our most productive source of sales', in the words of CEO Rick Goings.[6] Considering that its sales reps organise more than 13 million product parties worldwide each year, Tupperware's decision to quickly halt sales through Target and refocus its marketing plan on direct sales is understandable.

Sometimes companies discover that a strategy has been too successful, even before the year is up, as in the case of Tupperware.

A particular challenge is distinguishing ineffective or unsuitable strategies and programmes from ineffective or mishandled implementation so you can make changes during the next planning cycle. Did a programme fail to meet objectives because its planning was flawed or because its implementation was flawed? Have similar programmes worked well in the past, in other markets, in other segments or with other products? How do the current conditions differ from those previous situations, and what conclusions can you draw? At worst, annual control will reveal poor marketing performance and the need to address bad planning or bad implementation. At best, it will indicate superior marketing performance and confirm the soundness of the plan or the implementation – or identify an unintended result created by marketing strategy, which is what occurred at Tupperware.

Financial control

Businesses and non-profit organisations alike apply **financial control** to evaluate the marketing plan's interim and overall performance according to key financial measures such as sales (or contributions), profits, gross and net profit, costs and return on investment. To illustrate, some of the independent stores that carry Hallmark greeting cards use that supplier's systems to apply financial control at the product line level. The system pinpoints lines that are selling more slowly than in previous years so store owners can make decisions about discontinuing less profitable lines, adding products with more profit potential and improving cash flow.[7] Interim measurements show the progress of each programme and strategy toward full-year objectives; full-year financial results clarify the big picture of marketing performance. You can compare actual expenditures with planned budgets; actual sales and costs with forecasts; and profit objectives with profit results at multiple levels (by product, market, segment, channel and so forth).

Costs are an especially important part of financial control for start-ups and fast-growing companies. For example, its tightly controlled cost structure is a major competitive advantage for Tiger Motorcycles, based in Thailand. The company buys nearly all of its equipment and parts from local suppliers rather than from higher-priced import sources. By adhering to its low-cost targets, Tiger can keep its manufacturing expenses 20 per cent below those of Japanese competitors such as Suzuki, Yamaha and Honda. In turn, Tiger products are priced lower to appeal to value-conscious consumers in rural Thai markets – which has helped the company become the nation's fourth-largest seller of motorcycles and put it in position to attract more market share with expanded product offerings.[8]

Productivity control

The purpose of **productivity control** is to evaluate the marketing plan's performance relative to the efficiency of key marketing processes and activities. Whereas financial control is concerned with specific financial measures of performance, productivity control focuses on improvements to process and activities that either decrease costs or increase output. Different organisations apply productivity control in different ways (and at different intervals); some common business examples include:

- *Overall plan productivity*. Has the current plan yielded better results with smaller-than-usual marketing budgets? Has the current plan maintained expected results without budget increases? Have implementation costs increased without corresponding increases in marketing results?

- *Advertising and sales promotion productivity*. Without higher budgets, are reach and brand/product awareness increasing over time? With lower budgets, are reach and brand/product awareness levels sustained? Which sales promotions yield the best response for the investment? ING Direct, a financial services firm, has found online advertising to be particularly productive. The company spends 10 per cent of its marketing budget on Web advertisements – and brings in 40 per cent of its customers that way. For chief marketing officer David Lewis, the deciding factor in advertising productivity is his company's cost of acquiring a new customer.[9]

- *Sales force productivity*. Is the sales force contacting more prospects and making more sales without higher budgets? With lower budgets, is the sales force maintaining productivity on the same measures? Which sales representatives and territories are most productive relative to budgeted investments?

- *Product and development productivity*. Are more new products being generated on a stable development budget? Are more new products moving from the concept stage to commercialisation, resulting in higher sales and profit potential? Are some products more productive (yielding higher profitability relative to their costs) than others? Should some products be dropped because they are less productive? The pharmaceutical firm GlaxoSmithKline is particularly concerned with product development productivity, given the high cost of creating new drugs and bringing them to market. Although it has many more potential drugs moving through the first stages of development than in the past, the firm is also dropping less promising drugs earlier in the process.[10]

- *Channel productivity*. Are some channels more important for long-term sales and profit productivity, as Tupperware discovered? Do some channels require disproportionately high investment for the level of return? Can results be maintained with lower channel costs? As one example, Procter & Gamble dropped its Millstone Coffee Personal Blends website due to low productivity: although some customers liked being able to order coffees blended to taste, this direct channel generated insufficient return relative to the investment.[11]

- *Price productivity*. Did a price promotion stimulate sufficient revenues to offset the lower profit margin? Did a reduced price stimulate sufficient sales to bring a product to the breakeven point earlier than originally planned? Did a price increase yield higher total profit despite lower unit sales?

- *Segment and customer productivity*. Are the marketing costs for some targeted segments or customers too high relative to the payback? Which segments and customers yield the best returns for the investment? Are some segments or customers so unproductive in generating returns that they should be dropped?

Global companies often look at productivity from the perspective of whether effective marketing strategies or tactics can be transferred successfully to other products or markets. Unilever, for instance, has increased advertising efficiency by adapting one campaign for use in many countries. Its 'Dirt is Good' campaign for Omo laundry detergent first appeared in Hungary and later was adapted for Sweden, Portugal, Greece and other countries.[12]

Strategic control

Strategic control is used to evaluate marketing's performance in managing strategic areas such as the marketing function itself, stakeholder relationships, social responsibility and ethics. Applied annually or semi-annually – generally by marketing management and top executives – strategic control shows whether marketing is doing its job; successfully forging key stakeholder relationships; and achieving social responsibility and ethics objectives. The purpose is to assess strengths and weaknesses in these areas, identify where improvement is needed and build on success when developing future marketing plans.

MARKETING IN PRACTICE: WALKERS

The marketers planning the UK launch of Walkers Sensations Crackers, a premium crisps product, forecast sales of up to £18 million for the first nine months and prepared a full schedule of advertising and promotions to build awareness and stimulate product trial. After the launch, they studied the early sales results and decided that their new product forecast was not nearly optimistic enough. 'Consumers were going mad for it; we had the production lines going 24 hours a day, seven days a week, and still we couldn't keep up with demand', remembers Jon Goldstone, Walkers' marketing director.[13] He halted the advertising campaign during its second week to allow production to catch up with demand; sales continued strong and the actual nine-month total reached £48 million.

The marketing staff were swept up in the excitement of this extraordinary success, and Goldstone was determined to maintain the marketing momentum internally and externally. He had his staff begin planning several new snack flavours as line extensions to make the most of high consumer awareness and preference for the Walker Sensations brand. This approach worked: a year after the initial product launch, only one of 30 employees in the marketing department had left – and the company was inundated with job applications from top candidates. Moreover, the line extensions were selling well and other divisions were asking for advice in planning similar products for other countries.[14]

To assess the marketing function's performance, your organisation can conduct a **marketing audit** – a formal, detailed study of the planning process, plan implementation, personnel skills, use of resources and responsiveness. This chapter's practical marketer checklist offers questions to ask when assessing marketing planning and implementation. As part of the marketing audit, management should look at the skills and motivation of marketing personnel. The market-leading UK baked goods company Walkers effectively dealt with the challenge of keeping marketing staff motivated – and consumers excited about the brand – following the highly successful introduction of Walkers Sensations Crackers.

The Walkers Sensations example also illustrates the importance of evaluating effectiveness in starting and strengthening relationships with customers and other stakeholders. Once Jon Goldstone saw how well the first product was accepted, he decided to introduce new flavours so customers would stay interested in the brand. Customer relationships are at the heart of any company's success, which is why strategic control should evaluate marketing performance in acquiring and retaining new customers, building loyalty, increasing satisfaction and supporting positive perceptions. Moreover, it is important to examine performance in managing relationships with shareholders, suppliers, channel partners and other groups that can significantly affect the organisation's ability to achieve objectives.

Finally, use strategic control to assess marketing's performance with regard to social responsibility and ethics. Is marketing effectively conveying the organisation's involvement in socially responsible causes? Are societal objectives being set and achieved? Are marketing decisions being made and implemented in an ethical manner? What else can marketing do to support positive perceptions of the organisation as socially responsible and committed to strict ethical standards?

Contingency planning

To supplement implementation plans, many marketers develop contingency plans linked to the forecasts, schedules and budgets representing the most pessimistic and the most optimistic scenarios they may face during the planning period. For example, the Kirin Brewery in Japan recently developed contingency plans in case production at its Tokyo-area plants was interrupted by summertime power cuts. Kirin's managers knew that the Tokyo Electric Power Co. was having difficulty getting all its generating plants ready to meet peak demand during the hot months – just the time when consumers buy more beer. So the managers were ready with plans to move some production to other plants far from Tokyo and to reschedule production in Tokyo-area plants to weekends when power demand is lower and power cuts less likely.[15]

In addition, marketing managers need to prepare contingency plans for coping with large-scale emergencies brought on by uncontrollable external factors such as: natural disasters, an outbreak of a disease, terrorism, sabotage, computer system failures or transport cuts, unusual competitive pressures or the sudden withdrawal of a key supplier or customer. A severe, prolonged crisis may physically threaten employees, customers or other stakeholders; damage facilities and equipment; destroy products and supplies; and shut down channels. Less severe emergencies may disrupt (but not cripple) internal operations, as in Kirin's case, or negatively affect marketing activities.

Figure 12.4 presents the main components of contingency planning for marketing. Note that top management may incorporate marketing contingency plans into a comprehensive organisation-wide contingency plan. Contingency plans may also be the outcome of a sophisticated scenario-planning process in which strategists develop detailed descriptions of future situations to anticipate and plan for shifts in uncontrollable external forces, industry trends, technological developments and organisational resources.[16]

Planning action	Purpose
Identify emergency situations and analyse their potential consequences for marketing	To understand the marketing activities, people and operations most likely to be disrupted by each possible emergency
List advance preparations that can be made to minimise disruptions and restore normalcy	To have materials and procedures ready in the event an emergency erupts
Establish warning signs of impending crises	To help recognise when an emergency is developing and provide triggers for contingency plan implementation
Assign specific actions, responsibilities and priorities for containment and customer service	To prevent the crisis from becoming more severe by organising and coordinating an effective initial response to contain the problem and continue serving customers
Create a contingency communication plan	To keep internal and external stakeholders informed about the situation, the response and future steps
Resolve the crisis and analyse how well the contingency plan worked	To improve the contingency planning process by eliminating ineffective actions and using lessons learned for better advance preparation

FIGURE 12.4 Contingency planning for marketing

Some extreme crises are, of course, completely unprecedented and therefore nearly impossible to anticipate for contingency planning purposes. Consider the repercussions of severe acute respiratory syndrome (SARS).

MARKETING IN PRACTICE: RESPONSE TO SARS

After deadly outbreaks of severe acute respiratory syndrome (SARS) in Asian countries, travel businesses serving those destinations experienced a rapid and dramatic drop in sales. Hong Kong's Cathay Pacific Airways responded to the crisis by quickly cutting costs to minimise the financial damage: it eliminated many flights and grounded 22 jets. At the same time, the airline launched a new marketing campaign featuring sharply lower airfares to attract bargain-hunting travellers and rebuild revenues. Even after the epidemic was contained and no new cases were reported, passenger loads to and from the region remained extremely light; by one industry estimate, the number of passengers flying to Asia-Pacific destinations that summer dropped by more than 30 per cent compared with the previous summer. Cathay slowly restored some flights and put jets back into service one by one. However, as a result of the SARS crisis, the airline reported its worst-ever six-month loss and revenues remained lower than forecast for months afterward.[17]

At the opposite end of the spectrum, some businesses suddenly found their products in uncommonly high demand. In India, companies that sell surgical face masks could barely keep up with orders. 'Our export of masks has gone up by at least four to five times over the previous year', observed Vikas Narang, export director of Global Products. A manager for Apothecaries Sundries Manufacturing Co. agreed: 'New orders are pouring in every day. We never anticipated this kind of demand for masks made here.'[18] Working overtime and drawing on all supply sources helped these companies make sales and meet customers' needs during the worst of the SARS crisis.

CHAPTER SUMMARY

1. *Outline the marketing control process and explain its purpose.*

   The process of marketing control consists of: (1) setting standards and measurement intervals to gauge progress toward marketing objectives; (2) measuring interim results after implementation; (3) comparing measured results with standards and diagnosing any deviations; and (4) taking action as needed. The purpose is to pinpoint where results are below or above expectations, understand why and decide to leave the programmes and implementation unchanged; make changes to solve problems; or apply lessons learned to improve progress toward standards and, ultimately, objectives. The decisions made at the end of the process feed back to the beginning, providing feedback for changing standards, measurement intervals or even objectives.

2. *Identify the levels of marketing control that an organisation may apply.*
Organisations may apply marketing control at the macro and micro levels to measure interim progress. These levels of marketing control include: business unit; marketing mix strategies; product or product line; customer segment; geography; manager; programme; and brand.

3. *Explain the types of marketing control and how they are used.*
Marketers can apply four types of marketing control. Annual plan control is used to evaluate the current marketing plan's performance in preparation for developing next year's marketing plan. Financial control is used to evaluate the marketing plan's performance according to key financial measures such as sales and profits. Productivity control is used to evaluate the marketing plan's performance relative to the efficiency of key marketing processes and activities. Strategic control evaluates effectiveness in managing strategic areas such as the marketing function, stakeholder relations and social responsibility/ethics.

KEY TERM DEFINITIONS

annual control Type of marketing control used to evaluate the current marketing plan's full-year performance as a foundation for creating next year's marketing plan

financial control Type of marketing control used to evaluate the current marketing plan's performance according to specific financial measures such as sales and profits

marketing audit Formal, detailed study of the marketing function to assess strengths, weaknesses and areas needing improvement

marketing control Process of setting standards and measurement intervals to track progress toward objectives, measuring post-implementation interim results, diagnosing any deviations and making adjustments if needed

productivity control Type of marketing control used to evaluate the marketing plan's performance in managing the efficiency of key marketing activities and processes

strategic control Type of marketing control used to evaluate the marketing plan's effectiveness in managing strategic areas such as the marketing function, stakeholder relationships and social responsibility/ethical performance

THE PRACTICAL MARKETER CHECKLIST NO. 12: EVALUATING PLANNING AND IMPLEMENTATION

The marketing planning process

Were marketing plan objectives consistent with higher-level objectives?

Were strategies and programmes matched to objectives and consistent with the overall strategy, mission, targeting and positioning?

Were the appropriate personnel (internal and external) involved in the planning process?

Did programmes clearly target specific customer segments?

Was any programme in conflict with another programme or with objectives?

Were decisions about strategies and programmes made after investigating multiple options?

Were programmes and implementation responsibilities clearly delineated and communicated?

Did strategy and programmes reflect a thorough understanding of the organisation's situation, environment, markets and customers?

Did programmes reflect approved product, channel, price and IMC strategies?

Were customer service and internal marketing strategies consistent with marketing-mix strategies?

Were marketing forecasts, schedules, budgets and metrics coordinated and realistic?

Were marketing personnel prepared with contingency plans for responding to significant threats and opportunities?

How can the marketing planning process be improved in the future?

Plan implementation

Did each programme deliver the expected results on schedule and within budget?

How did each programme affect relations with customers and other targeted stakeholders?

Were all strategies and programmes integrated into a cohesive, practical plan?

Did marketing personnel effectively manage available resources, internal activities and value chain activities during implementation?

Did marketing personnel systematically measure interim results and make comparisons with standards at appropriate intervals?

How did marketing personnel deal with interim results that deviated from standards?

How did marketing personnel handle competitive pressures and customer response during implementation?

Were the appropriate internal personnel involved in implementation?

How did implementation involve and affect value chain partners?

How can implementation be improved in the future?

 ## ONLINE RESOURCES

Planning, strategy and implementation

- Biz/Ed (catalogue.bized.ac.uk/roads/market.html) – From the Institute for Learning and Research Technology at the University of Bristol, has links to information about marketing planning and strategic management.

- Strategy + Business (www.strategy-business.com) – From Booz Allen Hamilton, has analytical articles and white papers about strategy, planning, implementation, marketing and e-commerce.

- International Mass Retailing Association (www.imra.org/public/pages/index.cfm? pageid=3756) – Presents ideas for contingency planning in the retail industry, many of which can be applied to other industries.

QUESTIONS FOR DISCUSSION AND ANALYSIS

1. How would a non-profit organisation apply financial control to its marketing plan implementation?

2. Given the dynamic and uncertain nature of the business environment, why would marketers bother drafting contingency plans?

3. Why is the outcome of this year's marketing control an important input to next year's marketing plan?

APPLY YOUR KNOWLEDGE

Build on your research and responses for the 'Apply your knowledge' exercises in Chapters 11 and 5 to answer the following questions about your chosen company's marketing control:

• What quarterly or annual financial performance results has this company announced in the past few months? How does this performance compare with the budgets, metrics, schedules and forecasts you previously researched for this company?

• If the company's actual financial performance is different from the planned results, what corrective actions have been taken?

• Did this company recently report marketing performance results such as changes in share or customer acquisition? How do these compare with the metrics, schedules and forecasts you researched? What marketing control steps, if any, do you think this company should take right now – and why?

• On the basis of what you know of this company, identify a single issue that could interfere with achieving marketing plan objectives and explain how you would address this in a contingency plan.

• Prepare a brief oral or written report summarising your ideas.

BUILD YOUR OWN MARKETING PLAN

Finalise your marketing plan by selecting the levels at which you will apply marketing control and the types of marketing control that are most important for your product and situation. How often will you measure results and what standards are most important for determining interim progress? What would you do to diagnose a situation in which actual expenditures for a particular marketing programme exceed budgeted costs? What corrective action might you take if actual monthly unit sales for an important channel fall below your forecast? Look closely at the assumptions you have factored into your measurement standards: which should you reconsider if actual performance deviates significantly from your plan? Is it important to apply marketing control by segment, geography, manager and/or brand? How will you do this? And how will you apply productivity control to the implementation of your marketing plan? Get ready for implementation by documenting your conclusions in *Marketing Plan Pro* software or in a written marketing plan.

CLOSING CASE: KOLA REAL MEASURES RESULTS ONE BOTTLE AT A TIME

Coca-Cola, Pepsi-Cola and . . . Kola Real? Since the Ananos family founded Kola Real in 1988, they have relentlessly pursued market share in Latin American nations, despite considerable competition from the world's largest carbonated drink marketers and smaller local firms. Their strategy is to offer more value for the money: large sizes of Kola Real sell for much less than their global brand counterparts. In the early days, family members did just about everything themselves, from developing the special cola recipe to pasting labels on to bottles. They kept overhead and marketing costs low – a practice that continues today – and, as the business became profitable in its home country of Peru, they bought bottling plants and planned more formally for expansion to other regions.

Kola Real's owners apply marketing control at both macro and micro levels, monitoring interim company-wide results and results by country, product and channel. For example, when the Ananos family decided to expand into the Mexican market, they set a five-year goal of achieving 10 per cent market share, measured by sales volume. Before the end of the second year, they had already captured 5 per cent, despite a minuscule advertising budget and increasingly intense competitive pressure. For comparison, consider that Coca-Cola's share is more than 70 per cent; Pepsi's share is roughly 21 per cent; and smaller brands such as Chiva Cola and El Gallito account for the remainder.

Market share remains an important measure of competitive success for Kola Real, and by this measure it is making excellent progress: its share is 21 per cent in Peru, 14 per cent in Venezuela and 13 per cent in Ecuador. Channel penetration through intensive distribution is another vital measure of progress. During the first 18 months of operation in Mexico, Kola Real built up a channel network of 100,000 stores on its way to a total of 900,000 outlets selling colas in rural and urban areas. On a macro level, the company forecast an overall one-year 30 per cent increase in the number of litres sold to support its aggressive growth strategy and then measured interim results monthly to track progress.

Meanwhile, Coca-Cola and Pepsi are fighting to retain market share by cutting prices, increasing advertising budgets and using both trade and consumer sales promotion. The stakes are high: 11 per cent of Coca-Cola's worldwide sales come from the Mexican market, so every point of market share lost to Kola Real is costly – especially at a time when price wars are cutting into profits. Against this competitive backdrop, the Ananos family is counting every bottle sold, every channel member enlisted and every fraction of market share gained in implementing its plans for growth.[19]

Case questions

1. Why would Kola Real use an intensive distribution strategy in Mexico, and what additional standards might be set for monitoring progress toward signing a total of 900,000 outlets?

2. What contingency plans would you recommend that the owners prepare for Kola Real in Mexico, and why?

ENDNOTES

1. Based on information from Nina De Roy, 'Ducati's Motorcycles Face Tough Road', *Wall Street Journal*, 11 June 2003, p. B5E; Mark Haines, 'Ducati North America – CEO Interview', *The America's Intelligence Wire*, 2 June 2003, n.p.; John Tagliabue, 'How Ducati Roared Onto the Internet', *New York Times*, 18 April 2001, p. H14; 'Ducati Motor Holding Announces Third Quarter 2003 Results', Ducati news release, 6 November 2003, www.ducati.com.

2. Quoted in Jack Neff, 'S.C. Johnson to Bag Ziploc TableTops', *Advertising Age*, 25 November 2002, p. 3.

3. Christine Bittar, 'S.C. Johnson Comes Clean', *Brandweek*, 20 October 2003, p. 4; Neff, 'S.C. Johnson to Bag Ziploc TableTops'.

4. Rick Whiting, 'Gain the Financial Edge', *InformationWeek*, 2 June 2003, pp. 52ff.

5. 'Porsche Sets Another Record', *CNN.com*, 12 November 2003, www.cnn.com/2003/business/11/12/porsche.reut.

6. Quoted in 'Global Business Briefs: Tupperware Corp.', *Wall Street Journal*, 18 June 2003, p. D4.

7. Jeff Bailey, 'Big Firms Can Share Some Helpful Wisdom', *Wall Street Journal Online*, n.d., www.startupjournal.com.

8. Shawn W. Crispin, 'Thailand's Tiger Motorcycles Give Japan Rivals a Solid Race', *Wall Street Journal*, 8 October 2003, p. B11C.

9. Matthew De Paula, 'Forget Click Rates, Now View-Throughs Matter', *Banking Wire*, 19 August 2003, p. 24.

10. Reed Abelson, 'For Glaxo, the Answers Are in the Pipeline', *New York Times*, 4 May 2003, sec. 3, p. 4.

11. Roger O. Crockett, 'Online Extra: Where Customisation Goes Sour', *Business Week Online*, 2 December 2002, www.businessweek.com.

12. Agnes Csonka, 'Claiming "Dirt Is Good", Locally Devised Detergent Ad Goes Global', *Europe Intelligence Wire*, 16 June 2003, n.p.

13. Quoted in Claire Murphy, 'And For My Next Trick', *Marketing*, 30 October 2003, pp. 22ff.

14. Murphy, 'And For My Next Trick'.

15. Todd Zaun, 'This Summer, Tokyo Heat Wave Could Set Managers' Blood Boiling', *Wall Street Journal*, 27 June 2003, p. A10.

16. See Craig S. Fleisher and Babette E. Bensoussan, *Strategic and Competitive Analysis* (Upper Saddle River, NJ: Prentice Hall, 2003), pp. 284–97.

17. Edward Wong, 'Even After SARS, Airlines Suffer on Asian Routes', *New York Times*, 12 August 2003, pp. C1ff.

18. Quoted in Sumeet Chatterjee, 'Thanks to SARS, Business is Soaring', *Yahoo! News India*, 4 May 2003, in.news.yahoo.com/030504/43/2401e.html.

19. Based on information from David Luhnow and Chad Terhune, 'Latin Pop: A Low-Budget Cola Shakes Up Markets South of the Border', *Wall Street Journal*, 27 October 2003, pp. A1ff.; 'Cola Down Mexico Way', *The Economist*, 11 October 2003, pp. 69–70; Greg Hernandez, 'Kola Real Dedicates 2nd Soft Drinks Plant', *The America's Intelligence Wire*, 15 July 2003, n.p.

The fictitious company Lost Legends Luxury Chocolatier is planning to market premium gourmet chocolates to adults in the United Kingdom and, later, in Western Europe. Although many confectionery companies target the children's chocolate sweets market, fewer are active in the adult segment and fewer still in upmarket chocolates. This sample marketing plan illustrates how the marketing director for Lost Legends Luxury Chocolatier is preparing to enter the market. Notice how the contents, order of topics and section headings are tailored to fit the company's situation. Also notice that details (such as product by product pricing, programme schedules and budgets) are not in the main body of this plan but would be available in the appendix of an actual plan for readers who want more specifics. Check the *Marketing Plan Pro* software on the CD that accompanies this text for sample marketing plans that include complete forecasts and financial information.

EXECUTIVE SUMMARY

Lost Legends Luxury Chocolatier is a new company planning to market premium gourmet chocolates to adults in the United Kingdom and Western Europe. In monetary terms, this market is smaller than the children's chocolate sweets market; however, confectioners offering gourmet, premium-priced chocolates under well-regarded brands can potentially earn higher profit margins by targeting specific segments of the consumer and business markets. We will target three consumer segments and three business segments at the high end of the gift, holiday and affordable personal luxury market. Our Belgian Legends product line will be introduced in September to allow time for building brand awareness and product trial prior to the Christmas season, when our seasonal Limited Edition Legends line will be featured.

Our financial objectives relate to first-year turnover in the UK market, a minimum level of sales for each retail outlet, achieving breakeven within 15 months and aiming for 10 per cent gross profit margin by the end of our second year. Our marketing objectives relate to first-year brand awareness among consumers and businesses, arranging for retail distribution, launching the e-commerce website and planning for new products to be introduced in the second year. Our societal objectives relate to buying only Fairtrade Marked cocoa and using recycled materials in product packaging.

Key strengths are our family recipes, patented roasting process, cost-effective hand production and glamorous history. Weaknesses include lack of brand awareness and image, limited resources and lack of channel relationships. Our marketing plan will address three major opportunities: higher demand for premium chocolates; growing interest in treats with mystique; and growing interest in socially responsible products. The main threats we must counter are intense competition, market fragmentation and uncertain supply prices.

CURRENT MARKETING SITUATION

The company was founded by the British descendants of a nineteenth-century Bruges chocolate maker who was famous for his unusually dark and intensely flavoured chocolates. In this pre-automation era, he mixed small batches using the finest ingredients; kneaded and tempered the chocolate to achieve a smooth, refined texture; and poured his confections into hand-made moulds one at a time. Dozens of his recipes were handed down from generation to generation as the family moved from Bruges to the London area, but the chocolates were never produced commercially – until now. After experimenting with roasting cocoa beans and updating the recipes as they prepared for a St Valentine's Day party, two entrepreneurial family members were inspired to patent the roasting process and launch a new business. The name 'Lost Legends Luxury Chocolatier' was chosen because it captured the romance of dark, rich Belgian chocolates made in the old-fashioned way from treasured recipes.

Europe has a long tradition of chocolate making, from leading brands such as Suchard-Tobler, Nestlé, Thorntons, Cadbury, Godiva, Perugina and Lenôtre to locally owned and operated gourmet chocolatiers. The top brands enjoy high awareness and high customer loyalty. Upmarket stores such as Harrods and Fortnum and Mason also sell private-label branded chocolates as well as domestic and imported upmarket brands, which adds to the competitive pressure. Nonetheless, a number of smaller companies are successfully targeting specific niches within the adult chocolate market by offering all-natural chocolates; lower-calorie or lower-fat chocolates; holiday chocolates; and gift chocolates.

In this environment, Lost Legends Luxury Chocolatier will compete at the higher end of the gift, holiday and affordable personal luxury market. Our positioning is based on the hand-made, top-quality nature of our premium chocolates made from the finest, freshest ingredients; our distinctive product and package differentiation; our exclusive brand image; carefully controlled production output; and highly selective distribution. An integral part of our marketing strategy will be the use of Fairtrade Marked cocoa, a programme ensuring that growers receive a fair price for their cocoa. By actively promoting socially responsible sourcing of top-quality cocoa (and other ingredients), we can encourage positive associations with our brand and products – and encourage other gourmet chocolate makers to do the same.

MARKET SUMMARY

Although North and South America are the largest global markets in terms of chocolate sales, chocolate sales in Europe have been growing steadily. From 1996 to 2003, UK chocolate sales increased by 13 per cent and overall European chocolate sales increased by 15 per cent. By itself, the United Kingdom accounts for nearly 30 per cent of European chocolate consumption. Looking ahead, Eastern European nations are expected to experience the most rapid growth in chocolate sales, so we will explore opportunities in that region after establishing our brand and building sales in our home market of the United Kingdom and then in Western Europe.

Looking at customer buying patterns, chocolate sales are subject to seasonality. Sales increase markedly before holiday periods such as Easter, Christmas and St Valentine's Day. On the other hand, sales can drop in extremely hot weather because (1) stores must keep chocolate products chilled, which reduces the opportunity for impulse purchases; and (2) customers tend to buy sweets that are less perishable and retain their quality. We plan to introduce our first products in September, building awareness and word of mouth so we can attract buyers during the critical year-end holiday period.

Consumer market

The three consumer market segments targeted by Lost Legends Luxury Chocolatier are middle- to high-income adults who: (1) like (or want) to reward themselves or their families with the affordable luxury of gourmet chocolates; (2) view upmarket chocolates as a suitable gift; (3) buy fine chocolates as a tradition on St Valentine's Day, at Christmas or another holiday.

According to research, men were the main purchasers of gift chocolates in the past. Today, however, women account for the majority of purchases in this segment, and they are increasingly interested in product and packaging as expressions of personality. Not surprisingly, the high-disposable-income adults in our targeted segments have sophisticated tastes, high expectations and demanding standards. But we will give buyers of premium chocolate another reason to feel good about Lost Legends Luxury Chocolatier: they will be buying a brand that is socially responsible as well as top quality, an uncommon benefit combination among upmarket brands. Thus, as shown in Figure A1.1, we can plan to provide features that deliver valued benefits for the different needs of these targeted consumer segments.

Targeted segment	Characteristics and needs	Feature/benefit
Adults with middle to high income levels who buy fine chocolates for themselves or their families	• Appreciate premium chocolates • Prefer the cachet of luxury brands • Like small indulgences • Willing to splurge for themselves or loved ones	• Customers can select type and quantity of chocolates to accommodate tastes and budget • Premium brand image enhances perception of chocolates as special treat for individual or family • Fairtrade Marked cocoa balances self-indulgence with social responsibility
Adults, primarily women, with middle to high income levels who buy fine chocolates for gifts	• Seek a gift that reflects personality of giver or recipient • Seek a gift with high perceived value • Seek a gift to delight the senses • Seek a gift that is unique yet not excessively extravagant • Seek a gift with emotional overtones • Seek a gift that is socially responsible	• Lavish/distinctive gift packaging adds to visual appeal, personality, perceived value • Top-quality, limited-edition chocolates make our products unique and uncommon • Fairtrade Marked cocoa balances gift status with a sense of social responsibility
Adults with middle to high income levels who buy fine chocolates for holidays	• View holidays as occasions to enjoy special treats • Have or want to create a regular custom of enjoying special treats on certain holidays	• Seasonal and holiday packaging adds to our product's appeal for special occasions • Limited-edition line reinforces exclusivity • Fairtrade Marked cocoa combines holiday custom with social responsibility

FIGURE A1.1 Targeted segments in consumer market

Business market

The business market segments targeted by Lost Legends Luxury Chocolatier consist of professionals and businesspeople who select or give gifts: (1) to clients and other business contacts; (2) to colleagues or managers on holiday occasions; (3) customised by product, packaging or business logo. These segments represent a significant opportunity to build repeat purchasing and loyalty among businesses that require unique corporate gifts with wide appeal for various occasions. Many small chocolate shops accept or invite customised orders but Lost Legends Luxury Chocolatier will aggressively target this segment and seek to build longer-term customer relationships spanning gift-giving occasions.

Targeted segment	Characteristics and needs	Feature/benefit
Professionals and executives who give gifts to clients and other business contacts, or who are responsible for selecting such gifts	• Want a gift with high perceived status and value • May influence selection but not actually purchase gifts • May give gifts but not actually make the purchase • May make the purchase but not actually give the gift	• Purchasers can select type and quantity of chocolates to accommodate budget and occasion • Premium brand image enhances perception of chocolates as gift • Fairtrade Marked cocoa balances luxury with social responsibility
Professionals and businesspeople who give gifts to colleagues or managers at holiday times	• Seek a gift with high perceived status and value • Seek a gift that is recognised as unique and exclusive • Seek a gift that is socially responsible	• Lavish gift packaging adds to the visual appeal and perceived value • Top-quality, limited-edition chocolates make our products unique and unusual • Fairtrade Marked cocoa balances gift status with a sense of social responsibility
Professionals and businesspeople who give customised gifts	• Want to reinforce corporate name in a tangible and memorable way • Want to give a gift that is not available to the general public • Want recipients to anticipate high-quality customised gifts • Want recipients to feel good about the social responsibility aspect of the gift	• Chocolates and packaging can carry business logo as a visual reinforcement of corporate name • Special packaging customised for particular businesses reinforces the uniqueness and exclusivity of the gift • Fairtrade Marked cocoa combines gift-giving custom with social responsibility

FIGURE A1.2   Targeted segments in business market

Figure A1.2 summarises the features and benefits we can deliver to satisfy the needs of these targeted segments of the business market.

Market trends and growth

The overall European chocolate confectionery market is projected to grow at an annual compound rate of 3.5 per cent during this decade, a positive trend that indicates strong demand for our type of product. The UK chocolate confectionery market continues to show steady growth in monetary terms and volume output. Last year, the industry produced more than 525,000 tonnes of chocolates with a wholesale value of £2.4 billion and a retail value of £3.7 billion. Although the volume increase was only 1.4 per cent higher than the previous year, the whole-sale value was 2.5 per cent higher and the retail value was 2.4 per cent higher than the previous year. Annual per capita UK chocolate consumption is approximately 10 kg (valued at £69). Figure A1.3 shows industry-wide four-year sales forecasts for the European market, including the UK.

Gourmet chocolate brands clearly have higher wholesale and retail value than mass market chocolates, although per capita consumption does not match that of mass market chocolates. National advertising and sales promotions support sales of Cadbury, Nestlé, Mars and other mainstream chocolate marketers. Cadbury, for instance, spends heavily to launch new chocolate products or build sales during Easter and other holiday periods.

Further, product proliferation at the mass end and the premium end of the European chocolate market is adding to competitive pressure. Smaller companies are making speciality chocolate products for niche markets, such as chocolates for people who want to avoid dairy products, chocolates for people who are diabetic and chocolates for people who prefer natural or organic flavourings and ingredients. Established companies constantly introduce variations of truffles, bonbons, pralines and other favourites to satisfy customers' variety-seeking behaviour and encourage loyalty.

	2005	2006	2007	2008
Units (kg thousands)	2,745	2,795	2,850	2,900
Revenues (£ millions)	12,000	12,500	12,940	13,400

FIGURE A1.3 Forecast sales growth in European chocolate market

Large and small competitors are making e-commerce an important part of their marketing plans. UK customers (and those in other countries) can now buy gourmet chocolates directly from chocolate makers and, if intended as gifts, have products shipped directly to recipients. Another trend is toward incorporating premium branded chocolates into elaborate desserts served in exclusive restaurants. Finally, more competitors are customising their packaging or even their products for corporations and for weddings and other occasions.

Marketing research

To stay in touch with our targeted segments and track emerging market trends, we are commissioning qualitative research that will investigate perceptions, attitudes and behaviour related to premium chocolate products in general and Lost Legends Luxury Chocolatier in particular. We will use both secondary and primary research to support new product development, plan public relations activities, understand our competitive situation and monitor progress toward awareness objectives. In addition, we will commission marketing research to examine customer and channel satisfaction and identify opportunities and threats to which we must respond. Finally, we will solicit feedback through our website and through manufacturer's representatives as part of our ongoing research.

CURRENT PRODUCT OFFERINGS

Initially we will offer two main product lines, both based on modern adaptations of family recipes and a proprietary cocoa bean-roasting process we recently developed. The first, Belgian Legends, features 12 chocolates named for Belgian cities, such as: Antwerp (delicate, fruity flavour) and Bruges (dark and rich, sprinkled with *fleur de sel*). This product line will be available all year and both the chocolates and packaging can be customised for corporate gift giving. In subsequent years, we will add between two and four new varieties in this line and retain the best-selling eight to ten chocolates from the previous year, as measured by volume. We will also offer special packaging for three important holiday seasons: Easter, Christmas and St Valentine's Day.

This strategy has the following advantages: (1) the product line and packaging are freshened and updated on a regular basis; (2) customers can find their favourites year after year, holiday after holiday; (3) the product line and the names of individual chocolate varieties reflect our family's background and tradition. The strategy supports steady year-round purchasing and encourages impulse and gift purchases during peak selling periods.

The second product line, Limited Edition Legends, features chocolates in one of two seasonal shapes and matching packaging: seashells for summer and snowflakes for winter. Each season we will bring back the seashell or snowflake favourites in new packaging. By restricting production and distribution of these limited-edition chocolates – and planning each seasonal announcement as a media event, similar to those for new wine vintages – we will build customer anticipation and demand. Premium chocolates have been offered in limited editions for some time, but mainstream manufacturers such as Nestlé and Mars have brought the practice to a wider audience by offering limited editions of well-known chocolates such as Kit Kat.

Our limited edition strategy has the following advantages: (1) the temporary introduction of seasonal varieties will give sales a strong, relatively predictable boost during specific periods; (2) loyal customers will be able to buy some favourite chocolates in every season; (3) the perceived value as a gift will be higher because these varieties are not available throughout the year. As a result, we can capture customer interest in between the peak holiday periods and fulfil consumer and corporate needs for unique, value-added gifts.

BUSINESS ENVIRONMENT

Lost Legends Luxury Chocolatier will begin operations in an environment shaped by national and transnational political–legal forces; economic uncertainty; growing concerns about social responsibility and ecology; powerful social–cultural forces; and strong competition. This section discusses how the business environment is likely to affect our marketing and performance and this is followed by a SWOT analysis of our strengths, weaknesses, opportunities and threats.

- *Political–legal forces*. As chocolate makers, we must comply with prevailing local, national and (when we export) transnational laws and regulations governing product quality, labelling, ingredients and many other aspects of the business. If we decide to introduce an 'organic' chocolate product, we must abide by EU rules for organic certification. On the other hand, the European Court of Justice has ruled that chocolate containing minute amounts of vegetable fat to supplement cocoa butter content need not be labelled 'chocolate substitute', although all ingredients must be clearly listed on the label.

- *Economic uncertainty*. Economic conditions are not uniform throughout the European market, which will affect our ability to forecast sales and profits during the first year. Industry records show that demand falls slightly but not dramatically during economic downturns, because buying premium chocolate allows consumers to indulge themselves in a small way. We must also monitor the economic climate in Ghana, where we source our Fairtrade Marked cocoa beans.

- *Social responsibility and ecology*. The Fairtrade Marked system, designed to ensure that growers are equitably compensated for their cocoa beans, is emblematic of a larger movement toward socially responsible business operations, with which we will be associated. We will also take steps to keep production and packaging ecologically friendly.

- *Social–cultural trends.* Our products take advantage of the trend toward supporting small, local brands in a world dominated by giant multinational corporations. Buyers of premium chocolate are also part of the backlash against the trend toward healthier food. Nestlé, for example, is removing transfatty acids from its Rolo and Toffee Crisp sweets; Cadbury is re-examining the product formulations that include high fructose corn syrup. However, Lost Legends Luxury Chocolatier is moving in the opposite direction: we are deliberately using the best ingredients to create fine chocolate products intended as special treats, not as a steady diet.

- *Competition.* We must confront competition from major brands such as Lindt, Thorntons, Neuhaus, Perugina, Nestlé, Cadbury and Godiva, among others. These companies have established brands and sizeable advertising budgets yet they are not immune to industry competition and the effect of economic conditions on product sales. Thorntons, for instance, is seeking growth by expanding distribution to sell chocolates through Tesco and Safeway as well as through its own shops and franchised stores. Meanwhile, Duc d'O and other speciality chocolate makers are promoting their products through new packaging, increased advertising and new point-of-purchase displays. Lost Legends Luxury Chocolatier will preserve our upmarket status by restricting distribution to selected shops, using our heritage and sense of social responsibility to differentiate our products, promoting our patented roasting method and our commitment to hand-made quality.

SWOT analysis

Lost Legends Luxury Chocolatier can leverage several core competencies and key strengths in addressing potentially lucrative opportunities in both consumer and business market segments. Yet as a new and unknown company, we must counter a few critical weaknesses that could threaten our ability to serve the targeted segments using a growth strategy. Figure A1.4 summarises the SWOT analysis.

Strengths

Among the internal capabilities that support our ability to achieve long-term and short-term objectives are:

- *Unique, time-tested recipes.* No other chocolatier sells the unusually rich, flavourful chocolates we can offer, updated from dozens of original recipes developed in the Steenstraat section of Bruges – a city renowned for delicious hand-made chocolates.

Strengths	Weaknesses
• Unique, time-tested recipes • Patented roasting process • Cost-effective hand production • Glamorous history	• Lack of brand awareness, image • Limited resources • Lack of channel relationships

Opportunities	Threats
• Higher demand for premium chocolates • Growing interest in treats with mystique • Growing interest in socially responsible products	• Intense competition • Market fragmentation • Uncertain supply prices

FIGURE A1.4 Lost Legends Luxury Chocolatier SWOT analysis

- *Patented roasting process.* Our legally protected, proprietary process for roasting cocoa beans results in a distinctively rich flavour and complex aroma that add sensory appeal to the finished product.
- *Cost-effective production.* Drawing on family records and supplier connections, we have perfected a cost-effective method for producing consistently high-quality chocolates by hand.
- *Glamorous history.* Publicising the legend of our family's original recipes and generations of chocolate making will evoke vivid images of old-fashioned quality and enhance the brand's glamour.

Weaknesses

Some of the internal factors that might prevent Lost Legends Luxury Chocolatier from achieving our objectives include:

- *Lack of brand awareness and image.* Lost Legends Luxury Chocolatier is a new company and therefore has no brand awareness in its targeted segments. We must effectively position our brand, create a premium image and communicate product benefits in order to build positive perceptions and attract customers.
- *Limited resources.* Much of our first-year budget is committed to funding production and internal operations, leaving limited funds for paid marketing messages. We will therefore put more emphasis on special packaging, public relations, sales promotion and our Internet presence.
- *Lack of channel relationships.* Our competitors either own their own shops or have long-established relationships with leading retailers serving affluent

customers. We are in the process of convincing exclusive speciality shops, top department stores and other appropriate channel members that our products are compatible with their merchandise assortments and will be profitable to carry.

Opportunities

We plan to exploit the following key opportunities:

- *Higher demand for premium chocolates.* More people see premium gourmet chocolates as an affordable luxury and therefore buy such products for themselves and for gifts. The European market is familiar with premium chocolates and accustomed to paying more for brands that are perceived to offer the highest quality and taste. Also, corporate demand for top-quality chocolates is rising more quickly than consumer demand due to interest in status products that can be given as gifts to almost any business contact (unless restricted by religious or cultural custom).
- *Growing interest in treats with mystique.* Research suggests that customers (both consumers and business buyers) want more than a chocolate treat – they want to know the story behind the product and share in the product's mystique. Our company's connection with the family's legendary Bruges chocolates is an intriguing story to be publicised; the unique recipes, limited-edition products and special packaging add to the mystique.
- *Growing interest in socially responsible products.* The use of Fairtrade Marked cocoa (and coffee) will appeal to consumers who like the idea of supporting socially responsible products. It will also differentiate our products from those of companies using cocoa beans not grown by Fairtrade Marked farmers.

Threats

We have to plan to face the following threats as we begin marketing our chocolates:

- *Intense competition and market fragmentation.* In addition to the major luxury chocolate makers with established brands, national advertising campaigns and sizeable market share, many smaller, local chocolate makers are attracting loyal customers. The resulting market fragmentation threatens our ability to build a solid customer base effectively and efficiently.
- *Uncertain supply prices.* Initially, we will be buying supplies in limited quantities and will not qualify for the most favourable volume discounts. Also, cocoa prices can vary widely according to crop conditions, weather and other factors. Thus, we must allow for an extra margin when we set retail prices and recalculate breakeven and profit levels as we come to know our supply prices.

Key issues

Because weather is an uncontrollable environmental factor, it has a major effect on chocolate sales and cocoa bean production. Heatwaves generally hurt sales and can affect chocolate product production; cool weather allows both channel members and consumers more flexibility in storing chocolates. Lost Legends Luxury Chocolatier will forecast modest sales for the hottest summer months and be ready to increase production output if the weather is not extremely warm. Dry or unusually cold weather conditions in Ghana will hurt cocoa bean production, making this key ingredient scarce and expensive. We must therefore be prepared to buy from alternative sources of Fairtrade Marked cocoa if our primary growers cannot fulfil their contracts, if we are to meet our first-year sales objectives.

Product and package design are becoming increasingly important drivers of gift chocolate purchasing. Some companies are targeting niche markets such as golf-ball-shaped chocolates for men who play golf. Others are packaging premium gift chocolates in keepsake boxes that communicate status and elegance. We will monitor these trends and research opportunities in both niches during the coming year.

MISSION, DIRECTION AND OBJECTIVES

The mission of Lost Legends Luxury Chocolatier is to bring the family's expertise and tradition of making top-quality, premium chocolates to adult consumers and business buyers who buy luxury sweets for themselves or as gifts. All of our chocolate products will be updates or variations of cherished family recipes and produced by hand from the finest, freshest ingredients. We are committed to contracting for Fairtrade Marked cocoa, coffee and other ingredients from socially responsible sources. Our priority is to build our brand first in the UK market and then gradually expand our focus to other European markets.

Our initial year's direction is controlled growth through the establishment of the brand, development of two main product lines and targeting adults in consumer and business segments. In the second year, we will pursue growth through both market penetration and market development. Because of ongoing plans for limited-edition chocolate products, our growth will depend on product development as well. Based on this mission and direction, we have formulated the following primary objectives for our marketing plan:

- *Financial objectives*. The main financial objectives for Lost Legends Luxury Chocolatier are to (1) achieve first-year turnover of £500,000 in the UK market, (2) achieve full-year retail sales of at least £10,000 per outlet in the retail channel, (3) reach the breakeven point for UK operations within 15 months and (4) achieve 10 per cent gross profit margin in our second year of operation.
- *Marketing objectives*. The main marketing objectives are to (1) generate first-year brand awareness of 35 per cent within consumer segments and 40 per cent within business segments, (2) place our products in 50 exclusive shops and high-end

department stores located in affluent areas of the United Kingdom, (3) have our UK e-commerce website fully operational when the first product lines are launched and (4) research and develop between two and four new Belgian Legends variations, based on family recipes and traditions, for introduction in the second year.

- *Societal objectives.* The main societal objectives are to (1) support socially responsible trade by buying all cocoa and coffee from Fairtrade Marked sources and identifying Fairtrade Marked sources for other ingredients and (2) increase the proportion of recycled materials used in product packaging from 25 per cent at start-up to 35 per cent by the end of the first full year.

TARGETING AND POSITIONING

As shown in Figures A1.1 and A1.2, we are targeting specific segments of the consumer and business markets. In demographic terms, these are adults with middle to high income levels; professionals; and business people. In behavioural terms, the targeted consumer segments consist of adults who buy fine chocolates for themselves, for the holidays or as gifts. The targeted business segments consist of business people who buy fine chocolates as gifts, customised or not. Because the corporate gift market is growing faster than the consumer chocolate market – and because of the potential for higher customer lifetime value – we will put more emphasis on the targeted business segments.

We will use differentiated marketing to reinforce the positioning of Lost Legends Luxury Chocolatier as a marketer of gourmet chocolates hand-made from 'legendary' family recipes using strictly fresh, high-quality ingredients drawn from socially responsible sources. This positioning sets us apart competitively and helps establish a positive, upscale image in the minds of the consumers and business customers we are targeting.

PRODUCT AND BRAND STRATEGY

Both of our initial product lines are based on updates of traditional family recipes and use our proprietary, patented cocoa bean-roasting process. The 12 chocolates in the Belgian Legends line are named for Belgian cities: Antwerp, Bruges . . . The chocolates in the Limited Edition Legends line will be shaped like seashells (for the summer season) and snowflakes (for the winter season).

Packaging for both product lines will carry through the Belgian theme with stylised nineteenth-century artwork of the major cities on the boxes and foil wrappings; velvet and satin ribbons; and choice of ornate holiday or seasonal ornaments to top each box. Our Lost Legends Luxury Chocolatier packaging will be instantly recognisable because of the distinctive colours and graphics. Customised orders will allow for corporate logos on each chocolate and on the packaging (foil wrapping, ribbon and/or box). Limited-edition chocolates will also be individually wrapped in foil that is changed from season to season, adding to the feeling of luxury and exclusivity. Although some packaging will be retained from year to year, we will build customer anticipation by introducing elaborate new packaging for each holiday (Christmas, St Valentine's Day and Easter) and each new limited-edition line. Figure A1.5 summarises the main elements of our product strategy.

Product mix	(1) Offer Belgian Legends line year round (2) Offer Limited Edition Legends line seasonally (one for summer, one for winter)
Product life cycle	(1) Retain the top-selling 8–10 chocolates in Belgian Legends line each year (2) Replace the slowest-selling chocolates yearly with new flavours/variations (3) Bring back Limited Edition Legends in summer and winter to extend growth part of the life cycle
New product development	(1) Develop at least two new Belgian Legends flavours or variations each year by updating family recipes (2) Track customer preferences and market trends as input for new product decisions
Quality and performance	(1) Use only the finest and freshest ingredients (2) Hand-produce chocolates that meet highest customer standards for competitively superior taste and texture
Features and benefits	(1) Offer a range of flavours and variations to satisfy different customers' tastes (2) Offer year-round, holiday and customised packaging to satisfy needs for gift status
Brand	(1) Emphasise the 'legends' concept to communicate the long family heritage of gourmet chocolate (2) Link the Lost Legends Luxury Chocolatier brand to attributes such as: exclusivity; superior taste and quality; freshest ingredients; socially responsible sourcing
Design and packaging	(1) Offer chocolate in distinctive shapes and combinations that convey a sense of luxury and tradition (2) Create packaging that communicates the Bruges background and tradition of our chocolates (3) Offer special seasonal packaging for Limited Edition line (4) Offer special holiday packaging for Belgian Legends line (5) For corporate orders, design custom chocolates, foil wrapping and packaging with company logos

FIGURE A1.5 Summary of product strategy

The coming year's product development efforts will focus on researching and creating new chocolates to replace the slowest sellers in the Belgian Legends line. All new products must fit the high-quality tradition of our family recipes yet incorporate new flavours or other product elements that will trigger repeat purchasing from current customers and attract new customers. Also, every new product should take advantage of our proprietary cocoa-roasting process and our commitment to socially responsible sourcing of ingredients.

The competitively distinctive 'legends' concept is central to our brand strategy. For identity purposes, the Lost Legends Luxury Chocolatier name will appear on every package, along with the name of the product line (Belgian Legends or Limited Edition Legends). Packaging, public relations and other aspects of our marketing will emphasise the 'legends' concept. We want customers to associate our brand with a decades-old family history of making top-quality chocolates by hand in the Bruges tradition, using the finest, freshest ingredients. And we want them to respond to our brand's association with social responsibility, as demonstrated through purchases of Fairtrade Marked cocoa and coffee.

(In an actual marketing plan, more information about individual products, design, packaging and new product development would be shown here, with additional detail being shown in an appendix.)

CHANNEL AND LOGISTICS STRATEGY

One of our major first-year objectives is to establish strong relationships with 50 upmarket shops that cater to affluent UK customers and have temperature-controlled storage for our chocolates. By restricting distribution to only one retail store in a given area of the country, we can strengthen our luxury image and more effectively reach higher-income customers. We will also use exclusive distribution to our advantage by educating store personnel about our patented roasting process, our Fairtrade Marked ingredients, our recipes and our family 'legends'. During the initial product introduction period, we will provide channel members with sample chocolates and display packaging; posters publicising the 'legends' concept; product nutrition information; and literature about Fairtrade Marked sourcing.

To reinforce exclusivity, we will phase in Limited Edition Legends during each season. In the first week, only the top 20 per cent of our retail outlets (measured by volume) will receive the snowflake or seashell chocolates. During the second week, the next 20 per cent of the outlets will receive these seasonal chocolates. By the third week, all of our outlets will carry the product line. This approach rewards retailers that do the best job of selling our chocolates and gives their customers access to seasonal chocolates before anyone else.

We will also have our own UK e-commerce website operational by the time we launch the Belgian Legends line. The site will follow the 'legends' theme in describing our company background, recipes and hand-production methods. We will allow visitors to view each product and package in a larger format and check ingredients, nutrition information and other details before buying. The site will have separate ordering pages for consumer and business buyers and allow pre-orders for seasonal and holiday offerings (to be fulfilled through retail partners). Although non-UK buyers will be able to order online for direct delivery, we will open a separate European website during our second-year expansion, when we work with retailers outside the United Kingdom.

Our logistics strategy will cover: obtaining quality ingredients (including cocoa and coffee from Fairtrade Marked sources) and packaging components on schedule and in sufficient quantities; maintaining constant, optimal product temperature and protective packaging when delivering to retail outlets; checking that retailers store and display chocolates under proper conditions; and using shipping containers that preserve product quality when fulfilling orders placed online or by corporate customers.

(In an actual marketing plan, more information about channel relationships and logistics would be shown here with additional detail being shown in the appendix.)

PRICE STRATEGY

The price strategies for the two product lines will differ. On the basis of our research, we will make Belgian Legends available in 200g, 300g and 500g packages with introductory retail prices of £12, £17 and £28. Our wholesale prices will be 50 per cent lower than the retail prices, not including quantity pricing for retailers who sell a higher volume of our products. The Limited Edition Legends line will be priced at £1 higher per package, reflecting the limited period of availability and allowing Lost Legends Luxury Chocolatier to recoup higher costs related to these seasonal products. Holiday packaging will add between £1 and £2 to retail prices, depending on the package and ornaments selected. These prices support our premium positioning and the high value that our products represent.

For comparison, the following is a sample of competitive prices:

- Large UK chocolate maker offers a satin gift box with 1,800g of assorted fine chocolates for £60 and a smaller, star-shaped satin gift box with 280g of chocolates for £12. Its Christmas chocolates are priced according to packaging and assortment sizes. The company provides a special Web page for corporate orders.

- Family-owned chocolate retailer sells 12 hand-made truffles for £9.95; a gift box of 36 chocolates for £16.99; and charges varying prices for chocolates in gift boxes and Christmas packaging.

- Speciality gift company sells a 150g box of gourmet chocolates for £6 and a 400g box for £12. Chocolates in more deluxe packaging are priced at £17 for 300g and £30 for 550g.

Corporate orders will be priced higher depending on the amount of customisation required, the size of the order and the delivery instructions. We will charge more if chocolates, foil wrapping and packaging are all customised with corporate logos. For customers' convenience, we will pack and address all corporate orders; include a business card or a seasonal greeting; and despatch all gifts for a nominal delivery fee. Once a corporate customer has provided names and addresses of gift recipients, we will keep the information on file and automatically provide it for updating when the customer places another order.

By aggressively pursuing these more profitable corporate orders, we expect to attain our objective of breaking even on UK operations within 15 months. However, the timing is subject to change if the cost of cocoa (or other ingredients) rises dramatically. As shown in the financial details section, our pricing is planned to support the objective of attaining 10 per cent gross profit margin on our second-year turnover.

(In an actual marketing plan, more information about pricing, costs and breakeven would be shown here, with additional detail being given in the appendix.)

IMC STRATEGY

Given the company's start-up costs, our IMC strategy will rely less on paid advertising than on public relations, sales promotion, personal selling and direct marketing. We will be using a push strategy to make our products available in carefully selected retail outlets and will educate retail sales staff about our company and products. Our IMC messages will use the emotional appeal of status, incorporate the 'legends' concept and be consistent with our product's upscale, superior-quality positioning. We are choosing media that will bring our messages to the attention of prospective channel members and executives who buy or influence the ourchase of corporate gifts. Consumer advertising in upmarket magazines will be considered in our second year of operation.

We are designing public relations programmes to support our financial and societal objectives and to achieve our marketing objectives of (1) generating first-year brand awareness of 35 per cent within consumer segments (and 40 per cent within business segments) and (2) placing our products in 50 exclusive shops and department stores. As shown in Figure A1.6, we will use a combination of public relations activities to communicate with the key stakeholders of channel members, business customers and consumers.

Technique	Activities
Advertising	• Targeted magazine advertising to build brand awareness and acceptance among channel members and corporate customers • Channel-only campaign to announce seasonal products as part of push strategy • No advertising specifically targeting consumer segments
Public relations	• Media interviews, special events and news releases to build brand awareness and positive word of mouth among consumers, businesses, channel members • Communicate 'legends' concept and link it with the image of Lost Legends Luxury Chocolatier products • Communicate use of Fairtrade Marked cocoa to enhance public perception of company as socially responsible • Gather information about each public's attitudes and perceptions to shape messages and policies
Sales promotion	• Channel sales promotion to pave the way for personal selling by manufacturer's representatives, as part of push strategy • Selective consumer sales promotion in the form of product samples distributed through luxury hotels and restaurants • Participate in industry trade shows • Sales force promotion to reward manufacturer's reps for placing Lost Legends Luxury Chocolatier in upscale shops, part of push strategy
Personal selling	• Contract with manufacturer's sales reps to visit targeted retail stores and place Lost Legends Luxury Chocolatier products, part of push strategy • Arrange for periodic personal or telephone follow-up to gather feedback from channel, business customers
Direct marketing	• Encourage corporate customers, in particular, to visit the website and order customised products • Encourage consumers to visit the website to learn more about the 'legends' concept, see the two product lines, locate nearby stores and send queries or comments to management • To build relationships, invite website visitors to sign up for a quarterly e-mail newsletter and receive announcements about seasonal product availability

FIGURE A1.6 Summary of IMC components

Our sales promotion programmes will encourage channel participation and reward the outside manufacturer's representatives handling our products for arranging distribution through appropriate upmarket shops and department stores. The only consumer sales promotion we will use during the first year is arranging for luxury hotels and restaurants around the country to give away product samples. Our direct marketing effort will centre on the website, with separate sections devoted to product and company information, the 'legends' behind our family recipes, corporate ordering, store locations and social responsibility activities. We will also invite visitors to e-mail feedback and subscribe to our free quarterly newsletter.

(In an actual marketing plan, more information about IMC programmes, messages and schedules would be shown here, with additional detail being given in the appendix.)

CUSTOMER SERVICE AND INTERNAL MARKETING

Our customer service strategy is designed to create and sustain positive relationships with channel members, corporate customers and consumers. We recognise that customers who buy premium chocolates expect perfection, as do our retailers. Therefore we will empower the manufacturer's reps who call on our retailers to replace chocolates if necessary and take other steps to settle any channel complaints. We are holding monthly briefing sessions to keep our reps and our employees fully informed about our products, marketing programmes, product line performance and future plans. Further, we will keep reps and employees updated about the latest products and promotions by sending them the company's quarterly e-mail newsletter at least one week before customers receive it.

We have formulated a separate plan for delivering pre-purchase service, post-purchase service and service recovery to our business buyers (*see Appendix: this sample marketing plan has no appendix, but the previous pages have explained what it would contain*). Two service agents will be responsible for answering business customers' questions before orders are placed; monitoring order fulfilment; communicating with customers about delivery schedules; tracking deliveries; contacting customers after the sale to check on satisfaction; and handling any questions or complaints as quickly as possible. On the basis of our interaction with business customers, we will adjust offerings, policies and procedures to improve our service over time and build our share of this potentially profitable market.

(In an actual marketing plan, additional information about these support strategies and implementation would be shown here and in the appendix.)

MARKETING PROGRAMMES

Given below are summaries of our main integrated marketing programmes leading up to our product line introductions in September and mid-November and continuing during the year-end holiday period. Associated schedules, budgets and responsibilities are included in the appendix.

- *August*. Our push strategy will be strongest one month before the Belgian Legends line is introduced, to prepare channel members for the new product. Employees and manufacturer's reps will visit each participating retailer to provide product training, samples and display materials. Full-page colour advertisements in major confectionery and chocolate industry magazines will introduce the brand and the 'legends' concept. Simultaneously we will start our public relations efforts with media interviews and news releases focusing on the 'legends' concept and the family's treasured Bruges-style chocolate recipes. One special media event planned for August is the arrival of a shipment of Fairtrade Marked cocoa. In addition to inviting television and radio reporters, we will create video and audio news releases for distribution around the country.

- *September*. To launch the new product line, Lost Legends Luxury Chocolatier's founders and family members will travel to each retail outlet in an elegant horse-drawn coach and present the manager or owner with an ornate package containing all Belgian Legends varieties. This public relations event will focus attention on the legendary family heritage of chocolate making and the old-fashioned gourmet quality of our products. During this month participating upmarket hotels and restaurants will receive their first deliveries of Belgian Legends samples, also delivered by family members arriving by coach. Manufacturer's reps will follow up to ensure that every channel member has sufficient inventory and marketing material for the launch.

- *October*. We will place colour advertisements in business magazines to generate response from professionals and executives who buy premium chocolate as gifts for clients, colleagues and other business contacts. All advertisements will include the Fairtrade Marked logo and a brief description of this trade programme. Our e-commerce website will also be prominently featured, along with the store location function. Our public relations programme for the month will emphasise the company's commitment to socially responsible Fairtrade Marked sourcing. Our manufacturer's reps will participate in a sales contest to pre-sell the Limited Edition Legends line, which is launched in mid-November. The first issue of our e-mail newsletter will be sent out this month.

- *November*. The home page on our website will promote Christmas gifts, especially the seasonal Limited Edition Legends chocolates and special holiday packaging. Our channel advertising will promote the Limited Edition Legends line for holiday gift giving and encourage early ordering by each group of retailers. Public relations activities will draw media attention to the original family recipes on which our products are based. We will also send samples to opinion leaders in the media and the entertainment world to stimulate positive word of mouth.

- *December*. Our website will feature a new home page with suggestions for last-minute chocolate gifts for consumers and business contacts. Manufacturer's reps will visit every participating retailer to check on inventory, provide sales assistance, deliver additional display materials and provide other support as needed. More media interviews will showcase the 'legends' concept and our family's long tradition of gourmet chocolate making. Marketing research will gauge interim awareness levels and attitudes among the targeted consumer and business segments. Our quarterly e-mail newsletter will offer chocolate gift ideas and include a reminder that the Limited Edition Legends line will be sold only until St Valentine's Day. Internally, we will be preparing to make the summer line of Limited Edition Legends chocolates and developing new products for the coming year.

(In an actual marketing plan, additional programme details would be shown in the appendix.)

FORECASTS AND FINANCIAL DETAILS

As shown in Figure A1.3, sales forecasts for the European chocolate market indicate higher growth from 2005 to 2008. We are forecasting £500,000 in annual company turnover during our first full year of operation, with a minimum of £10,000 in sales per participating retail outlet. Our forecasts call for annual turnover increases of 20 per cent to 30 per cent during the next three years. We expect to reach the breakeven point on UK operations within 15 months and then achieve 12 per cent gross profit margin by the end of our second year.

Due to constant variations in the price of cocoa and other ingredients, we can only estimate our cost of goods and then only two or three months in advance. As our volume increases and we buy supplies in larger quantities, we will be able to stabilise variable costs for up to six months. Therefore, the financial plans shown in the appendix are considered estimates and subject to revision during the year.

(In an actual marketing plan, additional forecast and financial details would be shown in the appendix.)

IMPLEMENTATION AND CONTROL

To ensure that our two product lines are launched on time, we will adhere to week by week programme schedules and assign management responsibilities for: supervising manufacturer's reps; coordinating sales promotion activities; and briefing the public relations, advertising, research and website experts.

Among the metrics we have selected to monitor progress toward our objectives are:

- unit and monetary sales (analysed weekly by product, product line, channel, outlet)

- customer perceptions of and attitudes to brand (twice-yearly research)

- business customer retention and profitability (quarterly analysis)

- competitive standing (annual research)

- channel member participation and satisfaction (quarterly analysis)

- image as socially responsible company (annual research)

- use of recycled materials in packaging (twice-yearly analysis)

- order fulfilment speed, accuracy (monthly analysis).

We will review interim progress weekly during the first year of operation, comparing actual results with forecasts, schedules and budgets and adjusting activities if needed. We have also developed a comprehensive contingency plan to ensure a continuous supply of Fairtrade Marked cocoa beans in the event our growers in Ghana are unable to fulfil their contracts due to unfavourable weather conditions.

(In an actual marketing plan, additional details about implementation and control would be shown in the appendix.)

SOURCES FOR SAMPLE PLAN

Based on information in: Ed Levine, 'Chocolate for the Inner Child', *Business Week*, 8 December 2003, pp. 104–5; 'Chocolate: Europe Still the Leader', *International Food Ingredients*, June–July 2003, p. 20; 'Court Ruling Ends Chocolate Case', *Duty-Free News International*, 1 February 2003, p. 8; 'As Majors Work to Create Healthier Products', *Candy Industry*, July 2003, p. 11; Renee M. Kruger, 'Premium Gourmet: Premium Chocolate Reigns as the Supreme Affordable Luxury', *Confectioner*, January–February 2003, p. 48; 'Luxury Goods', *Grocer*, 22 March 2003, p. S14; Mark Kleinman, 'Brand Health Check: Thorntons – Thorntons Pins Hopes on Strategy Overhaul', *Marketing*, 18 September 2003, p. 13; 'Cheer Up Sales with Fairtrade', *Grocer*, 22 March 2003, p. S32; Renee M. Kruger, 'Chocolate Candy: Longtime Leading Brands Have Some New Tricks', *Confectioner*, January–February 2003, p. 24; Renee Kruger, 'Thinking out of the Boxed Chocolates', *Confectioner*, September 2002, pp. 34ff; Barry Callebaut, 'New Roles for Chocolate', *International Food Ingredients*, December 2002, pp. 39ff.; the Biscuit, Cake, Chocolate and Confectionery Alliance (www.bccca.org.uk); the Fairtrade Foundation, www.fairtrade.org.uk.

Glossary

advertising Non-personal promotion paid for by an identified sponsor

affective response Customer's emotional reaction, such as being interested in or liking a product

affordability budget method Method in which senior managers set the total marketing budget on the basis of how much the organisation can afford or will be able to afford during the period covered by the plan

annual control Type of marketing control used to evaluate the current marketing plan's full-year performance as a foundation for creating next year's marketing plan

attitudes Consumer's assessment of and emotions about a product, brand or something else

audience fragmentation Trend toward smaller audience sizes due to the multiplicity of media choices and vehicles

available market All the customers within the potential market who are interested, have adequate income to buy and adequate access to the product

Balanced Scorecard Broad organisational performance measures that seek to balance financial performance and performance affecting other stakeholders

behavioural response How the customer acts in responding to an IMC stimulus, such as seeking or buying a product

benefits Need-satisfaction outcomes that a customer expects or wants from a product

brand equity Extra value that customers perceive in a brand, which builds long-term loyalty

brand extension Widening the product mix by introducing new products under an existing brand

branding Giving a product a distinct identity and supporting its competitive differentiation to stimulate customer response

breakeven point Point at which a product's revenues and costs are equal and beyond which the product earns increasingly higher levels of profit as more units are sold

budget Time-defined allotment of financial resources for a specific programme, activity or product

business (organisational) market Companies, institutions, non-profit organisations and government agencies that buy goods and services for organisational use

business strategy Strategy determining the scope of each unit and how it will compete, what market(s) it will serve and how unit resources will be allocated and coordinated to create customer value

buying centre Group of managers or employees that is responsible for purchases within an organisation

cannibalisation Situation in which one product takes sales from another marketed by the same organisation

category extension Widening the mix by introducing product lines in new categories

cause-related marketing Marketing a brand or product through a connection to benefit a social cause or non-profit organisation

cognitive response Customer's mental reaction, such as awareness of a brand or knowledge of a product's features and benefits

competitive parity budget method Method in which senior managers establish a total marketing budget at least equal to that of competitors

concentrated marketing Targeting one segment with one market mix

consumer market People and families who buy goods and services for personal use

core competencies Organisational capabilities that are not easily duplicated and that serve to differentiate the organisation from competitors

customer lifetime value Total long-term revenue (or profit) that an organisation estimates it will reap from a particular customer relationship

customised marketing Tailoring marketing mixes to individual customers within targeted segments

demand How many units of a particular product will be sold at certain prices

derived demand Principle that the demand forecast for a business product ultimately derives from the demand forecast for a consumer product

differentiated marketing Targeting different segments with different marketing mixes

direct channel Marketing channel used by an organisation to make its products available directly to customers

direct marketing The use of two-way communication to engage targeted customers and stimulate a direct response that leads to a sale and an ongoing relationship

diversification strategy Growth strategy in which new products are offered in new markets or segments

econometric modelling method Use of sophisticated econometric models incorporating anticipated customer response and other variables to determine marketing budgets

elastic demand Relationship between change in quantity demanded and change in price in which a small percentage change in price produces a large percentage change in demand

elasticity of demand How demand changes when a product's price changes

emotional appeal Appeal in an advertising message intended to touch the audience's feelings.

environmental scanning and analysis The systematic and ongoing collection and interpretation of data about internal and external factors that may affect marketing and performance

ethnographic research Observing customer behaviour in real-world situations

exclusive distribution Channel arrangement where one intermediary distributes the product in an area

external audit Examination of the situation outside the organisation, including political–legal factors, economic factors, social–cultural factors, technological factors, ecological factors and competitive factors

features Specific attributes that contribute to a product's functionality

field marketing Working with outside agencies on sales promotions that take place in stores, shopping districts and office locations

financial control Type of marketing control used to evaluate the current marketing plan's performance according to specific financial measures such as sales and profits

financial objectives Targets for achieving financial results such as revenues and profits

fixed costs Business costs such as rent and insurance that do not vary with production and sales

forecast Projection of the estimated level of sales and costs during the months or years covered by a marketing plan

frequency The number of times people in the target audience are exposed to an advertisement in a particular media vehicle during a certain period

goals Longer-term targets that help a business unit (or the organisation as a whole) achieve performance

indirect channel Marketing channel in which intermediaries help producers make their products available to customers

inelastic demand Relationship between change in quantity demanded and change in price in which a small percentage change in price produces a small percentage change in demand

integrated marketing communication (IMC) Coordinating content and delivery of all marketing messages in all media to ensure consistency and to support the chosen positioning and objectives

intensive distribution Channel arrangement in which as many intermediaries as possible distribute the product in an area

intermediaries Businesses or individuals that specialise in distribution functions

internal audit Examination of the situation inside the organisation, including resources, offerings, previous performance, important business relationships and key issues

internal marketing Coordinated set of activities and policies designed to build employee relationships within the organisation and reinforce internal commitment to the marketing plan and to good customer service

lifestyle The pattern of living reflecting how consumers spend their time or want to spend their time

line extension Lengthening a product line by introducing new products

logistics Flow of products, associated information and payments through the value chain

maintenance strategy Non-growth strategy to sustain revenues, profits or market share at current levels or defend against deterioration

market The group of potential buyers for a specific product

market development strategy Growth strategy in which existing products are offered in new markets and segments

market penetration strategy Growth strategy in which existing products are offered to customers in existing markets

market segmentation Process of grouping consumers or businesses within a market into segments based on similarities in needs, attitudes or behaviour that marketing can address

market share The percentage of unit or monetary sales in a particular market accounted for by one company, brand or product

marketing audit Formal, detailed study of the marketing function to assess strengths, weaknesses and areas needing improvement

marketing control Process of setting standards and measurement intervals to track progress toward objectives, measuring post-implementation interim results, diagnosing any deviations and making adjustments if needed

marketing (distribution) channel Set of functions performed by the producer or participating intermediaries in making a product available to customers

marketing objectives Targets for achieving results in marketing relationships and activities

marketing plan Internal document outlining the marketplace situation and the marketing strategies and programmes that will help the organisation achieve its business and organisational goals

marketing planning Structured process that links the mission statement, organisational strategy and business strategy to marketing decisions and actions

marketing strategy Strategy used to determine how the marketing-mix tools of product, place, price and promotion – supported by service and internal marketing strategies – will be used to meet objectives

mass customisation Developing products tailored to individual customers' needs on a large scale

metric Numerical standard used to measure a performance-related marketing activity or outcome

mission statement Statement of the organisation's fundamental purpose, pointing the way toward a future vision of what it aspires to become

motivation Internal force driving a consumer's behaviour and purchases to satisfy needs and wants

niche market Sub-segment within a larger segment that has customers with distinct needs or requirements

objective and task budget method Method in which money is allocated according to the total cost of the tasks to be accomplished in achieving marketing plan objectives

objectives Shorter-term performance targets that lead to the achievement of organisational goals

opinion leader Person who is especially admired or possesses special skills and therefore exerts more influence over certain purchases made by others

opportunity External circumstance or factor that the organisation aims to exploit for higher performance

organisational (corporate) strategy Strategy governing the organisation's overall purpose, long-range direction and goals, the range of businesses in which it will compete and how it will create value for customers and other stakeholders

penetrated market All the customers in the target market who currently buy or previously bought a specific type of product

penetration pricing New product pricing strategy that aims for rapid acquisition of market share

percentage budget method Method in which senior managers set the overall marketing budget based on a percentage of the previous year's annual turnover, next year's expected turnover, the product's price or an average industry percentage

positioning Use of marketing to create a competitively distinctive place (position) for the product or brand in the mind of the target market

potential market All the customers who may be interested in that good or service

primary research Research undertaken to address a particular situation or question

product development strategy Growth strategy in which new products or product variations are offered to customers in existing markets

product life cycle Product's movement through the market as it passes from introduction to growth, maturity and decline

product line depth Number of variations of each product within one product line

product line length Number of individual products in each product line

product mix Assortment of product lines offered by an organisation

productivity control Type of marketing control used to evaluate the marketing plan's performance in managing the efficiency of key marketing activities and processes

psychographics Complex set of lifestyle variables related to activities, interests and opinions that marketers study to understand the roots and drivers of consumer behaviour

public relations (PR) Promoting a dialogue to build understanding and foster positive attitudes between the organisation and its stakeholders

pull strategy Approach to channel strategy that emphasises customer demand pulling products through the value chain

push strategy Approach to channel strategy that emphasises pushing (moving) the product through intermediaries in the value chain to customers

qualified available market All the customers within the available market who are qualified to buy based on product-specific criteria

quality Extent to which a good or service satisfies the needs of customers

rational appeal Appeal in an advertising message based on logic

reach The number or percentage of people in the target audience exposed to an advertisement in a particular media vehicle during a certain period

relationship marketing Marketing geared toward building ongoing relationships with customers rather than stimulating isolated purchase transactions

retailers Intermediaries that buy from producers or wholesalers and resell to consumers

retrenchment strategy Non-growth strategy to reduce operations by quitting markets, deleting products, downsizing marketing efforts, shrinking distribution or closing down

reverse channel Channel that allows for returning goods, parts or packaging

schedule Time-defined plan for coordinating and accomplishing tasks connected to a specific programme or activity

secondary research Information collected in the past for another purpose

segments Customer groupings within a market, based on distinct needs, wants, behaviours or other characteristics that affect product demand or usage and can be effectively addressed through marketing

selective distribution Channel arrangement in which a relatively small number of intermediaries distribute a product within an area

service recovery How the organisation recovers from a service lapse and satisfies the customer

skim pricing New product pricing strategy that aims for an upmarket impression on certain customer segments that are less price-sensitive and value innovative products

societal objectives Targets for achieving results in social responsibility areas

strategic control Type of marketing control used to evaluate the marketing plan's effectiveness in managing strategic areas such as the marketing function, stakeholder relationships and social responsibility/ethical performance

strength Internal capability or factor that can help the organisation achieve its objectives, capitalise on opportunities or defend against threats

subculture Discrete group within an overall culture that shares a common ethnicity, religion or lifestyle

sustainable marketing The establishment, maintenance and enhancement of customer relationships so that the objectives of the parties involved are met without compromising the ability of future generations to achieve their own objectives

SWOT analysis Evaluation of an organisation's primary strengths, weaknesses, opportunities and threats

target market All the customers within the qualified available market that an organisation intends to serve

targeting Determination of the specific market segments to be served, order of entry into the segment and coverage within segments

threat External circumstance or factor that may hinder organisational performance if not addressed

undifferentiated marketing Targeting the entire market with one marketing mix

value From the customers' perspective, the difference between the perceived benefits and the perceived price of a product

value (supply) chain Sequence of interrelated, value-added actions undertaken by marketers with suppliers, channel members and other participants to create and deliver products that fulfil customer needs

variable costs Costs for supplies and other materials, which vary with production and sales

weakness Internal capability or factor that may prevent the organisation from achieving its objectives or effectively addressing opportunities and threats

wholesalers Intermediaries that buy from producers and resell to other channel members or business customers

word of mouth People telling other people about a product, advertisement or some other aspect of an organisation's marketing

Index

IMPORTANT: READ CAREFULLY
WARNING: BY OPENING THE PACKAGE YOU AGREE TO BE BOUND BY THE TERMS OF THE LICENCE AGREEMENT BELOW.

This is a legally binding agreement between You (the user or purchaser) and Pearson Education Limited. By retaining this licence, any software media or accompanying written materials or carrying out any of the permitted activities You agree to be bound by the terms of the licence agreement below.

If You do not agree to these terms then promptly return the entire publication (this licence and all software, written materials, packaging and any other components received with it) with Your sales receipt to Your supplier for a full refund.

SINGLE USER LICENCE AGREEMENT

■ YOU ARE PERMITTED TO:

- Use (load into temporary memory or permanent storage) a single copy of the software on only one computer at a time. If this computer is linked to a network then the software may only be installed in a manner such that it is not accessible to other machines on the network.

- Make one copy of the software solely for backup purposes or copy it to a single hard disk, provided you keep the original solely for back up purposes.

- Transfer the software from one computer to another provided that you only use it on one computer at a time.

■ YOU MAY NOT:

- Rent or lease the software or any part of the publication.

- Copy any part of the documentation, except where specifically indicated otherwise.

- Make copies of the software, other than for backup purposes.

- Reverse engineer, decompile or disassemble the software.

- Use the software on more than one computer at a time.

- Install the software on any networked computer in a way that could allow access to it from more than one machine on the network.

- Use the software in any way not specified above without the prior written consent of Pearson Education Limited.

ONE COPY ONLY

This licence is for a single user copy of the software
PEARSON EDUCATION LIMITED RESERVES THE RIGHT TO TERMINATE THIS LICENCE BY WRITTEN NOTICE AND TO TAKE ACTION TO RECOVER ANY DAMAGES SUFFERED BY PEARSON EDUCATION LIMITED IF YOU BREACH ANY PROVISION OF THIS AGREEMENT.

Pearson Education Limited owns the software You only own the disk on which the software is supplied.